# Perfect Plants

# The Random House Book of
# Perfect Plants

## ROGER PHILLIPS & MARTYN RIX

Assisted by Peter Barnes, Anne Thatcher,
Alison Rix and Nicky Foy

Designed by Jill Bryan with
the help of Gillian Stokoe
and Debby Curry

Random House New York

# Acknowledgements

Most of the specimens photographed in the studio came from the following gardens and we would like to acknowledge the help we had from them and their staff.

The Crown Estate Commissioners at the Savill Gardens, Windsor Great Park; The Royal Botanic Gardens, Edinburgh; The Royal Botanic Gardens, Kew; The Royal Horticultural Society's Garden, Wisley; The University Botanic Garden, Cambridge; The Chelsea Physic Garden, London; Eccleston Square Garden, London; Washfield Nurseries, Hawkhurst, Sussex; Beth Chatto Gardens, Elmstead Market, Essex; David Austin Roses, Albrighton, West Midlands; Kelways, Langport, Sussex; Green Farm Plants, Bentley, Hants; Sandling Park, Hythe, Kent; The Vernon Pelargonium Nursery, Sutton, Surrey.
Among others who have helped in one way or another we would like to thank: Marilyn Inglis, Susie Stokoe, Ruth Grover, Meg Baker, Sam Phillips and Joanna Smith.

Text and photos © 1996 by Roger Phillips and Martyn Rix

Library of Congress Cataloging-in-Publication data is available
ISBN 0-679-77536-6

Random House Web address: http://www.randomhouse.com/

Printed and bound in Great Britain

9 8 7 6 5 4 3 2 1

First U.S. Edition

# Contents

The garden at Alton Towers in Staffordshire, England

# Introduction

This book is designed to cover all the basic groups of plants that are needed to establish and improve your garden. In general, we have chosen plants that are among the best in their class and the easiest to find. But rather than limit the gardener to only the commonest plants, we have also included a few rare and exotic things.

# The Text

The text is designed to be read in conjunction with the photographs. Between them, they will tell you all you need to know about each plant – from its height to flowering time – and most important, the winter temperature that each plant will stand. We have given temperature information in three forms: minimum temperatures in Centigrade and in Fahrenheit, and also the American zone rating.

# The Photographs

When shooting flowers in the garden or in the field, it is preferable to work from a tripod so that you can take the opportunity to use a slower shutter speed and thus use a smaller aperture, giving a greater depth of field. In practice, the best speed to shoot plants out of doors is normally $1/15$ sec, although if there is a strong wind you may have to go up to $1/30$, or in extremes, $1/60$ sec.

Our studio shots are taken with a Hasselblad using a normal lens and an aperture of f.22, with a large flash light source. The field shots have all been taken on a Nikon FM with a variety of lenses. The film used in both cases is Ektachrome 64 ASA.

# Trees

In this chapter, the plants are ordered from evergreen through to deciduous trees. The evergreens run from the larger trees to the smallest dwarf conifers, followed by the remaining evergreens. The deciduous trees run from the largest first, then cherries, magnolias and cornus, finishing with Japanese maples.

# Shrubs

The plants in this chapter have been arranged by flowering time, starting with very early-flowering shrubs such as the mahonias, camellias and rhododendrons, then on to the hydrangeas and very late-flowering shrubs. Then follows a group of shrubs noted for their show of berries and autumn colour. A section of largely tender shrubs, suitable for growing under glass in cold areas, is added at the end of the chapter.

# Roses

This chapter is divided into three sections, starting with old and species roses, followed by a section containing Modern Shrubs, Hybrid Teas, Floribundas, David Austin roses and Miniatures. The third section is devoted to Climbing roses. Each of the three sections is then arranged by colour, from whites through to yellows, oranges and reds to purples.

# Perennials

In this chapter all the hardy plants are arranged by their flowering times, starting with the very early ones – hellebores through peonies and irises, on to daylilies – then on to the very late-flowering plants such as daisies and asters. Most of the perennials we have chosen are hardy in eastern North America and northern Europe, but a selection of tender plants more suited to California and the Mediterranean will be found at the end of the chapter.

# Annuals

The annuals we have chosen here are a selection of the hundreds available; most are true annuals which can be sown in spring to flower throughout the summer. Some are perennials or soft shrubs that are usually grown as annuals; these are planted out as young plants and may need to be brought indoors as whole plants or as cuttings if they are to survive the winter frost.

*Tulipa praestans*

# Bulbs

The bulbs in this chapters have been arranged in five groups: spring-flowering followed by summer-flowering, autumn- and winter-flowering, and finishing with few tender bulbs.

# Alpines

The term 'alpines' covers a number of small or low-growing plants which are suitable for growing on rock gardens, or in a small, special place in the garden. Most, but not all alpines, grow wild in the mountains, and they are grouped here so that those shown on the same page will be happy in roughly the same kinds of conditions.

A cottage garden in Norfolk, England

Taxus baccata

Taxus baccata

Cupressus macrocarpa

CHAPTER ONE

# Trees

*The plants in this chapter have been ordered from evergreen trees through to deciduous trees. The evergreens run from the larger conifers to the smallest dwarf conifers, followed by the remaining evergreens. The deciduous trees run from the largest first; cherries and magnolias to cornus, finishing with Japanese maples.*

ENGLISH YEW *Taxus baccata*   An evergreen tree that grows up to 50ft (15m) tall, forming a dense rounded crown on a short stout trunk. Younger specimens remain shrubby for many years making it an excellent hedging shrub. The seeds, foliage and bark are very poisonous. Can be planted in reasonably well-drained soil between autumn and late spring. Will grow in deep shade or full sun and is hardy to -10°F (-23°C), US zones 6–10. Grows wild throughout Europe, western Asia and North Africa.

BLUE ATLAS CEDAR Best known as *Cedrus atlantica* 'Glauca' (now considered a subspecies of *C. libani*)   A large, slow-growing evergreen conifer that can reach 80ft (25m). Narrowly conical in shape, becoming broader with age. Happy in any moist well-drained fertile soil and prefers full sun. Hardy to -10°F (-23°C), US zones 6–9. Native to the mountains of North Africa.

ITALIAN CYPRESS *Cupressus sempervirens*   Can grow to about 60ft (18m) tall or more. As a young tree it has a columnar habit of growth which many specimens retain. Male flowers are tiny pale yellow cones that appear on the tips of branches in spring. Cones about 1–1¼in (2.5–4cm) in diameter. Hardy to 10°F (-12°C), US zones 8–9. Grows wild in the Mediterranean region and western Asia.

Pinus sylvestris

Pinus sylvestris

Cedrus atlantica 'Glauca'

**MONTEREY CYPRESS** *Cupressus macrocarpa* Can reach 60ft (18m) and as a young tree has a narrow conical habit of growth which later becomes broader and more irregular. Male flowers are tiny pale yellow cones that appear on the tips of the branches in the spring. The dark green leaves are tiny and scale-like with globular cones about 1–1¼in (2.5–3cm) in diameter. Hardy to 0°F (-18°C), US zones 7–9.

**MONKEY PUZZLE** *Araucaria araucana* A large, slow-growing evergreen conifer that grows to 80ft (25m) and has a rounded head above a distinctly patterned straight trunk. Prefers acid soil and plenty of sun. Hardy to 0°F (-18°C), US zones 7–10. Native to Chile.

**BREWER'S WEEPING SPRUCE** *Picea breweriana* Grows to 120ft (35m) but seldom exceeds 60ft (18m) in gardens. Its pendulous young shoots drooping on either side of the branches are distinctive. In late spring 1in (2.5cm) pink or yellow male flowers appear at the tips of the branches and erect pink female conelets form near the top of the tree. Needles ¾–1in (2–2.5cm) long. Hardy to -10°F (-23°C), US zones 6–9.

**WHITE SPRUCE** *Picea glauca* Can reach 60ft (18m) forming a conical crown. In late spring pink male flowers, 1in (2.5cm) wide, form at the tips of the branches, and erect pink female conelets of similar size form near the top of the tree. Needles ½–¾in (1–2cm) long. This specimen loses its compact habit and becomes rather gaunt when in shade. Hardy to -40°F (-40°C), US zones 3–9. Native to North America.

**BLUE COLORADO SPRUCE** *Picea pungens* var. *glauca* Can grow to about 100ft (30m), but only half this size in gardens. Forms a conical crown of vivid silvery-blue foliage. Pink male flowers, ¾in (2cm), appear at the tips of the branches and erect light green female conelets, 1½in (4cm), near the top of the tree in late spring. Needles up to 1in (2.5cm) long. Hardy to -40°F (-40°C), US zones 3–9.

**SCOTS PINE** *Pinus sylvestris* Can reach 100ft (30m). In spring, ¼in (5mm) pale yellow male flowers form in clusters near the tips of branches; less conspicuous purple female conelets of similar size appear in the upper branches. Leaves are twisted blue-green needles, 1½–3in (4–8cm) long, borne in pairs in a bundle. Oval cones are 1½–2in (4–5cm) long. Hardy to -40°F (-40°C), US zones 3–9.

*Araucaria araucana*          *Araucaria araucana*

*Picea pungens* var. *glauca*          *Cupressus sempervirens* (left) *C. macrocarpa*

*Picea glauca*          *Picea breweriana*

# TREES

Dwarf conifers growing at Bedgebury

*Picea pungens* 'Globosa'

SPREADING STAR FIR *Abies amabilis* 'Spreading Star'   An evergreen conifer with a low spreading habit of growth, eventually forming a mat 10–12ft (3–3.5m) wide and about 3ft (90cm) tall. Will grow best in acid soil in full sun. It can stand temperatures down to -10°F (-23°C), US zones 5–9. This fir is best planted in autumn or winter.

HUDSON BALSAM FIR *Abies balsamea* forma *hudsonia*   An evergreen forming a small roundish plant that grows slowly to about 2ft (60cm). Needs acid soil and full sun and will stand temperatures down to -40°F (-40°C), US zones 3–9. This fir is best planted in autumn or winter.

KOREAN FIR *Abies koreana* 'Silberlocke'   Grows to only 3ft (90cm). Insignificant conelets are borne on top branches and leaves are small dark green needles, white on the underside. Cones are deep purple, 4in (10cm) long, ripening to release seeds. Hardy to -20°F (-29°C), US zones 5–9.

DWARF SAWARA CYPRESS *Chamaecyparis pisifera* 'Aurea Nana' A slow-growing evergreen that eventually reaches 2–3ft (60–90cm). Prefers deep loamy soil, full sun and protection from cold winds. Hardy to -20°F (-29°C), US zones 5–10.

*Chamaecyparis pisifera* 'Golden Mop' A slow-growing golden-leaved evergreen with long trailing branches that eventually reaches 3–4ft (90–125cm). Prefers deep loamy soil, full sun and protection from cold winds. Hardy to -20°F (-29°C), US zones 5–10.

DWARF CHINA FIR *Cunninghamia lanceolata* 'Bánó' (also known as 'Compacta')   A small spreading plant that never develops a leading shoot and reaches only about 3ft (90cm) in height. The small insignificant flowers appear in spring and the dark glossy narrow leaves, to 2in (5cm) long, are typical of the species. The fruit is a round cone, up to 1in (2.5cm) long. Hardy to 0°F (-18°C), US zones 7–9. The wild form is suitable only for parks and large gardens, but the cultivar can be grown in the smallest of private gardens.

*Juniperus* x *media* 'Gold Coast'   An evergreen forming a spreading bush of irregular shape that grows to about 6ft (1.8m). Small flowers occasionally appear in the spring but are insignificant. The branches have mostly small golden-yellow scale-like leaves closely pressed to the slender shoots, but also some shoots with longer needle-like leaves about 1/4in (6mm) long. Best in a sunny position. Hardy to -30°F (-34°C), US zones 4–9.

*Juniperus horizontalis* 'Hughes'   An evergreen forming a trailing mat of foliage seldom more than 6in (15cm) tall, but several feet in spread after 10 years. Small leaves are scale-like and closely pressed to the slender shoots. The fruit is a black berry 1/4in (6mm) long, with a white bloom on the surface. Is hardy to -40°F (-40°C), US zones 3–9. Native to sea cliffs and stony places in North America. The variety 'Hughes' was introduced into cultivation in the 1970s.

*Juniperus squamata* 'Holger'   Grows to about 8ft (2.5m) after about 25 years and

is usually rather wider than tall. Very small insignificant flowers occasionally appear in spring. The leaves are small, sharply pointed needles about 1/4in (6mm) long. The fruit is a berry 1/4in (6mm) long. Hardy to -20°F (-29°C), US zones 5–9. Grows wild in much of Asia, from Afghanistan to China.

*Picea abies* 'Nidiformis'   A slow-growing evergreen that will eventually reach about 3ft (90cm). It has horizontally layered branches and is about twice as high. Flowers are very rarely produced. The small leaves are rigid, sharply pointed needles about 1/2in (1cm) long. Needs full sun; in shade it quickly loses its compact habit and becomes rather gaunt. Hardy to -40°F (-40°C), US zones 3–9.

*Picea pungens* 'Globosa'   An evergreen that only grows to about 3ft (90cm) tall and wide after 25 years. Unlikely to produce flowers or cones and valued for its vivid silvery-blue foliage. The leaves are stiff, sharply pointed needles up to 1in (2.5cm) long, marked with a white band on each of their four sides. Hardy to -40°F (-40°C), US zones 3–9. Native to south-western North America.

*Picea pungens* 'Koster's Prostrate'   This evergreen will only grow 1–2ft (30–60cm) tall after 25 years but will spread to 5ft (1.5m) or more fairly quickly. Stiff, sharply pointed needles up to 1in (2.5cm) long, marked with a white band on each of their four sides, giving a bright grey-green effect when viewed from a distance. Should be planted in autumn or early spring in full sun. Hardy to -40°F (-40°C), US zones 3–9.

*Juniperus* x *media* 'Gold Coast'

*Juniperus squamata* 'Holger'

*Chamaecyparis pisifera* 'Golden Mop'

*Chamaecyparis pisifera* 'Aurea Nana'

*Abies balsamea* forma *hudsonia*

*Picea pungens* 'Koster's Prostrate'

*Picea abies* 'Nidiformis'

*Abies amabilis* 'Spreading Star'

*Abies koreana* 'Silberlocke'

*Cunninghamia lanceolata* 'Bánó'

*Ilex aquifolium* 'Ferox Argentea'

SILVER QUEEN
HOLLY *Ilex
aquifolium* 'Silver
Queen'   Grows to
40ft (12m) or more.
Small white four-petalled
flowers, about ¼in (6mm)
wide, appear in the early summer.
'Silver Queen' is a male variety and so will
not produce berries, although its flowers
may pollinate a nearby female variety.
Leaves are 1–3in (2.5–8cm) long. Hardy
to 0°F (-18°C), US zones 7–10.

*Ilex* x *altaclerensis* 'Lawsoniana'   One of a
group of vigorous evergreens forming a
large shrub or medium-sized tree. Can
grow to 40ft (12m) or more. Small white
female flowers, about ¼in (6mm) wide,
appear close to the branches in early
summer. The leaves are oval, 2–4in
(5–10cm) long, leathery and a dull green
with a yellow central splash. Hardy to 0°F
(-18°C), US zones 7–10. It does not like
root disturbance.

*Ilex altaclerensis* 'Camelliifolia'   A large
tree with a pyramidal habit. Young stems
are purple and berries are
very freely produced.

GOLDEN KING HOLLY *Ilex*
x *altaclerensis* 'Golden King'
Can grow to
40ft (12m) or
more. Each
small white
female flower
is about ¼in
(6mm) wide.
Leaves are oval,
2–4in (5–10cm)
long. In spite of its
name is female,
producing red berries in winter. Hardy to
0°F (-18°C), US zones 7–10. Not
commonly affected by pests or diseases.

HEDGEHOG
HOLLY *Ilex
aquifolium* 'Ferox'
Can grow to 20ft
(6m) or more. This
is a male variety and
so will not produce
berries, although its
small white slightly scented
flowers may pollinate a nearby
female variety. The leaves are oval, 1–2in
(2.5–5cm) long, with margins strongly
waved and very spiny, but the most
unusual characteristic of this variety is
that the spines extend over the upper
surface of the leaf too. Hardy to 0°F
(-18°C), US zones 7–10.

*Ilex aquifolium* 'Ferox
Argentea'   Leaves
are similar to
'Ferox' but have a
clear cream margin.
It is excellent for
hedging, although
slower-growing than
other forms of English
Holly. Being variegated,
'Ferox Argentea' also makes
a distinctive lawn specimen.

*Ilex* x *meservae* Hybrid
between *I. aquifolium*
and *I. rugosa*   A very
hardy plant native to
northern Japan. 'Blue
Angel' is a selected
clone. Good in a
continental climate.

*Ilex* 'Nellie R. Stevens'
Is a hybrid of *Ilex
aquifolium* x *Ilex
cornuta* raised in
the US. A free-fruiting
female evergreen.

AMERICAN HOLLY *Ilex opaca*
Can grow to 40ft (12m) or more. Small,
inconspicuous white slightly scented
flowers, about ¼in (6mm) wide, appear in
early summer. Each tree produces either
male or female flowers which look very
similar, but only female bushes will
produce berries when pollinated by a
nearby male plant. Leaves are oval 1–3in
(2.5–8cm). Hardy to -10°F (-23°C), US
zones 6–10.

*Ilex opaca*

*Ilex* x *altaclerensis* ' Golden King'

*Ilex* 'Nellie R. Stevens'

*Ilex* x *altaclerensis* 'Lawsoniana'

*Ilex opaca*

*Ilex* 'Nellie R. Stevens'

*Koelreuteria paniculata*

*Quercus coccinea*

*Liquidambar styraciflua*

*Aesculus flava*

*Liriodendron tulipifera*

*Platanus* x *hispanica*

Autumn leaves photographed 27 October

*Castanea sativa*

*Castanea sativa*

*Populus alba* 'Richardii'

**SWEET BUCKEYE or YELLOW BUCKEYE** *Aesculus flava*   Grows up to 70ft (20m) after 70–80 years. In early summer, branches are covered with upright 'candles' of pale yellow flowers. In autumn the leaves turn to orange-brown before falling. The smooth round fruits are about 2in (5cm) across and each contains one or two shiny brown nuts. Hardy to -20°F (-29°C), US zones 5–10.

**GOLDENRAIN TREE** *Koelreuteria paniculata*   Slow-growing to 50ft (15m) after 50 years. Trees grown in woodland are more slender. The showy bright yellow flowers, 1/2in (1cm) wide, are borne in large complex clusters about 12in (30cm) long and wide in summer. Leaves to 18in (65cm) long, 8in (20cm) wide. The fruit is also an attractive feature of this tree. Hardy to -20°F (-29°C), US zones 5–9.

**SPANISH CHESTNUT** *Castanea sativa*
Can grow to 100ft (30m). Fast-growing with a distinctive deeply ridged spiral pattern on the trunk. Prefers acid or neutral soil, tolerates dry conditions but needs full sun. Hardy to -10°F (-23°C), US zones 6–10. Native to southern Europe, western Asia and North Africa.

**MAIDENHAIR TREE** *Ginkgo biloba*
A most interesting tree because its closest relatives are trees that are now only found as fossils; it seems that it is the sole survivor of a once-large family. It grows up to 100ft (30m) tall. Trees are either male or female and the flowers are small and green. Leaves 2–3in (5–8cm) long. A smelly yellow plum-like fruit containing a single large edible seed is produced by female trees. Hardy to -20°F (-29°C), US zones 5–10.

**SWEET GUM** *Liquidambar styraciflua*
Can reach 150ft (45m) but in gardens is rarely more than 60ft (18m). Insignificant greenish flowers are borne on short catkins in late spring and the shiny dark green leaves are 4–7in (10–18cm) long and wide. In autumn they turn shades of orange, red and purple for several weeks before falling. Hardy to -10°F (-23°C), US zones 6–10.

**TULIP TREE** *Liriodendron tulipifera*
A fast-growing tree that can exceed 150ft (45m) in height but in gardens reaches only 80ft (25m). The tulip-like flowers, each about 1 1/2in (4cm) long, appear in summer. The leaves are also unique, 3–8in

(8–20cm) long and wide. The fruit is a cone-like body 2–3in (5–8cm) long, made up of numerous overlapping scales. Hardy to -20°F (-29°C), US zones 5–8.

EUROPEAN HORNBEAM *Carpinus betulus* A medium-sized tree that grows to 80ft (25m). Happy in any soil including clay and chalk, and flourishes in full sun or light shade. Hardy to -30°F (-35°C), US zones 4–10. Native to Europe and western Asia.

LONDON PLANE *Platanus* x *hispanica* (also known as *P.* x *acerifolia*) A tough tree growing to 100ft (30m) or more in 100 years, it is well known for its flaking bark which is a patchwork of different shades of grey and pale green. The flowers appear in spring as do the leaves, 6–9in (15–23cm) when wide open. The leaves turn yellow and orange before falling. Hardy to -20°F (-29°C), US zones 5–8.

*Populus alba* 'Richardii' Grows to 50ft (15m) in 30–40 years. When mature it has a cream or pale grey trunk which is flecked with black marks. It sometimes develops suckers over a considerable area. The male flowers are silky red catkins, up to 4in (10cm) long, appearing on the higher branches in late winter before the leaves, 3–4in (8–10cm) long, open. Hardy to -30°F (-34°C) or lower, US zones 4–9.

SCARLET OAK *Quercus coccinea* Up to about 80ft (25m). Like other oaks it produces two sorts of flowers in late spring, insignificant female flowers and yellow-green tassel-like male flowers 2–3in (5–8cm) long. Leaves, 3–6in (8–15cm) long and up to 4in (10cm) wide, open bright yellow at the same time as the flowers. The fruit is an acorn 1/3–1in (8mm–2.5cm) long. Hardy to -30°F (-34°C), US zones 4–9.

TURKEY OAK *Quercus cerris* Up to 120ft (35m), but often reaches about 70ft (20m) after 70–100 years. In late spring it produces two sorts of flowers; insignificant females and abundant yellow-green tassel-like males 2–3in (5–8cm) long. Leaves 3–5in (8–12cm) long. The fruit is an acorn about 1in (2.5cm) long, in a mossy-looking cup, which ripens in October. Hardy to 0°F (-18°C), US zones 7–10.

*Liquidambar styraciflua*

*Carpinus betulus*

*Quercus cerris*

*Liriodendron tulipifera*

*Liriodendron tulipifera*

*Ginkgo biloba*

*Ginkgo biloba*

*Davidia involucrata*

*Fraxinus ornus*

*Sorbus aucuparia*

*Sorbus aria*

*Davidia involucrata*

*Parrotia persica*

*Gleditsia triacanthos*

**COMMON HACKBERRY or NETTLE TREE** *Celtis occidentalis* A medium-sized deciduous tree that grows to 50ft (15m) in height and width and has a rough corky bark. Happy in any well-drained soil, it is very wind- and drought-resistant but prefers full sun. Hardy to -30°F (-34°C), US zones 4–10. Native to North America.

**HANDKERCHIEF TREE** *Davidia involucrata* A deciduous tree that grows to 35ft (10.5m) high and 18ft (5.5m) wide. In late spring it is covered in a mass of white drooping scented bracts, or 'handkerchiefs', up to 7in (18cm) long. It will thrive in any deep moist soil, but prefers full sun and dislikes draughts. Hardy to -10°F (-23°C), US zones 6–10. Native to south-western China.

**FLOWERING ASH or MANNA ASH** *Fraxinus ornus* A medium-sized deciduous tree that grows to about 60ft (18m), commonly rather taller than wide. Unusually for an ash tree, it has showy flowers. Will grow in a sunny position in any soil type in areas of average rainfall. Hardy to -10°F (-23°C), US zones 6–9. Native to the Mediterranean region and western Asia.

**HONEY LOCUST** *Gleditsia triacanthos* A deciduous tree capable of growing to well over 100ft (30m). It has a broad spreading habit, but when mature is taller than it is wide. Best planted as a container-grown plant because the roots do not like to be disturbed. Prefers a sunny position with average rainfall. Hardy to -10°F (-23°C), US zones 7–10. Native to North America.

**PERSIAN IRONWOOD** *Parrotia persica* Deciduous tree growing to 40ft (12m), sometimes becoming multi stemmed. Flowers, consisting of a tuft of crimson

Robinia pseudoacacia 'Frisia'

Catalpa bignonioïdes

Catalpa bignonioïdes 'Aurea'

stamens, are only about ¼in(6mm) across but quite showy, appearing abundantly in late winter when the branches are leafless. The leaves are 3–5in (8–12cm) long, turning to shades of red and deep yellow in autumn. Hardy to 0°F (-18°C), US zones 7–9.

**FOXGLOVE TREE** *Paulownia tomentosa* A deciduous tree that grows to about 40ft (12m). Sweet-scented flowers, about 2in (5cm) long, in late spring. Leaves up to 10in (25cm) long. Needs shelter from strong winds as these may damage the leaves. The flower buds form in autumn and are easily damaged by frost as they begin to open in late spring. Hardy to 0°F (-18°C), US zones 7–9. Can be grown as a foliage plant for its dramatic large leaves. Native to China but now found wild in woods of North America.

**WHITEBEAM** *Sorbus aria* A member of the rose family, this deciduous tree of stiff upright habit grows to about 50ft (15m), eventually developing a rounded crown. Flowers, each about ⅓in (8mm) wide, are borne in rounded clusters which are up to 3in (8cm) wide in late spring. Leaves are up to 5in (12cm) long. Will grow on any soil in a sunny position. Hardy to 10°F (-23°C), US zones 6–9. Native to much of Europe, including the British Isles. Well suited to small gardens and chalk soils.

**MOUNTAIN ASH** or **ROWAN** *Sorbus aucuparia* A deciduous tree belonging to the rose family that grows to about 60ft (18m). Creamy white flowers, about ⅓in (8mm) wide, are borne in rounded clusters up to 6in (15cm) wide in late spring. The leaves grow to 9in (23cm) long, and in autumn turn to yellow or brown. Hardy to -40°F (-40°C) or lower, US zones 2–9. Susceptible to fireblight. Native to Europe.

**GOLDEN BLACK LOCUST** *Robinia pseudoacacia* 'Frisia' A deciduous tree, taller than wide, that may grow to 80ft (25m). 'Frisia' is slower-growing and more suitable for smaller gardens than the wild species, seldom exceeding 40ft (12m). In early summer, drooping clusters of scented white pea-like flowers appear. Each flower is about ¾in (2cm) wide and the clusters are up to 8in (20cm) long. Leaves are bright yellow, becoming rather deeper yellow in the summer. Hardy to -20°F (-29°C), US zones 5–9. The species is native to eastern North America.

**INDIAN BEAN TREE** *Catalpa bignonioïdes* A medium-sized tree that grows to 50ft (15m) in height and width. Happy in any soil but flourishes in deep fertile soil and full sun. Hardy to -20°F (-29°C), US zones 5–10. Native to North America.

**GOLDEN INDIAN BEAN TREE** *Catalpa bignonioïdes* 'Aurea' (below) A medium-sized tree that grows to 40ft (12m) in height and width. Happy in any soil but flourishes in deep fertile soil and full sun. Hardy to -20°F (-29°C), US zones 5–10. Native to North America.

Paulownia tomentosa

Celtis occidentalis

*Nyssa sylvatica*

*Rhus hirta*

*Dalea spinosa*

*Salix matsudana* 'Tortuosa'

*Morus nigra*

**KATSURA TREE** *Cercidiphyllum japonicum* Grows to 70ft (20m) with an elegant open and dainty habit, sometimes with a single trunk or itcan be multi-stemmed. Happy in any moist soil type except shallow chalk, and prefers light to full shade. Hardy to -20°F (-29°C), US zones 5–10. Native to Japan and China.

**JUDAS TREE** *Cercis siliquastrum* A large shrub that grows to 20ft (6m) in height and width or sometimes a small, taller, single-stemmed tree which grows to 40ft (12m). Should be grown in any type of well-drained soil and flourishes best in full sun. Hardy to 0°F (-18°C), US zones 7–10. Native to the Mediterranean.

**CALIFORNIAN SMOKE TREE** *Dalea spinosa* A deciduous shrub or small tree that grows to 12ft (3.5m) tall and wide. Leaves are small and narrow, grey-green, the flowers violet-blue and well-scented in spring. *D. spinosa* is a Californian desert plant suited to arid sites. It grows best in full sun. Hardy to 10°F (-12°C), US zones 8–10.

**SOFT TREE FERN** *Dicksonia antarctica* Up to 20ft (6m) or even 40ft (12m) in ideal conditions. Fronds can grow to 13ft (4m) long and 6ft (1.8m) wide, but are rarely more than half this size in cultivation. Best planted in damp weather on a shaded site in acid soil; needs even rainfall throughout the year. Plants collected recently under licence in the mountains of Tasmania have withstood 22°F (-6°C), US zone 9.

**EUCRYPHIA** *Eucryphia* 'Nymansay' An evergreen tree growing to a height of about 50ft (15m). Flowers, which are not produced for several years after planting, are 2¹⁄₂in (6cm) wide. Leaves are 1¹⁄₂–3¹⁄₂in (4–9cm) long. A moist soil in full sun or partial shade is best and some shelter from cold winds is desirable. Hardy to 0°F (-18°C), US zones 7–10 when established.

**COMMON LABURNUM** *Laburnum anagyroïdes* Grows up to 30ft (9m) with a compact rounded head of branches and is normally taller than it is wide. Flowers are about 1in (2.5cm) long and faintly scented. Leaves 3–5in (8–12cm) long and wide. Hardy to -20°F (-29°C), US zones 5–9. All parts of the plant are poisonous.

**BLACK MULBERRY** *Morus nigra* A broad widely branching tree that grows up to about 30ft (9m) tall. Flowers are small greenish catkins appearing in late spring, inconspicuous among expanding leaves which are up to 8in (20cm) long and wide. Origins are uncertain but has

been grown in British gardens since the
16th century and thought to come from
western Asia. Hardy to -20°F (-29°C), US
zones 5–9.

PEPPERIDGE or BLACK GUM *Nyssa
sylvatica* Although capable of reaching
100ft (30m), this tree usually grows to
about 60ft (18m). Insignificant yellowish-
green male and female flowers appear on
separate trees in early summer. Leaves
2–5in (5–12cm) long. Plant in early
autumn or late spring, preferably in a
container to avoid later root disturbance.
Gives wonderful autumn colour. Hardy to
-30°F (-35°C), US zones 4–10.

STAG'S HORN SUMAC *Rhus hirta*
(sometimes called *R. typhina*) Grows to
a height of 25ft (8m). In early summer,
male trees have clusters of small green
flowers and females have smaller clusters
about 6in (15cm) in length. Leaves are
1–2ft (30–60cm) long, colouring to
yellow, orange and crimson in autumn.
Hardy to -20°F (-29°C), US zones 5–9.
May also be grown for its foliage. Native
to eastern North America.

CORKSCREW WILLOW *Salix
matsudana* 'Tortuosa' Rather taller than
wide and growing to 40ft (12m), this tree
forms a broad rounded head with catkins
about 1½in (4cm) long which appear as
the leaves, 2–3in (5–8cm), open in spring.
Needs full sun. Hardy to -20°F (-29°C),
US zones 5–9. Prone to canker and rust
diseases in some areas but well suited to
small and medium-sized gardens.

FREMONTIA *Fremontodendron*
'California Glory' (above) A vigorous
evergreen growing to 30ft (9m). Flowers,
about 2in (5cm) wide throughout the
summer, become tinged with red as they
age. The leaves are 2–4in (5–10cm) long,
covered on the underside with pale brown
scurfy hairs that can irritate the skin. Not
tolerant of wet conditions. Hardy to 20°F
(-7°C), US zones 8–9. It is fast-growing
but often short-lived in cool areas, dying
quite suddenly for no obvious reason.

*Dicksonia antarctica*

*Cercis siliquastrum*

*Cercis siliquastrum*

*Cercidiphyllum japonicum*

*Eucryphia* 'Nymansay'

*Fremontodendron* (in the rear)

*Laburrnum anagyroïdes*

19

*Betula pendula*

*Betula pendula*

*Crataegus laevigata*

**SILK TREE** *Albizia julibrissin* A small deciduous tree that grows to 20–30ft (6–9m) and has a very broad head of branches Happy in well-drained soil or pots but flourishes best during warm summers. Hardy to 0°F (-18°C), US zones 7–10. Native to western Asia.

**SNOWY MESPILUS or ALLEGHENY SERVICEBERRY** *Amelanchier laevis* A small deciduous tree that grows to 30ft (9m) and has a small shrubby habit in cold areas. Prefers acid or neutral soil and flourishes in full sun or partial shade. Hardy to -10°F (-23°C), US zones 6–10. Native to North America.

**SILVER BIRCH** *Betula pendula* A deciduous tree that grows to 60ft (18m). Although fast-growing it only lives 60–100 years. Happy in any soil and quite tolerant of wet conditions, but must have full sun. Hardy to -30°F (-35°C), US zones 4–10. Native to northern Europe.

**ENGLISH HAWTHORN** *Crataegus laevigata* A small thorny deciduous tree that grows to 20ft (6m) and is suitable for hedging. Happy in any soil but prefers a sunny position. Hardy to -20°F (-29°C), US zones 5–9. Native to Europe.

**COCKSPUR THORN** *Crataegus crus-galli*  A small broad-headed tree growing to 30ft (9m). The spreading branches have thorns up to 3in (8cm) long and flowers appear in early summer. They have a characteristic smell that some like, but others may find unpleasant, especially close up. Leaves are up to 4in (10cm) long and turn to orange and red before falling. Hardy to -30°F (-35°C), US zones 4–9.

**JAPANESE CRAB-APPLE** *Malus floribunda*  Grows up to 25ft (8m) with a broad crown of arching branches. Each slightly scented flower is about 1in (2.5cm) wide and the leaves are 1–3in (2.5–8cm) long. Hardy to -20°F (-29°C), US zones 5–9.

**WILLOW-LEAFED PEAR** *Pyrus salicifolia*  Has clusters of small white flowers, each about ³/₄in (2cm) wide, which have a fairly strong and not very pleasant smell. The leaves are willow-like, 2–3in (5–8cm) long and about ¹/₂in (1cm) wide. Hardy to -20°F (-29°C), US zones 5–9. Prune by thinning the long shoots to make a graceful weeping shape.

*Crataegus laevigata*

*Malus floribunda*

*Albizia julibrissin*

*Pyrus salicifolia*

*Crataegus crus-galli*

*Amelanchier laevis*

*Pyrus salicifolia* at Knightshayes

*Cornus florida*

*Cornus florida*

*Cornus controversa* 'Variegata'

*Arbutus unedo*

*Cornus alternifolia*

*Cornus kousa*

*Cornus* 'Eddie's White Wonder'

STRAWBERRY TREE *Arbutus unedo*
A small evergreen tree or large shrub that grows to 30ft (9m) in height and width. Happy in any soil but must have full sun except in dry regions. Hardy to 10°F (-23°C), US zones 8–10. Native to the Mediterranean region.

'EDDIE'S WHITE WONDER' DOGWOOD *Cornus* 'Eddie's White Wonder'   A large deciduous shrub or small tree, a hybrid between the Flowering Dogwood and Nuttall's Dogwood (*Cornus nuttallii*), that grows 15–20ft (4.5–6m) in height and width. Prefers acid soil and light shade. Hardy to 0°F (-18°C), US zones 7–9.

PAGODA DOGWOOD *Cornus alternifolia*   A deciduous shrub or small tree that grows to 20ft (6m) in height and width with a strong spreading habit. Happy in any soil type and tolerant of wet conditions but needs full sun. The variegated form is especially pretty. Hardy to -20°F (-29°C), US zones 5–9. Native to eastern North America.

VARIEGATED GIANT DOGWOOD *Cornus controversa* 'Variegata'
A deciduous tree that grows to 50ft (15m) with distinctive tiered branches. Happy in any soil type and tolerant of wet conditions but needs full sun. Hardy to -20°F (-29°C), US zones 5–9. Native to China and Japan.

KOUSA DOGWOOD *Cornus kousa*
A large deciduous shrub or small tree that grows to 30ft (9m) with branches of mature specimens often rather layered

*Hamamelis* x *intermedia* 'Pallida'

*Hamamelis mollis*

and spreading. Prefers acid soil and light shade. Hardy to -20°F (-29°C), US zones 5–9. Native to China and Japan.

FLOWERING DOGWOOD *Cornus florida* A large deciduous shrub or small tree that grows to 20ft (6m). Prefers acid soil and light shade. Hardy to -20°F (-29°C), US zones 5–9. Native to eastern North America.

HYBRID WITCH HAZEL *Hamamelis* x *intermedia* 'Arnold Promise' (below) Grows to 20ft (6m) tall and wide. Strongly scented flowers about 1in (2.5cm) wide appear in winter on leafless branches. Leaves usually turn to shades of red, orange and yellow in autumn. Should be planted in the autumn or early spring in acid or neutral soil in full sun or light shade. Hardy to -20°F (-29°C), US zones 5–9. Hybrid witch hazels are the result of crossing Japanese and Chinese varieties.

HYBRID WITCH HAZEL *Hamamelis* x *intermedia* 'Pallida' Grows to 20ft (6m) tall and at least as wide. Strongly scented flowers about 1in (2.5cm) wide appear in winter on leafless branches. Leaves usually turn yellow in autumn. Should be planted in autumn or early spring in acid or neutral soil in full sun or light shade. Hardy to -20°F (-29°C), US zones 5–9.

HYBRID WITCH HAZEL *Hamamelis* x *intermedia* 'Ruby Glow' Grows to 20ft (6m) tall and 25ft (7m) wide. Sweetly scented flowers, about 1in (2.5cm) wide, appear in winter on leafless branches. Leaves usually turn shades of red and orange in autumn. Should be planted in the autumn or early spring in full sun or light shade. Hardy to -20°F (-29°C), US zones 5–9. Witch hazels are generally free of pests and diseases.

HYBRID WITCH HAZEL *Hamamelis* x *intermedia* 'Jelena' (right) Grows to 20ft (6m) tall and is at least as wide. Flowers, about 1in (2.5cm) wide, appear in winter on leafless branches and have less scent than some other varieties. Leaves usually turn shades of red, orange and yellow in autumn. Should be planted in autumn or early spring in full sun or light shade. Hardy to -20°F (-29°C), US zones 5–9.

CHINESE WITCH HAZEL *Hamamelis mollis* Grows to 20ft (6m) tall and is at least as wide. Sweetly scented flowers, about 1in (2.5cm) wide, appear in winter on leafless branches. Leaves usually turn yellow in autumn before falling. Should be planted in the autumn or early spring in full sun or light shade. Hardy to -20°F (-29°C), US zones 5–9. Native to western China, from where it was first introduced to Britain in the late 19th century.

MOUNTAIN SNOWDROP TREE *Halesia monticola* A deciduous tree or large spreading shrub that grows up to 30ft (9m) high and wide, but is much larger in the wild. Flowering in spring. It should have a position in full sun or partial shade. Hardy to -20°F (-29°C), US zones 5–9. Native to south-eastern North America.

*Hamamelis* x *intermedia* 'Ruby Glow'

*Halesia monticola*

*Halesia monticola*

Prunus dulcis in Wuxi, China

Prunus dulcis

Prunus avium

Prunus serrula

**WILD CHERRY** *Prunus avium*   A very tough deciduous tree of open habit; one of the fastest growing to about 60ft (18m). Flowers are 1in (2.5cm) wide, with five pure white petals borne in drooping clusters in early spring. The leaves are 2–5in (5–12cm) long; good autumn colour. Fruit is a small bitter or sweet cherry, at first red, later turning black. Hardy to -30°F (-35°C), US zones 4–9. Grows wild in much of Europe.

**ALMOND-PEACH** *Prunus* x *amygdalopersica*   A deciduous tree of spreading open habit that grows to 15ft (4.5m). Flowers, 2in (5cm) wide, borne in late winter or early spring. Leaves 2–4in (5–10cm) long. The fruit is like a peach but smaller and with dry flesh. Hardy to 10°F (-23°C), US zones 6–9. A hybrid between the almond and the peach first recorded in the early 17th century.

**ALMOND** *Prunus dulcis*   A small deciduous tree with erect main branches but becoming broader and bushier with age. Grows to 30ft (9m) high. Pink flowers, 1–2in (2.5–5cm) wide, appear in late winter or early spring. Other varieties have white or double flowers and some are grown for their fruit. Leaves 3–5in (8–12cm) long. Hardy to 0°F (-18°C), US zones 7–10.

**JAPANESE APRICOT** *Prunus mume*   A small deciduous tree with a rounded crown that grows to about 20ft (6m) and just as wide. The deep pink or white sweetly scented flowers, 1in (2.5cm) wide, borne in late winter on bare twigs. Leaves, 2–4in (5–10cm) long, oval or

Prunus sargentii

Prunus padus

rounded, with a long tapered tip. Fruits are small furry apricots but not sweet. Hardy to 0°F (-18°C), US zones 7–10. Native to Japan and China.

SARGENT'S CHERRY *Prunus sargentii*
A deciduous tree that grows to 80ft (25m) in the wild but seldom reaches more than 40ft (12m) in gardens. Flowers 1.5in (4cm) wide. Leaves 2–4in (5–10cm) long, oval with a long tapered tip. One of the first trees to change in early autumn, the leaves turn to orange and red before falling. Hardy to -20°F (-29°C), US zones 5–9. Native to Japan and Korea.

BIRD CHERRY *Prunus padus*
A deciduous tree of open habit that will grow to 40ft (12m) and is taller than it is wide. Almond-scented white flowers, $1/2$in (1cm) wide with five petals, are borne in late spring in drooping spikes 3–5in (8–12cm) long. The pointed oval leaves are 3–5in (8–12cm) long with finely toothed margins. Fruit is a small bitter black cherry $1/5$in (5mm) wide. Hardy to -30°F (-35°C), US zones 4–9. 'Colorata' is an attractive variety with pink flowers and purple leaves.

*Prunus* 'Okumiyako' (previously known as *Prunus serrulata* 'Longipes')
A deciduous tree with a spreading habit that grows to 15ft (4.5m). Flowers, 2in (5cm) wide, are borne in late spring and leaves are 3–5in (8–12cm) long. Hardy to -20°F (-29°C), US zones 5–9. At its best in the late spring, it is about the last of all the Japanese cherries to flower. Well-suited to average-sized gardens.

TIBETAN CHERRY *Prunus serrula*
Up to 40ft (12m) tall, it is grown mainly for its remarkable bark which, in young trees, is a burnished coppery-orange with horizonal markings. Small white flowers are $1/2$in (1cm) wide and leaves 3–4in (8–10cm) long. Hardy to -20F (-29C), US zones 5–9. Native to Tibet and western China.

*Prunus* x *amygdalopersica*

*Prunus* x *amygdalopersica* in Eccleston Square, London

*Prunus mume*

*Prunus padus*

*Prunus* 'Okumiyako'

*Prunus mume*

*Prunus* 'Tai Haku' photographed at Savill Gardens, Windsor

*Prunus* 'Shirofugen'

*Prunus* 'Shirotae'

*Prunus* 'Amanogawa'   A very narrow deciduous tree, that grows to about 26ft (8m) tall but only about 4ft (1.25m) wide, with fragrant semi-double shell-pink flowers. The pale green leaves are slightly bronzed when they unfold and turn yellow in autumn. Ideal for small gardens, making an attractive focal point. Hardy to -20°F (-29°C), US zones 5–9.

KANZAN CHERRY *Prunus* 'Kanzan' (also known as 'Sekiyama')   A deciduous tree of stiff habit at first (resembling a blown-out umbrella), but later becoming more spreading. It grows to about 30ft (9m), ultimately rather wider than tall. Double flowers, 2in (5cm) wide, are borne in late spring in drooping clusters of 2–4 flowers. The leaves, 3–5in (8–12cm) long, open a deep bronze colour but become green in summer, and turn to yellow and sometimes red before falling. Hardy to -20°F (-29°C), US zones 5–9. Susceptible to honey fungus and is not normally a long-lived tree.

*Prunus* 'Shirofugen'   A deciduous tree with a broad spreading habit, growing to about 25ft (8m). Pink buds open to semi-double white flowers 2in (5cm) wide and fade to purplish-pink. They are borne in long-stalked clusters of 2–4 flowers in late spring just as the young bronze leaves 3–5in (8–12cm) unfold. In the autumn they turn from green to yellow before falling, but the colour is not outstanding. Hardy to -20°F (-29°C), US zones 5–9. This is an old cultivar but has been grown in the West only since the early 20th century.

*Prunus* 'Shirotae'   A deciduous tree that grows to about 15ft (4.5m) and becomes considerably wider than tall with a flat top and layered branches. Flowers, 2in (5cm) wide, appear in spring in long-stalked drooping clusters of 2–4 flowers. Leaves are 3–5in (8–12cm) long, Hardy to -20°F (-29°C), US zones 5–9. No regular pruning is needed and, as with all cherries, it should be avoided as wounds are slow to heal and are liable to infection by various diseases. If essential, pruning should be done in mid-summer. 'Shirotae' is one of the Sato-zakura or 'Village Cherries' of Japan.

GREAT WHITE CHERRY *Prunus* 'Tai Haku'   This tree grows to about 30ft (9m) and is as wide as it is tall, with a flat top. Pink buds open to pure white showy single flowers, 2½in (6cm) wide, with large rounded petals. They are borne in mid-spring in long-stalked drooping clusters of 2–4 flowers. The leaves are 3–6in (8–15cm), opening to a deep purple or bronze colour becoming green in summer. Like many cultivated cherries, this tree does not produce fruit. Hardy to -20°F (-29°C), US zones 5–9. In the early 20th century the flowering cherry expert Collingwood Ingram recognized this variety in an English garden and it was subsequently reintroduced to Japan.

*Prunus* 'Ukon'  A deciduous tree with a broad spreading habit that grows to about 30ft (9m) in height. It is one of the very few Japanese cherries that can claim to have a yellow tint to the flowers. The flowers are about 2in (5cm) wide, opening from pink buds to semi-double cream petals tinged with pale green at the base. Flowers are borne in spring in clusters of 2–5 and leaves turning to red or red-brown before falling. Hardy to 20°F (-29°C), US zones 5–9. A striking and free-flowering small tree well suited to average-sized gardens.

*Prunus* x *yedoensis* 'Shidare Yoshino' (also known as *P.* x *yedoensis* forma *perpendens*) This tree grows to about 20ft (6m) tall, with branches that spread widely and arch almost to the ground. Pink buds open to slightly scented semi-double flowers, about 1in (2.5cm) wide, with pink-tinged white petals. They are borne in early spring in clusters of 2–5. Will grow on any soil and needs average rainfall and a sunny position. Hardy to -10°F (-23°C), US zones 6–9. Like other weeping trees, it is important to train up a leading shoot in order to encourage the formation of a tall enough trunk.

*Prunus* x *yedoensis* 'Shidare Yoshino'

*Prunus* x *yedoensis* 'Shidare Yoshino'

*Prunus* 'Ukon'

*Prunus* 'Amanogawa'

*Prunus* 'Kanzan'

*Magnolia wilsonii*

*Magnolia* x *soulangeana* 'Rustica Rubra'

*Magnolia* 'Elizabeth' A deciduous tree with a smooth grey bark, it is likely to grow to 40ft (12m) and is usually taller than wide. Fragrant flowers, up to 4in (10cm) wide, in late spring. Leaves are oval or elliptical 3–6in (8–15cm) long. The cone-like fruit is up to 4in (10cm) long. Plant in early autumn or late spring, preferably as a container-grown plant in a sunny but sheltered position. Hardy to 0°F (-18°C), US zones 7–9 or cooler.

BULL BAY *Magnolia grandiflora* A large evergreen shrub that will grow up to 30ft (9m) high and wide in cool areas, but in hot climates grows as a tree to 100ft (30m). Highly fragrant flowers, up to 10in (25cm) wide, are borne throughout summer. Should be planted in early autumn or late spring in deep fertile acid

or neutral soil in a sunny but sheltered position. Hardy to 0°F (-18°C), US zones 7–9. Native to south-eastern North America and first grown in Britain in the middle of the 18th century.

*Magnolia liliiflora* 'Nigra' A compact deciduous shrub, growing to 13ft (4m) high. From late spring into summer it produces a succession of slightly scented erect flowers up to 5in (12cm) long. Leaves are oval or elliptical and are 3–8in (8–20cm) long. Cone-like fruit is up to 4in (10cm) long. Hardy to 0°F (-18°C), US zones 7–9. Native to China but the variety 'Nigra' was first brought to Britain from Japan in the mid-19th century.

*Magnolia* 'Ricki' A much-branched deciduous shrub that grows to 10ft (3m) tall. Slightly sweet-scented flowers 5in (12cm) wide. Leaves oval or elliptical 3–6in (8–15cm) long. Cone-like fruit is about 3in (8cm) long. Needs a deep fertile acid or neutral soil and a sunny but sheltered position. Hardy to 0°F (-18°C), US zones 7–9. The later flowering means they are less liable to frost damage.

STAR MAGNOLIA *Magnolia stellata* A medium-sized deciduous shrub of twiggy habit growing up to 10ft (3m) tall, usually considerably wider than tall. Sweetly scented flowers are produced in great abundance, even on young trees. It should be planted in early autumn or late spring in deep fertile acid or neutral soil. Hardy to -20°F (-29°C), US zones 5–9. Originally from a small area of Japan and introduced into Britain in the late 19th century, it is now extremely rare in the wild.

*Magnolia* x *soulangeana* 'Rustica Rubra' A much-branched deciduous shrub or spreading tree up to 25ft (8m) tall, it bears slightly sweet-scented flowers about 5in (12cm) wide. Hardy to -10°F (-23°C), US zones 6–9. 'Rustica Rubra' appears to have arisen as a chance seedling in a Dutch nursery at the end of the 19th century.

*Magnolia wilsonii* Grows to 25ft (8m) and often as wide. In late spring produces strongly scented flowers 3–4in (8–10cm) wide. It should be planted in early autumn or late spring and will grow well in any moist soil in a sheltered and partly shaded position. Hardy to 0°F (-18°C), US zones 7–9. Native to western China, introduced into cultivation early in the 20th century.

*Magnolia* x *soulangeana* A much-branched deciduous shrub or spreading tree growing up to 25ft (8m) tall, usually wider than it is high. It produces an abundance of flowers before the leaves open. The roots are sensitive to disturbance, so avoid trying to move it. It needs a deep fertile acid or neutral soil, average rainfall and a sunny but sheltered position. Hardy to -10°F (-23°C), US zones 6–9. *Magnolia* x *soulangeana* is a group of hybrids between *M. denudata* and *M. liliiflora*, raised by the French nurseryman M. Soulange-Bodin in the 19th century.

*Magnolia* x *loebneri* 'Merrill' (left) A small deciduous tree growing to 25ft (8m) tall. Before the narrowly oval leaves, 3–5in (8–12cm) long, open in spring, the abundance of flowers, 4in (10cm) wide, are rarely all damaged by frost. Cone-like fruit 3in (8cm). Plant in early autumn or late spring, preferably as a container-grown plant on any good rich soil, even chalk, in a sunny but sheltered position. Hardy to 0°F (-18°C), US zones 7–9.

*Magnolia* x *loebneri* 'Leonard Messel' (above) A small vigorous deciduous tree growing to 25ft (8m) tall. Flowers, 4in (10cm) wide, appear in great abundance, even on young trees. Leaves narrowly oval 3–5in (8–12cm) long. Cone-like fruit 3in (8cm) long. Plant in early autumn or late spring, preferably as a container-grown plant. Unusually for a magnolia, it will grow well on any good rich soil. Hardy to 0°F (-18°C), US zones 7–9 or cooler.

*M.denudata* in Lion Grove Garden, China

*Magnolia* 'Elizabeth' photographed at Savill Gardens, Windsor

*Magnolia* x *soulangeana*

'Rustica Rubra'

¹/₂ life-size. Specimens from the Valley Gardens, Windsor, 13 May

*Magnolia liliiflora* 'Nigra'

*Magnolia* 'Ricki'

*Magnolia* x *soulangeana* 'Rustica Rubra'

*Magnolia grandiflora*

*Acer japonicum*

*Acer palmatum* 'Dissectum'

*Acer ginnala*

*Acer pseudoplatanus* 'Brilliantissimum'

*Acer negundo*

*Acer davidii*

*Acer palmatum* 'Atropurpureum'

*Acer palmatum* 'Osakazuki'

*Acer palmatum* 'Sango-kaku'

# MAPLE TREES

Acer saccharinum

Acer platanoides 'Crimson King'

PÉRE DAVID'S MAPLE *Acer davidii*
A deciduous tree that grows to about 50ft (15m). Happy on any soil type that is not too dry, it also tolerates light shade. Hardy to -10°F (-23°C), US zones 6–10. Native to western China. Should be planted in autumn or winter.

AMUR MAPLE *Acer ginnala*  A small deciduous tree or large spreading shrub that grows to about 15ft (4.5m). Happy on any soil type that is not too dry, it also tolerates light shade. Hardy to -20°F (-29°C), US zones 5–10. Native to Japan and China. Should be planted in autumn or winter.

SILVER MAPLE *Acer saccharinum*
A vigorous deciduous tree that grows up to 120ft (35m). Happy in any soil type, flourishing in moist conditions, it tolerates shade but prefers full sun. Hardy to -40°F (-40°C), US zones 3–10. Native to North America.

RED JAPANESE MAPLE *Acer palmatum* 'Atropurpureum'  A small spreading deciduous tree that grows to about 12ft (3.5m). Flourishes in moist acid soil sheltered from the wind, and prefers part shade. Hardy to -20°F (-29°C), US zones 5–10. Is best planted in damp weather in autumn or winter.

LACELEAF JAPANESE MAPLE *Acer palmatum* 'Dissectum'  A mushroom-shaped or rounded deciduous shrub that grows slowly to about 5ft (1.5m) with a habit that spreads to about the same width. Flourishes in moist acid soil sheltered from the wind; prefers part shade. Hardy to -20°F (-29°C), US zones 5–10. Is best planted in autumn or winter.

*Acer palmatum* 'Osakazuki'  A small deciduous shrub or tree that grows to 10ft (3m) tall with about the same width. Flourishes in moist acid soil sheltered from the wind and prefers part shade. Hardy to -20°F (-29°C), US zones 5–10

FULLMOON MAPLE *Acer japonicum*
A large deciduous shrub or small tree that grows to 25ft (8m). Prefers an acid or neutral soil that is not too dry; also tolerates light shade but a protected sunny position is needed for good autumn colour. Hardy to -20°F (-29°C), US zones 5–10. Native to Japan. Should be planted in autumn or winter, but small container-grown plants are often available and these may be planted at any time when the soil is moist.

GOLDEN FULLMOON MAPLE *Acer japonicum* 'Aureum' is also know as *Acer shirasawanum* forma *aureum* (above) A large deciduous shrub or small tree that grows to 20ft (6m) tall. Prefers an acid or neutral soil that is not too dry. It tolerates light shade, but needs to be protected from cold winds in spring. Hardy to -20°F (-29°C), US zones 5–10. Golden Fullmoon Maple is native to Japan. Should be planted in the autumn or in winter.

RED LACELEAF JAPANESE MAPLE *Acer palmatum* 'Dissectum Atropurpureum'  A rounded deciduous shrub that grows slowly to about 5ft (1.5m) tall with a habit that spreads to about the same width. It flourishes in moist acid soil sheltered from the wind, and prefers part shade. Hardy to -20°F (-29°C), US zones 5–10. It is best planted in autumn or winter.

CORAL-BARK MAPLE *Acer palmatum* 'Sango-kaku' (also known as 'Senkaki') A small deciduous tree that grows to 30ft (9m) in height, rather less wide than tall. Flourishes in moist acid soil sheltered from the wind and prefers part shade. Turns golden in autumn and has bright red twigs in winter. Hardy to -20°F (-29°C), US zones 5–10.

*Acer platanoides* 'Crimson King'
A deciduous tree that grows up to 70ft (20m) tall. Happy in any soil type and tolerates shade but prefers full sun. Hardy to -30°F (-35°C), US zones 4–10. Native to northern Europe.

*Acer pseudoplatanus* 'Brilliantissimum'
A fairly slow-growing deciduous tree that grows to 20ft (6m) with a rounded crown. Happy in any soil type and tolerates shade but prefers full sun. Hardy to -20°F (-29°C), US zones 5–10. Native to northern Europe.

BOX ELDER *Acer negundo*  A vigorous deciduous tree that grows to 50ft (15m) tall. It is happy in any soil type and tolerant of full sun or part shade. Hardy to -40°F (-40°C), US zones 3–10. *Acer negundo* should be planted in the autumn or winter.

CHAPTER TWO

# Shrubs

*The plants in this chapter are arranged by flowering time, starting with very early-flowering shrubs such as the mahonias, camellias and rhododendrons, then on to the hydrangeas and very late-flowering shrubs. Then follows a group of shrubs noted for their show of berries and autumn colour. A section of largely tender shrubs suitable for growing under glass in cold areas is added at the end.*

*Mahonia japonica*   A medium-sized shrub that grows to 5ft (1.5m) tall, eventually making a bush wider than tall. In winter it produces many arching spikes, 8in (20cm) long or more, of sweetly scented flowers about ¹/₂in (1cm) wide. The fruit is a blue-black berry. Hardy to 0°F (-18°C), US zones 7–10. Native to China.

*Mahonia* x *media* 'Charity'   An evergreen shrub that grows to 10ft (3m) tall. In late autumn and winter it produces spikes, 10in (25cm) long, of slightly scented flowers about ¹/₂in (1cm) wide. The fruit is a blue-black berry. Hardy to 0°F (-18°C), US zones 7–10. *M.* x *media* is a hybrid between *M. japonica* and

*M. lomariifolia*. The variety 'Charity' was raised in Britain in the mid-20th century.

## WINTER JASMINE
*Jasminum nudiflorum* (right) A medium-sized, deciduous shrub that grows to about 6ft (1.8m) tall, but twice as high if against a wall. In winter its green stems are wreathed in yellow flowers, each about 1in (2.5cm) wide. Hardy to 0°F (-18°C), US zones 7–10. Native to western China, from where Robert Fortune introduced it to Britain in the 19th century. This shrub is very showy in flower and is one of the most reliable and popular winter-flowering shrubs.

*Viburnum* x *bodnantense* 'Dawn' A medium-sized deciduous shrub that grows to 10ft (3m) tall, somewhat spare in habit. In late winter it bears compact clusters of small, strongly scented flowers, each about ¹/₂in (1cm) long, opening from red buds. Can be planted in autumn or spring. Hardy to -10°F (-23°C), US zones 6–9. *V.* x *bodnantense* is a hybrid raised in North Wales in this century.

*Garrya elliptica*   A large evergreen shrub that grows to 12ft (3.5m) tall and usually wider. Male and female flowers are carried on separate bushes. In winter, catkins develop which remain in beauty for several weeks; the male flowers are grey-green with a pink flush and may be 6in (15cm) or more in length; the females are shorter and less attractive, developing into lovely purplish fruits. The leaves are up to 3in (8cm) long and have greyish woolly hairs beneath. Hardy to 0°F (-18°C), US zones 7–10.

*Sarcococca confusa*   A compact and slow-growing evergreen shrub that grows up to 5ft (1.5m) tall and about as wide. In late winter it bears small clusters of highly fragrant but rather inconspicuous white flowers in the leaf axils. The fruit is a small black berry. Hardy to -10°F (-23°C), US zones 6–9, this shrub grows best in a partially shaded position. A fine foliage shrub for fairly dry shady places.

*Sarcococca hookeriana* var. *hookeriana* 'Purple Stem'   A compact evergreen shrub that grows to 5ft (1.5m) tall, the erect purple stems forming a thicket about as wide as tall. In late winter and early spring it bears small clusters of highly fragrant but rather inconspicuous flowers in the leaf axils. The fruit is a small

*Chimonanthus praecox* 'Luteus'

*Viburnum* x *bodnantense* 'Dawn'

*Mahonia* x *media* 'Charity'

*Mahonia japonica*

black berry. Hardy to -10°F (-23°C), US zones 6–9. *Sarcococca hookeriana* var. *hookeriana* is native to the Himalayas, from Nepal eastwards.

**CONTORTED HAZEL** *Corylus avellana* 'Contorta'   A large deciduous shrub that grows to 10ft (3m) tall, usually multi-stemmed and wider than tall. In late winter it produces an abundance of slender, drooping catkins about 2in (5cm) long, each consisting of many tiny male flowers producing quantities of pollen. The very small female flowers are paired within a bud from which each protrudes two crimson stigmas. Noted for its zig-zag stems resulting in a chaotic-looking shrub. Hardy to -20°F (-29°C), US zones 5–9.

*Prunus* x *subhirtella* 'Autumnalis'
An elegant, small deciduous tree that grows to 16ft (5m) tall. Intermittently throughout the winter and early spring it produces clusters of flowers, each about $^{1}/_{2}$in (1cm). The leaves take on orange and red tints in autumn. It can be planted in autumn or early spring. This tree should have a sunny position sheltered from strong winds. Hardy to -10°F (-23°C), US zones 6–9.

*Chimonanthus praecox* 'Luteus'
A deciduous shrub that grows up to 7ft (2m) tall and wide. Strongly scented flowers, each $^{3}/_{4}$–1in (2–2.5cm) wide, composed of several overlapping petals of a curious translucent waxy texture, appear on the bare branches in late winter. The fruit is a gourd-shaped capsule 1$^{1}/_{2}$in (4cm) long. Hardy to -10°F (-23°C), US zones 6–9.

**WINTER SWEET** *Chimonanthus praecox* (also known as *C. fragrans*)
A deciduous shrub that grows to 7ft (2m) tall and wide. The flowers, about $^{3}/_{4}$in (2cm) wide, appear on the bare branches in late winter, soon after Christmas. In some forms, the flowers have a maroon centre and in all, they have a strong and wonderful scent. The fruit is a gourd-shaped capsule 1$^{1}/_{2}$in (4cm) long. Hardy to -10°F (-23°C), US zones 6–9.

*Corylus avellana* 'Contorta'

*Garrya elliptica*

*Sarcococca hookeriana* var. *hookeriana*

*Sarcococca confusa*

*Prunus* x *subhirtella* 'Autumnalis'

*Clianthus puniceus*   A lax, partially evergreen shrub that grows up to 7ft (2m) tall with clusters of bright red (less commonly pink or white) pea-type flowers, each up to 3in (8cm) long, in early summer. The leaves are to 6in (15cm) long, divided into 15–25 small leaflets. The fruit is seldom seen, but is a pod 3in (8cm) long. Hardy to 10°F (-12°C), US zones 8–10. Native to northern New Zealand.

*Coronilla valentina* subsp. *glauca*   A small evergreen shrub that grows up to 4ft (1.25m) tall and about as wide. In spring, and often sporadically later in the year, it produces clusters of sweetly scented flowers, each ¹/₂in (1cm) long. The leaves are 2–3in (5–7cm) long and the fruit is a pod 1¹/₂in (4cm) long. Hardy to 10°F (-12°C), US zones 8–10. Native to southern Europe. Ideal for a hot and sunny corner and an excellent choice for a large pot on a patio.

*Erica canaliculata*

*Coronilla valentina*  subsp. *valentina* A low evergreen shrub that grows to 5ft (1.5m) tall. Scented flowers produced in spring. Hardy to 15°F (-9°C), US zones 8–10. Native to the Mediterranean, from eastern France to Albani, and North Africa, growing in scrub and on cliffs.

*Erica arborea* var. *alpina*   A medium-sized shrub that grows up to 12ft (3.5m) tall and wider, producing an abundance of dull white flowers, each about ¹/₈in (3mm) long, in conical clusters up to 12in (30cm) long, in early spring. The needle-like leaves are ¹/₄in (6mm) long. Hardy to 0°F (-18°C), US zones 7–10. *E. arborea* is native to much of the Mediterranean region, but var. *alpina* is confined to the mountains of eastern Spain. Worth

*Leptospermum scoparium*

*Erica arborea* var. *alpina*

*Leptospermum scoparium* 'Winter Cheer'

*Clianthus puniceus*

growing for its foliage which provides an unusual textural effect, enhanced by the flowers in early spring.

*Erica canaliculata*   A large evergreen shrub of erect growth that reaches 15ft (4.5m) tall, producing an abundance of fragrant pale pink or dull white flowers, each ¹/₈in (3mm) long, in conical clusters 12in (30cm) long in late winter. The needle-like leaves are ¹/₄in (6mm) long. Hardy to 20°F (-7°C), US zones 9–10. Native to South Africa, this shrub is too tender for many gardens but makes a fine conservatory shrub in cold areas.

*Leptospermum scoparium*   An evergreen shrub that grows to 7ft (2m) tall in cultivation but often taller in the wild. In the winter and spring it produces many small white flowers, each ¹/₂in (1cm) wide. The small dark green leaves are narrowly oval and up to ¹/₂in (1cm) long. It needs a well-drained acid or neutral soil and thrives in the dry summer conditions of California or the Mediterranean. Hardy to 10°F (-12°C), US zones 8–10. Native to Australia and New Zealand, and introduced to Britain in the 18th century.

*Leptospermum scoparium* 'Winter Cheer' A small evergreen shrub that grows up to 7ft (2m) tall in cultivation but taller and even tree-like in the wild. A profusion of flowers each ¹/₂in (1cm) wide, appear intermittently from autumn to spring in mild climates. Oval leaves about ¹/₂in (1cm) long, sometimes tinged with bronze when young. Thrives in a sunny position and benefits from a sheltered site by a south or west wall in cooler areas. Hardy to 10°F (-12°C), US zones 8–10. Native to Australia and New Zealand.

ROSEMARY *Rosmarinus officinalis* 'Severn Sea'   An erect evergreen shrub that grows to 4ft (1.25m) tall and usually wider. It bears clusters of pale blue flowers, each about ¹/₂in (1cm) long, in late spring. More compact with more

vividly coloured flowers than most varieties of *R. officinalis*. Delightfully aromatic leaves. Best in full sun and hardy to 20°F (-7°C), US zones 8–10. Native to Europe, Asia and North Africa.

*Pittosporum tenuifolium*   A small evergreen tree of elegant habit that grows up to 30ft (9m) tall. In spring it produces clusters of small deep chocolate-purple flowers, each ¹/₂in (1cm) wide with a strong honey scent, especially in the evening. The leaves are 1–2in (2.5–5cm) long. Hardy to 10°F (-12°C), US zones 8–10. Native to New Zealand. (*Not illustrated*)
   *Pittosporum tenuifolium* 'Variegatum' To 20ft (6m) with leaves edged white.

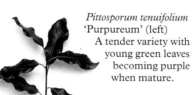

*Pittosporum tenuifolium* 'Purpureum' (left) A tender variety with young green leaves becoming purple when mature.

*Pittosporum tenuifolium* 'Warnham Gold'(right) To 20ft (6m) raised in England in this century.

*Pittosporum tobira*   A large shrub that grows to 20ft (6m) tall and wider when mature. In early summer it produces clusters of highly scented flowers, each about 1in (2.5cm) wide. The leaves are 2–4in (5–10cm) long. The fruit is a woody capsule that splits to reveal several sticky orange seeds. Hardy to 10°F (-12°C), US zones 8–10. Native to Japan, Taiwan and China, this is a handsome evergreen with attractive flowers and fruits, and thrives in coastal gardens.

*Coronilla valentina* subsp. *glauca*

*Coronilla valentina* subsp. *valentina*

*Pittosporum tobira*

*Rosmarinus officinalis* 'Severn Sea'

*Pittosporum tenuifolium* 'Variegatum'

# SHRUBS

**HIMALAYAN BOX** *Buxus wallichiana*
This shrub grows up to 15ft (4.5m) tall
and about as wide, with dense clusters of
flowers appearing in spring. Hardy to
10°F (-12°C), US zones 8–10. Grows
wild in the Himalayas, from Afghanistan
to Nepal. Although fairly hardy and very
distinct from European box, it is not
common in gardens because it is more
difficult to propagate. It is an attractive
shrub for a partially shaded corner.

*Elaeagnus* x *ebbingei* 'Gilt Edge'  A shrub
that grows up to 10ft (3m) tall and rather
wider than tall. This group of shrubs is
fairly fast-growing and wind-resistant,
useful for hedging and shelter, and for its
autumn flowering. It has clusters of 3–6
small bell-shaped, sweetly scented flowers.
Best in a sunny position and hardy to
10°F (-12°C), US zones 8–10, 'Gilt Edge'
is the variegated form raised by Waterer &
Crisp in 1961, much valued for its
handsome foliage.

*Elaeagnus macrophylla*  Growing up to
10ft (3m) tall and broader, this shrub

produces clusters of small bell-shaped,
sweetly scented flowers. It can be planted
in autumn or early spring in almost any
soil, except shallow chalk, in a sunny
position. Hardy to 0°F (-18°C), US zones
7–10. Native to Korea and southern Japan
and introduced to Britain in the late 19th
century. Like the rather similar hybrid
*E.* x *ebbingei*, it is most useful in exposed
seaside and windy sites.

*Griselinia littoralis*  This shrub grows up
to 50ft (15m) tall in the wild or in mild
areas, but more often reaches only 20ft
(6m) in cooler climates. In late spring it
produces inconspicuous flowers in
clusters 2–3in (5–8cm) long. Hardy to
10°F (-12°C), US zones 8–10, and native
to New Zealand from where it was
introduced to Britain in the mid-19th
century. Not seen at its best in cool inland
gardens, it makes a fine shrub in coastal
gardens where the climate is milder. The
flowers are not beautiful but the foliage
has a unique texture and colour.

*Griselinia littoralis* 'Variegata'  The
leaves have a broad irregular cream

margin, which is yellow when the leaves
first open. Occasionally, a branch will
sport to a form with the variegation
reversed.

*Photinia* x *fraseri* 'Robusta'  This shrub
grows up to 20ft (6m) tall and usually as
wide. In late spring it produces broad
clusters of flowers, each about ¹⁄₂in (1cm)
wide. Hardy to 0°F (-18°C), US zones
7 10. *P.* x *fraseri* is a hybrid first raised in
the US, but 'Robusta' originated in
Australia in this century. Valued for its
brightly coloured young foliage,
conspicuous well into the summer, this
shrub is hardier than the similarly
coloured pieris and, unlike them, grows
well in limy soils.

*Skimmia japonica*  This evergreen shrub
grows up to 7ft (2m) tall, but is often
more compact and usually rather wider
than tall. In spring it bears fragrant
flowers, each about ¹⁄₃in (8mm) wide.
Individual bushes have either male or
female flowers, the male being particularly
strongly scented. The leaves have a

*Skimmia laureola*

*Skimmia japonica*

*Skimmia japonica* 'Rubella'

*Photinia* x *fraseri* 'Robusta'

*Buxus wallichiana*

curious oily scent when bruised. Hardy to 0°F (-18°C), US zones 7–9 and native to Japan from where it was introduced to Britain in the mid-19th century. Popular both for its fragrance and its berries.

*Skimmia japonica* 'Rubella' This is a male clone which is a good pollinator for any female variety planted with it. One of the best for scent and is more colourful early in the flowering season.

*Skimmia laureola* This shrub is usually less than 3½ft (1m) tall, with aromatic leaves, sweetly scented flowers and black berries. Native of the Himalayas, from eastern Nepal to western China, and in the mountains to eastern China, especially as an undershrub in rocky places in forest from 5600–12600ft (1600–3600m). It flowers from April to June.

## WOOLLY WILLOW *Salix lanata*

A slow-growing deciduous shrub that grows to 5ft (1.5m) tall, bearing relatively large yellowish catkins, each about 1½in (4cm) long, in spring. Male and female catkins are borne on different bushes, the female being longer but less showy than the male. On female plants the catkins enlarge to about 3in (8cm) long before releasing masses of fluffy seeds. Hardy to -10°F (-23°C), US zones 6–9. Native to northern Europe including Scotland.

*Salix hastata* 'Wehrhahnii' A slow-growing deciduous shrub that reaches 7ft (2m) tall. The young shoots are a striking deep purplish-brown. A male clone, in spring it bears an abundance of silvery catkins, each about 1½in (4cm) long. Best in a sunny position and hardy to -10°F (-23°C), US zones 6–9. *S. hastata* is widely distributed in Europe and the cultivar 'Wehrhahnii' was found in Switzerland in the mid-20th century. It is very suitable for a damp corner.

*Elaeagnus* x *ebbingei* 'Gilt Edge'

*Elaeagnus macrophylla*

*Griselinia littoralis* 'Variegata'

*Salix lanata*

*Salix hastata* 'Wehrhahnii'

*Griselinia littoralis*

# SHRUBS

*Choisya* 'Aztec Pearl'   An evergreen shrub that grows to 24in (60cm) tall and usually wider, producing sweet-scented flowers, each about 1in (2.5cm) across, in spring and often with a second flush in late summer. Leaves strongly scented when crushed. Thrives in dry climates. Hardy to 10°F (-12°C), US zones 8–10. A hybrid between *C. arizonica* and *C. ternata*.

## MEXICAN ORANGE BLOSSOM
*Choisya ternata*   An evergreen shrub that grows to 10ft (3m) tall and wide. It produces sweet-scented flowers, each about ³/₄in (2cm) across, in the spring and a second flush in late summer and autumn. Best in a sunny position; in shade it grows well but flowers less freely. Hardy to 10°F (-12°C), US zones 8–10, but may lose its leaves at low temperatures.
*Choisya ternata* 'Sundance'   Grows to 5–6ft (1.5–1.8m) tall and wide. The young leaves are bright golden yellow, becoming slightly greener as they mature. *C. ternata* is native to Mexico. 'Sundance' was brought into cultivation in the late 20th century.

*Daphne mezereum* (left)
A deciduous shrub that grows up to 5ft (1.5m) tall. In early spring its stems are wreathed with clusters of sweet-scented lilac-pink or dark red-purple flowers, each about ¹/₂in (1cm) wide. The poisonous red berries are some-times borne in such abundance as to give a second season of interest. Hardy to -20°F (-29°C), US zones 5–10.

*Daphne bholua* 'Ghurka'   One of the showiest daphnes in the right conditions, this deciduous shrub grows to 12ft (3.5m) tall and produces clusters of very sweet-scented flowers in early spring. The fruit is a poisonous black berry. Hardy to -10°F (-23°C), US zones 6–10. Like other daphnes, this shrub is sometimes short-lived. *D. bholua* is native to the Himalayas and south-western China.

*Daphne* x *houtteana*   A semi-evergreen shrub that grows to 4ft (1.25m) tall and as wide. Clusters of 2–5 sweet-scented lilac-pink or dark red-purple flowers, each ¹/₂in (1cm) long, in early spring. Unusual purple foliage, at least some of which remains when the flowers appear. The fruit is a poisonous berry, seldom formed. Hardy to -10°F (-23°C); US zones 6–10.

*Daphne odora*   A small dome-shaped evergreen shrub that grows to 3ft (90cm) tall and usually wider. In winter and early spring it produces clusters of sweet-scented flowers, each with a narrow tube about ¹/₂in (1cm) long. The fruit is a poisonous berry. Native to China, but long cultivated in Japan, from where it was introduced to Britain in the 18th century (not illustrated).
*Daphne odora* 'Aureomarginata' (syn. 'Marginata')   The commonest form in cultivation; has leaves edged with a thin yellow line. Hardier than plain-leaved forms to 10°F (-12°C), US zones 8–10.

*Daphne retusa*   An evergreen shrub that grows to 3ft (90cm) tall and wider. In late spring and occasionally in autumn, it produces dense clusters of sweet-scented flowers. The leaves are tinged with purple and the fruit is a poisonous red berry. Hardy to -10°F (-23°C), US zones 6–10 and longer-lived than some daphnes.

Native to western China, from where it was introduced to cultivation at the beginning of the 20th century.

*Daphne sericea* f. *alba*   A small evergreen shrub that grows to 4ft (1.25m) tall, producing sweet-scented flowers, each about ¹/₂in (1cm) wide. Hardy to 10°F (-12°C), US zones 8–10. The species *D. sericea* is native to south-eastern Europe and was introduced to Britain in the 20th century. The white form *alba* is as attractive as the wild pink one and is a useful shrub for smaller gardens or as a focal point on a rock garden.

*Lonicera rupicola* var. *syringantha* (also known as *L. syringantha*) (right)   A twiggy deciduous shrub that grows to 5ft (1.5m) tall with an elegant spreading habit. Sweet-scented flowers in late spring, each about ¹/₂in (1cm) wide. Hardy to -10°F (-23°C), US zones 6–10 or lower. Native to Tibet and China. This shrub does not always flower freely but is most beautiful and worthwhile.

## FUCHSIA-FLOWERED GOOSEBERRY
*Ribes speciosum*   This is a spiny evergreen shrub (more or less deciduous in cool areas) that grows up to about 7ft (2m) tall, usually rather taller than wide. It makes an unusual informal hedge. Flowers in spring. Hardy to 0°F (-18°C), US zones 7–9 and in cold gardens will make a fine wall shrub. Native to California and Mexico.

*Daphne sericea* f. *alba*

*Daphne retusa*

*Daphne* x *houtteana*

*Daphne bholua* 'Ghurka'

*Daphne odora* 'Aureomarginata'

*Choisya ternata* 'Sundance'

*Choisya* 'Aztec Pearl'

*Choisya ternata*

*Ribes speciosum*

*Forsythia* x *intermedia* 'Lynwood'

*Pieris floribunda*

*Forsythia* x *intermedia* 'Karl Sax'
A deciduous shrub that grows to 6ft (1.8m) tall and usually as wide. In late winter and early spring it produces a profusion of flowers, each about 1in (2.5cm) long, with four broad and slightly wavy petals. Hardy to 0°F (-18°C), US zones 7–10. No regular pruning is required other than cutting away the old flowered shoots from mature bushes.

*Forsythia* x *intermedia* 'Lynwood'(right)
A medium-sized deciduous shrub that grows to 8ft (2.5m) tall and usually wider. In late winter and early spring it produces a profusion of flowers, each about 1in (2.5cm) long, and strong pruning results in long shoots wreathed in flowers. Best in a sunny position and hardy to 0°F (-18°C), US zones 7–10.

*Pieris* 'Firecrest' A vigorous evergreen shrub that grows to 7ft (2m) tall, of compact and upright growth. In early spring it produces drooping racemes about 4in (10cm) long, crowded with small white bell-shaped flowers. The young leafy shoots are bright scarlet in early spring, gradually changing through creamy-pink to dark green in summer, 3–5in (8–12cm) long. Hardy to 0°F (-18°C), US zones 7–9.

*Pieris* 'Forest Flame' A vigorous evergreen shrub that grows to 8ft (2.5m) tall. In early spring it produces drooping racemes about 4in (10cm) long, crowded with small white, bell-shaped flowers. Hardy to 0°F (-18°C), US zones 7–9.

*Pieris floribunda* An evergreen shrub that grows to 7ft (2m) tall. In early spring it produces erect clusters about 4in (10cm) long, of small white flowers, each pitcher-shaped and about 1/3in (8mm) long. The leaves are 2–3in (5–8cm) long, oval and slightly bristly on the margins. Hardy to 10°F (-23°C), US zones 6–9. Native to the south-eastern United States. Lacks the colourful young foliage of other species of pieris, but it is a beautiful and hardy evergreen shrub for a woodland situation.

*Pieris japonica* 'Grayswood' An evergreen shrub that grows to 5ft (1.5m) tall. In early spring it produces drooping racemes up to 6in (15cm) long, crowded with small milk-white pitcher-shaped flowers, each about 1/4in (6mm) long. The young leaves, 1 1/2–3in (4–8cm) long, are bronze in early spring, gradually becoming a slightly glossy dark green in summer. Hardy to 0°F (-18°C), US zones 7–9.

*Pieris japonica* 'Variegata' A compact evergreen shrub growing very slowly up to 10ft (3m) tall, rounded in habit and eventually wider than tall. In early spring it produces drooping racemes up to 4in (12cm) long, crowded with small milk-white pitcher-shaped flowers each 1/2in (1cm) long. The leaves are 1 1/2–2 1/2in (4–6cm) long, with a narrow cream margin and tinged coppery-pink when young. Hardy to 0°F (-18°C), US zones 7–9 or lower.

*Physocarpus opulifolius* 'Dart's Gold'
A compact deciduous shrub that grows to 5ft (1.5m) tall and usually wider. In spring it produces clusters of white or pink-tinged flowers, each about 1/3in (8mm) wide. The leaves are bluntly 3-lobed and bright yellow for most of the summer. Hardy to -10°F (-23°C), US zones 6–10. *Physocarpus opulifolius* is native to eastern North America.

BUFFALO CURRANT *Ribes odoratum*
A spreading deciduous shrub that grows to 7ft (2m) tall. Short racemes of small bright yellow flowers have a spicy scent and the leaves are 1–1 1/2in (2.5–4cm) wide. The fruit is a small deep purple berry. Best in a sunny position as it becomes very lax and untidy in shade. Hardy to -10°F (-23°C), US zones 6–9. Native to central North America.

FLOWERING CURRANT *Ribes sanguineum* A vigorous deciduous shrub that grows to 10ft (3m) tall. Drooping racemes of bright rose-pink flowers in spring. The leaves are 2–3in (5–8cm) wide, with a characteristic and slightly unpleasant smell when touched. Hardy to -10°F (-23°C), US zones 6–9. Native to western North America.

*Ribes sanguineum* 'Brocklebankii' A fairly erect deciduous shrub that grows to 5ft (1.5m) tall, grown mainly for its bright foliage. Drooping racemes of rose-pink flowers are produced in spring. The leaves are 2–3in (5–8cm) wide, producing a characteristic and unpleasant smell when touched; they may scorch in strong sun. The fruit is a small blue-black berry. Hardy to -10°F (-23°C), US zones 6–9.

*Forsythia* x *intermedia* 'Karl Sax'

Pieris japonica 'Grayswood'

Pieris japonica 'Variegata'

Pieris 'Firecrest'

Pieris 'Forest Flame'

Ribes sanguineum

Ribes sanguineum 'Brocklebankii' (left)
Physocarpus opulifolius 'Dart's Gold' (right)

Ribes odoratum

41

# SHRUBS

Spiraea
arguta

Prunus x cistena

Spiraea x cinerea
'Grefsheim'

¹/₃ life size. Specimens from Wisley, 24 April

*Spiraea thunbergii*

*Stachyurus praecox*

*Prunus cerasifera* 'Pissardii'

*Prunus tenella* 'Firehill'

*Corylopsis spicata*

42

# SPRING-FLOWERING SHRUBS

*Corylopsis pauciflora* (right) A small deciduous shrub that grows to 7ft (2m) tall and usually wider. In early spring it produces clusters of 1–3 pale yello, sweet-scented flowers, each about ¹⁄₂in (1cm) long, with 5 rounded petals in a bowl shape. Plant in autumn or early spring in a sheltered woodland position, in light or dappled shade. Hardy to 10°F (-12°C), US zones 8–10. Native to Japan and Taiwan.

*Corylopsis sinensis* A deciduous shrub that grows to 15ft (4.5m) tall and usually wider. The largest-flowered of the Chinese species, producing lemon-yellow flowers, each about ¹⁄₃in (8mm) long, in spring. Plant in any soil, except shallow chalk, in light or dappled shade. Hardy to 5°F (-15°C), US zones 7–10. Native to China, in scrub and forest at 5600–12600ft (1700–3800m). Grows especially well on the east coast of North America.

*Corylopsis spicata* A small deciduous shrub that grows up to 7ft (2m) tall and wider with spreading branches. In spring it produces drooping racemes of 6–12 flowers, each about ¹⁄₃in (8mm) long. The broadly oval or heart-shaped leaves are about 2in (5cm) long and distinctly greyish beneath. Hardy to 0°F (-18°C), US zones 7–10. Native to the island of Shikoku in southern Japan.

DWARF RUSSIAN ALMOND *Prunus tenella* 'Firehill' A deciduous shrub that grows to 5ft (1.5m) tall and spreading by suckers to a considerable width. The flowers, each about 1in (2.5cm) wide, with 5 oblong bright rose-pink petals, are borne in spring before the leaves, which are about 2in (5cm) long, narrowly lance-shaped and open crimson, becoming dull purple-brown later. The fruit is a small

purple cherry. Hardy to -20°F (-29°C), US zones 5–10.

PURPLE-LEAF SAND CHERRY
*Prunus* x *cistena* A small deciduous shrub with several dark stems that grows to 6ft (1.8m) tall and wide. The flowers, each just over ¹⁄₂in (1cm) wide, are borne in spring, before the leaves or as they open. The leaves are about 2in (5cm) long, narrowly lance-shaped and open crimson, becoming dull purple-brown later. The fruit is a small purple cherry. Hardy to -20°F (-29°C), US zones 5–10.

*Prunus cerasifera* 'Pissardii' (sometimes known as the Purple-leaved Plum) A small tree or shrub that grows to 12ft (3m), cultivated mainly for its foliage which comes out dark red and turns purple with age. It flowers early in spring just before the leaves open. Discovered by the gardener to the shah of Persia prior to 1880. Hardy to -30°F (-34°C), US zones 4–10.

*Stachyurus praecox* A deciduous shrub that grows to 16ft (5m) tall. Hanging spikes to 4in (10cm) long, bearing numerous small cup-shaped creamy-yellow flowers, each about ¹⁄₄in (6mm) wide, in early spring. Grows best in a partially shaded position and hardy to -10°F (-23°C), US zones 6–9. Native to Japan and western China. An unusual and most attractive shrub, well-suited to woodland conditions.

*Spiraea arguta* A spreading twiggy shrub that grows to 8ft (2.5m) high, with narrow leaves and flowers in clusters on the upper sides of the arching branches. Soon after flowering, pruning should aim to remove the faded flowers and encourage strong shoots from below the flowering point. Any soil, full sun. Flowering in spring. Hardy to -5°F (-20°C), US zones 6–10.

*Spiraea* x *cinerea* 'Grefsheim' A deciduous twiggy shrub that grows to 5ft (1.5m) high, probably a hybrid between *S. hypericifolia* and *S. cana*, introduced in 1954. Any soil, full sun. Hardy to -5°F (-20°C), US zones 6–10.

*Spiraea thunbergii* A deciduous or semi-evergreen shrub that grows to 5ft (1.5m) high, the most graceful of this group of spiraeas and the earliest to flower in spring. In cool climates it requires a warm autumn and a sheltered position to flower freely, to ensure the buds are formed on well-ripened shoots during the summer. Any soil. Hardy to -5°F (-20°C), US zones 6–10. Native to northern China, although now widely naturalized in southern Japan.

*Corylopsis sinensis*

*Corylopsis sinensis*

*Corylopsis pauciflora*

# SHRUBS

*Camellia* 'Cornish Snow'   A large evergreen shrub that grows to 15ft (4.5m). Flowers of about 1¹/₂in (4cm) appear in early spring. Hardy to 10°F (-12°C), US zones 8–10. *Camellia* 'Cornish Snow' is a hybrid between *C. cuspidata* and *C. saluenensis*. Its lax growth habit makes it less satisfactory than other camellias for planting in the open, but it is a first-rate shrub for planting against a wall, where it will need occasional trimming back and perhaps tying in to wires.

*Camellia* 'Cornish Spring'   A large shrub that grows to 12ft (3.5m) with small flowers 2in (5cm) wide appearing in early spring. It is hardy to 10°F (-12°C), US zones 8–10. *Camellia* 'Cornish Spring' is a hybrid between *C. cuspidata* and *C. japonica*, raised in Cornwall in 1950.

*Camellia reticulata* 'Captain Rawes'   Up to 12ft (3.5m) tall this evergreen shrub bears flowers about 5in (12cm) wide in late winter and early spring. Hardy to 20°F (-7°C), US zones 9–10. *Camellia reticulata* is native to western China and was first introduced to the West in the early 19th century by Robert Fortune. The variety 'Captain Rawes' was this original introduction.

*Camellia reticulata* 'Buddha'   An evergreen shrub that reaches 12ft (3.5m), with an open but bushy habit. In late winter and early spring single flowers about 5in (12cm) wide appear. This variety is hardy to 20°F (-7°C), US zones 9–10. The species *C. reticulata* is native to western China and was first introduced to the West in the early 19th century. The variety 'Buddha' was brought to America from China in 1950. Camellias are excellent shrubs for an unheated conservatory.

*Camellia* x *williamsii* 'Francis Hanger'   An evergreen shrub reaching 12ft (3.5m) with a fairly open habit. Its flowers are 3in (8cm) wide, leaves 2¹/₂–4in (6–10cm) long. 'Francis Hanger' is one of the very few white *Camellia* x *williamsii* cultivars. Hardy to 10°F (-12°C), US zones 8–10 or lower. The variety 'Francis Hanger' was raised at Wisley Gardens in England in the 1950s.

*Camellia* x *williamsii* 'Mary Christian'   An evergreen shrub reaching up to 15ft (4.5m). Its flowers, about 3in (8cm) wide, appear in spring. Leaves are 2¹/₂–4in (6–10cm) long. Hardy to 10°F (-12°C), US zones 8–10 or lower. This variety was raised at Caerhays in Cornwall in 1940.

*Camellia* x *williamsii* 'J C Williams' (above)   An evergreen shrub reaching 15ft (4.5m). The flowers, about 4in (10cm) wide, appear in spring in great abundance. Hardy to 10°F (-12°C), US zones 8–10 or

lower. The variety 'J C Williams' was raised at Caerhays, Cornwall in 1940 and was the first of the *williamsii* hybrids to be named from seed. Hardy to 10°F (-12°C), US zones 8–10. Introduced to Britain in the 20th century.

*Camellia* x *williamsii* 'Ballet Queen'   Growing up to 15ft (4.5m), this evergreen shrub is rather erect but bushy in habit. Flowers about 4in (10cm) wide appear in spring in great abundance. Like other double-flowered varieties, this camellia rarely fruits. This variety is hardy to 10°F (-12°C), US zones 8–10 or lower.

*Camellia* x *williamsii* 'Exaltation'   This evergreen shrub grows up to 15ft (4.5m), with a rather erect but bushy habit. In spring, flowers about 4in (10cm) wide appear. Camellias need a well-drained acid or neutral soil and enjoy plenty of humus. This variety is hardy to 10°F (-12°C), US zones 8–10 or lower. The variety 'Exaltation' was raised in Savill Gardens, Windsor, England in 1966.

*Camellia sasanqua* 'Chôjiguruma'   An evergreen, upright shrub that grows to 13ft (4m). Flowers appear in late autumn and early winter. Needs an acid soil in sun or part shade. Hardy to 20°F (-7°C), US zones 9–10. Raised in Japan in 1789.

*Camellia sasanqua* 'Narumigata'   This evergreen shrub grows to 15ft (4.5m) with delightful sweet-scented flowers, 2¹/₂–3in (6–8cm) wide. This variety occasionally produces a few rounded fruits, about 1in (2.5cm) wide, each containing 2–5 large seeds. Hardy to 10°F (-12°C), US zones 8–10. Introduced into cultivation in the 20th century.

*Camellia sasanqua* 'Chôjiguruma'

*Camellia sasanqua* 'Narumigata'

*Camellia reticulata* 'Captain Rawes'

# SINGLE CAMELLIAS

Camellia 'Cornish Snow'

Camellia x *williamsii* 'Francis Hanger'

Camellia *reticulata* 'Buddha'

Camellia x *williamsii* 'Exaltation'

Camellia x *williamsii* 'Ballet Queen'

Camellia x *williamsii* 'Mary Christian'

Camellia 'Cornish Spring'

*Camellia japonica* 'Adolphe Audusson'

*Camellia japonica* 'California'

*Camellia japonica* 'Bright Buoy' (below)
Evergreen shrub that grows up to 12ft
(3.5m). Its flowers are about 3in (8cm)
wide with overlapping petals,
surrounding a boss of golden stamens.
Camellias can be planted in the autumn
or late spring and need well-drained acid
or neutral soil. This variety is hardy to
20°F (-7°C), US zones 9–10, more tender
than most varieties of
*C. japonica*.

*Camellia japonica* 'Adolphe Audusson'
Evergreen shrub that reaches 20ft (6m).
In spring, semi-double flowers about 4in
(10cm) wide appear. Hardy to 10°F
(-12°C), US zones 8–10. Will grow in full
sun but may drop its buds in dry weather
and is more often grown in woodland
conditions of light shade. *Camellia
japonica* is native to Japan and was first
introduced to the West in the 18th
century.

*Camellia japonica* 'California'
A compact erect evergreen shrub that
reaches 12ft (3.5m). An abundance of
flowers about 4in (10cm) wide appear in
spring. Hardy to 10°F (-12°C), US zones

8–10. Little pruning is needed although
young plants can be lightly trimmed to
encourage them to bush out.

*Camellia japonica* 'Bob Hope'   A compact
medium-sized evergreen shrub that
reaches 10ft (3m). It is rather slower-
growing than other camellias. Its flowers
are 4in (10cm) wide. Hardy to 10°F
(-12°C), US zones 8–10.

*Camellia japonica* 'Guilio Nuccio'
A large evergreen shrub that reaches 20ft
(6m), and rather erect in habit. Flowers
can be up to 5in (12cm) wide and leaves
to 4in (10cm) long. Hardy to 10°F
(-12°C), US zones 8–10. Raised in
California in 1956.

*Camellia japonica* 'Lady Clare' (also
known as 'Akashigata')   An evergreen
shrub that grows to 7ft (2m) tall, lax and

pendulous in growth. Its semi-double
flowers are 4¹⁄₂in (11cm) wide and leaves
are up to 4in (10cm) long. Camellias can
be planted in autumn or late spring. This
variety is hardy to 10°F (-12°C), US
zones 9–10. Introduced from Japan in the
late 19th century, it remains popular. A
low-growing shrub of 2¹⁄₂ft (75cm) after
10 years, excellent for small gardens.

*Camellia* 'Leonard Messel'   A large evergreen shrub that reaches 20ft (6m), rather
erect in habit. Flowers are 4¹⁄₂in (11cm)
wide. Camellias enjoy plenty of humus
and average rainfall. This variety is hardy
to 10°F (-12°C), US zones 8–10.

*Camellia reticulata* 'Nuccio's Ruby'
An evergreen shrub that grows to 12ft
(3.5m). Flowers are semi-double, 5in
(12cm) wide, with wavy deep red petals.
Hardy to 20°F (-7°C), US zones 9–10.

*Camellia* 'Leonard Messel'

*Camellia japonica* 'Lady Clare'

*Camellia japonica* 'Jupiter'

*Camellia japonica* 'Rubescens Major' (above)   A compact evergreen shrub reaching up to 12ft (3.5m), bushy in habit. Flowers are about 4in (10cm) wide. Hardy to 10°F (-12°C), US zones 8–10.

*Camellia japonica* 'Jupiter'   A tall evergreen shrub reaching up to 15ft (4.5m) eventually. Flowers are single with overlapped petals blooming in spring. Upright, vigorous growth. Introduced to England in about 1900 by William Paul of Cheshunt.

*Camellia* x *williamsii* 'Anticipation' A rather erect, bushy evergreen shrub reaching 15ft (4.5m). Its flowers, about 4in (10cm) wide, appear in spring in abundance. Hardy to 10°F (-12°C), US zones 8–10 or lower. *Camellia* x *williamsii* is a hybrid between *C. japonica* and *C. saluenensis*. The variety 'Anticipation' was raised in New Zealand in 1962.

*Camellia* x *williamsii* 'Debbie' An evergreen shrub that grows up to 15ft (4.5m), with an erect but bushy habit. Flowers, about 4in (10cm) wide, appear in early spring in abundance and continue for several weeks. Camellias need a well-drained acid or neutral soil. Hardy to 10°F (-12°C), US zones 8–10 or lower.

*Camellia* x *williamsii* 'Anticipation'

*Camellia reticulata* 'Nuccio's Ruby'

*Camellia* x *williamsii* 'Debbie'

*Camellia japonica* 'Bob Hope'

*Camellia japonica* 'Guilio Nuccio'

47

Camellia japonica 'Margaret Davis'
A large evergreen shrub that grows up to 15ft (4.5m), with flowers about 4in (10cm) wide. Camellias will grow in full sun but may drop their flower buds in dry weather. Hardy to 10°F (-12°C), US zones 8–10. 'Margaret Davis' was raised in Australia in 1961.

Camellia x *williamsii* 'Jury's Yellow'
A large evergreen shrub that grows to 12ft (3.5m) and is rather erect in habit but compact. Its flowers are up to 4in (10cm) wide. This variety is hardy to 10°F (-12°C), US zones 8–10.

Camellia 'Nuccio's Carousel'  A large shrub that reaches 15ft (4.5m) and is erect in habit. Its flowers are about 4in (10cm) wide. Double and semi-double varieties often produce no seeds. Hardy to 10°F (-12°C), US zones 8–10. Raised in America in the late 20th century.

Camellia japonica 'Debutante' (also known as 'Sarah C. Hastie')  This evergreen shrub grows to 20ft (6m) and is erect in habit. 'Debutante' has double flowers that are about 4in (10cm) wide. Hardy to 10°F (-12°C), US zones 8–10.

Camellia japonica 'Berenice Perfection'
A large evergreen shrub that grows up to 20ft (6m) tall and is rather erect in habit. Flowers are about 4½in (11cm) wide and fruit is about 1in (2.5cm) long. Camellias can be planted in the autumn or late spring. They need a well-drained acid or neutral soil and enjoy plenty of humus and average rainfall. This variety is hardy to 10°F (-12°C), US zones 8–10.

Camellia japonica 'Tricolor' (right)
A large evergreen shrub that can reach 20ft (6m), and is rather erect in habit. Its flowers, about 4in (10cm) wide, appear in spring. The leaves grow to 4in (10cm) long. The fruit is a globose red-tinged green pod about 1in (2.5cm) long, containing a few large dark brown seeds. Hardy to 10°F (-12°C), US zones 8–10. 'Tricolor' was introduced from Japan around 1830 and is still popular today.

Camellia japonica 'Grace Bunton'

Camellia x *williamsii* 'Donation'  An evergreen shrub that grows to 12ft (3.5m) and is rather erect in habit. Its flowers are about 4½in (11cm) wide. Hardy to 10°F (-12°C), US zones 8–10 or lower. This variety is probably the most free-flowering of all cultivated camellias and thus the most popular.

Camellia japonica 'Otome'  This evergreen shrub grows up to 15ft (4.5m) and is rather erect in habit. The flowers that appear in late winter and early spring are single and are about 4½in (11cm) wide, with pale pink petals surrounding yellow stamens. Hardy to 10°F (-12°C), US zones 8–10.

Camellia japonica 'Augusto Leal de Gouveia Pinto' (above)  A large shrub that grows up to 20ft (6m). The flowers, about 4½in (11cm) wide, appear in spring. Hardy to 10°F (-12°C), US zones 8–10. This variety is thought to have originated in Portugal in the late 19th century as a sport on 'Mathotiana'.

Camellia japonica 'Grace Bunton'  This large evergreen shrub grows up to 15ft (4.5m) and has a rather erect habit. The flowers, up to 5in (12cm) wide, appear in spring in great abundance. The fruit is a globose red-tinged green pod about 1in (2.5cm) long, containing a few large dark brown seeds. Hardy to 10°F (-12°C), US zones 8–10. 'Grace Bunton' was raised in Virginia in 1950.

Camellia japonica 'Haku Rakuten'  A large evergreen shrub that grows up to 15ft (4.5m) tall and has an erect habit. The flowers, about 4in (10cm) wide, appear in spring. The fruit is a globose red-tinged green pod about 1in (2.5cm) long, containing a few large dark brown seeds. Hardy to 10°F (-12°C), US zones 8–10.

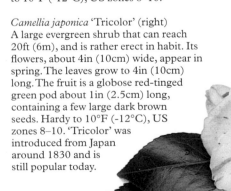

Camellia japonica 'Otome'

Camellia japonica 'Haku Rakuten'

Camellia x williamsii 'Jury's Yellow'

Camellia japonica 'Berenice Perfection'

Camellia x williamsii 'Donation'

Camellia japonica 'Margaret Davis'

Camellia 'Nuccio's Carousel'

Camellia japonica 'Debutante'

# SHRUBS

*Exochorda* x *macrantha* 'The Bride'

*Exochorda* x *macrantha* 'The Bride'

*Chaenomeles speciosa* 'Moerloosei'

*Actinidia kolomikta*
A deciduous shrub that grows to 30ft (9m) tall. The scented flowers ½in (1cm) wide, are borne in late spring. The leaves are oval, tinged with purple at first, but becoming variegated with the upper half silver, and later pink-tinged. This remarkable coloration is not developed by young plants, but a position in full sun encourages it. The fruit is seldom seen in cool climates, but is an oval yellowish berry about 1in (2.5cm) long. It is sweet and edible. Hardy to -20°F (-29°C), US zones 5–9.

FLOWERING QUINCE *Chaenomeles speciosa* 'Moerloosei' A deciduous shrub growing up to 7ft (2m) tall and wide. The flowers, each about 1½in (4cm) wide, appear in spring in small clusters, just as the leaves begin to open. They are very resistant to cold weather. The leaves are 1½–3in (4–8cm) long. The apple-like fruit is globose and yellow and has a delicious sweet scent when ripe. It is sometimes used for scenting drawers. Hardy to -20°F (-29°C), US zones 5–9.

*Chaenomeles* x *superba* A hybrid of *C. japonica* and *C. speciosa* which makes a vigorous, but generally small shrub. This cross has given rise to many of the garden hybrids grown today.

*Exochorda* x *macrantha* 'The Bride' A deciduous shrub that grows to 10ft (3m) tall. In late spring it produces spikes 4in (10cm) long of flowers, each 1¼in (3cm) wide, with five rounded petals. The leaves are narrowly oval, pale green and 2–3in (5–8cm) long. It thrives in a sunny position and is hardy to 0°F (-18°C), US zones 7–10. *Exochorda* x *macrantha* is a hybrid between *E. korolkowii* and *E. racemosa* raised in France by the Lemoine Nursery at the end of the 19th century.

*Chaenomeles* x *superba*

*Chaenomeles* x *superba* 'Rowallane' (left) A deciduous shrub growing to 5ft (1.5m) tall and wide against a wall, less in an open position. The flowers, each about 2in (5cm) wide, appear in spring in small clusters just as the leaves begin to open. The leaves are oblong or oval, 1½–3in (4–8cm) long. The apple-like fruit is globose and yellow and has a sweet scent when ripe. Hardy to -20°F (-29°C), US zones 5–9. Flowering quinces have a fairly compact habit and need little pruning.

JAPANESE HONEYSUCKLE
*Lonicera japonica*
A rampantly vigorous evergreen shrub that grows to 30ft (9m) tall. In summer it produces pairs of fragrant flowers, each about 1½in (4cm) long. The leaves are 1½–3in (4–8cm) long and the fruit is a black berry. Hardy to -20°F (-29°C), US zones 5–10. Native to China, Korea and Japan, it was introduced into cultivation at the beginning of the 19th century. Japanese honeysuckle is very beautiful and deliciously scented but it has become a widespread weed in some parts of North America, so must be planted with some forethought.

EARLY DUTCH HONEYSUCKLE
*Lonicera periclymenum* 'Belgica'
A beautiful and vigorous deciduous climbing shrub that grows to 20ft (6m) tall where support is available. In summer it produces flowers, each about 1½in (4cm) long, which have a delightful spicy fragrance in the evening. The leaves are 1½–2in (4–5cm) long and the fruit is a

*Akebia trifoliata*

red berry clustered at the shoot tips. Hardy to -10°F (-23°C), US zones 6–10. Native to most of Europe, *Lonicera* 'Belgica' has been ciltivated since the 17th century.

*Lonicera periclymenum* 'Graham Thomas' A vigorous deciduous climbing shrub that grows to 20ft (6m) tall where support is available. It produces clusters of flowers, each about 1¹/₂in (4cm) long, for several months in summer. In the evening, the shrub has a delightful spicy fragrance. The leaves are 1¹/₂–2in (4–5cm) long and the fruit is a red berry clustered at the shoot tips. Hardy to -10°F (-23°C), US zones 6–10. 'Graham Thomas' was found in the wild in England in this century.

*Lonicera* x *tellmanniana* A deciduous climbing shrub that grows to 20ft (6m) tall. In mid-summer it produces clusters of flowers, each about 2in (5cm) long. The leaves are 1¹/₂–3in (4–8cm) long. Hardy to 10°F (-12°C), US zones 8–10. Although unscented, this honeysuckle is very beautiful in flower and can be most effective when growing up into a tree or trained against a wall. A hybrid between the Chinese *L. tragophylla* and the American *L. sempervirens*, it was raised in Hungary early in this century.

*Akebia trifoliata* An evergreen climbing shrub of great vigour that can grow to 30ft (9m) tall and more in spread. Flowers are borne in late spring and early summer; each cluster has 1–3 female flowers, about 1in (2.5cm) wide, at the base and more smaller male ones at the apex. The leaves are 2–4in (5–10cm) long. The oblong pale purple fruit is 3–5in (8–12cm) long. Hardy to -20°F (-29°C), US zones 5–9.

*Akebia quinata* (below) An evergreen shrub of great vigour that can grow to 30ft (9m) tall and more in spread. The flowers are borne in late spring and early summer. Each cluster has 2–5 female flowers about 1in (2.5cm) wide at the base and rather smaller and paler male ones at the apex. The oblong purple fruit is 3–4in (8–10cm) long. Hardy to -20°F (-29°C), US zones 5–9. It may be grown through a substantial tree, trained up a pergola or to wires on a wall.

*Actinidia kolomikta*

*Lonicera* x *tellmanniana*

*Lonicera japonica*

*Lonicera periclymenum* 'Belgica'

*Lonicera periclymenum* 'Graham Thomas'

Phillyrea latifolia

Osmanthus x burkwoodii

Osmanthus decorus

Osmanthus yunnanensis

Osmanthus delavayi 'Latifolius'

Nothofagus antarctica

Kerria japonica

Osmanthus heterophyllus

Osmanthus delavayi

Kerria japonica 'Pleniflora'

¹/₃ life size. Specimens from Wisley, 24 April

*Abelia floribunda*   A semi-evergreen shrub that grows to 10ft (3m) or more tall and as wide, producing flowers up to 2in (5cm) long in early summer. Leaves 1–1¹⁄₂in (2.5–4cm) long. Thrives in a sunny, sheltered site and in cool areas is best grown against a wall. Hardy to 10°F (-12°C), US zones 8–10.

*Kerria japonica*   A medium-sized deciduous shrub that grows to 7ft (2m) tall, producing many flowers, each about 1in (2.5cm) wide, in late spring. Leaves 1¹⁄₂–3in (4–8cm) long. Best in a sunny position and in cooler areas will benefit from a sheltered site. Hardy to 10°F (-12°C), US zones 8–10. Native to much of China and is native or naturalized in Japan.

*Kerria japonica* 'Pleniflora'   This variety grows to 10ft (3m) tall. It is a particularly robust form but more stiff and less graceful in habit than the single-flowered wild forms.

*Nothofagus antarctica*   Deciduous shrub or tree that grows to 120ft (35m). Leaves aromatic, sticky when young, to 1in (2.5cm) long. Flowers in spring. Prefers moist soil, sun or part shade. Hardy to 0°F (-18°C), US zones 7–10. Native to southern Chile and Argentina in the subalpine zone of the Andes above the evergreen forest.

*Osmanthus decorus*   An evergreen shrub that grows to 13ft (4m). Fragrant flowers ¹⁄₄in (6mm) long and leaves 2–6in (5–15cm) in length. The fruit is egg-shaped, deep purple and often freely produced in gardens. Any soil, sun or shade. Hardy to -5°F (-20°C), US zones 6–10. Native to north-eastern Turkey and western Georgia.

*Osmanthus yunnanensis*   An evergreen shrub with narrow, holly-like leaves, to 30ft (9m) tall. Leaves to 8in (20cm) long. Flowers fragrant, small yellowish-white in spring. Hardy to 12°F (-10°C).

*Abelia floribunda*

*Weigela* 'Looymansii Aurea'

*Osmanthus delavayi*   A small, slow-growing dense evergreen shrub that grows to 6ft (1.8m) or more and eventually wider. Small fragrant white flowers, each about ¹⁄₂in (1cm) wide, produced in spring. Leaves to 1in (2.5cm) long. Hardy to 0°F (-18°C), US zones 7–9. 'Latifolius' is a taller-growing form with larger leaves.

*Osmanthus* x *burkwoodii*   A medium-sized but slow-growing evergreen shrub of dense habit that grows to 10ft (3m) tall and usually wider. Clusters of small fragrant white flowers, each about ¹⁄₃in (8mm) wide, produced in late spring. Leaves to 2in (5cm) long. Hardy to 0°F (-18°C), US zones 7–10.

*Osmanthus heterophyllus* (also known as *O. ilicifolius*)   A fairly slow-growing, dense evergreen shrub that reaches 10ft (3m) tall and wider. Hardy to 0°F (-18°C), US zones 7–9.

BEAUTY BUSH *Kolkwitzia amabilis*
A deciduous shrub that grows to 10ft (3m) tall and wide. Well-covered in spring to early summer with pairs of narrow bell-shaped flowers about 1in (2.5cm) long. Hardy to -30°F (-35°C), US zones 4–9. It is native to central China.

*Phillyrea latifolia*   An evergreen shrub that grows to 50ft (15m) in height, very elegant when old. Greenish flowers are produced in late spring and narrow leaves 8in–24in (20–60cm) long. Fruit is bluish-black and globose. Any soil, full sun. Hardy to 5°F (-15°C), US zones 7–10. Native to the Mediterranean region.

*Weigela florida*   An erect compact deciduous shrub that grows to 5ft (1.5m) tall, bearing flowers 1¹⁄₄in (3cm) long in early summer. Hardy to -10°F (-23°C), US zones 6–9. Native to China, Korea and southern Japa, and introduced into cultivation in the middle of the 19th century

*Weigela florida* 'Variegata'   Its variegated foliage extends the decorative value of this shrub for most of the summer.

*Weigela* 'Looymansii Aurea'
A deciduous shrub that grows to 5ft (1.5m) tall and somewhat wider. In early summer it bears clusters of flowers, each about 1¹⁄₄in (3cm) long. The leaves are narrowly oval, about 2–3in (5–8cm) long and light yellow in early summer, becoming greener as the season progresses. Hardy to -10°F (-23°C), US zones 6–9.

*Weigela florida* 'Variegata'

*Kolkwitzia amabilis*

*Rhododendron* 'Praecox'

*Rhododendron* 'Joanita'

*Rhododendron fortunei* subsp. *discolor*

*Rhododendron* 'Fragrantissimum'

*Rhododendron williamsianum* (right)
A compact and slow-growing
evergreen shrub that grows up to
3¹/₂ft (1m) and is rather wider
than tall. Its flowers are
about 2in (5cm) wide.
Hardy to 0°F (-18°C),
US zones 7–9. Native
to western China.

*Rhododendron augustinii*
One of the most beautiful
of all the rhododendrons
with magnificent blue flowers appearing
in April and May. Leaves are small and
hairy. It is fairly quick-growing, so makes
an ideal woodland shrub. Hardy to -10°F
(-23°C), US zones 6–9. Native to China.

*Rhododendron* 'Cilpinense'   Growing up
to 3ft (90cm), this shrub has flowers 2¹/₂in
(6cm) wide. Hardy to 10°F (-12°C), US
zones 8–9, but it should have a sheltered
position since its flowers are quickly
damaged by frost. Raised in England in
the 20th century.

*Rhododendron fortunei* subsp. *discolor*
A large late-flowering shrub that bears
enormous, spectacular trusses of fragrant
pink flowers, with seven-lobed corollas in
June and July. It has narrow leaves up to
8in (20cm) long and is a parent of many
well-known hybrids. Hardy to -10°F
(-23°C), US zones 6–9. Native to China.

*Rhododendron* 'Fragrantissimum'
A lax-habited evergreen shrub that is
usually rather wide and  grows up to 5ft
(1.5m). Its scented flowers are 3¹/₂in
(9cm) wide. Hardy to 20°F (-7°C), US
zones 9–10, it requires a conservatory in
cold areas or a sheltered position outside.

*Rhododendron* 'Joanita'   A compact
evergreen shrub that grows up to 5ft
(1.5m), it is usually wider than tall. Its
flowers, each about 2¹/₂in (6cm) wide,
appear in early summer. Hardy to 0°F
(-18°C), US zones 7–9.

*Rhododendron lacteum*   A large evergreen
shrub that grows up to 20ft (6m). Its
flowers, in a spherical truss, are about 2in
(5cm) wide and sometimes blotched with
maroon at the base. Hardy to 0°F
(-18°C), US zones 7–10.

*Rhododendron yakushimanum*   A very
compact and slow-growing evergreen
shrub that grows up to 8ft (2.5m) forming
a dome-shaped bush. The best forms such
as 'Koichiro Wada' do not exceed 5ft
(1.5m) in height. Its flowers are 2in (5cm)
wide. Hardy to -10°F (-23°C), US zones
6–9. Native of Yakushima, an island off
south Japan.

*Rhododendron ponticum*
A vigorous evergreen shrub that
grows up to 20ft (6m). Its flowers, each
about 2in (5cm) wide, are often speckled
with green or brown on the upper petal.
Hardy to -10°F (-23°C), US zones 6–9.
Has become a pest in parts of Ireland.

*Rhododendron* 'Praecox'   A compact
evergreen shrub that grows up to 5ft
(1.5m) and is usually rather wider than
tall. In late winter or early spring small
clusters of flowers about 1¹/₂in (4cm) wide
are produced. Hardy to 0°F (-18°C), US
zones 7–9.

*Rhododendron yunnanense*   This evergreen shrub grows up to 13ft (4m). In
spring it bears 1¹/₂in (4cm) wide, funnel-
shaped white, pink or mauve flowers,
usually spotted with red-brown within.
The leaves are aromatic when bruised.
Hardy to 10°F (-23°C), US zones 6–9.

*Rhododendron* 'Jalisco Goshawk'   A slow-
growing shrub that reaches up to 10ft
(3m) tall and is usually rather wider.
Loose clusters of flowers, about 4in
(10cm) wide, appear in early summer.
Hardy to 0°F (-18°C), US zones 7–9.

*Rhododendron* 'Christmas Cheer'   This
shrub may reach up to 12ft (3.5m). In late
winter or early spring it bears tight,
rounded clusters of widely funnel-shaped
pink and white flowers about 1¹/₂in (4cm)
wide, opening from deep pink buds.
Hardy to -10°F (-23°C), US zones 6–9. A
hybrid raised at Exbury Gardens, England
early this century, it is a hardy and reliable
variety, valued for its early flowers which
are very frost-resistant.

*Rhododendron yunnanense*

*Rhododendron lacteum*

*Rhododendron yakushimanum*

*Rhododendron ponticum*

*Rhododendron* 'Christmas Cheer'

*Rhododendron* 'Cilpinense'

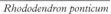

*Rhododendron* 'Jalisco Goshawk'

*Rhododendron augustinii*

# SHRUBS

'Arthur Bedford'

'Mrs Lionel de Rothschild'

'G A Sims'

'Thunderstorm'

'Anthony Waterer'

'Mrs Davis Evans'

'Frank Galsworthy'

'Sappho'

'Sigismund Rucker'

'Purple Splendour'

'Mrs Furnival'

¹/₅ life size. Specimens from Sandling Park, 2 June

*Rhododendron* 'Alice'  This evergreen shrub grows to 10ft (3m). Its flowers, about 3½in (9cm) wide, appear in late spring. Hardy to 0°F (-18°C), US zones 7–9. A vigorous hybrid raised in England in the early 20th century.

*Rhododendron* 'Anthony Waterer'  This evergreen shrub grows to 7ft (2m) and needs acid soil, in sun or partial shade. Hardy to -5°F (-20°C), US zones 6–10.

*Rhododendron* 'Arthur Bedford'  This evergreen shrub grows to 7ft (2m). Plant in acid soil, in sun or partial shade. Hardy to -5°F (-20°C), US zones 6–10.

*Rhododendron* 'Beauty of Littleworth'  A vigorous evergreen shrub that grows up to 13ft (4m) and is usually wider. Flowers, 4½in (11cm) wide, appear in late spring. Hardy to 0°F (-18°C), US zones 7–9.

*Rhododendron* 'Crest'  Compact evergreen shrub that grows up to 7ft (2m) and is usually wider. Clusters of flowers, 4in (10cm) wide, appear in late spring or early summer. Hardy to 0°F (-18°C), US zones 7–10.

*Rhododendron* 'Cynthia'  A large shrub that grows to 30ft (9m) and is usually wider than tall. Its flowers are about 3in (8cm) wide. Hardy to -10°F (-23°C), US zones 6–10.

*Rhododendron* 'Sigismund Rucker'  Evergreen shrub that grows to 10ft (3m). Flowers, about 2½in (6cm) across, appear in late May or early June. Plant in acid soil, in sun or partial shade. Hardy to -5°F (-20°C), US zones 6–10.

*Rhododendron* 'Frank Galsworthy'  An evergreen shrub that grows to 7ft (2m) and is usually wider than tall. Hardy to -5°F (-20°C), US zones 6–10.

*Rhododendron* 'G A Sims'  An evergreen shrub that reaches 7ft (2m). Plant in acid soil in sun or partial shade.  Hardy to -5°F (-20°C), US zones 6–10.

*Rhododendron* 'Mrs A T de la Mare'  A vigorous evergreen shrub of compact habit that grows up to 10ft (3m) and is usually wider than tall. Its flowers grow to 4in (10cm) wide. Hardy to 0°F (-18°C), US zones 7–9.

*Rhododendron* 'Mrs Davis Evans'  An evergreen shrub that grows to 10ft (3m). Its flowers are 3in (8cm) across, 16–20 in a truss. Plant in acid soil, in sun or partial shade. Hardy to -5°F (-20°C), US zones 6–10.

*Rhododendron* 'Surrey Heath'

*Rhododendron* 'Cynthia'

*Rhododendron* 'Mrs Furnival'   An evergreen shrub that grows to 7ft (2m). Flowers are 3in (8cm) wide, 10–14 in a truss. Hardy to -5°F (-20°C), US zones 6–10.

*Rhododendron* 'Mrs G W Leak'   A large but fairly compact evergreen shrub that grows to 7ft (2m). Flowers, 3½in (9cm) wide, appear in late spring. Hardy to 0°F (-18°C), US zones 7–10 or slightly lower.

*Rhododendron* 'Mrs Lionel de Rothschild' An evergreen shrub of compact habit that grows to 7ft (2m). Flowers are up to 4in (10cm) wide. Hardy to 0°F (-18°C), US zones 7–9.

*Rhododendron* 'Pink Pearl'   A vigorous evergreen shrub that grows to 10ft (3m) tall and usually wider. Flowers, 4in (10cm) wide, appear in early summer fading from pink to near white before falling. Hardy to -10°F (-23°C), US zones 6–9.

*Rhododendron* 'Purple Splendour'   An evergreen shrub that grows to 7ft (2m). Flowers, 3in (8cm) across, appear in early summer, up to 15 in a truss. Hardy to -5°F (-20°C), US zones 6–10.

*Rhododendron* 'Queen Elizabeth II'. A compact evergreen shrub that grows up to 10ft (3m), with flowers up to 4in (10cm) wide. Hardy to 0°F (-18°C), US zones 7–9.

*Rhododendron* 'Sappho'   A large evergreen shrub that grows up to 10ft (3m). Flowers, 3in (8cm) wide, appear in early summer. Hardy to 0°F (-18°C), US zones 7–9 or lower.

*Rhododendron* 'Sun of Austerlitz'   Evergreen shrub that grows to 7ft (2m), it prefers acid soil, in sun or part shade. Hardy to -5°F (-20°C), US zones 6–10.

*Rhododendron* 'Surrey Heath'   Up to 6ft (1.8m) tall and usually wider, this evergreen blooms in late spring, with flowers up to 2in (5cm) wide. Hardy to 0°F (-18°C), US zones 7–9.

*Rhododendron* 'Thunderstorm' An evergreen shrub that grows up to 10ft (3m) tall. Plant in acid soil, in sun or partial shade. Hardy to -5°F (-20°C), US zones 6–10.

Rhododendron 'Mayday'   A compact and slow-growing shrub that reaches 5ft (1.5m) and is rather wider. Flowers about 2½in (6cm) wide appear in early summer. Hardy to 0°F (-18°C), US zones 7–9.

*Rhododendron* 'Alice'

'Pink Pearl'   'Mrs A T de la Mare'   'Queen Elizabeth II'   'Alice'   'Sun of Austerlitz'   'Beauty of Littleworth'   'Mayday'

⅕ life size. Specimens from Eccleston Square, 14 May

'Mrs G W Leak'   'Crest'

¼ life size. Specimens from Hillier Arboretum, 14 May

Kurume azaleas at Sandling Park

*Rhododendron* 'Hinamoyo' (above)  This compact evergreen azalea grows up to 5ft (1.5m) and is usually wider than tall. Flowers, about 1½in (4cm) wide, appear in late spring. It grows well in moist soil in sun but is best suited to a partially shaded position. Hardy to 0°F (-18°C), US zones 7–10. 'Hinamoyo' is a hybrid introduced from Japan early in the 20th century.

*Rhododendron* 'Amoenum'  A compact, slow-growing evergreen shrub that grows up to 5ft (1.5m) and is usually wider. Its flowers are about ¾in (2cm) wide. Plant in autumn or spring in acid or neutral soil. Needs average rainfall and grows best in a partially shaded position. Hardy to 0°F (-18°C), US zones 7–9 or lower.

*Rhododendron* 'Mother's Day'  A hybrid evergreen azalea, probably the result of crossing Kurume Minode-Girl with an Indica azalea, raised by van Hecke in Belgium before 1970. Low spreading growth to 5ft (1.5m). Hardy to -5°F (-20°C), US zones 6–10.

*Rhododendron* 'Cowslip'  Rounded evergreen shrub that grows to 3½ft (1m). It flowers in spring and prefers moist, acid or non-chalky soil in part shade. Hardy to 5°F (-15°C), US zones 7–10. An excellent free-flowering dwarf shrub for a small garden.

*Rhododendron* 'Palestrina'  This compact evergreen azalea grows up to 3½ft (1m) tall and is usually rather wider. Flowers,

about 2in (5cm) wide, appear in late spring. Plant in autumn or spring in acid or neutral soil. Needs an average rainfall and is best suited to a partially shaded position. Hardy to 0°F (-18°C), US zones 7–10.

*Rhododendron* 'Temple Belle'  A compact evergreen shrub that grows up to 5ft (1.5m) and is usually rather wider than tall. Flowers, about 3in (8cm) wide, appear in late spring. An excellent free-flowering shrub for a small garden. Raised at Kew in around 1916 by crossing *R. williamsii* with *R. orbiculare*, so will tolerate some lime in the soil. Hardy to 0°F (-18°C), US zones 7–9. No regular pruning is required and it is seldom affected by pests and diseases.

*Rhododendron* 'Vuyk's Scarlet' A compact evergreen azalea that grows to 3ft (90cm) with a spreading habit. Flowers, about 2in (5cm) wide, appear in late spring. Plant in either autumn or spring, in acid or neutral soil and in partial shade. Hardy to 0°F (-18°C), US zones 7–10.

*Rhododendron* 'Cowslip'

*Rhododendron* 'Temple Belle'

*Rhododendron* 'Palestrina'

*Rhododendron* 'Vuyk's Scarlet'

*Rhododendron* 'Temple Belle'

*Rhododendron* 'Mother's Day'

*Rhododendron* 'Amoenum'

Azaleas at Sandling Park

# SHRUBS

tall. Each flower is about 3in (8cm) wide. The leaves are about 6in (15cm) long, bronze when opening and turning orange and red in autumn. Hardy to 0°F (-18°C), US zones 7–10. No regular pruning is required and it is seldom affected by pests and diseases.

*Rhododendron prinophyllum* A medium-sized deciduous azalea that grows up to 10ft (3m), and is usually rather wider than tall. Highly fragrant flowers, about 1¼in (3cm) wide, appear in late spring. Leaves, 2in (5cm) long, are bronze when opening and turn orange and red in autumn. Grows well in sun or part shade. Hardy to -20°F (-29°C), US zones 5–9.

*Rhododendron vaseyi* A deciduous azalea of open habit that grows up to 16ft (5m) tall, and is usually rather taller than wide. Flowers, up to 2in (5cm) wide, appear in early spring. Leaves, about 5in (12cm) long, open just after the flowers and turn red or orange in autumn. Native to North Carolina. Grows well in moist soil in a sunny or partially shaded position. Hardy to -10°F (-23°C), US zones 6–9.

Mollis azaleas at Sandling Park

*Rhododendron* 'Glory of Littleworth' A medium-sized deciduous or partially evergreen azalea that grows up to 6ft (1.8m), usually rather taller than wide. Sweetly scented flowers, about 2in (5cm) wide, appear in late spring. Its leaves are up to 4in (10cm) long and turn orange and red in autumn. One of the very few hybrids between an azalea and a rhododendron. Hardy to 0°F (-18°C), US zones 7–10.

*Rhododendron* 'Berryrose' A medium-sized deciduous azalea that grows to 10ft (3m), wider than tall. Flowers, 3in (8cm) wide, appear in late spring. Leaves, about 6in (15cm) long, are bronze when newly open, turning orange and red in autumn. Hardy to 0°F (-18°C), US zones 7–10.

*Rhododendron* 'Oxydol' A medium-sized deciduous azalea that grows up to 10ft (3m), usually rather wider than tall. Each flower is about 2½–3in (6–8cm) wide. Hardy to 0°F (-18°C), US zones 7–10. 'Oxydol' is a hybrid raised at Exbury Gardens in England in the 20th century.

*Rhododendron* 'Freya' A medium-sized deciduous azalea that grows to 5ft (1.5m), usually wider than tall. Sweetly scented flowers, 1¼in (3cm) wide, appear in late spring. Grows well in sun or partial shade. Hardy to -10°F (-23°C), US zones 6–10. No regular pruning is required and it is seldom affected by pests and diseases.

*Rhododendron* 'George Reynolds' A medium-sized deciduous azalea that grows to 10ft (3m), usually rather wider than tall. It has slightly fragrant flowers, about 3in (8cm) wide and leaves 6in (15cm) long. It should be planted in autumn or early spring in acid or neutral soil. Grows well in sun or partial shade. Hardy to 0°F (-18°C), US zones 7–10.

*Rhododendron* 'Phoebe' (left) A medium-sized deciduous azalea that grows up to 6ft (1.8m) and is usually rather wider than tall. Sweetly scented flowers, 1¼in (3cm) wide, appear in early summer. Leaves, up to 4in (10cm) long, often turn orange and red in autumn. Hardy to -10°F (-23°C), US zones 6–10. This hybrid was raised in Belgium in the 19th century.

*Rhododendron* 'Klondyke' A medium-sized deciduous shrub that grows up to 10ft (3m) tall, usually rather wider than

*Rhododendron* 'Exquiseta' (above) A deciduous azalea that grows up to 8ft (2.5m), with scented flowers. Hardy to -5°F (-20°C), US zones 6–10.

*Rhododendron* 'Berryrose'

*Rhododendron prinophyllum*

*Rhododendron* 'Klondyke'

*Rhododendron vaseyi*

*Rhododendron* 'Oxydol'

*Rhododendron* 'George Reynolds'

*Rhododendron* 'Freya'

*Rhododendron* 'Glory of Littleworth'

Kalmia latifolia at Winkworth Arboretum

Kalmia angustifolia 'Rubra'

*Agapetes serpens* An evergreen shrub that grows to 7ft (2m) tall with support and a lax spreading habit. From late winter to early summer it produces waxy textured flowers 1in (2.5cm) long. The oval leaves are about 1/2in (1cm) long and a dark glossy green. Plant in autumn or early spring in any moist, lime-free soil in a shady position. Hardy to 28°F (–3°C), US zones 9–10. Native to the eastern Himalayas, this shrub is valued for its long flowering season.

GULF MANZANITA *Arctostaphylos patula* An evergreen shrub with a smooth red-brown bark, growing slowly to 7ft (2m) tall. Flowers, 1/4in (6mm) long, are carried in drooping clusters of 30–40 in late spring. The leaves are 1–2in (2.5–5cm) long and the globose fruit is dark brown when ripe and about 1/2in (1cm) long. Plant in autumn or spring in any soil except chalk. Hardy to 0°F (-18°C), US zones 7–10. Native to western North America.

*Enkianthus campanulatus* A medium-sized deciduous shrub that grows to 12ft (3.5m) tall, producing clusters of flowers about 1/3in (1cm) long in late spring. The leaves are 1–2in (2.5–5cm) long. Hardy to 0°F (-18°C), US zones 7–10. Native to Japan. This shrub is quietly attractive when in flower but really comes into its own in autumn when it gives some of the most brilliant colour.

*Enkianthus perulatus* A compact deciduous shrub that grows to 6ft (1.8m) tall. Flowers about 1/3in (8mm) long and leaves 1–2in (2.5–5cm) long, turning to

brilliant red, orange and yellow in autumn. Plant in autumn or early spring. It should have a partially shaded situation, but in moist soil will stand a more sunny position. Hardy to 0°F (-18°C), US zones 7–10. Native to southern Japan.

*Gaultheria shallon* Low evergreen suckering shrub that can reach 7ft (2m) high, although usually only about 3.5ft (1m). Flowers in spring and summer. Fruit formed by the fleshy calyx is purple. Acid soil, partial or full shade. Hardy to -5°F (-20°C), US zones 6–10. Native to the west coast of North America, from Santa Barbara north to British Columbia, in redwood forests, woods and scrub in the coast ranges up to 2800ft (800m).

HIGHBUSH BLUEBERRY *Vaccinium corymbosum* A medium-sized deciduous shrub that grows to 10ft (3m) tall and usually as wide. In early summer it bears clusters of flowers, each up to 1/2in (1cm) long. The leaves are 1–3in (2.5–8cm) long and turn to various shades of red in autumn. The fruit is a blue-black berry about 1/3in (8mm) wide, edible with an excellent flavour. Grows well in a sunny or a partially shaded position and is hardy to -10°F (-23°C), US zones 6–9.

*Leucothoë davisiae* An evergreen shrub that grows to 5ft (1.5m) high. Leaves 1–21/2in (2.5–6cm) long. Flowering in summer and needs an acid moist soil, sun or part shade. Hardy to -5°F (-20°C), US zones 6–10. Native to central and northern California, from Fresno, north to Oregon, in bogs and swamps at 3500–8750ft (1000–2500m).

*Leucothoë fontanesiana* An evergreen shrub that grows to 5ft (1.5m), with arching branches forming a spreading clump. Native to US states of Virginia, Georgia and Tennessee, in damp woods in mountains. Flowering in May. Acid soil. Hardy to -5°F (-20°C), US zones 6–10.

SHEEP LAUREL *Kalmia angustifolia* 'Rubra' A small evergreen shrub that grows to 6ft (1.8m) tall, spreading by suckers to cover a considerable area. In early summer it produces rounded clusters of flowers 2in (5cm) wide, each flower is about 1/3in (8mm) wide. The leaves are up to 2in (5cm) long. Hardy to -20°F (-29°C), US zones 5–10. All parts of the plant are poisonous and it should be kept away from grazing animals. Native to eastern North America.

MOUNTAIN LAUREL *Kalmia latifolia* (below) A large but slow-growing evergreen shrub that grows to 12ft (3.5m) tall, developing into a broad, dense mass of foliage. It produces rounded clusters of flowers 2in (5cm) wide, with each flower about 1in (2.5cm) wide. The leaves are 2–5in (5–12cm) long. Hardy to -20°F (-29°C), US zones 5–10. Poisonous to animals. Native to eastern North America.

*Arctostaphylos patula*

*Vaccinium corymbosum*

*Gaultheria shallon* with *Davidia involucrata* growing behind

*Leucothoë davisiae*

*Enkianthus perulatus*

*Enkianthus campanulatus*

*Leucothoë fontanesiana*

*Agapetes serpens*

*Ceanothus impressus*

*Ceanothus* 'Cascade'

*Ceanothus* 'Blue Mound'

*Ceanothus* 'Puget Blue'

*Ceanothus* with *Exchordia* 'The Bride'

*Ceanothus thyrsiflorus*

*Ceanothus arboreus* 'Trewithen Blue'
A large evergreen shrub that grows to 24ft (7m) tall, often with a short stout trunk. The flower heads, each 3–4in (8–10cm) long, appear in late spring. The leaves are 2–4in (5–10cm) long and the fruit is black, about ¼in (6mm) long. This shrub is best planted in early autumn or late spring and grows best in an acid or neutral soil with good drainage. Hardy to 20°F (-7°C), US zones 9–10. When grown against a wall, it is best to fan-train it to form a structure of main branches tied to wires. As with all ceanothus any pruning or shaping should be done straight after flowering.

*Ceanothus* 'Blue Mound'  An evergreen shrub that grows to 2–4ft (60cm–1.25m) tall and much wider. The flower heads, each 1–2in (2.5–5cm) long, composed of many tiny 5-petalled flowers, appear in late spring and in some years it produces another flush of flowers in the autumn. The leaves are 1in (2.5cm) long and the fruit is black, less than ¼in (6mm) long. Hardy to 10°F (-12°C), US zones 8–10. In cool climates the ceanothus may be short-lived but they are generally free of pests and diseases. *C.* 'Blue Mound' is thought to be a hybrid of *C. griseus* and, possibly, *C. impressus.* It forms large mounds that make an excellent ground cover in larger gardens.

*Ceanothus* 'Concha'  An evergreen shrub that grows to 7ft (2m) tall. The flower heads, each 1–2in (2.5–5cm) long and composed of many tiny 5-petalled flowers, appear from deep red buds in late spring. The glossy leaves, about 1in (2.5cm) long, are narrowly oblong, rather blunt and with prominently impressed veins. Hardy to 10°F (-12°C), US zones 8–10. *C.* 'Concha' is a hybrid of garden origin, between *C. impressus* and *C. papillosus.* This variety is more compact than some others and is well suited to a small garden.

# CEANOTHUS

*Ceanothus* 'Eleanor Taylor'

*Ceanothus* 'Concha'

*Ceanothus* 'Eleanor Taylor' An evergreen shrub that grows to between 5–10ft (1.5–3m) tall and 10ft (3m) wide. Flowers light blue in spring. Hardy to 10°F (-12°C), US zones 8–10, but it may need some protection from cold winds. 'Eleanor Taylor' is thought to be a hybrid between *C. papillosus* var. *roweanus* and *C. impressus.*

### SANTA BARBARA CEANOTHUS

*Ceanothus impressus* A spreading evergreen shrub that grows to 6ft (1.8m) tall with flower heads, each about 1in (2.5cm) long, appearing in late spring. The small leaves are up to 1/2in (1cm) long and the fruit is black, about 1/4in (6mm) long. Hardy to 20°F (-7°C), US zones 9–10. *C. impressus* is native to southern California and was introduced to Europe in the middle of the 20th century. Though rather tender, it makes a good wall shrub in warmer parts of Britain

*Ceanothus arboreus* 'Trewithen Blue'

*Ceanothus* 'Delight'

*Ceanothus* 'Delight' An evergreen shrub growing up to 24ft (7m) tall, often with a short stout trunk. The flower heads, each about 1in (2.5cm) long and composed of many tiny 5-petalled flowers, appear in the late spring. The leaves, 1–2in (2.5–5cm) long, are narrowly oval and somewhat rough and the fruit is black, about 1/4in (6mm) long. Hardy to 0°F (-18°C), US zones 7–10. *C.* 'Delight' is a hybrid between *C. papillosus* and *C. rigidus.* It was raised in Yorkshire in the early 20th century and has proved to be one of the best for cooler gardens.

*Ceanothus* 'Puget Blue' An evergreen shrub that grows to 16ft (5m) tall against a wall, producing flower heads 1–2in (2.5–5cm) long, in late spring. The leaves are oblong, rounded at each end and with many fine teeth. They are 3/4in (2cm) long with strongly impressed veins. Hardy to 10°F (-12°C), US zones 8–10. When grown against a wall, fan-train it to form a structure of main branches tied to wires. Any pruning is done straight after flowering. *C.* 'Puget Blue' is of uncertain origin, but may be a hybrid between *C. impressus* and *C. papillosus.*

BLUE BLOSSOM *Ceanothus thyrsiflorus* A tall evergreen shrub that grows to about 25ft (7.3m) tall. Native to California and southern Oregon, near the coast in woods and canyons. The pure blue flower heads, each 3–4in (8–10cm) long, appear in late spring, occasionally with some later flowers. The leaves are 1–2in (2.5–5cm) long and the fruit is black, about 1/4in (6mm) long. Hardy to 12°F (-10°C), US zones 8–10. This ceanothus is not often grown but is most commonly seen in the creeping form var. *repens* and the weeping form 'Cascade'.

### WEEPING BLUE BLOSSOM

*Ceanothus* 'Cascade' A form or hybrid of *C. thyrsiflorus* that grows to 15ft (4.5m), with arching branches that give it a most attractive form. Hardy to 15°F (-9°C), US zones 8–10.

*W. floribunda* f. *macrobotrys*

*W. venusta*

*W. floribunda* 'Issai'

*W. sinensis* 'Black Dragon'

*W. floribunda* 'Rosea'

*W. sinensis*

¹/₅ life size. Specimens from Cannington, Somerset, England, 10 June

*Wisteria floribunda* 'Alba' arbor at Bodnant Gardens, north Wales

*Wisteria floribunda* 'Alba'  A deciduous climbing shrub that grows to 30ft (9m) tall, and bears racemes 24in (60cm) long made up of fragrant flowers, each ¾in (2cm) wide, as the leaves open in spring. The oblong leaves are 12in (30cm) long and divided into as many as 19 narrow lance-shaped leaflets. Can be planted in autumn or spring and will grow well in any fertile soil, thriving in a sunny position. Hardy to -10°F (-23°C), US zones 6–9. The long whippy shoots that develop should be shortened in late summer and it is often necessary to prune the whole plant hard in late winter to restrict its spread. *W. floribunda* is native to Japan. It is a very popular and beautiful climber grown against a wall or over a pergola where the flowers can hang free.

*Wisteria floribunda* 'Issai'  A form of *W. floribunda* or possibly a hybrid with *W. sinensis* or *W. venusta*, which flowers well as a young plant. Racemes about 12in (30cm) long. This shrub twines clockwise.

*Wisteria floribunda* f. *macrobotrys*
The racemes of *macrobotrys* are much longer than usual in this species, up to 5ft (1.5m) long.

*Wisteria floribunda* 'Rosea'  A pale-pinkish form known since 1903. Racemes of flowers grow up to 18in (45cm) long.

*Wisteria sinensis*  A deciduous shrub that grows to 70ft (20m) tall or more with support, bearing drooping racemes, up to 12in (30cm) long, of fragrant light lilac-blue flowers, each about ¾in (2cm) wide, opening more or less simultaneously before the leaves open in spring. The leaves are oblong, about 12in (30cm) long and divided into as many as 11 narrow lance-shaped leaflets. Thrives in a sunny position and hardy to -10°F (-23°C), US zones 6–9. Straggly shoots should be shortened in late summer and pruning in late winter is sometimes necessary to restrict spread. Native to China.

*Wisteria sinensis* 'Black Dragon'
A double-flowered, dark purple cultivar.

*Wisteria venusta*  A woody deciduous climber that grows to 40ft (12m) or more, recognized by its velvety hairy leaves. Short broad racemes, 4–6in (10–15cm) long, consist of flowers 1in (2.5cm) across that open simultaneously. Twines anticlockwise. Hardy to -5°F (-20°C), US zones 6–10. Long grown in Japan.

*Wisteria sinensis*

*Wisteria floribunda* f. *macrobotrys*

*Wisteria sinensis* 'Black Dragon'

'Maréchal Foch'

'Blue Hyacinth'

'Maud Notcutt'

'Esther Staley'

⅓ life size. Specimens from Kew, 30 May

LILAC *Syringa* x *hyacinthiflora* 'Blue Hyacinth' A deciduous suckering shrub that grows to 13ft (4m). Clusters of highly fragrant flowers, 6in (15cm) long, appear in spring. Hardy to -10°F (-23°C), US zones 6–9. *S.* x *hyacinthiflora* is a group of lilac hybrids first raised in France in the 19th century. 'Blue Hyacinth', however, was raised in California in the 20th century.

*Syringa* x *hyacinthiflora* 'Esther Staley' was raised by W.B. Clarke in 1948, and has pinkish flowers.

*Syringa* x *josiflexa* 'Guinevere'
A deciduous suckering shrub that grows to 13ft (4m). In late spring it bears clusters about 9in (23cm) long, with highly fragrant flowers, each about ½in (1cm) wide, opening from mauve buds. Hardy to -20°F (-29°C), US zones 5–9. No regular pruning is required but suckers should be pulled up and dead flower heads removed. Raised in Canada in the early 20th century.

*Syringa microphylla* 'Superba' This shrub grows up to 5ft (1.5m) tall. In early summer, and occasionally throughout the summer, it bears flower heads about 5in (12cm) long, with fragrant flowers, each about ¼in (6mm) wide. Hardy to -10°F (-23°C), US zones 6–9. *S. microphylla* is native to north and west China. 'Superba' is particularly free-flowering and has become a popular shrub, very suitable for small gardens.

*Syringa vulgaris* 'Aurea' A deciduous suckering shrub that grows up to 13ft (4m). In spring it has 6in (15cm) long clusters of highly fragrant flowers, each about ½in (1cm) wide. Hardy to -20°F (-29°C), US zones 5–9. Although it has small flowers, this variety is distinct in its yellow-green leaves. Native to eastern Europe and first introduced to England in the 16th century.

*Syringa vulgaris* 'Firmament'
A deciduous suckering shrub that grows up to 13ft (4m). It has clusters, about 6in (15cm) long, of highly fragrant flowers, each about 1in (2.5cm) wide. 'Firmament' is perhaps the truest blue lilac and the colour of the open flowers shows up well against the pinker buds.

*Syringa vulgaris* 'Katherine Havemeyer' A deciduous suckering shrub that grows to 13ft (4m), with highly fragrant, semi-double lavender-purple flowers, which become paler and increasingly pink with age. Raised in France in the early 20th century.

*Syringa vulgaris* 'Sensation'

'Lucie Baltet'

Syringa vulgaris 'Katherine Havemeyer'

**Syringa vulgaris 'Lucie Baltet'**
A deciduous suckering shrub that grows up to 13ft (4m), with highly fragrant light flowers, each about ³/₄in (2cm) wide, opening from deep rose-pink buds. Raised in France in the late 19th century but now seldom grown.

**Syringa vulgaris 'Primrose'** A large deciduous shrub that is especially prized for the exceptional pale yellow flowers that it produces in early summer. Introduced by De Maarse of Holland after the second world war.

**Syringa vulgaris 'Maréchal Foch'**
A deciduous suckering shrub that grows to 13ft (4m). In early summer it bears large oblong flower heads about 6in (15cm) long, with fragrant deep purple flowers, each about 1in (2.5cm) wide and opening from darker buds. 'Maréchal Foch' is a fine, strong-coloured variety, raised in France in the early 20th century.

**Syringa vulgaris 'Maud Notcutt'**
A deciduous suckering shrub that grows to 13ft (4m). In early summer it bears large flower heads, about 9–12in (23–30cm) long, with fragrant pure white flowers, each about 1in (2.5cm) wide. It is one of the showiest white varieties, raised in Britain in the mid-20th century.

**Syringa vulgaris 'Sensation'** A deciduous suckering shrub that grows to 13ft (4m). In early summer it bears conical flower heads about 6in (15cm) long, with fragrant purple flowers edged in white, each about ³/₄in (2cm) wide and opening from darker buds. 'Sensation' is a striking variety raised in Holland in the 20th century.

S. vulgaris 'Primrose' and 'Firmament'

Syringa vulgaris 'Aurea'

Syringa microphylla 'Superba'

Syringa x josiflexa 'Guinevere'

*Phlomis fruticosa*

*Euphorbia mellifera* An evergreen shrub or small tree that grows to 15ft (4.5m) tall. It produces clusters of small brown flowers, each about 2¹/₂in (6cm) wide, with a strong honey scent in late spring. Best in a sunny position and hardy to 10°F (-12°C), US zones 8–10. Native to Madeira and the Canary Islands, but is now very rare in the wild. Introduced into cultivation late in the 19th century.

JERUSALEM SAGE *Phlomis fruticosa* An evergreen shrub that grows 3–6ft (90cm–1.8m) tall, producing whorls of hooded golden-yellow flowers, each about 1in (2.5cm) long at the tips of the shoots, in early and midsummer. It prefers dry summer conditions and is well suited to cultivation in the Mediterranean region or California. Hardy to 10°F (-12°C), US zones 8–10. Native to much of the Mediterranean region.

*Berberis verruculosa* A member of the barberry family, the Berberidaceae, this slow-growing shrub grows to 6ft (1.8m) tall and about as wide, making a good small- or medium-sized hedge. The flowers, each to up ³/₄in (2cm) wide, open in early summer. Hardy to 0°F (-18°C), US zones 7–10 or lower. Native to western China and introduced into cultivation at the beginning of the 20th century.

*Berberis thunbergii* 'Aurea' A compact spiny deciduous shrub that grows to 2ft (60cm) tall and about as wide. The flowers are borne in spring, each about ¹/₂in (1cm) wide, 1–2 together. The leaves are bright yellow in early summer, becoming pale green later, in contrast to the bright berries. Hardy to -10°F (-23°C), US zones 6–10. *Berberis thunbergii* is native to Japan and China and was introduced in the late 19th century, while yellow-leafed 'Aurea' was introduced in the 20th century.

*Berberis thunbergii* 'Atropurpurea Nana' This dwarf variety was raised in the mid-20th century. It is very appropriate for small gardens, where its summer foliage makes a striking feature. It is compact enough to grow on a rock garden where the bright flowers of autumn-flowering gentians would contrast nicely.

*Berberis* x *stenophylla* 'Crawley Gem' An evergreen shrub that grows to 10ft (3m) tall. Flowers, each about ¹/₄in (6mm) wide, 5–15 in drooping clusters up to 2in (5cm) long, appear in spring. Hardy to 0°F (-18°C), US zones 7–10. *Berberis* x *stenophylla* is a hybrid between *B. darwinii* and *B. empetrifolia*, raised in the middle of the 19th century, but many varieties, such as 'Crawley Gem', have been raised since.

*Cotinus coggygria* 'Notcutt's Variety'

*Euphorbia mellifera*

DARWIN'S BARBERRY *Berberis darwinii* A compact spiny evergreen shrub that grows to 8ft (2.5m) tall and often as wide. The flowers, each about 1/2in (1cm) wide, 10–20 together in drooping clusters up to 2in (5cm) long, are borne in spring in great profusion. Best in a sunny site and hardy to 0°F (-18°C), US zones 7–10. Native to Chile.

PURPLE SMOKE BUSH *Cotinus coggygria* 'Notcutt's Variety' A deciduous shrub that grows to 15ft (4.5m) tall. In late spring and early summer it produces large airy clusters of misty flowers. But it is principally grown for its purple leaves. Grows well in areas with dry summers. Hardy to 0°F (-18°C), US zones 7–10. Native to much of the area from the Mediterranean to the Himalayas and China.

*Berberis* x *stenophylla* 'Crawley Gem'

*Berberis verruculosa*

*Berberis thunbergii* 'Aurea'

*Berberis thunbergii* 'Atropurpurea Nana'

2/5 life size. Specimens from Kew, 25 April

*Berberis darwinii*

*Berberis darwinii*

*Cistus* x *aguilari*    A medium-sized evergreen shrub that grows up to 7ft (2m). The flower, borne in early summer, is about 3in (8cm) wide. Cistuses thrive in dry summer conditions and do very well in seaside areas. Hardy to 10°F (-12°C), US zones 8–10. A hybrid between the Gum Cistus and *C. populifolius*, occurring in the wild in Spain and Morocco, it was first introduced into cultivation in the early 20th century.

*Cistus* x *cyprius* 'Albiflorus'    An evergreen shrub that grows to 7ft (2m). Flowers, borne in early summer, are 3in (8cm) wide. Hardy to 10°F (-12°C), US zones 8–10. *C.* x *cyprius*, a hybrid between the Gum Cistus and *C. laurifolius,* occurs in the wild in south-west Europe, and was first introduced into cultivation in the early 19th century. The unspotted form 'Albiflorus' was introduced later.

*Cistus* x *hybridus* (better known as *C.* x *corbariensis*)    A compact evergreen shrub that reaches 3ft (90cm) tall and generally wider. Flowers, each about 1.5in (4cm) wide, are borne in early summer. This is one of the hardiest cistuses, withstanding temperatures to 0°F (-18°C), US zones 7–10. A hybrid between *C. populifolius* and *C. salviifolius*, occurring in the wild in France and introduced into cultivation in the mid-17th century.

GUM CISTUS *Cistus ladanifer*    An evergreen shrub that grows to 5ft (1.5m). Flowers, 3–4in (8–10cm) wide, are borne in early summer. The leaves are up to 4in (10cm) long, narrowly lance-shaped and, like the stems, very sticky. Hardy to 10°F (-12°C), US zones 8–10 or slightly lower. *C. ladanifer* grows wild in southern Europe and North Africa. It was first introduced to Britain in the early 17th century.

*Cistus populifolius*    Growing up to 7ft (2m) tall, this shrub has small-stalked clusters of flowers 2in (5cm) wide, with five broad petals surrounding a boss of deep orange-yellow stamens, borne in early summer. Hardy to 10°F (-12°C), US zones 8–10. *C. populifolius* grows wild in south-west Europe and North Africa. It was introduced into cultivation in the middle of the 17th century.

*Cistus* 'Silver Pink' (below)    A compact evergreen shrub that grows to 2½ft (75cm) tall with similar spread. The flowers, about 3in (8cm) wide, are borne in early summer. Hardy to 10°F (-12°C), US zones 8–10, or slightly lower. *Cistus* 'Silver Pink' is thought to be a hybrid between *C. creticus* and *C. laurifolius*. It was raised at Hillier Nurseries in Britain in the early 20th century.

*Cistus* x *hybridus* (top), *Cistus* x *aguilari*

*Cistus* x *cyprius* 'Albiflorus'

*Cistus ladanifer*

*Cistus* x *purpureus*

*Cistus populifolius*

*Lupinus arboreus*

*Genista aetnensis*

*Cytisus battandieri*

*Cytisus* x *kewensis*

*Cytisus* x *praecox* 'Warminster'

*Cistus* x *purpureus*  This shrub grows up to 5ft (1.5m) tall. Flowers, 3in (8cm) wide with five broad, slightly wavy-edged petals surrounding a boss of deep orange-yellow stamens, are borne in early summer. Hardy to 10°F (-12°C), US zones 8–10. *Cistus* x *purpureus* is a hybrid between *C. creticus* and the Gum Cistus. It was first introduced into cultivation in the late 18th century.

*Cytisus battandieri*  A deciduous shrub that grows to 15ft (4.5m). In early summer it produces pineapple-scented flowers about ³/₄in (2cm) long in upright clusters 5in (12cm) long. The laburnum-like leaves are composed of three elliptic leaflets each about 2¹/₂in (6cm) long, covered with silky hairs especially when young. Hardy to 0°F (-18°C), US zones 7–10. Native to Morocco.

*Cytisus* x *praecox* 'Warminster'
A spreading evergreen shrub with small leaves but green twigs, growing to 5ft (1.5m) across. Flowers pale yellow, each about ¹/₂in (1cm) long, with a rather sharp scent, covering the whole plant in late spring.  Raised at Warminster, Wiltshire in

around 1867. 'Allgold', a more recent form of *C.* x *praecox* from Holland, is taller with deep yellow flowers. Hardy to 0°F (-18°C), US zones 7–10.

*Cytisus* x *kewensis*  A deciduous shrub that grows 1ft (30cm), with a spread of up to 5ft (1.5m) or more. In late spring it produces flowers, each about ¹/₂in (1cm) long and with the characteristic shape of flowers of the bean family, in great abundance. Hardy to 0°F (-18°C), US zones 7–10.

MOUNT ETNA BROOM *Genista aetnensis*  A deciduous shrub that grows to 20ft (6m). In summer it produces flowers, each about ¹/₂in (1cm) long. The green stems give the shrub an evergreen appearance. Hardy to 0°F (-18°C), US zones 7–10. Native to Sicily and Sardinia, from where it was introduced in the 19th century.

TREE LUPIN *Lupinus arboreus*
A vigorous evergreen shrub that grows to 8ft (2.5m) tall and usually as wide. In summer it produces upright spikes up to 10in (25cm) long, with many light or

sulphur-yellow flowers. Each flower is a typical bean shape, about ³/₄in (2cm) long. The flowers have a pleasant scent. The leaves are about 4in (10cm) wide, divided into nine narrow leaflets. Hardy to 0°F (-18°C), US zones 7–10.

SPANISH BROOM
*Spartium junceum* (right)  A vigorous broom-like deciduous shrub that grows to 10ft (3m) tall and usually wider. The whip-like green shoots give it the effect of an evergreen shrub. Over a long period from early summer to autumn they bear a succession of sweetly scented flowers, each about 1in (2.5cm) wide. Hardy to 10°F (-12°C), US zones 8–9. Native to Portugal and Mediterranean region.

*Viburnum plicatum* 'Mariesii'

*Viburnum* x *carlcephalum*

*Viburnum plicatum* 'Mariesii' A large deciduous shrub that grows up to 10ft (3m) tall, of broad spreading habit, with distinctly layered branches. In early summer it bears flat clusters, up to 4in (10cm) wide, of small fertile flowers surrounded by a ring of cream sterile flowers 1¹/₂in (4cm) wide. Hardy to -20°F (-29°C), US zones 5–9. The species *V. plicatum* is native to China, Japan and Taiwan and has been cultivated in England since the late 19th century. 'Mariesii' is a popular shrub of distinctive habit and very showy in flower.

*Viburnum plicatum* 'Pink Beauty'
A large deciduous shrub that grows up to 7ft (2m) tall. In early summer it bears clusters, up to 4in (10cm) wide, of small fertile flowers surrounded by a ring of cream sterile flowers about 1in (2.5cm) wide, which turn to pink as they mature. Small red berries turn black on ripening in the autumn. Hardy to -20°F (-29°C), US zones 5–9. 'Pink Beauty', a distinctive variant of *Viburnum plicatum*, is attractive in both flower and fruit and was raised in the US.

*Viburnum carlesii* 'Aurora' A compact deciduous shrub that grows up to 5ft (1.5m) tall and usually wider. In spring it bears rounded clusters up to 4in (10cm) wide of sweetly scented flowers, each about ¹/₂in (1cm) wide, which open from bright red buds. Hardy to -10°F (-23°C), US zones 6–9. *V. carlesii* is native to Korea and a small island of Japan. It was introduced into cultivation in the early 20th century. The variety 'Aurora' was raised in Northern Ireland and is notable for its vividly coloured flowers buds.

*Viburnum davidii* A compact evergreen shrub that grows up to 3¹/₂ft (1m) tall and usually wider. In early summer it bears rounded clusters, up to 3in (8cm) wide, of small off-white, sweetly scented flowers about ¹/₂in (1cm) wide. The fruit is a small, oval metallic-blue berry. Hardy to 0°F (-18°C), US zones 7–9. *V. davidii* is native to western China and was introduced to England in the early 20th century. It is an unusual shrub, not spectacular in flower but with distinctive foliage and berries.

**HOBBLE BUSH**
*Viburnum lantanoides*
(syn. *V. alnifolium*)
(left) A compact deciduous shrub that grows up to 10ft (3m) tall and usually wider. In early summer it bears domed clusters, up to 3in (8cm) wide, of small cream fertile flowers with a fringe of larger, sterile flowers about 1in (2.5cm) wide. The leaves are up to 8in (20cm) long, usually turning deep red or purple in autumn. The fruit is a small berry, at first red, finally black. Hardy to -20°F (-29°C), US zones 5–9. *V. lantanoides* is native to eastern North America.

SHEEP-BERRY *Viburnum lentago*
A deciduous shrub that grows up to 10ft (3m) tall and usually wider but occasionally a small tree twice this height. In early summer it bears sprays, up to 5in (12cm) wide, of flowers about ¹/₄in (6mm) wide. The leaves are up to 4in (10cm) long, shiny dark green and usually turning orange or deep red in autumn. The fruit is a small blue-black berry. Hardy to -20°F (-29°C), US zones 5–9. *V. lentago* is native to eastern North America.

SNOWBALL TREE *Viburnum opulus* 'Roseum' (also known as 'Sterile')
A deciduous shrub that grows up to 12ft (3.5m) tall and about as wide. In early summer it bears rounded clusters, up to 2¹/₂in (6cm) wide, of sterile flowers ³/₄in (2cm) wide. The maple-like, three-lobed leaves are up to 4in (10cm) long and usually turn purple and deep red in autumn. Hardy to -20°F (-29°C), US zones 5–9. The species *V. opulus* is native to Europe, western Asia and North Africa, and has long been cultivated.

*Viburnum rhytidophyllum* A large, wide evergreen shrub that grows to 20ft (6m) tall. In early summer it bears clusters up to 7in (18cm) wide, of not very pleasantly scented flowers, each about ¹/₄in (6mm) wide. The large oblong leaves are up to 7in (18cm) long. The fruit is a small oval

*Viburnum plicatum* 'Pink Beauty'

*Viburnum lantanoides*

*Viburnum carlesii* 'Aurora'

*Viburnum lentago*

berry, at first bright red, but finally glossy black. Hardy to 0°F (-18°C), US zones 7–9. *V. rhytidophyllum* is native to western China and was introduced to cultivation at the beinning of the 20th century. It is a striking foliage shrub, not spectacular in flower but with showy berries.

*Viburnum* x *carlcephalum*   A medium-sized deciduous shrub that grows up to 7ft (2m) tall and usually wider. In spring it bears rounded clusters to 5in (12cm) wide, of slightly scented flowers about ¹/₂in (1cm) wide. Hardy to -10°F (-23°C), US zones 6–9. *V.* x *carlcephalum* is a hybrid between *V. carlesii* and *V. macrocephalum*, first raised in England in the early 20th century. It is less fragrant than *V.* x *burkwoodii* but is more compact and has larger flower heads.

*Viburnum* x *burkwoodii* 'Park Farm Hybrid' (below)   A medium-sized evergreen shrub that grows up to 8ft (2.5m) tall and usually wider. In spring it bears compact clusters of sweetly scented flowers, each about ¹/₂in (1cm) wide, opening from pink buds. This shrub can be planted in the autumn or spring, grows well in full sun and is hardy to -10°F (-23°C), US zones 6–9. No regular pruning is required and it is seldom affected by pests and diseases. *Viburnum* x *burkwoodii* is a hybrid between *V. carlesii* and *V. utile* and was first raised in England in the early 20th century.

*Viburnum davidii*

*Viburnum davidii*

*Viburnum rhytidophyllum*

*Viburnum opulus* 'Roseum'

Deutzia longifolia 'Veitchii'

Deutzia x elegantissima 'Rosealind'

¹⁄₃ life size. Specimens from Wisley, 21 June

Deutzia pulchra

Philadelphus insignis

Philadelphus 'Etoile Rose'

*Deutzia* x *elegantissima* 'Rosealind'
A medium-sized deciduous shrub that grows to 5ft (1.5m) tall, of erect growth but when mature about as wide as high. In early summer it produces clusters of flowers about ³⁄₄in (2cm) wide. Hardy to 0°F (-18°C), US zones 7–10. *Deutzia*. x *elegantissima* is a group of hybrids between *D. purpurascens* and *D. sieboldiana*, raised by the French nurseryman Lémoine. 'Rosealind' was introduced in the late 20th century and is one of the most strongly coloured deutzias.

*Deutzia longifolia* 'Veitchii' A medium-sized deciduous shrub that grows up to 5ft (1.5m) tall and usually as wide. In early summer it produces clusters of flowers 1in (2.5cm) wide. This shrub can be planted in the autumn or early spring in sun or partial shade. Hardy to 0°F (-18°C), US zones 7–10. *D. longifolia* is native to western China, and it was introduced to Britain early in the 20th century. 'Veitchii' has larger flowers than the wild type.

*Deutzia pulchra* A medium-sized deciduous shrub that grows up to 8ft (2.5m) tall and usually as wide. In early summer it produces elongated clusters of pure white flowers ³⁄₄in (2cm) wide. Hardy to 10°F (-12°C), US zones 8–10, it will benefit from a sheltered site by a south or west wall. It only requires regular pruning every two or three years; cut out the oldest shoots immediately after flowering to encourage strong new growth. It is free from pests and diseases. *D. pulchra* is native to Taiwan and the Philippines.

*Philadelphus* 'Beauclerk' A medium-sized deciduous shrub that grows to 7ft (2m) tall and wider. In early summer it produces clusters of sweetly scented flowers 2¹⁄₂in (6cm) wide. Plant in autumn or early spring in a sunny position. Hardy to 0°F (-18°C), US zones 7–10. No regular pruning is required other than cutting out old flowering shoots. Sometimes infested with aphids. A hybrid raised in Britain in this century.

*Philadelphus* 'Avalanche' A medium-sized shrub that grows up to 6ft (1.8m) tall. In early summer it produces clusters of up to 7 sweetly scented flowers about 1in (2.5cm) wide, with 4 relatively narrow white petals. Hardy to 0°F (-18°C), US zones 7–10. Old flowering shoots should be cut out. It is free from diseases but is sometimes infested with aphids. Raised in France at the end of the 19th century.

*Philadelphus coronarius* A deciduous shrub that grows to 7ft (2m) tall and as wide as it is tall. In early summer it produces clusters of highly scented flowers, each about 1in (2.5cm) wide. Hardy to -10°F (-23°C), US zones 6–10. No regular pruning is required other than cutting out old flowering shoots. Thrives in very dry conditions.

*Philadelphus coronarius* 'Aureus' A deciduous shrub that grows to 7ft (2m) tall and as wide. This variety has bright pure yellow leaves in spring gradually turning green in summer.

*Philadelphus insignis* A vigorous deciduous shrub that grows to 12ft (3.5m) tall and usually wider. In summer it produces clusters of slightly scented flowers about 1¼in (3cm). It flowers later than most mock oranges. Hardy to 0°F (-18°C), US zones 7–10. Old flowering shoots should be cut out. It is free from diseases but is sometimes infested with aphids. *P. insignis* is native to California.

*Philadelphus* 'Etoile Rose' A small deciduous shrub that grows to 4ft (1.25m) tall and about the same width. In summer it produces abundant long-lasting large white flowers stained rose at the base, about 1½in (4cm) wide. This shrub can be planted in autumn or early spring in a a sunny position. Hardy to 0°F (-18°C), US zones 7–10 or lower. *P.* 'Etoile Rose' was raised in France at the beginning of the 20th century by Lemoine at Nancy.

*Philadelphus* 'Virginal' (below) A medium-sized deciduous shrub with a somewhat gaunt habit that grows to 6ft (1.8m) tall and wider. In early summer it produces abundant long-lasting clusters of white flowers about 1½in (4cm) wide. The leaves are 2in (5cm) long. This shrub can be planted in autumn or early spring in a sunny position. Hardy to 0°F (-18°C), US zones 7–10 or lower. *P.* 'Virginal' was raised in France at the beginning of the 20th century.

*Philadelphus* 'Avalanche'

*Philadelphus coronarius*

*Philadelphus coronarius* 'Aureus'

*Philadelphus* 'Beauclerk'

*Clematis alpina*
'Ruby'

*C. macropetala*
'Markham's Pink'

*C. alpina*
'Grandiflora'

*C. alpina*
'Inshraich Form'

*C. alpina*
'Pauline'

*C. montana*
'Elizabeth'

*C. montana*

*C. montana*
'Mayleen'

*C. montana*
'Pink Perfection'

*C. montana*
'Tetrarose'

*C. x vedrariensis*

*C. montana* var.
*rubens*

⅓ life size. Specimens from Eccleston Square and Kew, 19 May

*Clematis alpina* A member of the buttercup family, the Ranunculaceae. This deciduous climbing shrub grows up to 8ft (2.5m) tall. Flowers, each with four slender lance-shaped petal-like sepals up to 1.5in (4cm) long, surrounding a cluster of smaller oblong cream staminodes, appear in the late spring as the young leaves, 6in (15cm) long, open. Hardy to -10°F (-23°C), US zones 6–9. *Clematis alpina* is native to the mountains of central Europe from France east to Bulgaria.

*Clematis alpina* 'Grandiflora' This variety grows to 8ft (2.5m) tall with flowers to 2.5in (6cm) long. The origin of 'Grandiflora' is unknown.

*Clematis alpina* 'Inshraich Form' Raised at Jack Drake's Nursery near Aviemore, Scotland.

*Clematis alpina* 'Pauline' Introduced by Washfield Nurseries, Sussex in 1970. The long staminodes suggest that it may be a hybrid with *C. macropetala*.

*Clematis alpina* 'Ruby' This variety grows up to 8ft (2.5m) tall. Petal-like sepals up to 1 1/2in (4cm) long. Raised in England in the mid-20th century.

*Clematis armandii* An evergreen climbing shrub that grows to 20ft (6m) tall. Flowers, 1 1/2–2 1/2in (4–6cm) wide, appear in spring with sepals up to 1in (2.5cm) long. The leathery dark green leaves consist of three lance-shaped, prominently veined leaflets. The fruit is a cluster of silky plumes 1 1/2in (4cm) long, each with a seed attached at the base. Hardy to 10°F (-12°C), US zones 8–9. *C. armandii* is native to low mountains in central and western China, growing in open scrub and on river banks.

*Clematis cirrhosa* This shrub grows up to 13ft (4m) and has scented flowers. Hardy to 10°F (-12°C), US zones 7–9 and benefits from a warm position against a west or south wall, with a cool shaded root-run. No pruning is needed and it is seldom affected by pests or diseases. Native to much of the Mediterranean region, growing in open scrub and rocky places at low altitudes. Cultivated in Britain since the middle of the 16th century.

*Clematis tangutica* A vigorous deciduous shrub that grows up to 10ft (3m) tall. The lantern-shaped flowers appear in autumn. Each has four tapering lance-shaped petal-like sepals, to 2in (5cm) long. Hardy to -10°F (-23°C), US zones 6–9. *C. tangutica* is native to the mountains of northern China and was introduced to Britain at the end of the 19th century. It is best grown against a wall, through a tree or even cascading down a bank.

*Clematis macropetala* 'Markham's Pink' A deciduous climbing shrub that grows to 8ft (2.5m) or taller. Flowers, about 2 1/2in (6cm) wide, appear in late spring and early summer. Hardy to -10°F (-23°C), US zones 6–9.

*Clematis montana* A vigorous deciduous climbing shrub that grows to 20ft (6m) tall. Flowers, up to 2.5in (6cm) wide, appear in late spring. The fruit is an insignificant cluster of flattened seeds with silky tails. It will grow on any well-drained but fertile soil and needs average rainfall. Hardy to 0°F (-18°C), US zones 7–9. *C. montana* is native to the Himalayas and western China and was introduced to Britain in the early 19th century.

*Clematis montana* 'Elizabeth' This variety grows to 20ft (6m) tall and has flowers up to 3in (8cm) wide.

*Clematis montana* 'Mayleen' A form of *C. montana* with pale pink flowers.

*Clematis montana* 'Pink Perfection' A selection of *C. montana* var. *rubens*, its flowers are 2 1/2–3in (6–8cm) across. No pruning is required.

*Clematis montana* var. *rubens* This variety grows to 20ft (6m) tall. Flowers up to 2.5in (6cm) wide.

*Clematis montana* 'Tetrarose' Grows to 20ft (6m) tall. Flowers up to 3in (8cm) wide.

*Clematis* x *vedrariensis* A hybrid between *C. montana* var. *rubens* and *C. chrysocoma*, raised in France by Vilmorin *c.* 1914 Hardy to 5°F (-15°C), US zones 7–10.

*Clematis* x *durandii* A hybrid between the climbing *C.* x *jackmannii* and the herbaceous *C. integrifolia*, this scrambling shrub grows up to 8ft (2.5m) tall. The nodding blue-purple flowers, about 4in (10cm) wide, appear in summer and early autumn. Each has four overlapping oval petal-like sepals, surrounding a cluster of yellow stamens. The fruit is an insignificant cluster of flattened seed vessels.

*Clematis cirrhosa*

*Clematis tangutica*

*Clematis armandii*

*Clematis montana*

'Perle d'Azur'

'Comtesse de Bouchaud'

*Clematis rehderiana*

*Clematis* 'Rouge Cardinal' (below)
A vigorous deciduous climbing shrub that grows to 12ft (3.5m) tall. Flowers, 5–6in (12–15cm) wide with sepals about 3in (8cm) long, appear in the summer. Hardy to -10°F (-23°C), US zones 6–9, this clematis should be pruned hard, back to 1ft (30cm) from the ground in late winter. *Clematis* 'Rouge Cardinal' is a hybrid of garden origin introduced in the late 20th century.

*Clematis* 'Comtesse de Bouchaud'
A deciduous climbing shrub that grows to 12ft (3.5m) tall. Flowers 4in (10cm) wide appear in summer. Each has 6 overlapping, rounded petal-like sepals up to 2in (5cm) long, surrounding a cluster of cream stamens. Hardy to -10°F (-23°C), US zones 6–9, this clematis should be pruned hard, back to 1ft (30cm) from the ground in late winter.

*Clematis* x *durandii*   Growing to 8ft (2.5m) tall, this variety has nodding flowers about 4in (10cm) wide in summer and early autumn. Each has four overlapping, oval petal-like sepals, which surround a cluster of yellow stamens. Hardy to -10°F (-23°C), US zones 6–9. Should be pruned hard, back to about 1ft (30cm) from the ground in late winter.

*Clematis* 'Etoile Violette'   A deciduous climbing shrub that grows to 12ft (3.5m) tall. Flowers 4in (10cm) wide appear late summer. Hardy to -10°F (-23°C), US zones 6–9, this clematis should be pruned hard, back to 1ft (30cm) from the ground, in late winter. *Clematis* 'Etoile Violette' is a hybrid of garden origin, raised in France in the late 19th century.

*Clematis rehderiana*   This variety grows to 24ft (7m) tall where suitable support is available. The nodding, bell-shaped and sweetly scented flowers appear in late summer and autumn in large open clusters up to 1ft (30cm) long. Sepals are ³/₄in (2cm) long and leaves about 6in (15cm) long. Hardy to 0°F (-18°C), US zones 7–9. *C. rehderiana* is native to the mountains of western China and was introduced to cultivation at the end of the 19th century.

*Clematis viticella* 'Purpurea Plena Elegans'

# CLEMATIS

'Gravetye Beauty'

Clematis macropetala

*Clematis* 'Madame Julia Correvon' (above)   A deciduous climbing shrub that grows to 8ft (2.5m) tall. Flowers, 5¹/₂in (13cm) wide with sepals to 2in (5cm) long, appear in summer and early autumn. Hardy to -10°F (-23°C), US zones 6–9, this clematis should be pruned hard, back to 1ft (30cm) from the ground in late winter. 'Madame Julia Correvon' is a hybrid of garden origin, derived from *C. viticella* and raised in France at the start of the 20th century.

*Clematis* 'Gravetye Beauty'   A deciduous climbing shrub that grows to 8ft (2.5m) tall. Flowers, bell-shaped at first, spread to about 3in (8cm) wide and appear in summer and early autumn. Hardy to -10°F (-23°C), US zones 6–9, this clematis should be pruned hard, back to 1ft (30cm) from the ground in late winter. A hybrid of *C. texensis* and a large-flowered hybrid, it was raised in England in the early 20th century.

*Clematis macropetala*   A deciduous climbing shrub that grows to 8ft (2.5m) or taller. Flowers about 2¹/₂in (6cm) wide appear in the late spring and early summer. The fruit is an attractive cluster of silky plumes 1¹/₂in (4cm) long, each with a seed attached at the base. Hardy to -10°F (-23°C), US zones 6–9. *C. macropetala* is native to the mountains of northern China and Siberia.

*Clematis viticella* 'Kermesina' (right)   This deciduous climbing shrub grows up to 12ft (3.5m) tall. Flowers to 1in (2.5cm) long appear in summer and early autumn. Hardy to 0°F (-18°C), US zones 7–9. It should be pruned hard in late winter. *C. viticella* is native to southern Europe and has been cultivated since the 16th century. The variety 'Kermesina' was raised in France in the 19th century.

*Clematis* 'Perle d'Azur'   A vigorous deciduous climbing shrub that grows to 13ft (4m) tall. Flowers 4–6in (10–15cm) wide, with sepals about 2¹/₂in (6cm) long, appear in the summer. Hardy to -10°F (-23°C), US zones 6–9, this clematis should be pruned hard, back to 1ft (30cm) from the ground in late winter. 'Perle d'Azur' is a hybrid of garden origin, raised in France in the late 19th century.

*Clematis viticella* 'Purpurea Plena Elegans'   A deciduous climbing shrub that grows to

10ft (3m) tall. Flowers with sepals up to 1in (2.5cm) long. Hardy to 0°F (-18°C), US zones 7–9, this clematis should be pruned hard in late winter. The variety 'Purpurea Plena Elegans' was first recorded in the 17th century.

*Clematis florida* 'Sieboldii'   A deciduous climbing shrub that grows up to 8ft (2.5m) tall. Flowers about 3in (8cm) wide appear in summer and early autumn. Hardy to -10°F (-23°C), US zones 6–9, this clematis needs little pruning but it is worth removing the old flowering wood. *C. florida* is a native of central China but has long been cultivated in Japan, from where the variety 'Sieboldii' was introduced in the early 19th century.

Clematis x *durandii*

*Clematis* 'Etoile Violette'

*Clematis florida* 'Sieboldii'

*Clematis* 'Gypsy Queen'

'Mrs Spencer Castle'

'Lord Nevill'

'Jackmanii Rubra'

'Beauty of Richmond'

'Beauty of Worcester'

'The President'

'Belle of Woking'

'Vyvyan Pennell'

'Proteus'

¼ life size. Specimens from Treasures Nursery, Tenbury, England, 3 July

*Clematis* 'Beauty of Richmond'
A vigorous cultivar with flowers up to 6in (15cm) across, appearing from mid-summer. It will do well in any situation. Requires only light pruning. Hardy to -5°F (-20°C), US zones 6–10.

*Clematis* 'Belle of Woking'   One of the old hybrids, it produces large flowers during spring 6in (15cm) across. Prefers a sunny position. Requires only light pruning. Hardy to -5°F (-20°C), US zones 6–10.

*Clematis* 'Beauty of Worcester'   This cultivar produces double flowers on old wood from early to mid-summer and single flowers on young wood until early autumn. Prefers a sunny position. Hardy to -5°F (-20°C), US zones 6–10.

*Clematis* 'Gypsy Queen'   A vigorous hybrid that will eventually reach 16ft (5m) in height. Flowers, 5in (12cm) across, are freely produced in mid-summer and autumn; the colour of the sepals changes slightly as they age. Flourishes in full sun. Hard pruning required. Hardy to -5°F (-20°C), US zones 6–10.

*Clematis* 'Jackmanii Superba'   Growing to 16ft (5m) tall. Rich violet-purple flowers, about 4in (10cm) wide, appear in summer and early autumn. Hardy to -10°F (-23°C), US zones 6–9 or lower.

*Clematis* 'Jackmanii Rubra'   A fairly vigorous shrub with semi-double flowers during mid-summer, followed by single blooms until early autumn. Requires only light pruning. Hardy to -5°F (-20°C), US zones 6–10.

*Clematis* 'Lord Nevill'   A vigorous cultivar growing to 20ft (6m). Flowers up to 7in (18cm) across, are borne in mid-summer and early autumn. Requires only light pruning. Hardy to -5°F (-20°C), US zones 6–10.

*Clematis* 'Mrs Spencer Castle'
A moderately vigorous shrub growing to 16ft (5m) high. The large flowers appear in early summer and single blooms are borne on young wood in the autumn. Requires only light pruning. Hardy to -5°F (-20°C), US zones 6–10.

*Clematis* 'Nellie (or Nelly) Moser'   One of the best known and most popular of all the hybrids, this clematis grows to 12ft (3.5m) in height. The large flowers up to 7in (18cm) are freely produced in early, and again in late summer. It is best planted in a shady position to avoid bleaching of flower colour. Requires only light pruning. Hardy to -5°F (-20°C), US zones 6–10.

*Clematis* 'Jackmanii Superba'

*Clematis* 'Jackmanii Superba'

*Clematis* 'Niobe'   This climbing shrub grows to 16ft (5m) tall, with flowers 5–6in (12–15cm) wide, appearing in late summer and early autumn. Each has about 6 broad, rounded petal-like sepals up to 3in (8cm) long, surrounding a cluster of yellow stamens. Hardy to -10°F (-23°C), US zones 6–9. Raised in England in the late 20th century.

*Clematis* 'Proteus'   An old hybrid, first introduced under the name 'The Premier'. Moderately vigorous, with double flowers during early summer and a crop of single flowers towards the end of summer. It does best away from full sun or deep shade. Hardy to -5°F (-20°C), US zones 6–10.

*Clematis* 'The President'   A vigorous deciduous climbing shrub that grows to 12ft (3.5m) tall. Flowers, about 6–7in (15–18cm) wide with sepals 3in (8cm) long, appear in summer and early autumn. Hardy to -10°F (-23°C), US zones 6–9. It needs light pruning immediately after flowering. A hybrid of garden origin, it was raised in England in the late 19th century.

*Clematis* 'Ville de Lyon'   A vigorous deciduous climbing shrub that grows to 16ft (5m) tall. Flowers, 5in (12cm) wide with sepals up to 3in (8cm) long, appear in summer and autumn. Hardy to -10°F (-23°C), US zones 6–9. It should be pruned hard, back to 1ft (30cm) from the ground in late winter.

*Clematis* 'Vyvyan Pennell'   A vigorous deciduous climbing shrub that grows to 12ft (3.5m) tall. Flowers, up to 8in (20cm) wide, appear in summer and early autumn. Hardy to -10°F (-23°C), US zones 6–9. It needs only light pruning immediately after flowering. It is a garden hybrid, raised in England this century.

*Clematis* 'Ville de Lyon'

*Clematis* 'Nellie (or Nelly) Moser'

*Clematis* 'Niobe'

# SHRUBS

*Lavandula stoechas*

*Santolina pinnata*

*Santolina chamaecyparissus*

**LAVENDER** *Lavendula angustifolia*
A much-branded evergreen shrub that grows to 3¹/₂ft (1m) tall. In May–June, flowers ¹/₂in (1cm) long on spikes, which when bruised gently, release the characteristic lavender scent. Plant in well-drained soil in full sun. Hardy to 5°F (-15°C), US zones 7–10. Native to the Mediterranean region from the Balkans to Spain and North Africa.

*Lavandula angustifolia* 'Hidcote' Early flowering; grows to 2–2¹/₂ft (60–75cm); flowers bluish-violet.

*Lavandula angustifolia* 'Loddon Pink' Early flowering; grows to 2¹/₂ft (75cm) tall and usually wider.

*Lavandula angustifolia* 'Munstead' A small evergreen shrub that grows up to 2¹/₂ft (75cm) tall and usually wider. In early summer it produces long-stalked spikes of violet-blue flowers.

*Lavandula angustifolia* 'Nana Alba' Early flowering; grows to only 1ft (30cm) tall and wider.

*Lavandula angustifolia* 'Ariele' Late flowering; grows to 3¹/₂ft (1m) or a little more. The spikes are often branched. Probably a hybrid between *L. angustifolia* and *L. latifolia.*

*Lavandula dentata* A small evergreen shrub that grows up to 3ft (90cm) tall and usually wider. Flower spikes about 1¹/₂in (4cm) long, with small flowers over-topped by a few bluish bracts. This lavender is less strongly scented than most others. Leaves are up to 1¹/₂in (4cm) long. Hardy to 24°F (-5°C), US zones 8–10. It needs a sheltered position in cold areas. Native to the W. Mediterranean region.

*Lavandula lanata* A small evergreen shrub that grows to 2ft (60cm) tall. It produces long stalked spikes of flowers, each 1¹/₂–2¹/₂in (4–6cm) long, in late summer. The leaves are 2in (5cm) long. Hardy to 0°F (-18°C), US zones 7–10. *L. lanata* is native to Spain, from where it was introduced to Britain in the 19th century. Its striking foliage makes this shrub distinct from other lavenders.

*Lavandula latifolia* Differs from *L. angustifolia* in having greyer, hairier leaves, linear-lanceolate bracts and flowers, ¹/₂in (1cm) long.

*Lavandula pinnata* Native to dry hills on the Canary Islands. Leaves once pinnate. Hardy to 29°F (-2°C), US zones 9–10.

**FRENCH LAVENDER** *Lavandula stoechas* Up to 3ft (90cm) tall, this small evergreen shrub produces short-stalked spikes of small, deep purple flowers over-topped by showy purple bracts about 1¹/₂in (4cm) long in early summer. The

leaves are up to 1¹/₂in (4cm) long. Hardy to 10°F (-12°C), US zones 8–10. Native to the Mediterranean region, from where it was introduced to Britain in the 16th century.

*L. stoechas* subsp. *pedunculata* From the mountains of central Spain and Portugal, it has much longer stems.

*Lavandula multifida* Evergreen rounded shrub that grows to 3¹/₂ft (1m). From March onwards it produces deep purplish flowers, each 1¹/₂in (4cm) long, in a slender spike ³/₄–2¹/₂in (2–6cm) long. Hardy to 12°F (-10°C), US zones 8–10. Native to Italy, Sicily, North Africa, Spain and Portugal on dry and rocky hills.

**COTTON LAVENDER** *Santolina chamaecyparissus* A compact, slow-growing evergreen shrub that grows to 2ft (60cm) and is usually wider, making it suitable for miniature hedges or edging. In summer it bears long stalked, bright yellow button-like flower heads ³/₄in (2cm) wide. Hairy silver leaves are narrowly oblong, up to 1¹/₂in (4cm) long, divided into regularly arranged segments. Hardy to 0°F (-18°C), US zones 7–9.

*Santolina pinnata* Up to 2ft (60cm) tall, this shrub bears long stalked, white button-like flower heads ³/₄in (2cm) wide in summer. The leaves are oblong, up to 1¹/₂in (4cm) long. Hardy to 0°F (-18°C), US zones 7–9. Native to the western Mediterranean region, it was introduced to Britain in the 16th century.

*Santolina pinnata* subsp. *neapolitana* 'Edward Bowles' A compact and slow-growing evergreen shrub, growing up to 2ft (60cm) tall and usually wider. Long stalked, creamy-yellow flower heads ³/₄in (2cm) wide. The grey hairy leaves are narrowly oblong, up to 2in (5cm) long and divided into regularly arranged segments. Hardy to 0°F (-18°C), US zones 7–9. Native to central Italy on dry rocky slopes near the sea.

*Lavandula angustifolia* 'Loddon Pink'

# LAVENDERS

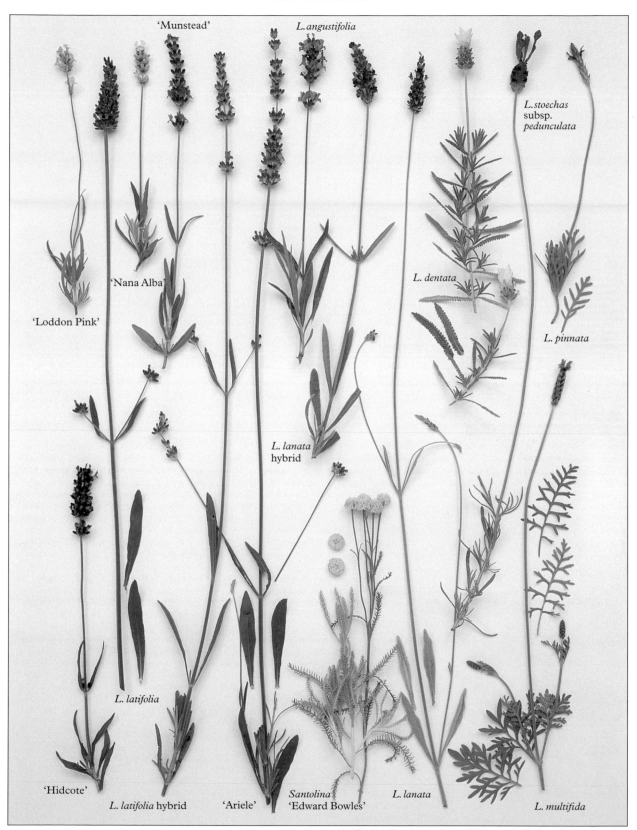

'Munstead'

*L. angustifolia*

'Nana Alba'

'Loddon Pink'

*L. dentata*

*L. stoechas*
subsp.
*pedunculata*

*L. pinnata*

*L. lanata*
hybrid

*L. latifolia*

'Hidcote'

*L. latifolia* hybrid

'Ariele'

*Santolina*
'Edward Bowles'

*L. lanata*

*L. multifida*

²/₅ life size. Specimens from Wisley and Chelsea Physic Garden

Potentilla in a walled garden with a view of the British countryside beyond

*Potentilla* 'Elizabeth' (below) A small twiggy deciduous shrub that grows to 3ft (90cm) tall, becoming a little wider than tall. For a long period in summer it produces a succession of flowers, each about 1in (2.5cm) wide. Best in a sunny position and hardy to -10°F (-23°C), US zones 6–9 or lower. Raised in Britain in the 20th century.

*Potentilla fruticosa* A medium-sized twiggy deciduous shrub that grows to 5ft (1.5m) tall and as wide, producing clusters of bright yellow flowers, each ³/₄–1in (2–2.5cm) wide, in summer. Best in a sunny position and hardy to -40°F (-40°C), US zones 3–8 or lower. Native to northern Europe, Asia and North America and has long been cultivated.

*Potentilla* 'Abbotswood' A small twiggy deciduous shrub of spreading growth, that grows to 2ft (60cm) tall and rather more in spread. For a long period in summer it produces clusters of flowers, each about ³/₄in (2cm) wide. Best in a sunny position and hardy to -10°F (-23°C), US zones 6–9 or lower. A selection of *P. davurica* which is native to northern China and has long been cultivated.

*Potentilla* 'Beesii' A small twiggy deciduous shrub that grows to 2ft (60cm) tall and usually as wide. In summer it produces clusters of flowers, each about 1in (2.5cm) wide. This shrub can be planted in autumn or early spring in a sunny position and is hardy to -10°F (-23°C), US zones 6–9. Raised from seeds collected in western China by George Forrest at the beginning of the 20th century.

*Potentilla* 'Princess' A small twiggy deciduous shrub of spreading habit that grows to 2ft (60cm) tall and considerably wider. In summer it produces a succession of pale pink flowers, an unusual colour in this group of plants. Each flower is about 1in (2.5cm) wide. Best in a sunny position and is hardy to -10°F (-23°C), US zones 6–9 or lower. Raised in Britain in the late 20th century.

*Potentilla* 'Red Ace' A small twiggy deciduous shrub that grows to 2ft (60cm) tall and becoming wider. It produces a succession of flowers, each about 1in (2.5cm) wide, in summer. Requires a sunny, moist or partially shaded position and is hardy to -10°F (-23°C), US zones 6–9 or lower. Raised in Britain in the 20th century. The flowers are sometimes a washed-out colour in dry weather.

*Potentilla* 'Tangerine' Flowers 1in (2.5cm) across. Raised at Slieve Donard Nursery in about 1955. Produced from a seed collected from a 'red form' on the border of Burma and Yunnan.

SHRUBBY GERMANDER *Teucrium fruticans* A lax evergreen shrub that grows to 7ft (2m) tall, bearing flowers, each about 1in (2.5cm) wide, in summer.

*Potentilla* 'Tangerine'

*Potentilla* 'Red Ace'

Needs well-drained soil and dry summer conditions. Hardy to 10°F (-12°C), US zones 8–9. Native to the Mediterranean region of southern Europe and North Africa and introduced into cultivation in the early 18th century.

*Convolvulus cneorum* (below)   A small evergreen shrub that grows to 2ft (60cm) tall and usually wider, producing clusters of flowers, each about 1½in (4cm) across, in late summer. Best in a sunny position, benefiting from a sheltered site in cooler areas and hardy to 10°F (-12°C), US zones 8–10. Native to the Mediterranean region, introduced into cultivation in the 17th century and grown primarily for its remarkable silvery foliage.

*Potentilla fruticosa*

*Potentilla* 'Abbotswood'

*Potentilla* 'Beesii'

*Potentilla* 'Princess'

*Teucrium fruticans*

Buddleja auriculata
B. lindleyana
Buddleja crispa
B. fallowiana var. alba
Buddleja 'Lochinch'
Buddleja nivea
B. davidii var. wilsonii

¹/₄ life size. Specimens from Chelsea Physic Garden, 13 September

*Buddleja alternifolia*

*Buddleja officinalis*

*Buddleja auriculata* An evergreen shrub that grows to 20ft (6m) with support. Sweetly scented flowers ¹/₃in (8mm) long are produced in autumn and winter. Leaves are thin, 4in (10cm) long. Hardy to 12°F (-10°C), US zones 7–10. Native to South Africa where it is widespread from the Cape north and eastwards. Grown primarily for its scent in winter.

*Buddleja crispa* A deciduous shrub that grows up to 13ft (4m) or more. Fragrant flowers, each ¹/₂in (1cm) long, in spring or summer to autumn if pruned in spring. Any well-drained soil, full sun, in cool climates on a wall. Hardy to 12°F (-10°C), US zones 7–10. Native to the Himalayas, from Afghanistan to Yunnan at 4200–14000ft (1200–4000m) in scrub and open hillsides.

*Buddleja davidii* A large and vigorous deciduous shrub growing up to 8ft (2.5m) tall and about the same width. Sweetly scented flowers in June–August. Variable in the wild. Hardy to 5°F (-15°C), US zones 7–10. Native to the Chinese provinces of east and west Sichuan and west Hubei, growing on shingle by rivers and streams at 4550–9100ft (1300–2600m). This is one of the best shrubs to attract butterflies to the garden.

*Buddleja davidii* var. *wilsonii* A deciduous shrub that grows to 7ft (2m) high with fragrant lax-flowered delicate panicles. Thrives in well-drained, chalky or limestone soil in full sun and should be pruned hard in spring. Hardy to 5°F (-15°C), US zones 7–10.

*Buddleja davidii* var. *nanhoensis* 'Nanho Blue' A deciduous shrub that grows to 5ft (1.5m), more elegant than var. *davidii* with smaller leaves and shorter spikes of flowers.

*Buddleja davidii* 'Black Knight' A large and vigorous deciduous shrub growing up to 8ft (2.5m) tall and about the same width. Sweetly scented flowers. Hardy to -20°F (-29°C), US zones 5–10. It was raised in Holland in the late 1950s.

*Buddleja davidii* 'Fortune' A shrub growing up to 7ft (2m) high with rather open habit, introduced in 1936 by Schmidt. Panicles up to 15in (40cm) long.

*Buddleja davidii* 'Royal Red' A large and vigorous deciduous shrub growing up to 8ft (2.5m) tall and about the same width. Sweetly scented flowers appear over a long period from early summer. The leaves are 5–12in (12–30cm) long and covered with white hairs on the lower surface. Hardy to -20°F (-29°C), US zones 5 10.

*Buddleja davidii* 'Variegata' A variegated

form of 'Royal Red' raised by Good and Reese and introduced in 1941.

*Buddleja davidii* 'White Bouquet' A rare, rather low-growing cultivar raised by Tarnok in 1942.

*Buddleja davidii* 'White Cloud' A cultivar that will grow up to 10ft (3m) high and produces small but dense panicles of flowers.

*Buddleja* 'Dartmoor' A hybrid probably between *B. davidii* and var. *nanhoensis*, growing up to 12ft (3.5m). The flowers appear in summer on distinct branched panicles.

*Buddleja fallowiana* var. *alba* A large and vigorous deciduous shrub growing 7–10ft (2–3m) tall. In late summer clusters of sweetly scented flowers, $^{1}/_{2}$in (1cm) long, form long arching wands up to 15in (40cm) in length. Hardy to 10°F (-12°C), US zones 8–10. Native to western China and introduced to Britain in the early 20th century.

*Buddleja lindleyana* A deciduous shrub that grows to 6ft (1.8m). Flowers, each $^{1}/_{2}$in (1cm) long, with a curved tube, in a long spike to 8in (20cm) long open a few at a time in late summer. Any soil; full sun. Hardy to 5°F (-15°C), US zones 8–10. Native to China. Naturalized in south-eastern North America.

*Buddleja* 'Lochinch' A vigorous deciduous shrub, growing 5–8ft (1.5–2.5m) tall and often rather more in width. Sweetly scented flowers are borne in spikes up to 9in (23cm) long on the current year's growth. The individual flowers are nearly $^{1}/_{2}$in (1cm) long. Hardy to 0°F (-18°C), US zones 7–10. This buddleja flowers on the current season's growth and should be pruned back hard each spring.

*Buddleja nivea* A deciduous shrub that grows to 10ft (3m). Flowers $^{1}/_{3}$in (8mm) long in a narrow spike or panicle to 6in (15cm). Leaves are ovate to lanceolate 4–10in (10–25cm) long with white woolly undersides and stems . Hardy to 5°F (-15°C), US zones 7–10. Native to western Sichuan and Yunnan in scrub at 4550–12600ft (1300–3600m).

*Buddleja* x *weyeriana* 'Golden Glow' A shrub that grows up to 10ft (3m) tall. The sweetly scented flowers, about $^{1}/_{2}$in (1cm) long with narrow tube and four spreading lobes, are borne over a long period from early summer in ball-like clusters arranged in loose spikes on the current year's growth. Hardy to -10°F (-23°C), US zones 6–10. Excellent shrub for seaside locations or a sunny border.

*Buddleja officinalis* An evergreen shrub that grows up to 8ft (2.5m). The scented flowers are in terminal panicles 3in (8cm) long, in early spring. Hardy to 15°F (-9°C), US zones 9–10. It makes an excellent conservatory plant. Native to south-west China.

*Buddleja alternifolia* A deciduous shrub or small tree to 20ft (6m). Flowers in spring all along the previous year's growth. Prune after flowering. Grows well on any soil including chalk. Hardy to -5F° (-20°C), US zones 8–10. From China.

*Buddleja* 'Dartmoor'

'Variegata'

'Royal Red'

'Fortune'

'Black Knight'

'Nanho Blue'

*Buddleja davidii*

'Golden Glow'

'White Cloud'

'White Bouquet'

$^{1}/_{4}$ life size. Specimens from  Kew Gardens, London, 12 September

*Richea scoparia*

*Hebe* 'Great Orme'

*Hebe vernicosa*

*Hebe* 'Margery Fish'

*Hebe macrantha*

**Hebe brachysiphon** An evergreen shrub that grows to 6ft (1.8m) high. In mid-summer it produces an abundance of short spikes up to 1¹/₂in (4cm) long, densely packed with pure white flowers, each about ¹/₄in (6mm) wide. It is very well-adapted to conditions in coastal gardens. Hardy to 0°F (-18°C), US zones 7–10. It is native to the South Island of New Zealand.

**Hebe carnosula** A medium-sized evergreen shrub that grows 1–2ft (30–60cm) tall and usually wider. In mid-summer it produces short spikes of 1in (2.5cm) long, densely packed with flowers, each about ¹/₄in (6mm) wide. Leaves are ¹/₂–³/₄in (1–2cm) long, rounded and distinctly cupped or concave. Hardy to 0°F (-18°C), US zones 7–10. This shrub is at its best in early summer when in flower.

**Hebe cupressoides** 'Boughton Dome' A compact, evergreen shrub growing slowly up to 18in (45cm) high and usually wider. In mid-summer it produces short spikes of white or very pale mauve flowers, each about ¹/₄in (6mm) wide. The leaves are tiny and scale-like, dark greyish-green and slightly aromatic. Hardy to 0°F (-18°C), US zones 7–10. It is native to New Zealand.

**Hebe** 'County Park' A hardy, low-growing and fairly compact plant, forming a mat about 8in (20cm) high and 18–24in (45–60cm) wide. The greyish leaves have red edges and in early summer, spikes of violet flowers appear. Hardy to 5°F (-15°C), US zones 7–10. It was raised from a good form of *H. pimeleoides*, from which it differs in several ways but mainly in being more compact.

**Hebe macrantha** Native to mountain areas in the northern part of South Island,

New Zealand. It is easily recognized by its large, pure white flowers, produced 2–6 to a raceme in summer. Hardy to 25°F (-4°C), US zones 9–10.

**Hebe** 'Margery Fish' (syn. 'Primley Gem') A low bush about 2ft (60cm) high and up to 3¹/₂ft (1m) in width. The flowers are violet-blue with white tubes, borne in racemes 2–3in (5–8cm) long. Hardy to 12°F (-10°C), US zones 8–10. Originated at Paignton Zoo in Devon before 1966, but was distributed by the late Margery Fish from her garden at Lambrook Manor, Somerset.

**Hebe** 'Great Orme' A medium-sized evergreen shrub that grows up to 4ft (1.25m) tall when mature and rather wider. In mid-summer it produces an abundance of flower spikes up to 3in (8cm) long. Each flower is about ¹/₄in (6mm) wide. Hardy to 20°F (-7°C), US zones 9–10. A garden hybrid introduced in the 20th century.

**Hebe** 'Autumn Glory' (right) A small evergreen shrub that grows to 2ft (60cm) high with rather sparse, erect branches which are purplish-brown when young. In late summer and into the autumn it produces a succession of short spikes about 1¹/₂in (4cm) long, with strikingly coloured flowers each about ¹/₄in (6mm) wide. Hardy to 10°F (12°C), US zones 8–10.

*Hebe* 'County Park'

*Hebe brachysiphon*

*Hebe ochracea* 'James Stirling'

*Hebe carnosula*

*Hebe* 'Ettrick Shepherd'

*Hebe cupressoides*

*Hebe ochracea* 'James Stirling'   An evergreen shrub growing slowly up to 1ft (30cm) high and usually wider. In mid-summer it produces short spikes of flowers, each about ¼in (6mm) wide. The leaves are tiny and scale-like and of a curious ochre colour, becoming almost yellow at the shoot tips. Hardy to 0°F (-18°C), US zones 7–10. This shrub is at its best in early summer when in flower.

*Hebe vernicosa*   An evergreen shrub growing slowly up to 18in (45cm) high and rather wider. In early summer it produces short spikes up to 2in (5cm) long, with many flowers each about ¼in (6mm) wide. The oval leaves are about ½in (1cm) long and a very glossy bright green. The bright glossy domes of foliage are well suited to rock gardens. Hardy to 0°F (-18°C), US zones 7–10, possibly lower.

*Hebe* 'Ettrick Shepherd'   Of uncertain origin, known since 1953. The flowers open purple or magenta but fade quickly to white, to produce a bicoloured raceme. Hardy to 12°F (-10°C), US zones 8–10.

*Richea scoparia*   An evergreen shrub that grows to about 3.5ft (1m) high, although in the wild it may exceed 7ft (2m). Dense spikes of flowers of variable colour are produced in summer; in the wild, shrubs with red, pink or white flowers may be found. Hardy to 5°F (-15°C), US zones 7–10. Native to Tasmania in mountains to 4500ft (1800m).

*Abelia* x *grandiflora*

*Clerodendrum bungei* growing with *Albizia*

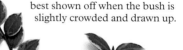

*Myrtus communis* subsp. *tarentina*

*Abelia* x *grandiflora*   A semi-evergreen shrub that grows to 6ft (1.8m) tall and as wide, producing clusters of flowers, each about ³/₄in (2cm) long, from mid-summer to autumn. It prefers a sunny, sheltered site and in cool areas benefits from a warm position against a south- or west-facing wall. Hardy to 0°F (-18°C), US zones 7–10. It was first raised in Italy in the middle of the 19th century.

*Clerodendrum bungei*   A deciduous shrub that grows up to 6ft (1.8m) tall. In cold climates the stems are often killed down to the ground each year (like a fuchsia) but they regrow freely in the following spring. In late summer it produces fragrant flower heads up to 8in (20cm) wide. The leaves have an unpleasant odour when bruised. Hardy to 10°F (-12°C), US zones 8–10. Native to China.

*Jasminum humile* 'Revolutum'
A medium-sized, more or less evergreen shrub that grows to about 6ft (1.8m) tall. In summer it produces clusters of flowers each about 1in (2.5cm) wide. Hardy to 10°F (-12°C), US zones 8–10. Native to much of the Himalayas and western China, from where 'Revolutum' was introduced to England in the 19th century. This shrub is showy in flower.

### COMMON WHITE JASMINE
*Jasminum officinale*   A medium-sized deciduous climbing shrub that grows to 20ft (6m) tall when grown against a wall. In summer it produces clusters of several sweetly scented flowers each about 1in (2.5cm) wide. Hardy to 0°F (-18°C), US zones 7–10. Native to the Caucasus, the Himalayas and western China; introduced to England in the 16th century.

*Jasminum* x *stephanense*   A deciduous climbing shrub that grows to about 10ft (3m) tall or more with the support of a wall. It produces clusters of scented flowers, each about 1in (2.5cm) wide, in summer. Hardy to 10°F (-12°C), US zones 8–10. A hybrid between the Chinese *J. beesianum* and *J. officinale*, raised in France early in this century.

*Salvia microphylla*   An evergreen shrub that grows to 3–4ft (90–125cm) high. Flowers, 1in (2.5cm) long, through summer and autumn. Native to Mexico, it was first introduced to cultivation in the early 19th century. Hardy to 10°F (-12°C), US zones 8–10.

*Salvia officinalis* 'Icterina'   A deciduous shrub that grows to 24in (60cm) tall, bearing clusters of light purple flowers flowers, each about ³/₄in (2cm) long in summer. The leaves, which are strongly sage-scented, are greyish-green and variegated with golden yellow. It grows best in full sun and is hardy to 0°F (-18°C), US zones 7–9. Native to southern Europe and has been cultivated since the 16th century as a culinary herb.

*Salvia officinalis* 'Purpurascens'   The attractive purple-leaved variety.

*Trachelospermum asiaticum*   A twining evergreen climbing shrub that grows to 20ft (6m) tall. Clusters of highly fragrant flowers, each about ³/₄in (2cm) wide in mid- to late summer. Hardy to 10°F (-12°C), US zones 8–9, perhaps lower with the protection of a wall. Native to Japan and Korea. An excellent climber for a conservatory and in mild areas an attractive cover for a warm wall.

*Trachelospermum jasminoides*   A twining evergreen shrub that grows to 24ft (7m) tall. In mid- to late summer it bears clusters of highly fragrant flowers, each about 1in (2.5cm) wide. Hardy to 20°F (-7°C), US zones 9–10, perhaps lower with protection. Native to China and Taiwan, it was introduced to Britain in the early 19th century.

*Myrtus communis* subsp. *tarentina*   An evergreen shrub that grows to 5ft (1.5m) tall and as wide, producing clusters of flowers, each ³/₄in (2cm) wide, tinged pink in the bud in late summer. The leaves are aromatic when bruised. Very successful in seaside gardens and hardy to 0°F (-18°C), US zones 7–10. Native to the Mediterranean region.

*Myrtus luma* 'Glanleam Gold' (below)
An evergreen shrub that grows to 15ft (4.5m) tall, producing white flowers, each about 1in (2.5cm) wide, in late summer. The variegated leaves are aromatic when bruised. Hardy to 0°F (-18°C), US zones 7–10. The species *M. luma* is native to Chile. This shrub is excellent in seaside gardens and the beautiful flaky bark is best shown off when the bush is slightly crowded and drawn up.

*Jasminum* x *stephanense*

*Salvia officinalis* 'Icterina' with *Salvia officinalis* 'Purpurascens'

*Jasminum officinale*

*Salvia microphylla* growing amongst *Opuntia* in southern Spain

*Jasminum humile* 'Revolutum'

*Trachelospermum asiaticum*

*Trachelospermum jasminoides*

'Madame Cornelissen'

'Rufus'

'Variegata'

'Versicolor'

'Tom Thumb'

'Corallina'

*Fuchsia magellanica* var. *molinae*

⅓ life size. Specimens from Wisley, 26 September

*Fuchsia* 'Corallina'  A lax spreading bush that grows up to 3½ft (1m) tall. Hardy to 15°F (-9°C), US zones 8–10. An old hybrid raised in Exeter, Devon in 1844.

*Fuchsia* 'Tom Thumb'  A bushy deciduous shrub that grows to 3ft (90cm) tall, upright in growth. In late summer it produces flowers, each about 1½in (4cm) long. Hardy to 10°F (-12°C), US zone 8 or slightly lower. No regular pruning is required other than cutting away any old damaged shoots, but plants grown in cold areas will die back to the roots in many winters. A hybrid raised in the middle of the 19th century.

*Fuchsia* 'Lady Thumb'  A compact deciduous shrub that grows to 2ft (60cm) tall. In late summer it produces flowers, each about 1in (2.5cm) long, along the current year's growth. Best in a sunny position and benefiting from a sheltered site in cooler areas, it is hardy to 10°F (-12°C), US zones 8–10, possibly lower when established. Raised in Britain in the 20th century as a sport on the well-known 'Tom Thumb'.

*Fuchsia* 'Madame Cornelissen' A vigorous deciduous shrub that grows to 3ft (90cm) tall, producing characteristic pendulous flowers, each about 2in (5cm) long, along the current year's growth in late summer. Benefits from a sheltered site by a south or west wall, this shrub is hardy to 10°F (-12°C), US zones 8–10, possibly lower when established. Raised in Belgium in the 19th century and remains one of the most popular of the hardy fuchsias.

*Fuchsia* 'Mrs Popple'  A compact deciduous shrub that grows up to 3ft (90cm) tall, usually taller than wide. In late summer it produces flowers, each about 1½in (4cm) long. Hardy to 10°F (-12°C), US zones 8–10, possibly lower when established. Raised in Britain in the early 20th century and remains one of the most popular of the hardy fuchsias, although it may need some protection over the roots in cold areas.

*Fuchsia* 'Riccartonii'  A deciduous shrub that grows up to 6ft (1.8m) tall or more. Flowers are produced in summer, 1in (2.5cm) long. Hardy to 10°F (-12°C), US zones 8–10, even lower when established. Raised in Scotland in the 19th century and is believed to be a variant of *F. magellanica*. This shrub is one of the less hardy forms of this species and it may need some protection over the roots in cold areas. It is vigorous in growth and well suited to use for hedging or as a specimen shrub.

*Fuchsia* 'Lady Thumb'

*Fuchsia magellanica* var. *macrostema*

*Fuchsia magellanica* var. *conica* (right)
A compact deciduous shrub that grows to
3ft (90cm) tall and usually rather wider.
In late summer it produces characteristic
pendulous flowers, about 1in (2.5cm)
long, along the current year's growth.
Hardy to 10°F (-12°C), US zones 8–10,
perhaps lower where the root is protected
in winter. Native to southern Chile, from
where it was introduced to Britain in the
early 19th century.

*Fuchsia* 'Rufus'   A vigorous, bushy
upright-growing cultivar, raised in the US
in 1952. Easy to grow; free-flowering over
a long season. Hardy to 10°F (-12°C), US
zones 8–10.

*Fuchsia magellanica* var. *gracilis* 'Variegata'
A compact deciduous shrub that grows up
to 5ft (1.5m) tall or more in mild climates,
and about as wide. Flowers, about 1in
(2.5cm) long, appear in late summer. The
fruit is an oblong berry ¾in (2cm) long,
black when ripe. Plant in autumn or early
spring in any soil in a sunny position.
Hardy to 10°F (-12°C), US zones 8–10,
provided that the root is protected in
winter. Native to southern Chile, from
where it was introduced into cultivation in
the early 19th century.

*Fuchsia magellanica* var. *gracilis*
'Versicolor'   A compact deciduous shrub
that grows up to 5ft (1.5m) tall or more in
mild climates and about as wide. Flowers
about 1in (2.5cm) long. Hardy to 10°F
(-12°C), US zones 8–10, provided that
the root is protected in winter. Native to
southern Chile, from where it was
introduced to Britain in the early 19th
century. Less hardy than other forms of
the species and is likely to be killed back
to the roots in cold areas.

*Fuchsia magellanica* var. *macrostema*
A compact deciduous shrub that grows to
5ft (1.5m) tall or more in mild climates
and about as wide. Flowers about 1½in
(4cm) long. Best in a sunny position and
in cooler areas will benefit from a
sheltered site by a south- or west-facing
wall. Hardy to 10°F (-12°C), US zones
8–10, lower where the root is protected in
winter. The plant then behaves as an
herbaceous perennial. Native to southern
Argentina and Chile, from where it was
introduced into cultivation in the early
19th century.

*Fuchsia magellanica* var. *molinae*
(syn. *Fuchsia magellanica* var. *alba*)
Native of the island of Chiloe. Flowers
very pale pink. A graceful but shy-
flowering variety, said to be the hardiest
variety of all fuchsias, perhaps to 5°F
(-15°C), US zones 7–10.

*Fuchsia* 'Mrs Popple'

*Fuchsia* 'Riccartonii'

Caryopteris x *clandonensis*   A small deciduous shrub that grows to 3ft (90cm) tall and often as wide. Flowers, each about ¼in (6mm) long, are borne in late summer and the leaves are 1–2in (2.5–5cm) long. Best in a sunny position, this plant is hardy to 0°F (-18°C), US zones 7–10. A hybrid between *C. incana* from China and Japan and *C. mongolica* from northern China. An attractive late-flowering small shrub for a sunny border.

*Cestrum aurantiacum*   A deciduous shrub that grows to 20 ft (6m) with suitable support, but more often a bushy plant that grows to 7ft (2m). Clusters of flowers, each about ¾in (2cm) long, appear in late summer and autumn. The leaves are 3–6in (8–15cm) long with an unpleasant odour when bruised. All parts of this plant are thought to be somewhat poisonous if eaten by animals. Hardy to 20°F (-7°C), US zones 9–10. Native to Guatemala and was introduced to Britain in the middle of the 19th century.

*Cestrum elegans* (also known as *C. purpureum*)   A deciduous shrub that grows to 10 ft (3m) with suitable support. The flowers, each about ¾in (2cm) long, appear in spring and summer, or sporadically throughout the year. Leaves are 5in (12cm) long with an unpleasant odour when bruised. Poisonous to animals. Hardy to 10°F (-12°C), US zones 8–10. Native to Mexico.

*Cestrum parqui*   A deciduous shrub that grows to 7 ft (2m) tall. The flowers, sweetly scented at night, each about ¾in (2cm) long, appear in the late summer and autumn. The leaves are up to 5in (12cm) long and have an unpleasant odour when bruised. The fruit is a small black berry but is not always produced by cultivated plants. Poisonous to animals. Hardy to 20°F (-7°C), US zones 9–10. Native to Chile.

ROSE OF SHARON *Hypericum calycinum*   A small semi-evergreen shrub that grows to 18in (45cm) tall, spreading widely by suckering underground stems. Flowers, each 3–4in (8–10cm) wide, in late summer, and leaves 2–3in (5–8cm) long. Grows vigorously in sun or partial shade. Hardy to -10°F (-23°C), US zones 6–10. Invaluable for covering dry banks or poor ground beneath mature trees.

*Hypericum* 'Hidcote'   A compact semi-evergreen shrub that grows to 6ft (1.8m) tall and as wide, producing clusters of flowers, each about 3in (8cm) wide, over a long period in the summer. The leaves are 2–3in (5–8cm) long. Hardy to 10°F (-12°C), US zones 8–10. No regular

*Hypericum* 'Rowallane'

*Hypericum* 'Hidcote'

*Hypericum* x *moserianum*

*Hypericum calycinum*

½ life size.  Specimens from Wakehurst Place, 2 September

*Hypericum* 'Hidcote'

*Hypericum* 'Rowallane'

pruning is required, but plants are sometimes partially killed back in the winter and the damaged stems should be pruned out in the early spring. Thought to be a hybrid between *H. calycinum* and one of the Chinese species.

*Hypericum* x *moserianum*   An evergreen shrub that grows to 20in (50cm), but usually dying back to ground level in winter. Flowers, to 2½in (6cm) across, in summer and autumn. Leaves to 2in(5cm) long. Will grow in any soil in sun or partial shade. Hardy to 12°F (-10°C). A hybrid between *H. patulum* and *H. calycinum*, raised at Moser's Nurseries at Versailles in around 1887.

*Hypericum* 'Rowallane'   A compact semi-evergreen shrub that grows to 6ft (1.8m) tall and as wide. Clusters of flowers, each about 3in (8cm) wide, in summer and leaves 2–3in (5–8cm) long. Hardy to 20°F (-7°C), US zones 9–10. Thought to be a hybrid between two Chinese species, originating in Northern Ireland in the 20th century. This shrub is very showy in flower and, although tender, is considered to be one of the best hypericums.

*Solanum crispum* 'Glasnevin'   A vigorous evergreen or semi-evergreen shrub that grows to 30ft (9m) tall, best grown as a climber, although not self-clinging. Flowers, each about 1in (2.5cm) wide, in summer and autumn. Leaves to 5in (12cm) long. Hardy to 10°F (-12°C), US zones 8–9. This is a beautiful shrub for a warm wall; also suitable for a large conservatory and is notable for its long flowering season.

*Solanum jasminoides* 'Album'   A vigorous semi-evergreen climbing shrub that grows to 30ft (9m) tall, with long twining stems. Flowers, each about 1in (2.5cm) wide, in early summer. It grows well in full sun and is at its best when grown against a south- or west-facing wall. Hardy to 10°F (-12°C), US zones 8–9. *S. jasminoides* is native to Brazil.

*Cestrum parqui*

*Cestrum aurantiacum*

*Solanum crispum* 'Glasnevin'

*Cestrum elegans*

*Solanum jasminoides* 'Album'

*Caryopteris* x *clandonenensis*

*Hydrangea aspera*

*Hydrangea serrata* 'Bluebird'

*Hydrangea arborescens* 'Annabelle'

*Hydrangea quercifolia*

*Hydrangea macrophylla* 'Lanarth White'

*Hydrangea paniculata* 'Praecox'

*Hydrangea paniculata* 'Tardiva'

*Hydrangea aspera* subsp. *sargentiana*

*Hydrangea* 'Preziosa'

*Hydrangea paniculata* 'Grandiflora'

*Hydrangea petiolaris*

Hydrangeas at Trebah, Cornwall

*Hydrangea arborescens* 'Annabelle'  This shrub grows up to 4ft (1.25m) tall, producing clusters of sterile flowers in late summer and well into the autumn. Hardy to -10°F (-23°C), US zones 6–9. *H. arborescens* is native to much of eastern North America, from where it was introduced to Britain in the 18th century. The variety 'Annabelle' is a selected form with particularly large flower heads.

*Hydrangea aspera* subsp. *sargentiana* A deciduous shrub that grows to 7ft (2m) or more, often gaunt in cultivation. Sterile white or pink flowers in a head to 8in (20cm) wide in late summer. Will grow in sun or part shade, with shelter. Hardy to 0°F (-18°C), US zones 7–10. Native to western Hubei, China, in scrub at 5250–6300ft (1500–1800m).

*Hydrangea aspera*  A deciduous shrub that grows up to 12ft (3.5m) tall. In late summer and autumn it produces broad flat clusters of small fertile flowers, surrounded by a zone of showier pale purple, tooth-ray florets, each about ³/₄in (2cm) wide. The leaves are narrowly oval or lance shaped, up to 8in (20cm) long and very hairy. Hardy to 0°F (-18°C), US zones 7–10, but once growth has begun in spring it is easily damaged by late frosts. *H. aspera* is native to much of the central and eastern Himalayas and Taiwan. Plants now called 'Villosa Group' came from China early in the 20th century.

*Hydrangea paniculata*  Erect shrub that grows to 20ft (6m) tall, flowering from July to October. Leaves up to 5in (12cm) long. Thrives in moist, rich soil. Hardy to -12°F (-25°C), US zones 5–10. Native to south-eastern China (rare), Sakhalin and Japan in open forest and by streams. Illustrated here are: 'Grandiflora', a clone in which most of the flowers are sterile, giving a dense, rather rounded head;

'Praecox', which flowers 6 weeks earlier than 'Grandiflora' and originated in Hokkaido; 'Tardiva', a large-flowering clone usually flowering in early autumn and is the earliest-flowering clone in cultivation.

*Hydrangea macrophylla* 'Generale Vicomtesse de Vibraye' (above) A deciduous shrub that grows up to 5ft (1.5m) tall and about as wide. In late summer and autumn it produces large clusters of sterile florets, rosy-purple on alkaline soils. Hardy to 0°F (-18°C), US zones 7–9. *H. macrophylla* is native to central Japan and was introduced to Britain in the 19th century. This variety was selected for its colour and large flower heads.

*Hydrangea macrophylla* 'Lanarth White' A deciduous shrub that grows up to 4ft (1.25m) tall and about as wide. A 'Lace-cap' hydrangea, it produces large clusters

of sterile florets surrounding a central mass of small flowers in late summer and autumn. Hardy to 0°F (-18°C), US zones 7–9. Selected for its compact growth and large flower heads, this variety is a great success in seaside gardens.

*Hydrangea* 'Preziosa'  A cross between *H. macrophylla* and *H. serrata*, it was raised in Germany in 1961. The flowers are pink at first later turning deep red.

CLIMBING HYDRANGEA *Hydrangea petiolaris*  A deciduous shrub that can reach to 60ft (18m) tall or even more in the wild. In mid-summer it produces large flat clusters, containing many small, fertile, creamy-white flowers surrounded by several showier sterile florets, as much as 9in (23cm) wide. Hardy to -10°F (-23°C), US zones 6–9. A magnificent large climber for the difficult situation of a shady wall.

*Hydrangea quercifolia*  A low deciduous shrub that grows up to 5ft (1.5m) tall and generally much wider. In late summer and autumn it produces large conical clusters of florets which often turn purplish-pink as they age. The leaves are broadly oval, up to 6in (15cm) long and, unusually for a hydrangea, are strongly lobed, turning to red and purple in the autumn. Hardy to -10°F (-23°C), US zones 6–9.

*Hydrangea serrata* 'Bluebird'  A vigorous deciduous shrub that grows up to 5ft (1.5m) tall and about as wide. In late summer and well into the autumn it produces clusters of fertile flowers. It will grow in any soil (but the ray florets tend to be purple on alkaline soils). Hardy to 0°F (-18°C), US zones 7–9. The species *H. serrata* is native to Japan, just extending into Korea. 'Bluebird' is a form selected for its colour and particularly large flower heads.

*C.x watereri*

*C. lacteus*

'Rothschildianus'

*C.* 'Hybridus
Pendulus'

*C. franchetii* var.
*sternianus*

'Pink Champagne'

'Cornubia'

'Jeurgl'

*C. conspicuus*

*C. simonsii*

*C. salicifolius*
var. *floccosus*

'Gnom'

*C. horizontalis'*
'Variegatus'

*C. microphyllus*

*C. horizontalis*

¹/₃ life size. Specimens from Goatcher's Nursery, Sussex, 30 October

# COTONEASTER BERRIES

*Cotoneaster bullatus* A deciduous shrub that grows to 10ft (3m) tall, producing clusters of flowers, each about ¹/₂in (1cm) wide, in early summer. Leaves to 3in (8cm) long, turning to orange and red. The red berries, ¹/₄in (6mm) long, are borne in clusters 2in (5cm) wide. Hardy to -10°F (-23°C), US zones 6–10.

*Cotoneaster cochleatus* An evergreen shrub that grows to 1ft (30cm) tall, but spreading to 6ft (1.8m) or more. Flowers, each about ¹/₄in (6mm) wide, in early summer. Leaves ¹/₃in (8mm) long and red berries ¹/₄in (6mm) long in autumn. Hardy to -10°F (-23°C), US zones 6–10.

*Cotoneaster* 'Cornubia' A large semi-evergreen shrub that grows to 20ft (6m) tall, producing large clusters of slightly unpleasantly scented flowers, each about ¹/₂in (1cm) wide, in early summer. Red berries, ¹/₂in (1cm) in length, are borne in clusters 2in (5cm) or more wide, making the bush very showy in autumn. Hardy to -10°F (-23°C), US zones 6–10.

*Cotoneaster conspicuus* An evergreen shrub that grows to 7ft (2m) in cultivation. Red berries are displayed along the long hanging shoots in autumn. Hardy to 5°F (-15°C), US zones 7–10. Native to China.

*Cotoneaster franchetii* var. *sternianus* A medium-sized semi-evergreen shrub that grows to 10ft (3m) tall. In early summer it produces clusters of pink-tinged white, slightly unpleasantly scented flowers, each about ¹/₄in (6mm) wide. The leaves, up to 1in (2.5cm) long, turn orange before falling and orange-red berries, ¹/₄in (6mm) long, are borne in abundant clusters 2in (5cm) wide. Hardy to -10°F (-23°C), US zones 6–10.

*Cotoneaster horizontalis* A deciduous shrub that grows to 1ft (30cm) tall (taller against a wall) and up to 6ft (1.8m) in spread with a distinctive habit. In early summer it produces pink-tinged white flowers, ¹/₄in (6mm) wide, scattered over the shoots. The glossy leaves turn to orange and red in autumn. The berries are ¹/₄in (6mm) long. Hardy to -10°F (-23°C), US zones 6–10. '*Variegatus* has white-edged leaves.

*Cotoneaster* 'Jeurgl' This evergreen shrub grows to 20in (50cm) high and is probably a hybrid between *C. dammeri* and *C. rotundifolius*.

*Cotoneaster simonsii* An erect, semi-evergreen shrub that grows to 13ft (4m). Hardy to -5°F (-20°C), US zones 6–10. Native to the Khasia Hills, Assam, India.

*Cotoneaster* 'Hybridus Pendulus' (syn. 'Pendulus') A deciduous shrub of unknown origin with prostrate stems that are pendulous when grafted as a standard.

*Cotoneaster lacteus* A large evergreen shrub that grows up to 16ft (5m) tall and usually as wide. In early summer it produces large clusters of rather small flowers, each about ¹/₄in (6mm) wide. Orange-red berries, ¹/₄in (6mm) long, are borne in wide clusters. Hardy to -10°F (-23°C), US zones 6–10.

*Cotoneaster microphyllus* An evergreen shrub that grows to 1ft (30cm) tall and spreading to 5ft (1.5m). Flowers, each about ¹/₄in (6mm) wide, appear in early summer. Leaves ¹/₃ to ²/₃in (8–16mm) long. A profusion of red berries, ¹/₄in (6mm) long, in autumn. Hardy to -10°F (-23°C), US zones 6–10.

*Cotoneaster* 'Pink Champagne' A hybrid close to *C. salicifolius* with yellow berries becoming pinkish.

*Cotoneaster* 'Rothschildianus' A hybrid between *C. salicifolius* and *C. frigidus* 'Fructo-luteo' raised at Exbury in 1930. A graceful shrub up to 16ft (5m).

*Cotoneaster salicifolius* var. *floccosus* (also known as *C. floccosus*) Shrub that grows up to 13ft (4m) tall and usually as wide. Clusters of flowers, each about ¹/₄in (6mm) wide. Leaves up to 3¹/₂in (9cm) long. Masses of red berries, ¹/₄in (6mm) long, in clusters 2in (5cm) wide, appear in autumn. Hardy to -10°F (-23°C), US zones 6–10.

*Cotoneaster* 'Gnom' A seedling of *C. salicifolius*, forming an evergreen carpet. Leaves to about ³/₄in (2cm).

*Cotoneaster* x *watereri* A group of hybrids between *C. frigidus* and *C. henryanus*. Evergreen or semi-evergreen shrubs that grow to 16ft (5m).

*Cotoneaster horizontalis*

*Cotoneaster bullatus*

*Cotoneaster cochleatus*

*Cotoneaster* 'Cornubia'

Pyracantha growing on a cottage wall in Dorset

Pyracantha 'Orange Glow'

Pyracantha rogersiana 'Flava'

Pyracantha rogersiana

Euonymus europaeus

Euonymus alatus

*Euonymus alatus*   A large but slow-growing deciduous shrub that grows to 10ft (3m) tall and usually considerably wider. The branches often bear two or four broad corky wings, which give an unusual effect, especially after a light fall of snow. In early summer it produces clusters of insignificant yellow-green flowers, each about ¼in (6mm) wide. The leaves are 1–2½in (2.5–6cm) long, turning to brilliant scarlet and orange tints before falling. Hardy to -10°F (-23°C), US zones 6–10.

*Euonymus europaeus*   A large deciduous shrub that grows to 15ft (4.5m) tall and usually as wide. In early summer it produces clusters of insignificant yellow-green flowers, each about ½in (1cm) wide. The leaves are 1–3½in (2.5–9cm) long. The fruit is a small red four-lobed capsule, which eventually splits to reveal vivid orange-coated seeds within. Hardy to -10°F (-23°C), US zones 6–10. When fruiting freely, this shrub is one of the most spectacular in autumn.

*Euonymus fortunei* 'Emerald 'n' Gold'   A dense low-growing evergreen shrub up to 20in (50cm) tall and rather wider. It is very suitable for ground cover or even dwarf hedge and stands clipping well. It rarely, if ever, flowers. The leaves are 1–2in (2.5–5cm) long. Best in a sunny position and in cooler areas will benefit from a sheltered site. Hardy to -10°F (-23°C), US zones 6–10. *E. fortunei* is native to Japan and China.

*Euonymus fortunei* 'Silver Queen' (above)   A dense small evergreen shrub that grows up to 3ft (90cm) tall and rather wider. Suitable for ground cover or even a dwarf hedge, rarely flowering. The leaves are 1–2½in (2.5–6cm) long and the shrub is highly valued for its attractive variegated foliage which gives all-year colour in sun or shade alike. Hardy to -10°F (-23°C), US zones 6–10. 'Silver Queen' was raised in Britain in the late 19th century.

*Euonymus japonicus* 'Latifolius Albomarginatus' (also known as 'Macrophyllus Albus') An evergreen shrub that grows to 16ft (5m) tall and is suitable for hedging as it stands clipping well. Clusters of small pale green flowers, about ¼in (6mm) wide, are produced in early summer and its glossy broadly oval leaves are 1–3in (2.5–8cm) long, variegated with a wide irregular white margin. Hardy to 10°F (-12°C), US zones 8–10. The handsome foliage of this variety is useful in brightening up a shady corner.

*Euonymus japonicus* (left) A large dense evergreen shrub that grows up to 16ft (5m) tall and usually wider. Highly valued in coastal gardens where its tolerance of salty winds makes it invaluable for hedging and shelter belts. In early summer it produces clusters of small pale green flowers about ¼in (6mm) wide. The fruit is a small reddish capsule which splits to show the orange seed. Hardy to 10°F (-12°C), US zones 8–10.

*Pyracantha* 'Orange Glow' An evergreen shrub that grows up to 16ft (5m) tall and usually wider. In late spring it produces clusters of hawthorn-like flowers and leaves up to 3in (8cm) long. The fruit is a bright reddish-orange berry, often produced in great abundance and lasting well into winter if not eaten by birds. It benefits from a sheltered site by a south or west wall. Hardy to 0°F (-18°C), US zones 7–10. *P.* 'Orange Glow' arose as a chance seedling in Holland in the 20th century.

*Pyracantha rogersiana* An evergreen shrub that grows up to 13ft (4m) tall and usually wider. In late spring it produces clusters of hawthorn-like flowers. The fruit is a small slightly flattened red berry. Will benefit from a sheltered site by a south or west wall. Hardy to 0°F (-18°C), US zones 7–10. *P. rogersiana* is native to western China.

*Pyracantha rogersiana* 'Flava' An evergreen shrub that grows up to 13ft (4m) tall and usually wider. In late spring it produces clusters of hawthorn-like flowers. The fruit is a small slightly flattened clear yellow berry. Hardy to 0°F (-18°C), US zones 7–10. No regular pruning is required except when trained against a wall; then the long shoots can be trimmed back after flowering.

*Euonymus fortunei* 'Emerald 'n' Gold'

*E. japonicus* 'Latifolius Albomarginatus'

*Euonymus fortunei* 'Silver Queen'

*Euonymus alatus*

Hamamelis x intermedia 'Pallida' (text page 23)

Hamamelis x intermedia 'Diane'

Aronia arbutifolia

Cornus kousa var. chinensis (text page 22)

Fothergilla major

¹/₃ life size. Specimens from Savill Gardens, Windsor, 30 October

**RED CHOKEBERRY** *Aronia arbutifolia*
A deciduous shrub that grows 6–10ft (1.8–3m) tall with a bushy habit, sometimes throwing up sucker shoots thereby developing into an extensive clump. The small flowers, each about ¹/₂in (1cm) wide, are borne in late spring. Hardy to -10°F (-23°C), US zones 6–9. Native to eastern North America, this is a first-rate shrub for autumn colour, valuable for its tolerance of a wide range of soil types including peaty and wet soils.

*Disanthus cercidifolius* A deciduous shrub that grows to 15ft (4.5m) tall. As the leaves fall, it produces flowers which have a slight but unpleasant scent. Hardy to 0°F (-18°C), US zones 7–10. Native to southern Japan where it grows in damp woodland, this shrub is grown entirely for its foliage. It is quietly attractive in summer but comes into its own in the autumn and is well worth growing for this season alone.

*Fothergilla major* An evergreen shrub that grows to 10ft (3m) tall, producing spikes of small white flowers in late spring. Hardy to 0°F (-18°C), US zones 7–10. Native to south-eastern US, this shrub is attractive in spring when in flower but also gives spectacular autumn colour.

*Hamamelis x intermedia* 'Diane' This shrub grows to 20ft (6m) tall and wide. Strongly scented flowers appear in winter on leafless branches. Leaves usually turn to shades of red, orange and yellow in autumn. Should be planted in acid or neutral soil, in full sun or light shade. Hardy to -20°F (-29°C), US zones 5–9.

**VIRGINIA CREEPER** *Parthenocissus quinquefolia* A vigorous deciduous climber that grows to 60ft (18m) tall and capable of a similar spread. Grown for its foliage, the stems cling to walls by adhesive-tipped tendrils and the leaves turn to brilliant crimson and orange before falling. Hardy to -10°F (-23°C), US zones 6–10 or lower. Native to eastern North America.

**BOSTON IVY** *Parthenocissus tricuspidata*
A deciduous, climber that grows to 60ft (18m) tall and wide where space is available. Inconspicuous greenish flowers, each about ¹/₄in (6mm) wide. The leaves, on stems that cling to the wall by adhesive-tipped tendrils, are variable in size and shape, turning bright crimson before falling. Hardy to 0°F (-18°C), US zones 7–10. In spite of its name, Boston Ivy is native to Japan, Korea and China.

*Prunus padus* 'Colorata' A deciduous tree growing to about 20ft (6m). The

Vitis vinifera 'Purpurea'

Vitis coignetiae

almond-scented flowers are about ½in (1cm) wide. The leaves are purple when young, bronze-green in summer. Hardy to -30°F (-35°C), US zones 4–9. Susceptible to honey fungus and often not long-lived. The Bird Cherry grows wild in Europe and much of Asia. The variety 'Colorata' was found in Sweden in the 20th century.

HIGHBUSH BLUEBERRY *Vaccinium corymbosum* 'Triumph'  A deciduous shrub up to 10ft (3m) tall and as wide. In early summer it bears clusters of small narrowly bell-shaped white flowers. The leaves turn to various shades of red in the autumn. The fruit is a blue-black berry about ⅓in (8mm) wide, edible with an excellent flavour. Hardy to -10°F (-23°C), US zones 6–9. Native to eastern North America.

*Vitis coignetiae*  A deciduous climbing shrub that grows to 80ft (25m) tall, given suitable support. Small greenish-yellow flowers and handsome, prominently veined leaves, very broadly rounded with three low triangular lobes. In autumn they turn to brilliant shades of orange and red. Hardy to -10°F (-23°C), US zones 6–9. Native to Japan and Korea.

*Vitis vinifera* 'Purpurea'  A deciduous climbing shrub that grows to 30ft (9m) tall or more, given suitable support. Small greenish-yellow flowers and handsome leaves that are rich red-purple in early summer, becoming dark purple later in the year. Hardy to -10°F (-23°C), US zones 6–9. *V. vinifera* is native to south-east Europe and western Asia, and has been cultivated since time immemorial.

*Viburnum sargentii* (above)  A small deciduous shrub that grows to 5ft (1.5m) tall and about as wide. In early summer it bears flat clusters, about 3in (8cm) wide, of small fertile flowers surrounded by a ring of larger cream sterile flowers ¾in (2cm) in width. The leaves usually turn orange and red in autumn. Translucent red berries ripen in bunches in late summer. Hardy to -20°F (-29°C), US zones 5–9. Native to north-eastern Asia.

*Vaccinium corymbosum* 'Triumph'

*Prunus padus* 'Colorata'

*Vaccinium corymbosum*  (text page 62)

*Parthenocissus tricuspidata*

*Parthenocissus quinquefolia*

*Disanthus cercidifolius*

*Hedera helix* 'Cavendishii' (above)
A slow-growing climbing shrub that grows to 10ft (3m) tall and capable of spreading widely. Broad leaves about 1¹/₂in (4cm) wide. Hardy to -10°F (-23°C), US zones 6–10. No regular pruning is required other than to keep the plant within bounds. 'Cavendishii' is a neat and attractively variegated form introduced in the 19th century. A fine choice for a not-too-shady wall, it makes good ground cover and can be used in hanging baskets.

PERSIAN IVY *Hedera colchica*
A vigorous evergreen climbing shrub that grows up to 30ft (9m) tall or more. In late autumn it produces clusters of small greenish flowers which provide a late supply of nectar for many insects. The leaves are up to 8in (20cm) long. The fruit is a small black berry. Hardy to 10°F (-12°C), US zones 8–10 or slightly lower. Persian Ivy is native to the Caucasus, from where it was introduced to Britain in the 19th century. This shrub is valued for its large leaves and is a fine choice for a shady wall.

*Hedera helix* 'Glacier'(above)   A slow-growing evergreen climbing shrub that grows to 10ft (3m) tall or more. The leaves are 1–2in (2.5–5cm) wide, variegated with a fine white marginal zone. Hardy to -10°F (-23°C), US zones 6–10. 'Glacier' is a strikingly coloured form introduced in the mid-20th century. This shrub is frequently grown in hanging baskets and pots, but is quite hardy and suitable for outdoor cultivation and makes good ground cover.

*Hedera helix* 'Buttercup'   A relatively slow-growing evergreen climbing shrub that grows to 10ft (3m) tall, capable of spreading widely with suitable support. The leaves are 1¹/₂–2in (4–5cm) wide, suffused bright yellow in summer and becoming greener in autumn and winter. This shrub can be planted in autumn or early spring. Hardy to -10°F (-23°C), US zones 6–10. The Common Ivy *Hedera helix* is native to much of Europe, including Britain.

*Hedera helix* 'Sagittifolia'   A slow-growing evergreen shrub that grows to 10ft (3m) tall, capable of spreading widely with suitable support. The leaves are 1–2in (2.5–5cm) long. Hardy to -10°F (-23°C), US zones 6–10. No regular pruning is required other than to keep the plant within bounds. 'Sagittifolia' is a distinctive form introduced in the 20th century valued for the curiously arrow-shaped leaves. An excellent pot-plant which also makes good ground cover.

*Hedera colchica* 'Dentata Variegata'
A vigorous climbing variegated form of *H. colchica* 'Dentata'. Stiff branches and large leaves with small, widely spaced teeth. Said to be good for acid soils.

*Hedera colchica* 'Sulphur Heart' (also known as 'Paddy's Pride') (below)
A vigorous evergreen climbing shrub that grows to 30ft (9m) tall or more. In late autumn it produces clusters of small greenish flowers. The leaves are up to 8in (20cm) long and the fruit is a small black berry. Hardy to 10°F (-12°C), US zones 8–10 or slightly lower. This shrub is valued not for its flowers but for the large and colourful variegated leaves which can brighten up a large expanse of shady wall. It is free from pests and diseases.

ALGERIAN IVY *Hedera algeriensis* 'Gloire de Marengo' (often included in *Hedera canariensis*) (above)   A vigorous evergreen climbing shrub that grows up to 30ft (9m) tall or more. Small greenish flowers in late autumn and leaves to 6in (15cm) long and wide. The fruit is a small black berry. This shrub grows well in full or part shade and, in cooler areas, will benefit from a sheltered site on a north wall. Hardy to 10°F (-12°C), US zones 8–10 or slightly lower. The Algerian Ivy is native to North Africa

*Fatsia japonica*   A large evergreen shrub that grows up to 12ft (3.5m) tall and usually rather wider. In late autumn it produces large branched clusters of globose white flower heads composed of many tiny flowers, each about 2¹/₂in (6cm) wide. The long-stalked leathery leaves are 12in (30cm) wide. The pea-sized fruit is black when ripe. Hardy to 10°F (-12°C), US zones 8–10. Native to southern Japan and particularly appropriate to town gardens where its handsome foliage makes a bold statement against walls.

*Hedera colchica* 'Dentata Variegata'

*Hedera colchica*

*Hedera helix* 'Sagittifolia'

*Hedera helix* 'Buttercup'

Mixed ivies growing on a wall

*Hedera helix* 'Cavendishii'

*Fatsia japonica*

*Acacia dealbata*

*Acacia baileyana*

*Acacia verticillata*

*Bauhinia variegata*

*Correa* 'Mannii'

*Correa* 'Mannii'

**COOTAMUNDRA WATTLE**
*Acacia baileyana* A large, dense, rapidly growing spreading shrub or small tree that reaches 27ft (8m) tall. Scented flower heads produced from winter to spring. Prefers well-drained soil, but tolerates drought and wet. Hardy to 25°F (-4°C), US zones 9–10. Native to Australia.

**SILVER WATTLE, MIMOSA** *Acacia dealbata* A large, fast-growing upright shrub or tree, that grows to 35ft (10m) in cultivation, but up to 100ft (30m) in the wild. Scented flower heads are produced in winter. Prefers well-drained, preferably moist soil, but tolerates drought and wet. Hardy to 12°F (-10°C), US zones 8–10.

**PRICKLY MOSES** *Acacia verticillata* An upright or spreading bristly shrub that grows to 20ft (6m) tall, with roots that smell of garlic. Rod-like flower heads are produced from winter to spring. Needs well-drained, moist soil and some shade. Hardy to 25°F (-4°C), US zones 9–10. Native to Australia.

**ORCHID TREE** *Bauhinia variegata* A deciduous greenhouse shrub or small tree that grows to 20ft (6m) tall and wider, bearing flowers, about 4in (10cm) wide, in late winter and spring. Hardy to 40°F (5°C), and may survive in some areas within US zone 10. Native to the warmer parts of eastern Asia and introduced into cultivation in the late 18th century.

*Correa* 'Mannii' (syn. *C.* x *harrisii*) An evergreen shrub that grows to 4ft (1.25m) tall, producing flowers, about 1¹/₂in (4cm) long, from late summer to early spring. Best in a sunny position, thriving in dry summer conditions; in cooler areas it benefits from the protection of a greenhouse. Hardy to 20°F (-7°C), US zones 9–10. This genus is native to Australia; 'Mannii' is an old cultivar of hybrid origin, raised in 1840, by crossing *C. reflexa* and *C. pulchella*.

*Correa* 'Marian's Marvel' An evergreen shrub with strongly pendulous flowers that are pink at the neck with a lime-green skirt. Hardy to 25°F (-4°C), US zones 9–10. Native to Australia.

*Correa pulchella* An evergreen greenhouse shrub that grows to 3ft (90cm) tall. It produces flowers, 1¹/₄in (3cm) long, from summer to autumn, and intermittently throughout the year. Best in a sunny position, thriving in dry summer conditions. Hardy to 32°F (0°C), US zone 10.

*Correa* 'Marian's Marvel'

*Correa pulchella*

*Correa schlechtendalii*

*Piptanthus nepalensis*

*Correa schlechtendalii*   An erect greenhouse evergreen shrub that grows to 6ft (1.8m) tall, producing flowers, about 1in (2.5cm) long, from summer to autumn, and intermittently throughout the year. Best in a sunny position, it needs protection in cooler areas. Hardy to 32°F (0°C), US zone 10.

*Piptanthus nepalensis* (also known as *P. laburnifolius*)   A deciduous or partially evergreen shrub, often short-lived, that grows to 8ft (2.5m) tall, producing flowers, 1¹/₂in (4cm) long, in early spring. It is very attractive when the stems are festooned with drooping seed-pods. Hardy to 0°F (-18°C), US zones 7–10.

LAURESTINUS *Viburnum tinus* 'Eve Price'   A compact evergreen shrub that grows to 5ft (1.5m) tall, and makes a good small hedge. In early summer it bears rounded clusters, to 3in (8cm) wide, of slightly scented flowers, each about ¹/₂in (1cm) wide, followed by blue berries which last until the next flowering season. Hardy to 10°F (-12°C), US zones 8–9. Native to the Mediterranean region.

*Viburnum tinus* 'Eve Price'

*Aloysia triphylla*

*Crinodendron hookerianum*

*Cantua buxifolia*

*Fabiana imbricata*

*Crinodendron patagua*

*Rubus cockburnianus* 'Golden Vale'

LEMON VERBENA *Aloysia triphylla* (syn. *Lippia citriodora*)  A bushy, deciduous shrub that grows to 10ft (3m) tall and as wide. It bears tiny flowers in early summer and its leaves have a very strong and refreshing scent of lemon. Best in a sunny, sheltered position. Hardy to 10°F (-12°C), US zones 8–10. Native to southern South America.

*Cantua buxifolia*  An evergreen shrub that grows to 4ft (1.25m) tall, arching in growth, and as wide. It bears flowers, about 1½in (4cm) wide, in spring. Grows best in a sheltered, sunny position and needs protection in cool areas. Hardy to 20°F (-7°C), US zones 9–10. Native to the mountains of northern South America and introduced into cultivation in the middle of the 19th century.

*Crinodendron hookerianum*  (also known as *Tricuspidaria lanceolata*)  An evergreen shrub that grows to 15ft (4.5m) tall and usually wider, producing many flowers each about 1in (2.5cm) long, in late spring. Best in a sheltered and partially shaded position; in full sun the leaves may scorch. Hardy to 10°F (-12°C), US zones 8–10. Native to Chile in South America.

*Crinodendron patagua*  A large evergreen shrub or small tree that grows to 30ft (9m) tall, occasionally much more in ideal conditions, and usually rather wider than tall. In late summer it produces flowers, each about ¾in (2cm) long. Best in a sheltered and partially shaded position and benefits from the shelter of a wall. Hardy to 10°F (-12°C), US zones 8–10. Native to Chile in South America.

*Desfontainia spinosa*  A medium-sized, evergreen shrub that grows to 10ft (3m) tall and usually wider. The flowers, each about 1½in (4cm) long, appear over a long period in late summer and autumn. Best in an open or partially shaded position, and in cooler areas will benefit from a sheltered site by a wall. Hardy to 10°F (-12°C), US zones 8–10. Native to much of South America.

CHILEAN FIRE BUSH *Embothrium coccineum*  A large evergreen shrub or small tree that grows to 30ft (9m) tall, producing flowers, each about 1½in (4cm) long, in spring and early summer. Best in a sheltered but open position in woodland, under a tall tree canopy or on the edge of a glade. Hardy to 10°F (-12°C), US zones 8–10. Grows wild in South America, from southern Argentina to Chile and was introduced into cultivation in the 19th century.

*Fabiana imbricata*   A small evergreen shrub with a spreading habit that grows to 6ft (1.8m) tall in the wild, but rarely more than 2ft (60cm) in cultivation. In early summer the branches are wreathed in dull white or mauve flowers, about 1in (2.5cm) long. Best in a sunny position, benefiting from shelter in cooler areas. Hardy to 10°F (-12°C), US zones 8–10. Native to the Andes of South America, from Bolivia to Chile.

*Rubus* 'Benenden'   A vigorous deciduous shrub that grows to 13ft (4m) tall, usually rather taller than wide. In early summer it bears flowers like wild roses, each about 2¹/₂in (6cm) wide. Best in a sunny or partially shaded position. Hardy to 0°F (-18°C), US zones 7–9. Raised in England in the mid-20th century and well suited to a semi-wild garden or to a mixed shrubbery.

*Rubus cockburnianus* 'Golden Vale'   A deciduous shrub that grows to 8ft (2.5m) tall, grown both for its foliage and for the effect of the leafless white canes in the winter. Flowers are borne in early summer and the leaves are to 8in (20cm) long. Best in a sunny position. Hardy to -10°F (-23°C), US zones 6–9. The best stem effect is gained if the old stems are cut down in the autumn. Native to central China.

*Rubus tricolor*
A vigorous creeping evergreen or semi-evergreen shrub only a few inches tall, but spreading rapidly to form an extensive mat of almost indefinite growth. In early summer it bears white, bramble-like flowers, each about 1in (2.5cm) wide.

Best grown in partial shade. Hardy to 0°F (-18°C), US zones 7–9. Native to western China and introduced into cultivation in the early 20th century.

*Grevillea rosmarinifolia* (below)   A small, evergreen shrub that grows 2–6ft (60cm–1.8m) tall, and wider. In summer it produces clusters of flowers, about ¹/₂in (1cm) long, with a long, red style protruding a further ³/₄in (2cm). Grows best in a peaty acid or neutral soil in a sunny position and benefits from a sheltered site in cooler areas. Hardy to 10°F (-12°C), US zones 8–10. Native to south-eastern Australia.

*Embothrium coccineum*

*Rubus* 'Benenden'

*Desfontainia spinosa*

*Rubus tricolor*

**CALIFORNIAN ALLSPICE**
*Calycanthus occidentalis* (below)
A deciduous shrub that grows to 12ft (3.5m) tall, bearing unusually coloured flowers, with a curious fruity scent, each about 2in (5cm) wide, over a long period in summer. The shoots and wood are aromatic when scratched but the leaves have an unpleasant scent. Best in a sunny position. Hardy to 10°F (-12°C), US zones 8–10.

**TREE ANEMONE** *Carpenteria californica* (below) An evergreen shrub that grows to 7ft (2m) tall and as wide, producing flowers 2–3in (5–8cm) wide, in clusters of 3–7, in early summer. Best planted in early autumn or late spring, thriving in areas with dry summers and needing the protection of a warm wall in cool climates. Hardy to 0°F (-18°C), US zones 7–10. Native to California.

**BEAUTYBERRY** *Callicarpa bodinieri* var. *giraldii* A deciduous shrub that grows to 7ft (2m) tall, bearing inconspicuous flowers, 1/2in (cm) wide, in summer. The leaves turn to unusual rosy-pink shades in autumn and the attractive fruit is a mauve or purple berry about 1/8in (3mm) wide, borne in tight clusters along the stems. Hardy to -10°F (-23°C), US zones 6–9. Native to China.

**MADAGASCAR PERIWINKLE**
*Catharanthus roseus* (syn. *Vinca rosea*)
A tender perennial that grows to 1ft (30cm) tall and as wide, bearing flowers, each about 1 1/4in (3cm) wide, in early summer. Best in a sunny position. Hardy to 32°F (0°C), US zone 10. Native to Madagascar, but widely cultivated and sometimes naturalized elsewhere.

*Chionanthus virginicus* A small deciduous tree or shrub that grows to 20ft (6m) tall, producing clusters of slightly scented, white flowers, about 1in (2.5cm) long, in late spring and early summer. The blue-black, olive-like fruit is seldom seen, as single trees produce flowers of one sex only. Needs as much sun as possible. Hardy to -10°F (-23°C), US zones 6–9. Native to eastern North America; a closely related species occurs in China.

*Clerodendrum trichotomum* A bushy deciduous shrub that grows to 20ft (6m) tall, and usually wider. It is at its best in late summer and autumn. In summer it produces strongly fragrant flowers, about 1in (2.5cm) wide. Hardy to 10°F (-12°C), US zones 8–10 or slightly lower. Native to China and Japan and introduced into cultivation in the 19th century.

**CRAPE MYRTLE** *Lagerstroemia indica*
A small deciduous tree or large shrub that grows to 25ft (8m) tall; when shrubby usually rather wider than tall. In late summer it produces flowers, each about 1 1/2in (4cm) wide and the leaves colour well in autumn. Requires the sunniest position possible and benefits from a sheltered site or a cool greenhouse in cooler areas. Hardy to 10°F (-12°C), US zones 8–10. Native to China and Korea.

**ROSE ACACIA** *Robinia hispida*
A lax deciduous shrub that grows to 10ft (3m) tall, spreading by suckers. The slightly untidy growth is compensated for by beautiful flowers, each about 1 1/2in (4cm) wide, produced in early summer. Best in a partially shaded position and hardy to -10°F (-23°C), US zones 6–9, but in cool areas will benefit from the extra warmth of a sunny wall. Native to the south-eastern United States.

*Stephanandra tanakae* A deciduous shrub that grows to 7ft (2m) tall, forming a mound rather wider than tall and bearing flowers, each less than 1/2in (1cm) wide, in summer. The leaves often colour well before falling and this plant is grown mainly for its elegant habit and distinctive foliage. Best in a partially shaded or more open position. Hardy to -10°F (-23°C), US zones 6–9. Native to Japan.

*Tamarix aphylla* (syn. *T. tetrandra*)
A deciduous shrub that grows to 10ft (3m) tall, of loose and open habit and usually wider than tall. Flowers are produced in spring on the previous year's shoots. Best in a sunny position. Hardy to -10°F (-23°C), US zones 6–10 and very tolerant of seaside conditions. Native to south-eastern Europe and western Asia, and introduced in the early 19th century.

**OLEASTER** *Elaeagnus angustifolia* (below) A small deciduous tree or large shrub that grows to 24ft (7m) tall, and as wide. This plant is quite fast-growing and wind-resistant, with attractive greyish foliage, making it useful for hedging and shelter. In early summer it produces scented flowers, each with a slender tube 1/2in (1cm) long. Best in a sunny position. Hardy to -40°F (-40°C), US zones 3–10.

*Lagerstroemia indica*

*Tamarix aphylla*

*Catharanthus roseus*

*Clerodendrum trichotomum*

*Stephanandra tanakae*

*Robinia hispida*

*Callicarpa bodinieri*

*Carpenteria californica*

*Chionanthus virginicus*

# TENDER SHRUBS

FEIJOA *Acca sellowiana* (also known as *Feijoa sellowiana*)   An evergreen shrub that grows 7–10ft (2–3m) tall and wide; in warm climates it is a small tree that grows to 20ft (6m), rather taller than wide. The flowers appear in midsummer and are about 1¹/₂in (4cm) wide; petals are sweet and edible. Hardy to 10°F (-12°C), US zones 8–10. Native to Brazil and Uruguay in South America.

*Brachyglottis monroi* (also known as *Senecio monroi*) A compact evergreen shrub that grows to 3ft (90cm) high, and rather wider when mature. It is particularly well suited to seaside gardens. The flowers, about 1in (2.5cm) wide, are borne in flat heads, 3–6in (8–15cm) wide, in the summer. Hardy to 10°F (-12°C), US zones 8–10 or lower. Native to New Zealand's South Island.

*Escallonia* 'Langleyensis' (right)   A small, evergreen shrub of compact growth that reaches 8ft (2.5m) tall and as wide. Suitable for use as hedging, it produces flowers, each about ¹/₂in (1cm) wide, in summer and early autumn. Best in a sunny position, benefiting from a sheltered site in cold areas. Hardy to 10°F (-12°C), US zones 8–10 and very tolerant of salt-laden coastal winds.

*Eucryphia milliganii*   Native to mountainous areas in Tasmania, this species forms a compact shrub up to 10–13ft (3–4m) tall, but smaller in cultivation. The small simple leaves are evergreen and the white flowers are about ³/₄in (2cm) wide, smaller than the otherwise similar *E. lucida*. Introduced in 1929, it requires an open but sheltered site in lime-free and moist soil. Hardy to 10°F (-12°C), US zones 8–10.

*Escallonia* 'Iveyi'   A vigorous evergreen shrub of compact growth and handsome glossy foliage that grows to 10ft (3m) tall, producing flowers, about ¹/₂in (1cm) long, in summer. Best in a sunny position, benefiting from a sheltered site by a south- or west-facing wall in cold areas. Hardy to 0°F (-18°C), US zones 7–10 and very tolerant of coastal winds.

*Ozothamnus ledifolius* (also known as *Helichrysum ledifolium*)   A small, evergreen shrub that grows to 3ft (90cm) tall, bearing flower heads, each about ¹/₂in (1cm) wide, in summer. The bush has a slightly sweet scent. Tolerant of dry summers and best in a sunny position, benefiting from shelter in cooler areas. Hardy to 10°F (-12°C), US zones 8–10. Native to Tasmania.

CAPE LEADWORT *Plumbago auriculata* (syn. *P. capensis*)   An easily grow, evergreen greenhouse shrub that reaches 12ft (3.5m) tall, somewhat scrambling in habit and needing some support. Over a long period, from summer to early winter, it bears clusters of flowers, about ¹/₂in

(1cm) wide. Best in a sunny position, but will tolerate some shade. Hardy to 45°F (7°C), the warmer parts of US zone 10. Native to South Africa.

*Eucryphia glutinosa*
A deciduous shrub that grows to 20ft (6m) tall, bearing single or double flowers, 2–2¹/₂in (5–6cm) wide, that are attractive to bees, in late summer. Few shrubs give more interest to the late summer and autumn than this one; the leaves turn to shades of orange and red before falling. Hardy to 0°F (-18°C), US zones 7–10. Native to Chile in South America.

*Eucryphia glutinosa* double forms (above)   When raised from seeds, double flowers sometimes appear.

*Acca sellowiana*

*Escallonia* 'Iveyi'

*Eucryphia glutinosa*

*Eucryphia milliganii*

*Brachyglottis monroi*

*Ozothamnus ledifolius*

*Plumbago auriculata*

*Plumbago auriculata*

GOLD GUINEA VINE *Hibbertia scandens*  A vigorou, evergreen shrub that grows to 10ft (3m) tall, and climbs by twining stems. From early summer well into autumn it produces flowers, 2–3in (5–8cm) wide. Best in a sunny position, benefiting from protection by a warm wall in cooler areas. Hardy to 32°F (0°C), US zone 10. Native to south-eastern Australia.

*Citrus aurantium*

CRIMSON BOTTLEBRUSH *Callistemon citrinus*  An evergreen shrub that grows to 10ft (3m) high, producing flower clusters about 4in (10cm) long, and leaves that have a strong lemon scent when crushed. Hardy to 10°F (-12°C), US zones 8–10. Very tolerant of drought conditions and best protected against a warm wall in cool gardens. Native to eastern Australia and introduced into cultivation in the late 18th century.

*Callistemon* 'Widdecombe Gem'  A medium-sized evergreen shrub that grows to 6ft (1.8m) high, producing flower clusters to 2in (5cm) long, and leaves that have an aromatic scent when crushed. Drought-tolerant and hardy to 10°F (-12°C), US zones 8–10; best protected in cool gardens. A selection from *C. sieberi* which is native to the mountains of south-eastern Australia.

SEVILLE ORANGE *Citrus aurantium*  An evergreen shrub or small tree that grows to 20ft (6m) tall, bearing strongly scented, white flowers, each about 1¼in (3cm) wide, sporadically throughout the year. The fruit is a bitter orange about 3in (8cm) in diameter. Well adapted to dry summer conditions and thriving in sunshine, this plant is hardy to 20°F (-7°C), US zones 9–10.

CITRON *Citrus medica*  A tender evergreen shrub or small tree that grows to 15ft (4.5m) tall. In early summer and sporadically later, it bears strongly scented, pink-flushed white flowers, each about 2in (5cm) wide, and spectacular fruits. Thrives in a sunny position, well adapted to dry summer conditions. Hardy to 20°F (-7°C), US zones 9–10.

*Echium nervosum*  A half-hardy evergreen shrub that grows to 4ft (1.25m) tall, bearing dense spikes, up to 6in (15cm) long, of tubular flowers, about ½in (1cm) wide, in late winter. Prefers a sheltered, sunny position. Hardy to 20°F (-7°C), US zones 9–10. Native to Madeira, it was introduced in the 18th century.

*Olearia cheesemanii* (also known as *Olearia arborescens* var. *angustifolia*)  An evergreen that grows to 10ft (3m) tall, producing clusters of flowers, 6in (15cm) wide. Best in a sunny position, benefiting from a sheltered site in cooler areas. Hardy to 10°F (-12°C), US zones 8–10 and tolerant of seaside conditions. Native to New Zealand.

*Olearia macrodonta*  An evergreen shrub that grows to 10ft (3m) tall and usually wider, making an excellent hedge. In early summer it produces flat clusters of flower

*Citrus aurantium* put out for the summer

*Citrus medica*

heads, 6in (15cm) across. Best in a sunny position, benefiting from a sheltered site in cooler areas. Hardy to 0°F (-18°C), US zones 7–10 and very tolerant of seaside conditions. Native to New Zealand.

BEAD TREE *Melia azedarach*
A deciduous tree that grows to 30ft (9m) tall, bearing starry, pale purple or lilac-pink flowers, about ³/₄in (2cm) wide, in spring. The tree gets its common name from the conspicuous pale yellow fruits, ¹/₂in (1cm) long, containing hard seeds formerly used as rosary beads. Hardy to 20°F (-7°C), US zones 9–10.

*Hibbertia scandens*

*Echium nervosum*

*Melia azedarach*

*Olearia cheesemanii*

*Olearia macrodonta*

*Callistemon citrinus*

*Callistemon 'Widdecombe Gem'*

¹/₃ life size. Specimens from Wisley, 15 July

*Plumiera rubra*

*Plumiera rubra* (white)

*Gardenia augusta*

*Tibouchina organensis*

*Senna corymbosa*

*Lantana camara* 'Goldsonne'

*Lantana montevidensis*

FLOWERING GUM *Eucalyptus ficifolia* One of several hundred species of gum tree, this is a fairly fast-growing evergreen that will grow to 25ft (8m) tall, producing large clusters of flowers in spring and summer. A position in full sun is best and when established, gum trees are very tolerant of drought conditions. Hardy to 20°F (-7°C), US zones 9–10. Native to western Australia.

CAPE JASMINE *Gardenia augusta* 'Veitchii' (syn. *Gardenia jasminoides*) A compact greenhouse shrub that grows to 3ft (90cm) tall and usually wider, bearing highly fragrant, double white flowers, each about 2$\frac{1}{2}$in (6cm) wide, from summer to early winter. Best in a partially shaded position. Hardy to 60°F (15°C), US zone 11 and warmer. Native to China and Japan.

*Lantana camara* 'Arlequin' This evergreen shrub is a dwarf cultivar of *Lantana camara*, bearing dark pink and yellow

*Lantana camara* 'Arlequin'

*Eucalyptus ficifolia*

*Lotus berthelotii*

*Lotus maculatus*

*Luculia gratissima* var. *rosea*

flowers. Hardy to 32°F (0°C), US zone 10. Native to tropical America.

*Lantana camara* 'Goldsonne'
A German cultivar useful for growing in pots outside in summer.

*Lantana montevidensis*   An evergreen shrub that grows up to 1½ft (45cm) tall, bearing clusters of flowers, each about ½in (1cm) wide, more or less all year round, but mainly in summer. Best in a sunny position, thriving in dry summer conditions. Hardy to 50°F (10°C), parts of US zone 10. Native to South America and introduced into cultivation in the early 19th century.

*Lotus berthelotii*   A silvery cascading sub-shrub with stems that grow to 3½ft (1m) or more, producing bright red and black flowers, 1in (2.5cm) long, mainly in spring. For a tall pot or hanging basket, with well-drained but moisture-retentive soil. Hardy to 32°F (0°C), US zone 10. It is now very rare in the wild, but is widely cultivated. Native of the Cape Verde Islands and Tenerife in the Canary Islands, growing on cliffs in the cloud forest at up to 4200ft (1200m).

*Lotus maculatus*   A low-growing perennial forming a mat up to 6in (15cm) tall and 2ft (60cm) wide, producing curiously shaped flowers, about ¾in (2cm) long, in summer. Best planted in the late spring in a sunny position. Hardy to 10°F (-12°C), US zones 8–10. Native to the Canary Islands and introduced into cultivation in the 19th century.

*Luculia gratissima* var. *rosea*   A tender shrub that grows to 15ft (4.5m) tall and

wider, bearing clusters of highly fragrant flowers, about 1½in (4cm) long, in autumn and winter. Best in a sunny or partially shaded position. Hardy to 32°F (0°C), US zone 10. Native to the Himalayas. Although not commonly cultivated, this beautiful shrub has pleasantly scented flowers with a curious crystalline texture, well suited to cultivation in a conservatory.

FRANGIPANI *Plumiera rubra*
A member of the periwinkle family Apocynaceae, this rather gaunt deciduous shrub grows to 12ft (3.5m) tall. It is not particularly easy to grow but worth some effort for its large, deliciously scented flowers, produced in late summer and autumn. These are light rosy-pink or white with a yellow throat, about 4in (10cm) wide. (Other cultivars are deep red or yellow.) Best in a partially shaded position and hardy to 55°F (13°C), US zone 10. Native to tropical parts of Central America and introduced into cultivation in the late 17th century.

*Senna corymbosa* (syn. *Cassia corymbosa*)
A tender deciduous shrub that grows up to 13ft (4m) tall and as wide, producing light yellow flower clusters, each about 1in (2.5cm) wide. Best in a sheltered, sunny position or within the protection of a conservatory. Hardy to 10°F (-12°C), US zones 8–10. *S. corymbosa* is native to South America.

*Tibouchina organensis*   A shrub that grows to 16ft (5m) tall, bearing silky flowers, up to 4½in (11cm) wide, in mauve, indigo or violet. Hardy to 32°F (0°C), US zone 10. Native to Brazil.

*Fuchsia* 'Koralle'

*Fuchsia* 'Thalia'

*Fuchsia* 'Roos Breytenbach'

¹/₂ life size. Specimens from Eccleston Square, August 22

*Fuchsia boliviana*  A large deciduous shrub (evergreen in frost-free areas) that grows to 20ft (6m) tall. It produces drooping clusters of trumpet-shaped flowers, each about 1in (2.5cm) long, opening into four spreading sepals, ¹/₂in (1cm) long, in late summer. Best in a sunny position. Hardy to 30°F (-3°C), US zone 10 or slightly lower. Native to South America from Peru to Argentina.

*Fuchsia* 'Cascade'  Medium-sized single blooms, with tube and sepals white, flushed carmine and petals deep carmine. Trailing growth in a cascade, as the name implies. Hardy to 25°F (-4°C), US zones 9–10. Raised in the United States in 1937.

*Fuchsia* 'Jack Shahan'  A deciduous shrub that grows to 5ft (1.5m) tall, producing flowers, about 2in (5cm) long, in late summer. Best in a sunny position. Hardy to 20°F (-7°C), US zone 9 or slightly lower. A hybrid raised in the 20th century, hardy only in mild areas but is an excellent plant for a basket in a cool greenhouse.

*Fuchsia fulgens* 'Rubra Grandiflora'  A tuberous-rooted low shrub, with soft woody stems, producing flowers, 2¹/₂–4in (6–10cm) long, in bunches in late summer. Easily grown and free-flowering in warm, sunny humid conditions and rich well-drained soil. Hardy to 25°F (-4°C), US zones 9–10. Native to Mexico.

*Fuchsia* 'Koralle'  A deciduous shrub that grows to 3ft (90cm) tall, producing clusters of flowers, about 2¹/₂in (6cm) long, in late summer. Has purple-tinted, velvety-green leaves. Hardy to 32°F (0°C), US zones 9–10 or slightly lower. A hybrid of *Fuchsia triphylla*, it was raised in Germany early in the 20th century.

*Fuchsia* 'Orient Express' (right)  A bushy deciduous shrub that grows to 3ft (90cm) tall, producing clusters of flowers, each about 2¹/₂in (6cm)

long, in late summer. Best in a sunny position. Hardy to 32°F (0°C), US zones 9–10 or slightly lower. A hybrid of *Fuchsia triphylla*, it was raised in England in the late 20th century.

*Fuchsia* 'Roos Breytenbach'  A single-flowered plant with a long, pale orange tube and smaller red sepals and petals. Hardy to 25°F (-4°C), US zones 9–10. Raised by Stannard in 1993.

*Fuchsia* 'Red Spider'  A deciduous shrub that grows to 5ft (1.5m) tall, producing flowers, each about 2in (5cm) long, in late summer. Hardy to 20°F (-7°C), US zone 9 or slightly lower. A hybrid raised in the 20th century, this plant is hardy only in mild areas but is an excellent plant for bedding out or for pots.

*Fuchsia* 'Thalia'   A bushy deciduous shrub that grows to 3ft (90cm) tall, producing clusters of flowers, each about 3in (8cm) long, in late summer. Best in a sunny position, benefiting from a sheltered site by a south- or west-facing wall in cooler areas.  Hardy to 32°F (0°C), US zones 9–10 or slightly lower. A hybrid of *Fuchsia triphylla*, it was raised in Germany early in the 20th century.

*Fuchsia* 'Trumpeter'   A bushy deciduous shrub that grows to 3ft (90cm) tall, producing clusters of flowers, about 2½in (6cm) long, in late summer. Hardy to 32°F (0°C), US zones 9–10 or slightly lower. No regular pruning is required other than cutting away any old, damaged shoots and shorten the rest in early spring. A hybrid of *F. triphylla*, it was raised in the 20th century.

*Fuchsia* 'Koralle' (left), *Fuchsia* 'Thalia' (right)

*Fuchsia fulgens* 'Rubra Grandiflora'

*Fuchsia* 'Cascade'

*Fuchsia* 'Jack Shahan'

*Fuchsia* 'Trumpeter'

*Fuchsia boliviana*

*Fuchsia* 'Red Spider'

121

*Campsis grandiflora*

**CHINESE TRUMPET VINE** *Campsis grandiflora* A self-clinging woody climber, that grows to 30ft (9m) tall, and is capable of covering a large wall. In late summer and autumn it bears clusters of reddish-orange, trumpet-shaped flowers, each about 3in (8cm) long. Plant in autumn or spring in a sheltered, sunny position. Hardy to 0°F (-18°C), US zones 7–10. Native to China.

*Mandevilla* x *amoena* 'Alice du Pont' (syn. *Mandevilla* 'Splendens Hybrid') Pink flowers to 4in (10cm) wide. Hardy to 32°F (0°C), US zone 10.

**COMMON PASSION FLOWER** *Passiflora caerulea* A vigorous, more or less evergreen climbing shrub that grows to 15ft (4.5m) tall or more and is capable of a similar spread where space is available. For a long period in summer it produces flowers, each about 3–4in (8–10cm) wide. Plant in autumn or spring in sun with suitable support. Hardy to 10°F (-12°C), US zones 8–10. Native to Brazil and Argentina.

*Passiflora racemosa* (syn. *P. princeps*) An evergreen vine that grows to 33ft (10m)

outside in warm countries, but nearer to 16ft (5m) under glass. Flowers usually borne in pairs, in pendulous groups up to 1ft (30cm) long, throughout summer and autumn. Sepals to 1 1/2in (4cm) long and 1/2in (1cm) wide; petals similar but smaller. Hardy to 45°F (7°C), US zone 10, for short periods. Native to Brazil, it was introduced into cultivation in 1815.

**PINK TRUMPET VINE** *Podranea ricasoliana* A fast-growing evergreen climbing shrub that reaches 16ft (5m) tall where suitable support is available. It produces clusters of slightly scented flowers, each about 2 1/2in (6cm) long, over a long period from early summer to autumn. Best in a sunny position. Hardy to 40°F (5°C), US zone 10. Native to South Africa.

*Solandra grandiflora* A member of the potato family Solanaceae, this robust evergreen climber of scrambling habit grows to 15ft (4.5m) tall, usually rather wider than tall where adequate support is present. In early summer it bears flowers, each about 5in (12cm) wide, opening light yellow, but soon changing to a deeper buff yellow. Best in a sunny

position. Hardy to 50°F (10°C), the warmer parts of US zone 10. Native to the West Indies and introduced into cultivation in the late 18th century.

*Solandra maxima* Yellow flowers with a purple-brown line down the centre of each lobe. Native to Central America and Venezuela and introduced into cultivation in the early 19th century.

*Streptosolen jamesonii* A more or less evergreen shrub that grows to 10ft (3m) tall, scrambling in habit and with suitable support, taller than wide. In spring and summer and occasionally at other times of year, it bears clusters of funnel-shaped flowers, each about 1in (2.5cm) wide. Best in a sunny position. Hardy to 45°F (7°C), in the warmer parts of US zone 10. Native to South America.

**GOLDEN TRUMPET TREE** *Tabebuia chrysotricha* A deciduous tree that grows to 30ft (9m) tall and as wide, bearing flowers, about 3in (8cm) long, in late winter or early spring. Best in a sunny position. Hardy to 60°F (15°C), the warmer parts of US zone 10. Native to South America and introduced into cultivation in the late 19th century.

*Podranea ricasoliana*

*Streptosolen jamesonii*

*Passiflora caerulea*

*Tabebuia chrysotricha*

*Passiflora racemosa*

*Mandevilla* x *amoena* 'Alice du Pont'

*Solandra grandiflora*

*Solandra maxima*

*Beaumontia grandiflora*

*Brugmansia* 'Grand Marnier'

*Cestrum* 'Newellii'

*Thunbergia grandiflora*

*Solanum rantonettii*

*Solanum wendlandii*

HERALD'S TRUMPET *Beaumontia grandiflora* An evergreen twining shrub that grows to 25ft (8m) tall, bearing fragrant flowers, each up to 5in (12cm) long, in early summer. Grows best in a well-lit position but out of direct sun. Hardy to 45°F (7°C). In most areas it should be grown in a greenhouse, but in parts of US zone 10 it can be tried outdoors. Native to tropical east Asia.

*Brugmansia* 'Grand Marnier' (syn. *Datura* 'Grand Marnier') Grows to 12ft (3.5m) tall and as wide, bearing flowers, each 1ft (30cm) or more in length, in late summer and autumn. All parts of this plant are poisonous and it should be handled with care. Thrives in dry summers and is best in a sunny position. Hardy to 20°F (-7°C), US zones 9–10.

*Brugmansia suaveolens* (syn. *Datura suaveolens*) A tender evergreen shrub that grows to 15ft (4.5m) tall and as wide. The flowers, about 1ft (30cm) long, with a heady evening scent, are borne in the late summer and autumn. All parts of this plant are poisonous and it should be handled with care. Best in a sunny position, thriving in dry summer climates. Hardy to 20°F (-7°C), US zones 9–10. Native to Brazil.

*Brunfelsia uniflora* (syn. *B. hopeana*) An evergreen greenhouse shrub that grows to 2ft (60cm) tall and wider, bearing rounded, deep purple or violet flowers, about 1¼in (3cm) wide and yellow in the throat, from winter or early spring to summer. Best in a partially shaded position. Hardy to 50°F (10°C). Native to tropical South America.

*Cestrum* 'Newellii'   An evergreen shrub of lax, arching habit that grows to 10ft (3m) tall, bearing flowers, about ³/₄in (2cm) long, in spring and summer. The leaves have an unpleasant odour when bruised and all parts of this plant are thought to be somewhat poisonous to animals. Thrives in dry summer conditions and should have a sunny position. Hardy to 10°F (-12°C), US zones 8–10.

BLUE POTATO BUSH *Solanum rantonettii*   An evergreen shrub that grows to 6ft (1.8m) tall. Rounded in habit and rather wider than tall, it bears flowers, each about 1in (2.5cm) wide, in summer. Best in a sunny position and hardy to 40°F (5°C), US zone 10. Suitable for a conservatory or outdoors in the warmest climates. Native to South America.

POTATO CREEPER *Solanum seaforthianum*   An evergreen climbing shrub that grows to 10ft (3m) tall and wider, for a large conservatory or outdoors in the warmest climates. Over a long period from late spring to autumn, it bears flowers, each about 1in (2.5cm) wide, which may be purple, violet, pinkish or white. Hardy to 40°F (5°C), US zone 10. Native to South America.

POTATO VINE *Solanum wendlandii*   A more or less evergreen climber for a large conservatory, or outdoors in the warmest climates. Scrambling stems grow to 15ft (4.5m) tall, and wider with adequate support. In late summer and into autumn, it bears flowers, about 2in (5cm) wide. Best in a sunny position and hardy to 40°F (5°C), US zone 10. Native to Central America.

*Thunbergia grandiflora*   A large twining shrub producing blue-violet flowers, 2³/₄ (7cm) wide, either solitary or in bunches, in summer. Hardy to 32°F (0°C), US zone 10. Native to northern India.

*Brunfelsia uniflora*

*Solanum seaforthianum*

*Brugmansia suaveolens*

*Lapageria rosea*

*Bouganvillea glabra*

*Rhodochiton atrosanguineum*

*Jasminum grandiflorum*

*Bouganvillea glabra* An evergreen shrub that grows to 15ft (4.5m) tall, bearing clusters of flowers, each about 2in (5cm) wide, in summer. The actual flowers are small, tubular and white, but are surrounded by large coloured bracts. Hardy to 20°F (-7°C), US zones 9–10. This plant withstands dry summer conditions well; plants in a conservatory may become infested with glasshouse whitefly. Native to South America and first introduced into cultivation in the 19th century.

*Clerodendrum thompsoniae* An evergreen shrub that grows to 12ft (3.5m) tall, scrambling in habit and taller than wide, given some support. In summer it bears clusters of flowers, about ³/₄in (2cm) long in a contrasting bell-shaped white calyx. Best in a partially shaded position. Hardy to 50°F (10°C), US zone 10. Native to tropical West Africa, this is a spectacular shrub for a conservatory, flowering over a long period in the summer, but common greenhouse pests may be a problem.

CHILEAN BELLFLOWER *Lapageria rosea* A twining elegant evergreen climber that grows to 15ft (4.5m) tall. Suitable for a cool greenhouse or outdoors in warmer climates. Flowers, in shades of pink or red, about 3¹/₂in (9cm) long, are borne in summer and autumn. Best in a partially shaded position and hardy to 20°F (-7°C), US zones 9–10. Native to Chile.

*Gloriosa superba* 'Rothschildiana' A tuberous-rooted perennial climbing by tendrils to 8ft (2.5m) tall, bearing flowers, to 4in (10cm) long, in early summer. Best

in a sunny position. Hardy to 32°F (0°C), US zone 10, requiring the protection of a greenhouse in all but warm areas. *Gloriosa superba* is native to tropical Africa and Asia, introduced into cultivation in the late 18th century. 'Rothschildiana' has larger, more brilliantly coloured flowers.

WAX PLANT *Hoya carnosa* A tough yet attractive twining evergreen shrub that grows to 20ft (6m) tall or more and wider unless trained on horizontal wires. In late summer and autumn it bears flowers, a little over ¹/₂in (1cm) wide, that are white or pale pink with a dark red centre. Flowers are not always freely produced by young plants. Best in a partially shaded position. Hardy to 20°F (-7°C), US zones 9–10. Native to subtropical parts of eastern Asia.

MOONFLOWER, BELLE DE NUIT *Ipomoea alba* (also known as *Calonyction aculeatum*) A perennial climber, woody at the base, that grows from 16–100ft (5–30m) tall. It produces nocturnal fragrant white flowers, 3¹/₂–6in (9–15cm) long, with a tint of green on the outside, in summer. Not hardy below 32°F (0°C), US zone 10.

MORNING GLORY *Ipomoea purpurea* An annual or short-lived perennial that grows to 16ft (5m) tall, bearing deep blue or purple flowers, about 3in (8cm) long, in summer. Seeds are normally sown in early spring. Best in a sunny position. Not hardy below 32°F (0°C), US zone 10. Thought to be native to Mexico but widely grown and naturalized elsewhere. This morning glory is a popular climber in temperate and warmer regions.

*Ipomoea tricolor* 'Heavenly Blue'

*Ipomoea purpurea*

*Ipomoea alba*

MORNING GLORY *Ipomoea tricolor* 'Heavenly Blue'   A climbing annual or perennial that grows to 12ft (3.5m) tall and bears flowers, each about 3in (8cm) wide, in summer. Best in a warm sunny position. Not hardy below 32°F (0°C), US zone 10. Native to Mexico and Central America, and introduced into cultivation in the 19th century. This is a beautiful climber for a sunny wall, equally suitable for a conservatory.

SPANISH JASMINE *Jasminum grandiflorum*   An evergreen shrub that grows to 7ft (2m) tall and usually wider, bearing fragrant flowers, to 2in (5cm) wide, in late summer and autumn. Best in a sunny position and effective when

trained on wires to a wall. Hardy to 10°F (-12°C), US zones 8–10, but best grown with a minimum temperature of 45°F (7°C), US zone 10. Probably native to the Himalayas, but long cultivated in southern Europe.

*Rhodochiton atrosanguineum*   An unusual and elegant climbing perennial that grows to 10ft (3m) tall, bearing flowers, about 2¹⁄₂in (6cm) long, throughout summer and autumn. This plant is best grown as an annual, from seeds sown in early spring. Best in a sunny position, it should have support to allow it to climb tall enough to show off the flowers. Hardy to 20°F (-7°C), US zones 9–10. Native to Mexico.

*Gloriosa superba* 'Rothschildiana'

*Clerodendrum thompsoniae*

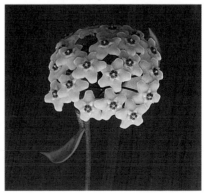

*Hoya carnosa*

*Acalypha wilkesiana* 'Musaica'

*Acalypha wilkesiana*

*Codiaeum variegatum* var. *pictum*

*Pentas lanceolata* (red form)

**JACOB'S COAT** *Acalypha wilkesiana*
An evergreen greenhouse shrub that grows to 7ft (2m) tall and usually as wide. Intermittently, it bears red flower catkins, up to 8in (20cm) long. However, it is grown mainly for its leaves which are a rich coppery green, edged and splashed with red, up to 8in (20cm) long. Best in a partially shaded position. Hardy to 60°F (15°C), hot areas of US zone 10. *Acalypha wilkesiana* is native to tropical islands of the Pacific Ocean. First introduced to Britain in the 19th century.

*Acalypha wilkesiana* 'Musaica' Leaves green, marked orange and red. A fine foliage shrub for a warm greenhouse or conservatory.

*Codiaeum variegatum* var. *pictum* A shrub that grows to 6ft (1.8m) tall, bearing brightly coloured leaves, variegated with white, yellow or red, in a variety of shapes. The flowers are small, white and insignificant. Hardy to 32°F (0°C), US zone 10. Plant in well-drained fertile, lime-free soil. Native of south India, Ceylon and Malaysia.

**CORAL TREE** *Erythrina crista-galli*
A deciduous shrub or tree that grows to 15ft (4.5m) tall, producing erect clusters to 1ft (30cm) long, bearing flowers, each about 2in (5cm) long, in summer. Thrives in sunshine, benefiting from shelter in cooler areas. The woody base of the plant should be protected with dry bracken or other material in the winter. Hardy to 10°F (-12°C), US zones 8–10 and native to Brazil.

**OLEANDER** *Nerium oleander* A large, evergreen shrub that grows to 12ft (3.5m) tall. In summer it produces clusters of flowers which may be clear pink, red, white or even pale yellow, single or double. Each flower is about 1½in (4cm) wide and all parts of this plant are poisonous. Best in a sunny position, thriving in dry summer conditions. In cool areas it may be grown in a tub outdoors in the summer and moved into a greenhouse for the winter. Hardy to 10°F (-12°C), US zones 8–10 and native to much of the Mediterranean region.

*Nerium oleander* 'Variegata' Variegated leaves.

*Jasminum polyanthum* An evergreen shrub that grows to 20ft (6m) tall and wider, bearing highly fragrant flowers, to 1½in (4cm) wide, from late summer and into winter. Grows best in a sunny position and is most effective when trained through wires on a wall. Hardy to 10°F (-12°C), US zones 8–10. Native to western China.

*Pentas lanceolata* A member of the madder family Rubiaceae, this bushy evergreen shrub grows to 4ft (1.25m) tall and as wide, bearing dense clusters of rosy-pink or red flowers, each about ½in (1cm) wide, in late summer and autumn. Best in a light but partially shaded position. Hardy to 50°F (10°C), the warmest parts of US zone 10. Native to an area from Saudi Arabia to east Africa, it was introduced into cultivation in the 19th century. A delightful small shrub for a conservatory. This shrub produces flowers in a range of red and mauve and white, as well as shades of pink.

**POINSETTIA** *Euphorbia pulcherrima* 'Double Red' A member of the spurge family Euphorbiaceae, this tender shrub can grow to 10ft (3m) tall, but is usually kept to only 15in (40cm) by dwarfing in a pot. From early winter to early spring, it bears a cluster of showy bright red bracts,

*Pentas lanceolata*

*Erythrina crista-galli*

about 4in (10cm) long. Hardy to 40°F (5°C), US zone 10. Native to Mexico. One of the most popular pot plants for Christmas decoration.

*Euphorbia pulcherrima* 'Top White' Clusters of showy, creamy-white oval bracts, surrounding a few inconspicuous yellow flowers at the top of each main stem.

CASTOR-OIL PLANT *Ricinus communis* A tender shrub or tree, most often grown as a half-hardy annual, that grows to 5ft (1.5m) tall, bearing small, rather insignificant flowers in summer. In some varieties the leaves are a rich red or purple and it is a spectacular foliage plant. However, the seeds are poisonous. Hardy to 32°F (0°C), US zone 10. Native to North Africa and the Middle East.

*Jasminum polyanthum*

*Nerium oleander* 'Variegata'

*Euphorbia pulcherrima* 'Top White'

*Euphorbia pulcherrima* 'Double Red'

*Nerium oleander*

*Ricinus communis*

*Abutilon*
'Kentish Belle'

*Penstemon cordifolius*

*Abutilon* x *milleri*

*Abutilon* 'Ashford Red'

*Abutilon megapotamicum* 'Variegatum'

*Abutilon megapotamicum*

²/₅ life size. Specimens from Chelsea Physic Garden, 17 October

*Abutilon* cultivars   Members of the hibiscus family Malvaceae, these partially evergreen shrubs grow to 6ft (1.8m) tall. They produce broadly bell-shaped flowers, about 1¹/₂in (4cm) wide, over a long period in summer and early autumn. Best planted in early spring and in warm summers generous watering will be beneficial. Thrives in full sun and will benefit from the protection of a sunny wall in cooler areas. Hardy to 20°F (-7°C), US zones 9–10. Sometimes infested with whitefly, abutilons are inclined to be short-lived, but are excellent conservatory shrubs and are also suitable for use in containers outside in the summer. Shown here are:

*Abutilon* 'Ashford Red'   Rounded, dusky red petals in a pale green calyx. Thought to be a hybrid between *A. darwinii* and *A. striatum*, it was introduced in the 20th century.

*Abutilon* 'Cynthia Pike'

*Abutilon* 'Louis Marignac'

*Abutilon* 'Nabob'

*Abutilon* 'Silver Belle'

# ABUTILONS

*Abutilon* 'Canary Bird' (right) Rounded bright yellow petals and a central boss of deep red stamens in a pale green calyx. Thought to be a hybrid between *A. darwinii* and *A. striatum*, it was introduced in the 20th century.

*Abutilon* 'Cerise Queen' Rounded rich deep pink petals in a pale green calyx. Thought to be a hybrid between *A. darwinii* and *A. striatum*, it was introduced in the 20th century.

*Abutilon* 'Kentish Belle' Rounded orange petals heavily veined with red in a pale green calyx. A hybrid of *Abutilon megapotamicum*, it was introduced in the 20th century.

*Abutilon* 'Cynthia Pike' Slightly spreading apricot-yellow petals with a deep red calyx. A hybrid of complex origin, perhaps involving *Abutilon megapotamicum*, it was introduced in the 20th century.

*Abutilon* 'Louis Marignac' In-curved pale pink petals in a pale green calyx. A hybrid of complex origin, it was raised by Lemoine at Nancy in France in the late 19th century.

*Abutilon* 'Nabob' In-curved dark red petals in a green calyx. A hybrid of complex origin, it was raised in the late 19th century.

*Abutilon* 'Silver Belle' Wide spreading white petals and a boss of deep yellow stamens in a green calyx. A hybrid of complex origin raised in the 20th century.

*Abutilon megapotamicum* Grows to 6ft (1.8m) tall, bearing flowers with bright yellow petals and a central cluster of maroon stamens in a large crimson calyx. Flowers are about 3/4in (2cm) wide and 1 1/2in (4cm) long and are produced from red buds over a long period in summer and early autumn. Hardy to 10°F (-12°C), US zones 8–10. Native to southern Brazil.

*Abutilon megapotamicum* 'Variegatum' Introduced in the 20th century, this is a striking and neat shrub for a sunny wall, conspicuous even when not flowering.

*Abutilon* x *milleri* Grows to 5ft (1.5m) tall, producing flowers with pointed orange-yellow petals, each in a contrasting red cup-shaped calyx, over a long period in summer and early autumn. Hardy to 20°F (-7°C), US zones 9–10. A hybrid between *A. megapotamicum* and *A. pictum*, it was introduced in the 20th century.

*Penstemon cordifolius* Native to California from San Louis Obiso southwards, it is found in scrub, canyons and rocky slopes below 3500ft (1000m) flowering from May to July. Flowers sometimes yellow. Well-drained soil, dry in summer. Hardy to 24°F (-5°C), areas of zones 9 and 10 and warmer.

*Abutilon* 'Canary Bird'

*Abutilon* 'Cerise Queen'

*Hibiscus syriacus* 'Red Heart'

*Hibiscus syriacus* 'Dorothy Crane'

*Hibiscus syriacus* 'Diana' (above) A member of the mallow family Malvaceae, this deciduous shrub grows to 7ft (2m) tall and as wide. It is valued for its late season. Thriving in a sunny position and benefiting from a sheltered site in cooler areas, it produces white flowers, up to 5in (12cm) wide, in late summer and early autumn. Hardy to -10°F (-23°C), US zones 6–10. Native to the Himalayas and China and introduced into cultivation by the 16th century. 'Diana' was raised in North America.

*Hibiscus syriacus* 'Dorothy Crane' Grows to 10ft (3m) tall, producing white flowers up to 4in (10cm) wide. 'Dorothy Crane' was raised by Notcutt's Nursery in England.

*Hibiscus syriacus* 'Mauve Queen' Grows to 10ft (3m) tall, producing rich blue-mauve flowers up to 4in (10cm) wide. 'Mauve Queen' was raised by Notcutt's Nursery in England.

*Hibiscus syriacus* 'Red Heart' Grows to 10ft (3m) tall, producing large white flowers up to 4in (10cm) wide. 'Red Heart' was raised in France.

*Hibiscus syriacus* 'William R Smith' Very large, pure white single flowers.

*Hibiscus syriacus* 'Mauve Queen'

*Hibiscus syriacus* 'William R Smith'

*Alyogyne huegelii* A tall open shrub with stems that grow to 8ft (2.5m) tall, producing flowers 2½–4in (6–10cm) across, usually bluish-mauve, but sometimes deep purple, white or yellow (the beautiful silvery, bluish-mauve of the form shown here, called 'Santa Cruz', is impossible to reproduce on colour film!). Flowers in summer. Hardy to 32°F (0°C), US zone 10. Native to southern Australia.

*Alyogyne hakeiformis*
A tall shrub with narrow, fleshy leaves, growing to 8ft (2.5m) tall, producing funnel-shaped flowers around 3in (8cm) long, usually bluish-mauve with a red eye, rarely pale yellow, only opening in hot sun. Flowers in summer. Hardy to 32°F (0°C), US zone 10. Native to western and south Australia.

HARDY PLUMBAGO *Ceratostigma willmottianum* This tender shrub grows to 4ft (1.25m) tall, with flowers, about 1in (2.5cm) wide, in clusters from summer to autumn. In cool climates it dies back in winter and needs a sunny, sheltered position. Hardy to 0°F (-18°C), US zones 7–10, withstanding dry summer conditions well. Native to western China.

*Colquhounia coccinea* (left) A deciduous shrub that grows to 10ft (3m) tall, rather lax in growth. In the late summer and autumn it produces compact spikes about 6in (15cm) long. Best in a sunny position, benefiting from a sheltered site. Hardy to 10°F (-12°C), US zones 8–10, given protection. Native from the Himalayas to western China.

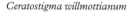

*Ceratostigma willmottianum*

*Alyogyne huegelii* 'Santa Cruz'

*Alyogyne hakeiformis*

*Lavatera maritima*

*Hibiscus syriacus* 'Blue Bird'

*Hibiscus rosa-sinensis* 'Tylene'

*Lavatera* 'Barnsley'

*Lavatera* 'Barnsley'  A vigorous deciduous woody-based plant that grows to 8ft (2.5m) tall. For much of the summer it produces a succession of large flowers, each about 3in (8cm) wide, almost white with a prominent red centre. Best in a sunny position and in cold areas may be killed back to ground level. Hardy to 0°F (-18°C), US zones 7–10.

*Lavatera maritima*  A soft spreading shrub with stems that grow to 6ft (1.8 m) tall, producing flowers 1–2¹/₂in (2.5–6cm) wide, from February to June or October in cool climates. For poor, well-drained soil in a hot, sunny position. Hardy to 25°F (-4°C), US zones 9–10. Native to the western Mediterranean from Corsica, Sardinia and North Africa, west to Spain, growing in dry, rocky places, usually near the sea.

*Hibiscus mutabilis*  A large deciduous shrub with stems that grow to 3¹/₂ft (1m) tall, producing flowers 4–5in (10–12cm) wide, in late summer and early autumn. For any good soil in a sheltered position, warm and wet in summer. Hardy to 32°F (0°C), US zone 10. Native to southern Japan and the coasts of southern China, growing in scrub. Cultivated in the southern United States as the 'Confederate Rose Mallow'.

*Hibiscus rosa-sinensis* 'Butterfly'  A member of the mallow family Malvaceae, this tender shrub grows rather slowly to 6ft (1.8m) tall. Upright in habit and taller than wide, it bears relatively small, bright yellow single flowers, each about 4in (10cm) wide, in summer. Best in a sheltered sunny position or in a cool greenhouse, it is hardy to 32°F (0°C), US zone 10. Native to tropical Asia and introduced into cultivation in the early 18th century.

*Hibiscus rosa-sinensis* 'Carnival'  A beautiful pale apricot, single-flowered cultivar with a darker centre.

*Hibiscus rosa-sinensis* 'Diamond Head'  Grows to 8ft (2.5m) tall and about as wide, bearing large fully double flowers, each about 6in (15cm) wide and very deep blackish-red in colour.

*Hibiscus rosa-sinensis* 'Carnival'

*Hibiscus rosa-sinensis* 'White Wings'

*Hibiscus rosa-sinensis* 'Butterfly'

*Hibiscus rosa-sinensis* 'Lady Bird'

*Hibiscus rosa-sinensis* 'Gray Lady'
A large-flowered variety with an attractive central pink flush.

*Hibiscus rosa-sinensis* 'Lady Bird'
Single red blooms with prominent white-yellow veins, up to 8in (20cm) across.

*Hibiscus rosa-sinensis* 'Norman Lee'
Single flowers, about 8in (20cm) across with a red centre, a pink zone shading to orange and a yellow edge.

*Hibiscus rosa-sinensis* 'Tylene'   Single blue flowers, zoned and veined with white, with a small pink eye, up to 7in (18cm) across.

*Hibiscus rosa-sinensis* 'White Wings'
Grows to 8ft (2.5m) tall and about as wide, bearing single white flowers, each about 5in (12cm) wide, with rather narrow petals and a red centre.

*Hibiscus syriacus* 'Blue Bird'   A large deciduous shrub that grows to 10ft (3m) tall and usually as wide, producing flowers, each about 4in (10cm) wide, in late summer and early autumn. Best in a sunny position, benefiting from a sheltered site by a south or west wall in cooler areas. Hardy to -10°F (-23°C), US zones 6–10. Native to the Himalayas and China, and introduced into cultivation by the 16th century.

*Hibiscus mutabilis*

*Hibiscus rosa-sinensis* 'Gray Lady'

*Hibiscus rosa-sinensis* 'Diamond Head'

*Hibiscus rosa-sinensis* 'Norman Lee'

'Celestial'

'Celestial'

'Fantin-Latour'

'Frau Dagmar Hartopp'

CHAPTER THREE

# Roses

*This chapter is divided into three sections, starting with old and species roses followed by a section containing Modern Shrubs, Hybrid Teas, Floribundas, David Austin roses and Miniatures. The third section is devoted to Climbing roses. Each of the three sections is then arranged by colour, from whites through to yellows, oranges and reds to purples.*

ROSE 'BOULE DE NEIGE'
A Bourbon that grows to 6ft (1.8m) tall and 4ft (1.25m) wide, making it a slender, upright shrub. The scented double blooms that reflex in good weather to form a ball, appear continuously from midsummer to autumn and hang in clusters. Hardy to -20°F (-29°C), US zones 5–10. A cross between 'Blanche Lafitte' and 'Sappho', raised by Lacharme in France and launched in 1867.

ROSE 'MAIDEN'S BLUSH', 'Small Maiden's Blush' An Alba that grows to 8ft (2.5m) tall and 6ft (1.8m) wide. The flowers, which have a lovely scent, bloom beautifully in the summer. Tolerant of poor soils, some shade and hardy to -30°F (-35°C), US zones 4–10. Identified in Europe since 1797; this is a smaller version of Rose 'Great Maiden's Blush', which has been known since the 15th century or possibly earlier.

ROSE 'CELESTIAL', 'Celeste' An Alba that grows to 6ft (1.8m) tall and 4ft (1.25m) wide, forming a large rounded

bush. The wonderful sweetly scented, semi-double flowers bloom in summer. Tolerates poor soils, some shade and is hardy to -30°F (-35°C), US zones 4–10. Originated in Holland around the end of the 18th century, possibly as early as 1759; illustrated by Redouté under the name *Rosa damascena* 'Aurore'.

ROSE 'DUCHESSE DE MONTEBELLO' A Gallica that grows to 5ft (1.5m) tall and 3ft (90cm) wide, it is a vigorous shrub with a spreading habit. Scented flowers in summer. Tolerates poor soils, some shade and is hardy to -30°F (-35°C), US zones 4–10. Raised by Laffay in France and known since 1829.

ROSE 'FRAU DAGMAR HARTOPP', 'Fru Dagmar Hastrup' A Hybrid Rugosa that grows to 5ft (1.5 m) tall and 4ft (1.25m) wide, with a wide bushy habit. Flowers with some scent bloom continuously from midsummer to autumn. Tolerates poor soil, some shade, salty winds and hardy to -30°F (-35°C), US zones 4–10. Raised from a *Rosa rugosa* seedling by Hastrup in Denmark and launched in 1910.

ROSE 'BLANC DOUBLE DE COUBERT' A Hybrid Rugosa that grows to 7ft (2m) tall and 4ft (1.25m) wide, with a dense bushy habit. Fragrantly scented flowers bloom throughout the summer. Tolerates poor soil, some shade, salt winds and is hardy to -30°F (-35°C), US zones 4–10. A cross between a *Rosa rugosa* and 'Sombreuil', or possibly a sport from *Rosa rugosa* 'Alba'. Raised in France by Cochet-Cochet and launched in 1892.

*ROSA RUGOSA* 'ALBA' This white form of *Rosa rugosa* is a strong-growing bush. It is particularly notable for its shiny orange-red hips, which appear in late summer, making an attractive contrast to the flowers that remain. It can grow up to 7ft (2m) tall and wide. US zones 4–10.

ROSE 'FANTIN-LATOUR' A China or Hybrid Tea, sometimes thought of as a Centifolia, grows to 7ft (2m) tall and 4ft (1.25m) wide, with a large spreading habit. The well-scented blooms are produced only at midsummer. Tolerates poor soil and is hardy to 0°F (-18°C), US zones 7–10. Categorized as a Centifolia by Beverley Dobson but its precise origins and background are unknown.

ROSE 'MADAME HARDY'
A Damask that grows to 7ft (2m) tall and 5ft (1.5m) wide. It is a strong shrub with long shoots and wonderfully scented flowers in summer. Tolerates poor soils, some shade. Hardy to -20°F (-29°C), US zones 5–10. A Damask, possibly crossed with an Alba or a Centifolia, raised by Hardy, the curator of the Luxembourg Gardens in Paris, and launched in 1832.

ROSE 'OLD BLUSH', 'Parson's Pink China', 'Monthly Rose' (below) A China rose that grows to 6ft (1.8m) tall and 4ft (1.25m) wide, it can be trained as a climber, reaching a height of 10ft (3m). Flowers, with a good scent reminiscent of apples or sweet peas, bloom continuously from summer to winter. Tolerates poor soil, a northerly aspect, some shade and is hardy to 0°F (-18°C), US zones 7–10. One of the original China roses, which, together with 'Slater's Crimson China', 'Hume's Blush Tea-scented China' and 'Parks' Yellow Tea-scented China' are known as the 'four stud Chinas', the important ancestors of the Hybrid Teas and most other modern roses.

'Duchesse de Montebello'

'Boule de Neige'

'Madame Hardy'

'Maiden's Blush'

'Blanc Double de Coubert'

*Rosa rugosa* 'Alba'

ROSE 'CHAPEAU DE NAPOLEON',
'Crested Moss', 'Cristata', *Rosa centifolia*
'Cristata'   A Moss rose that grows to 5ft
(1.5m) tall and 4ft (1.25m) wide,
producing beautifully scented flowers in
summer. Tolerant of poor soil and hardy
to -20°F (-29°C), US zones 5–10. A sport
of *Rosa centifolia* that is said to have been
found on the wall of a convent at
Fribourg, Switzerland around 1820.
Introduced to France by Vibert in 1826.

ROSE 'PRÉSIDENT DE SÈZE', 'Mme
Hébert'   A Gallica that grows to 4ft
(1.25m) tall and 3ft (90cm) wide,
producing large wonderfully scented
double blooms in summer. Tolerates poor
soils and is hardy to -30°F (-35°C), US
zones 4–10, but hates wet weather when
in full flower. Raised by Hébert in France
and launched in 1836.

ROSE 'MRS JOHN LAING'
A Hybrid Perpetual that grows to 4ft
(1.25m) tall and 3ft (90cm) wide, with a
short sturdy habit and a very fragrant
scent. Tolerates poor soil, hardy to -20°F
(-29°C), US zones 5–10 and impervious
to rain. Raised from a seedling of
'François Michelon', by Bennett in
Britain and launched in 1887. Bennett
reputedly received $45,000 for the rights
to this rose in the US.

ROSE 'FERDINAND PICHARD'
A Hybrid Perpetual that grows to 8ft
(2.5m) tall and 5ft (1.5m) wide, with a
vigorous bushy habit. Fragrant flowers
grow in tight clusters from midsummer
into autumn. Tolerates poor soil and is
hardy to -20°F (-29°C), US zones 5–10.
A Hybrid Perpetual, sometimes classed as
a Bourbon, it was raised by Tanne in
France and launched in 1921.

ROSE 'GÉNÉRAL KLÉBER'
A Damask-Hybrid Moss that grows to
5½ft (1.6m) tall and 4ft (1.25m) wide,
producing clusters of large fully double
scented flowers in summer. Tolerates poor
soil and is hardy to -20°F (-29°C), US
zones 5–10. Raised by Robert in France
and launched in 1856, 'Général Kléber'
was named after the famous French
general who commanded Napoleon's
army in Egypt and was assassinated in
Cairo in 1800.

ROSE 'ISPAHAN', 'Isfahan', 'Pompon
des Princes'   A Damask that grows to 6ft
(1.8m) tall and 3ft (90cm) wide, with a
bushy upright habit. The medium-pink
double blooms with a wonderful scent are
summer-flowering over a long period and
grow in clusters. Tolerates poor soils and is
hardy to -20°F (-29°C), US zones 5–10.
Known since before 1832.

ROSE 'KÖNIGIN VON DÄNEMARK',
'Queen of Denmark', 'Dronningen af
Danmark', 'Reine du Denmark, 'Belle
Courtisanne'   An Alba rose that grows
up to 7ft (2m) tall and 4ft (1.25m) wide,
with a sweet-scented flowers. A lax bush
with branches often weighted down by its
numerous flowers. Tolerates poor soils,
some shade and is hardy to -30°F
(-35°C), US zones 4–10.

ROSE 'LOUISE ODIER'   A Bourbon
that grows to 5ft (1.5m) tall and 4ft
(1.25m) wide. This strong bushy upright
shrub produces richly scented flowers
continuously from midsummer to
autumn. Tolerant of some shade and
hardy to -20°F (-29°C), US zones 5–10.
Raised by Margottin in France and
launched in 1851.

*ROSA GALLICA* 'VERSICOLOR'
'Rosa Mundi'   A Gallica rose that grows
up to 5ft (1.5m) tall and 3ft (90cm) wide.
It is a suckering shrub, producing flowers
in summer. Tolerates poor soil, some
shade and is hardy to -30°F (-35°C), US
zones 4–10, but is susceptible to mildew.
A variegated sport of *Rosa gallica*
'Officinalis', 'Versicolor' has been known
since 1581. Legend has it that it was
named after Fair Rosamund, mistress of
Henry II.

'Louise Odier'

'Président de Sèze'

'Chapeau de Napoleon'

'Général Kléber'

ROSE 'COMTE DE CHAMBORD'
(above)   A Portland that grows to 5ft
(1.5m) tall and 2ft (60cm) wide, with an
upright habit and a sweet scent, repeating
throughout summer and often well into
autumn. This variety tolerates poor soil, is
hardy to -30°F (-35°C), US zones 4–10
and is disease-resistant. A cross between
'Baronne Prévost' and a Portland Rose,
raised by Moreau-Robert in France and
launched in 1860.

'Mrs John Laing'

'Königin von Dänemark'

'Ispahan'

'Ferdinand Pichard'

*Rosa gallica* 'Versicolor'

*Rosa gallica* 'Officinalis'

'Cardinal de Richelieu'

'Thérèse Bugnet'

ROSE 'THÉRÈSE BUGNET'
A Rugosa that grows to 6ft (1.8m) tall and 6ft (1.8m) wide, with a hardy bushy habit. The fragrantly scented flowers bloom continuously throughout summer. Tolerates poor soil, some shade, salt winds and is hardy to -30°F (-35°C), US zones 4–10. Rose 'Thérèse Bugnet' is a complex Rugosa hybrid, raised by Bugnet in Canada and launched in 1950.

*ROSA RUGOSA* The wild Rugosa rose grows to 7ft (2m) tall and 6ft (1.8m) wide. A vigorous thorny shrub with a very fragrant scent that flowers continuously throughout summer and autumn. Tolerates poor soil, some shade, salt winds and is hardy to -30°F (-35°C), US zones 4–10. Native of eastern Siberia, northern China, Korea and Japan, and naturalized throughout northern and eastern Europe.

ROSE 'CARDINAL DE RICHELIEU' A compact shrub with a wonderful scent that grows to 5ft (1.5m) tall and 3ft (90cm) wide and flowers in summer. This variety tolerates poor soils and is hardy to -30°F (-35°C), US zones 4–10, but needs generous feeding and careful pruning if it is to grow happily and successfully. A triploid Gallica-China hybrid raised by Laffay in France and launched in 1840.

ROSE 'TUSCANY SUPERB', 'Superb Tuscan' (below) A vigorous Gallica that grows to 5ft (1.5m) tall and 3ft (90cm) wide. The double blooms flower in summer and have a wonderful scent. Tolerates poor soils and is hardy to -30°F (-35°C), US zones 4–10. Thought to be a sport or seedling of Rose 'Tuscany', and known since 1837.

'Charles de Mills'

ROSE 'CHARLES DE MILLS', 'Bizarre Triomphant' (left) A Gallica that grows to 5ft (1.5m) tall and 4ft (1.25m) wide. An erect, vigorous shrub that produces scented flowers in shades of crimson, fading to mauve and purple in summer. Tolerant of poor soils and hardy to -30°F (-35°C), US zones 4–10.

*ROSA GALLICA* 'OFFICINALIS', 'Apothecary's Rose', 'Red Rose of Lancaster', 'Rose of Provins' A Gallica that grows to 5ft (1.5m) tall and 3ft (90cm) wide, producing scented semi-double blooms in the summer. Tolerant of poor soils, some shade and hardy to -30°F (-35°C), US zones 4–10. Thought to be the oldest form of *Rosa gallica* in cultivation, generally believed to have been brought from Damascus to Provins in northern France by Thibault in 1250. It has been grown in that area in vast quantities for medicinal purposes, thus giving rise to its common name.

'Rose de Rescht'

'ROSE DE RESCHT' A Damask that grows to 4ft (1.25m) tall and 2ft (60cm) wide. A leafy, bushy shrub, producing wonderfully scented double blooms, flowering repeatedly in summer and autumn. Tolerates poor soils, some shade and is hardy to -20°F (-29°C), US zones 5–10, with good disease resistance. A Damask possibly crossed with a Gallica or a Portland, introduced from Iran in the 1940s.

ROSE 'PORTLAND ROSE', 'Scarlet Four Seasons', 'Duchess of Portland', 'Duchesse de Portland' A Portland that grows to 2ft (60cm) tall and 2ft (60cm) wide, with a small bushy habit. Blooms, with some scent, flowering repeatedly in summer and again in autumn. Tolerant of poor soil and hardy to -30°F (-35°C), US zones 4–10. Possibly a cross between *Rosa gallica* and 'Autumn Damask', known since about 1790.

*Rosa rugosa* on dunes by the sea of Okhots in northern Japan

'Portland Rose'

'Pascali'

'Nevada'

'Winchester Cathedral'

'Margaret Merril'

**ROSE ' FRÜHLINGSGOLD'**
A Hybrid that grows to 8ft (2.5m) tall and 5ft (1.5m) wide. Sweetly scented flowers in early summer are often followed by another crop in late summer. Tolerates poor soil, some shade and temperatures of -30°F (-35°C), US zones 4–10. A cross between *Rosa pimpinellifolia* 'Hispida' and 'Joanna Hill', raised by Kordes in Germany and launched in 1937.

**ROSE 'GOLDEN WINGS'**  A Shrub that grows to 7ft (2m) tall and 4ft (1.25m) wide, with a compact habit. Sweetly scented flowers from midsummer to autumn. Tolerant of poor soils and hardy to -20°F (-29°C), US zones 5–10. A cross between 'Sœur Thérèse' and *Rosa pimpinellifolia* 'Grandiflora' crossed with 'Ormiston Roy', raised by Shepherd in the US and launched in 1956.

**ROSE 'PASCALI', 'Blanche Pasca'**
A Hybrid Tea that grows to 3ft (90cm) tall and 2ft (60cm) wide; however the climbing variety can reach to 7ft (2m). Blooming abundantly throughout the summer, this rose will tolerate poor soils and temperatures of -10°F (-23°C), US zones 6–10. A cross between 'Queen Elizabeth' and 'White Butterfly', raised by Lens in Belgium and introduced by Dickson in 1963.

**ROSE 'JACQUELINE DU PRÉ'**
A large Modern Shrub rose with a good musk scent that grows to 6ft (1.8m) tall and 5ft (1.5m) wide. Very free-flowering, repeating continuously throughout the summer. It will tolerate poor soils and temperatures of -20°F (-29°C), US zones 5–10. A cross between 'Radox Bouquet' and 'Maigold'. Raised by Harkness in Britain and launched in 1989.

**ROSE 'MARGARET MERRIL'**
A Floribunda that grows to 2.5ft (75cm) tall and 2ft (60cm) wide, with an excellent scent, repeating almost continuously throughout summer. Tolerant of poor soils and hardy to -30°F (-35°C), US zones 4–10. Susceptible to blackspot. A cross between 'Rudolph Timm' and 'Dedication', raised by Harkness in Britain and launched in 1977.

**ROSE 'NEVADA'**  A Hybrid Moysii that grows to 8ft (2.5m) tall and 8ft (2.5m) wide. Lightly scented, flowering profusely in summer and intermittently into autumn, this disease-resistant rose will tolerate poor soil and hardy to -20°F (-29°C), US zones 5–10. Probably a cross between 'La Giralda' and *Rosa moysii* or possibly with a *Rosa pimpinellifolia* hybrid. Raised by Dot in Spain and launched in 1927.

'Nozomi'

'Iceberg'

'Frühlingsgold'

ROSE 'POLAR STAR', 'Polarstern' (below) A Hybrid Tea that grows to 4ft (1.25m) tall and 2ft (60cm) wide with a bushy habit and blooms throughout summer. This slightly scented variety will tolerate poor soils and temperatures of -10°F (-23°C), US zones 6–10. Raised by Tantau in Germany, launched in 1982.

ROSE 'ICEBERG', 'Fée des Neiges', 'Schneewittchen' A Floribunda that grows to 3ft (90cm) tall and 2ft (60cm) wide. Very free-flowering, repeating almost continuously throughout summer, with some scent. Hardy to -30°F (-35°C), US zones 4–10, susceptible to blackspot. A cross between 'Robin Hood' and 'Virgo', raised by Kordes in Germany and launched in 1958.

ROSE 'NOZOMI' A climbing Miniature or ground-cover rose that grows to 3ft (90cm) tall and 6ft (1.8m) wide, with a rampant, spreading habit and a slight scent. This variety will tolerate poor soil, some shade and is hardy to -10°F (-23°C), US zones 6–10. A cross between 'Fairy Princess' and 'Sweet Fairy', raised by Onodera in Japan and launched in 1968.

ROSE 'WINCHESTER CATHEDRAL' An English Rose that grows to 4ft (1.25m) tall and as wide, this is a vigorous, bushy sweetly scented shrub that flowers continuously throughout summer. Hardy to -20°F (-29°C), US zones 5–10 with good disease resistance. A sport from 'Mary Rose'. Raised by David Austin in Britain and launched in 1988.

'Jacqueline du Pré'

'Golden Wings'

'Graham Thomas'

'Graham Thomas'

ROSE 'GRAHAM THOMAS' A tall English Rose that grows to 6ft (1.8m) tall and 4ft (1.25m) wide, with a bushy habit. Tea rose-scented flowers bloom in summer and repeat again at the end of the season. Tolerant of poor soils and hardy to -20°F (-29°C), US zones 5–10. A cross between 'Charles Austin' and a hybrid between 'Iceberg' and an English Rose, raised by David Austin in Britain and launched in 1983.

ROSE 'ARTHUR BELL' A Floribunda that grows to 2½ft (75cm) tall and 2ft (60cm) wide, with a bushy habit and a strong scent. Repeats throughout summer and tolerant of poor soils. Hardy to -30°F (-35°C), US zones 4–10. It should be pruned hard to encourage late flowering. A cross between 'Cläre Grammerstorf' and 'Piccadilly', raised by McGredy in Britain and launched in 1965.

ROSE 'BUFF BEAUTY' A Hybrid Musk shrub rose that grows to 5ft (1.5m) tall and as wide, with a delicious scent. Flowers throughout summer into autumn. Tolerant of poor soils, some shade and hardy to -20°F (-29°C), US zones 5–10, with good disease resistance. A cross between an unknown and 'William Allen Richardson' raised by Bentall in Britain and launched in 1939.

ROSE 'GOLDEN SUNBLAZE', 'Rise 'n' Shine' A Miniature or patio rose that grows to 1½ft (45cm) tall, producing clusters of slightly scented flowers throughout summer. Hardy to -10°F (-23°C), US zones 6–10. A cross between 'Little Darling' and 'Yellow Magic', raised by Moore in the US and launched in 1978.

'Golden Sunblaze'

'Elina'

'Buff Beauty'

'Chinatown'

ROSE 'CHINATOWN', 'Ville de Chine' A Floribunda that grows to 4ft (1.25m) tall and 3ft (90cm) wide. Free-flowering strongly scented blooms repeat continuously all summer, becoming a little lighter with age and flushed with pink. Tolerant of poor soils and hardy to -30°F (-35°C), US zones 4–10. A cross between 'Columbine' and 'Cläre Grammerstorf', raised by Poulsen in Denmark and launched in 1963.

ROSE 'ELINA', 'Peaudouce' A Hybrid Tea that grows to 3ft (90cm) tall and 2ft (60cm) wide, with a bushy upright growth. Flowers, with some scent, bloom continuously throughout summer. This variety will tolerate poor soils and is hardy to -10°F (-23°C), US zones 6–10. A cross between 'Nana Mouskouri' and 'Lolita', raised by Dickson in Northern Ireland and launched in 1985.

ROSE 'FREEDOM' A Hybrid Tea that grows to 2¹/₂ft (75cm) tall and 2ft (60cm) wide, with abundant lightly scented flowers blooming throughout summer. Disease-resistant and hardy to -10°F (-23°C), US zones 6–10. A cross between 'Eurorose'and 'Typhoon' x 'Bright Smile', raised by Dickson in Northern Ireland and introduced by Harkness in 1984.

ROSE 'GRANDPA DICKSON', 'Irish Gold' A Hybrid Tea that grows to 2¹/₂ft (75cm) tall and 2ft (60cm) wide. Slightly scented blooms throughout summer. Hardy to -10°F (-23°C), US zones 6–10, with good disease resistance. A cross between 'Perfecta' x 'Governado Braga de Cruz' and 'Piccadilly', raised by Dickson in Northern Ireland and introduced into the US by Jackson and Perkins in 1966.

ROSE 'MOUNTBATTEN' A Floribunda that grows to 5ft (1.5m) tall and 3ft (90 cm) wide. Free-flowering with a good scent repeating throughout summer. Excellent dark-green healthy foliage. Tolerant of poor soils, good disease resistance and hardy to -30°F (-35°C), US zones 4–10. Best in a sunny position. A cross between 'Peer Gynt' and a seedling x 'Southampton', raised by Harkness in Britain and launched in 1982.

ROSE 'PEACE', 'Mme A Meilland' 'Gloria Dei' A Hybrid Tea that grows to 5ft (1.5m) tall and 3ft (90cm) wide. Flowers with some scent, bloom throughout summer, often varying in colour depending on the soil, season and weather. Tolerant of poor soils and hardy to -10°F (-23°C), US zones 6–10. Raised by Meilland in France and introduced there in 1943, but introduced to US by Conrad-Pyle on Armistice Day in 1945.

'Arthur Bell'

'Freedom'

'Mountbatten'

'Grandpa Dickson'

'Peace'

The garden of Sharon Van Enoo near Los Angeles

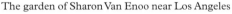

'Anne Harkness'

ROSE 'AMBER QUEEN', 'Prinz Eugen von Savoyen' A Floribunda that grows to 2½ft (75cm) tall and 2ft (60 cm) wide, with a good scent, very free-flowering and repeating almost continuously throughout summer. Hardy to -30°F (-35°C), US zones 4–10. A cross between 'Southampton' and 'Typhoon', it was raised by Harkness in Britain and launched in 1984.

ROSE 'ANNE HARKNESS' A tall Floribunda that grows to 3½ft (1m) tall and 2ft (60 cm) wide, with a slight scent, very free-flowering, repeating almost continuously and best in late summer. Tolerant of poor soils, hardy to -30°F (-35°C), US zones 4–10. A cross between 'Bobby Dazzler' and 'Chanelle' x 'Piccadilly', raised by Harkness in Britain and launched in 1979.

ROSE 'WHISKY MAC', 'Whisky' A Hybrid Tea that grows to 4ft (1.25m) tall and 2ft (60cm) wide. Strongly scented flowers bloom abundantly throughout the summer. Hardy to -10°F (-23°C), US zones 6–10, but susceptible to some mildew and frost damage. It was raised by Tantau in Germany and launched in 1967.

ROSE 'CHICAGO PEACE' A Hybrid Tea that grows to 4ft (1.25m) tall and 3ft (90cm) wide, with an upright bushy habit. Abundant flowers throughout summer and a good scent. Tolerant of poor soils and hardy to -10°F (-23°C), US zones 6–10, with good disease resistance. A sport of 'Peace' and identical to it except in colour, raised by Johnston in the US and introduced by Conard-Pyle and Universal Rose Selection in 1962.

ROSE 'FRAGRANT DELIGHT' A free-flowering Floribunda with a good scent that grows to 3ft (90cm) tall and 2ft (60 cm) wide, which repeats almost continuously throughout summer. Hardy to -30°F (-35°C), US zones 4–10. A cross between 'Chanelle' and 'Whisky Mac', raised by Tysterman in the US and launched by the Wisbech Plant Co. in Britain in 1978.

ROSE 'JUST JOEY' A Hybrid Tea that grows to 2½ft (75cm) tall and 2ft (60cm) wide. Flowers with a good scent appear continuously throughout summer. Hardy to -10°F (-23°C), US zones 6–10. A cross between 'Fragrant Cloud' and 'Dr A J Verhage', raised by Cants in Britain and launched in 1972.

ROSE 'SOUTHAMPTON', 'Susan Ann' A Floribunda with some scent that grows to 3ft (90cm) tall and 2ft (60 cm) wide, with an upright habit. Very free-flowering, repeating throughout the summer. Tolerant of poor soils and hardy to -30°F (-35°C), US zones 4–10, with good disease resistance. 'Southampton' is a cross between 'Ann Elizabeth' x a seedling, raised by Harkness in Britain and launched in 1972.

ROSE 'SUNSPRITE', 'Korresia', 'Friesia', 'Fresia' A Floribunda with a good, fresh scent that grows to 2½ft (75cm) tall and 2ft (60 cm) wide. Very free-flowering, of strong bushy habit and repeating all summer. Tolerant of poor soils and hardy to -30°F (-35°C), US zones 4–10. A cross between 'Friedrich Wölein' and 'Spanish Sun', raised by Kordes in Germany and launched in 1977.

ROSE 'SWEET DREAMS' A delicate, cup-shaped Floribunda or patio rose that grows to 1½ft (45cm), with a slight scent. Flowers continuously throughout the summer. Hardy to -10°F (-23°C), US zones 6–10. It was raised by Frycr in Britain and launched 1987.

'Anne Harkness'

'Amber Queen'

'Whisky Mac'

'Southampton'

'Sunsprite'

¹/₃ life size. Specimens from Wisley Garden, 18 July

'Fragrant Delight'

'Just Joey'

'Chicago Peace'

'Sweet Dreams'

ROSE 'ALEXANDER'  A very large-growing Hybrid Tea that reaches 7ft (2m) tall and 4ft (1.25m) wide, with an upright habit. Slightly scented flowers bloom continuously throughout summer. Tolerant of poor soils, some shade and hardy to -10°F (-23°C), US zones 6–10. A cross between 'Super Star' and 'Ann Elizabeth' x 'Allgold', raised by Harkness in Britain and launched in 1972.

ROSE 'BLAST OFF'  A Floribunda that grows to 3ft (90cm) tall and 2ft (60 cm) wide, with an upright bushy habit. It can be grown as a shrub or in pots or tubs. The large, loose, spicily scented blooms are very freely produced, repeating almost continuously throughout the summer. Hardy to -20°F (-29°C), US zones 5–10. A cross between 'Orangeade' and 'Little Artist', raised by Moore and launched in 1995.

ROSE 'ANISLEY DICKSON', 'Dicky'  A Floribunda that grows to 2½ft (75cm) tall and 2ft (60 cm) wide. Very free-flowering with a good scent, repeating almost continuously throughout the summer. Tolerant of poor soils and hardy to -30°F (-35°C), US zones 4–10. A cross between 'Coventry Cathedral' and 'Memento', raised by Dickson in Northern Ireland and launched in 1983.

ROSE 'PICCADILLY'  A Hybrid Tea that grows to 2½ft (75cm) tall and 2ft (60cm) wide, although the climbing variety can grow to 7ft (2m). Slightly scented flowers bloom continuously throughout summer. Tolerant of poor soils and hardy to -10°F (-23°C), US zones 6–10, but susceptible to blackspot. A cross between 'McGredy's Yellow' and 'Karl Herbst', it was raised by McGredy and launched in 1960.

ROSE 'ANGELA RIPPON'  A Miniature or patio rose that grows to 12in (30cm) tall, producing slightly scented flowers continuously throughout the summer. This variety is hardy to -10°F (-23°C), US zones 6–10. A cross between 'Rosy Jewel' and 'Zorina', it was raised by deRuiter in Holland and launched in 1978.

ROSE 'MATANGI'  A Floribunda that grows to 3ft (90cm) tall and 2ft (60 cm) wide, with an upright, sturdy habit. It is a good example of the 'hand-painted' roses; the slightly scented double blooms are very free-flowering, repeating throughout summer. Tolerant of poor soils and hardy to -30°F (-35°C), US zones 4–10. A cross between a seedling and 'Picasso', raised by McGredy in New Zealand' and launched in 1974.

ROSE 'ANNA FORD'  (above)  A Miniature or patio rose that grows to 1½ft (45cm) tall with a dense bushy habit. Semi-double flowers bloom continuously throughout the summer and this variety tolerates some shade. It is hardy to -10°F (-23°C), US zones 6–10. A cross between 'Southampton' and 'Darling Flame', raised by Harkness in Britain and launched in 1980.

ROSE 'FRAGRANT CLOUD'  A Hybrid Tea that grows to 3ft (90cm) tall and 2ft (60cm) wide, bearing large double flowers with an excellent scent. Blooms abundantly throughout summer. Hardy to -10°F (-23°C), US zones 6–10, but susceptible to blackspot. A cross between a seedling and 'Prima Ballerina', it was raised by Tantau in Germany and launched in 1967.

'Anisley Dickson'

'Blast Off'

'Alexander'

ROSE 'TRUMPETER' A Floribunda that grows to 2ft (60cm) tall and 1½ft (45 cm) wide, with a compact bushy habit. It can be grown as a shrub or in pots or tubs. Free-flowering with little scent and repeating throughout summer. Hardy to -30°F (-35°C), US zones 4–10. A cross between 'Satchmo' and a seedling, raised by McGredy in New Zealand and launched in 1977.

ROSE 'REMEMBER ME' (below) A Hybrid Tea that grows up to 3½ft (1m) tall and 2ft (60cm) wide, with an upright bushy habit. The large double flowers, with a slight scent, bloom abundantly throughout the summer. This variety tolerates poor soils and is hardy to -10°F (-23°C), US zones 6–10. A cross between 'Ann Letts' and 'Dainty Maid' x 'Pink Favourite', raised by Cocker in Scotland and launched in 1984.

'Angela Rippon'

'Matangi'

'Alexander'

'Trumpeter'

'Piccadilly'

'Fragrant Cloud'

149

'Tip Top'

ROSE 'CORNELIA' (above)  A Hybrid Musk shrub rose that grows to 5ft (1.5m) tall and as wide, with a vigorous spreading habit. Perpetual flowering throughout summer into autumn, with a sweet, musky, pervasive scent. Tolerant of poor soils, some shade and hardy to -20°F (-29°C), US zones 5–10, with good disease resistance. Raised by Pemberton in Britain and launched in 1925.

ROSE 'BLESSINGS'  A Hybrid Tea that grows to 2½ft (75cm) tall and 2ft (60cm) wide, although the climbing variety reaches 15ft (4.5m). Dense, upright growth with slightly scented flowers blooming throughout summer. Tolerant of poor soils and hardy to -10°F (-23°C), US zones 6–10, but susceptible to mildew. A cross between 'Queen Elizabeth' and a seedling, raised by Gregory in Britain and launched in 1967.

ROSE 'ELIZABETH OF GLAMIS', 'Irish Beauty'  A Floribunda that grows to 2½ft (75cm) tall and 2ft (60 cm) wide, with an upright habit. Very free-flowering, repeating almost continuously throughout the summer. Hardy to -30°F (-35°C), US zones 4–10, but susceptible to blackspot and mildew. A cross between 'Spartan' and 'Highlight', raised by McGredy in Northern Ireland and launched in 1964.

ROSE 'FRÜHLINGSMORGEN'
A Hybrid Pimpinellifolia that grows to 7ft (2m) tall and 4ft (1.25m) wide. A tall, upright shrub with some scent that flowers in spring and often again in late summer. Tolerant of poor soils, some shade and is hardy to -30°F (-35°C), US zones 4–10. This individual is a cross between *Rosa pimpinellifolia altaica* and 'E G Hill' x 'Catherine Kordes', raised by Kordes in Germany and launched in 1932.

ROSE 'GENTLE TOUCH'
A Miniature or patio rose that grows to 1ft (30cm) tall, with a compact habit. It produces slightly scented blooms continuously throughout summer. Hardy to -10°F (-23°C), US zones 6–10. Raised by Dickson in Northern Ireland and launched in 1986.

ROSE 'HERITAGE'  An English Rose that grows to 4ft (1.25m) tall and as wide, with a strong, vigorous habit. Flowers with a strong, slightly lemony scent, appear throughout summer. Tolerates poor soil and is hardy to -20°F (-29°C), US zones 5–10. A cross between an unnamed seedling and 'Wife of Bath' x 'Iceberg', raised by David Austin in Britain and launched in 1984.

ROSE 'PAUL SHIRVILLE'  A Hybrid Tea that grows to 3ft (90cm) tall and 2ft (60cm) wide, with a slightly spreading habit. Large double flowers bloom throughout summer with a good scent. Tolerant of poor soils. Hardy to 10°F (-23°C), US zones 6–10, but susceptible to blackspot. A cross between 'Mischief' and 'Compassion', raised by Harkness in Britain and launched in 1983.

ROSE 'PINK PARFAIT'
A Grandiflora or Floribunda that grows to 2½ft (75cm) tall and 2ft (60 cm) wide, with an upright bushy habit. The flowers repeat throughout summer and have little or no scent. Tolerant of poor soils and hardy to -30°F (-35°C), US zones 4–10, with good disease resistance. A cross between 'First Love' and 'Pinocchio', raised by Swim in the US and launched in 1960.

ROSE 'TIP TOP'  A small Floribunda or Miniature that grows to 1½ft (45cm) tall and as wide. The loose, semi-double blooms are free-flowering, repeating throughout summer and have some scent. Hardy to -30°F (-35°C), US zones 4–10, but susceptible to blackspot. Raised by Tantau in Germany and launched in 1963.

ROSE 'FELICIA' (below)  A Hybrid Musk shrub rose that grows to 5ft (1.5m) tall and 9ft (2.75m) wide with a strong, bushy habit. Sweetly scented flowers throughout summer and autumn. This variety will tolerate poor soils and is hardy to -20°F (-29°C), US zones 5–10. A cross between 'Trier' and 'Ophelia', raised by Pemberton in Britain and launched in 1928.

'Elizabeth of Glamis'

'Elizabeth of Glamis'     'Pink Parfait'

¹/₃ life size. Specimens from Wisley Gardens, 18 July

'Gentle Touch'

'Paul Shirville'

'Blessings'

'Heritage'

'Frühlingsmorgen'

'Savoy Hotel' in Queen Mary's Rose Garden, Regent's Park, London

'Savoy Hotel'

'Sexy Rexy'

'Chaucer'

'Mary Rose'

'Queen Elizabeth'

'City of London'

'Redouté'

'Fritz Nobis'

ROSE 'CHAUCER' An English Rose that grows to 3½ft (1m) tall and 3ft (90cm) wide, with a vigorous, upright bushy habit. Flowers with good myrrh-like scent repeat throughout summer. It will tolerate -20°F (-29°C), US zones 5–10, but susceptible to mildew. A cross between 'Duchesse de Montebello' and 'Constance Spry', raised by David Austin in Britain and launched in 1970.

ROSE 'CITY OF LONDON' A tall Floribunda rose that grows to 4ft (1.25m) tall and 3ft (90cm) wide. The large, loose, slightly scented blooms are very free-flowering and repeat throughout summer. Tolerant of poor soils and hardy to -30°F (-35°C), US zones 4–10. Hard pruning encourages late flowering. A cross between 'New Dawn' and 'Radox Bouquet', raised by Harkness in Britain and launched in 1987.

ROSE 'MARY ROSE' An English Rose that grows to 4ft (1.25m) tall and as wide with a vigorous bushy, branching habit. Flowers, with a slight sweet scent, flourish throughout summer. Hardy to -20°F (-29°C), US zones 5–10, with good disease resistance. A cross between 'Wife of Bath' and 'The Miller', raised by David

Austin in Britain, launched in 1983 and named to mark the recovery of Henry VIII's flagship from the Solent.

ROSE 'FRITZ NOBIS' A Shrub rose that grows to 7ft (2m) tall and 4ft (1.25m) wide, with a vigorous habit. The beautifully scented blooms, which are like those of an Old Rose and flower only once in summer, make a beautiful show. This variety tolerates poor soils and some shade. Hardy to -20°F (-29°C), US zones 5–10. A cross between 'Joanna Hill' and 'Magnifica', raised by Kordes in Germany and launched in 1940.

ROSE 'QUEEN ELIZABETH', 'The Queen Elizabeth Rose' A Floribunda or Grandiflora that grows to 6ft (1.8m) tall and 2½ft (60 cm) wide, with a very tall, upright habit. Free-flowering, repeating in summer, with some scent. This variety tolerates poor soils and is hardy to -30°F (-35°C), US zones 4–10. A cross between 'Charlotte Armstrong' and 'Floradora', raised by Lammerts in the US and launched in 1954.

ROSE 'REDOUTÉ' An English Rose that grows to 4ft (1.25m) tall and as wide, with a vigorous bushy habit. Flowers with

a slight, sweet scent appear all summer. Hardy to -20°F (-29°C), US zones 5–10, with good disease resistance. A sport of 'Mary Rose', raised by David Austin in Britain, launched in 1992 and named after Empress Josephine's celebrated rose painter Pierre Joseph Redouté.

ROSE 'SAVOY HOTEL' A Hybrid Tea that grows to 3ft (90cm) tall and 2½ft (75cm) wide, producing large double flowers that bloom throughout summer, and have a very good scent. Tolerant of poor soils and hardy to -10°F (-23°C), US zones 6–10, with good disease resistance. A cross between 'Silver Jubilee' and 'Amber Queen', raised by Harkness in Britain and launched in 1989.

ROSE 'SEXY REXY', 'Heckenzauber' A Floribunda rose that grows to 3ft (90cm) tall and 2ft (60 cm) wide, with a bushy habit. The bushes are very free-flowering, repeating throughout summer and have some scent. This variety will tolerate poor soils and is hardy to -30°F (-35°C), US zones 4–10 and has good disease resistance. A cross between 'Seaspray' and 'Dreaming', raised by McGredy in New Zealand and introduced by Sealand in 1984.

'Marguerite Hilling'

'Aloha'

**ROSE 'PINK BELLS'**
(above) A Miniature
or small shrub ground-
cover rose that grows to
1¹/₂ft (45cm) tall, with a dense,
spreading habit and slight scent.
Tolerant of poor soil, some shade and
temperatures of -10°F (-23°C), US zones
6–10, with good disease resistance.
A cross between 'Mini-Poul' x 'Temple
Bells' and a twin of 'White Bells', raised
by Poulsen in Denmark and launched
in 1983.

**ROSE 'ALOHA'** A Hybrid Tea that
grows to 5ft (1.5m) tall and 4ft (1.25m)
wide with an upright habit, making it a
superb shrub or low climber. The
beautifully scented flowers bloom
throughout summer. Tolerant of poor
soils and hardy to -10°F (-23°C), US
zones 6–10, with good disease resistance.
A cross between 'Mercedes Gallart' and
'New Dawn', raised by Boerner in the US
and launched in 1949.

**ROSE 'BONICA'** A ground-cover or
Modern Shrub rose that grows to 3ft
(90cm) tall and 5ft (1.5m) wide, with a
spreading, arching habit. Very free-
flowering, repeating throughout the
summer with some scent. Tolerant of poor
soils, hardy to -20°F (-29°C), US zones
5–10, with good disease resistance. A
cross between *Rosa sempervirens* x 'Mlle
Marthe Carron' and 'Picasso', raised by
Meilland in France and launched in 1982.

**ROSE 'FERDY'** A ground-cover or
Shrub rose that grows to 6ft (1.8m) tall
and 5ft (1.5m) wide. The small double
blooms that flower continuously
throughout the summer have a slight
scent. It tolerates poor soils, hardy to
-20°F (-29°C), US zones 5–10, with good
disease resistance. A cross between a
climbing seedling and 'Petite Folie', raised
by Suzuki in Japan and launched in 1984.

**ROSE 'MARGUERITE HILLING'**
A Hybrid Moysii that grows to 7ft (2m)
tall and as wide. The large single blooms

that flower profusely in early summer and intermittently on into autumn are mid-pink with a light scent. Tolerant of poor soils and hardy to -20°F (-29°C), US zones 5–10, with good disease resistance. A sport of 'Nevada' discovered by Graham Thomas and launched by Hilling in Britain in 1959.

ROSE 'SILVER JUBILEE'   A Hybrid Tea that grows to 3½ft (1m) tall and 2ft (60cm) wide. Slightly scented flowers throughout summer. This variety tolerates temperatures of -10°F (-23°C), US zones 6–10 and has good disease resistance. A cross between 'Mischief' and a seedling, raised by Cocker in Scotland and launched in 1978.

ROSE 'THE FAIRY'   A dwarf Polyantha now used as a ground-cover rose that grows to 2ft (60cm) tall and 4ft (1.25m) wide with a dense, spreading habit. The small, loose double flowers that bloom continuously throughout the summer have little scent. Tolerates poor soil, some shade, hardy to -10°F (-23°C), US zones 6–10, with good disease resistance. A cross between 'Paul Crampel' and 'Lady Gay', raised by Bentall in Britain and launched in 1932.

ROSE 'BALLERINA' (above)   A small Hybrid Musk shrub that grows to 4ft (1.25m) tall and 2½ft (75cm) wide. Large clusters of delicate, small, slightly scented single blooms, pale to medium pink with white centres, flower throughout summer into autumn and early winter. Tolerant of poor soils, some shade and temperatures of -20°F (-29°C), US zones 5–10. A *Rosa multiflora* seedling, probably raised by Pemberton and launched by Bentall in Britain in 1937.

'Ferdy'

'The Fairy'

'Silver Jubilee'

'Bonica'

'Ballerina'

'Raubritter'

'Raubritter'

'Lavender Lassie'

'Prima Ballerina'

'Gertrude Jekyll'

'Blue Moon'

'Regensberg'

'Flower Carpet'

'Charmian'

ROSE 'BLUE MOON', 'Blue Monday'
A Hybrid Tea that grows to 3½ft (1m) tall
and 2ft (60cm) wide, although the
climbing variety can reach 8ft (2.5m).
It has an excellent scent and will tolerate
temperatures of -10°F (-23°C), US zones
6–10. One of the best of the so-called
'blue' group, raised by Tantau in Germany
and launched in 1965.

ROSE 'CHARMIAN'   An English Rose
that grows to 4ft (1.25m) tall and as wide,
with a spreading, rather arching habit.
The large, fully double blooms that flower
continuously throughout the summer,
have a strong scent. This variety will
tolerate poor soil and -20°F (-29°C), US
zones 5–10. A cross between an unnamed
seedling and 'Lilian Austin', raised by
David Austin in Britain and launched
in 1982.

ROSE 'FLOWER CARPET'
A ground-cover Shrub rose that grows to
1½ft (45cm) tall and 4ft (1.25m) wide,
with a dense, spreading habit. The double
blooms that flower continuously
throughout the summer have little scent.
This variety will tolerate temperatures of
-20°F (-29°C), US zones 5–10. Raised by
Noack in Germany and launched in 1990.

ROSE 'LAVENDER LASSIE'
A Hybrid Musk shrub rose that grows to
5ft (1.5m) tall and 4ft (1.25m) wide.
Scented flowers flourish throughout the
summer into autumn. This variety will
tolerate poor soils, some shade and
temperatures of -20°F (-29°C), US zones
5–10. A cross between 'Hamburg' and
'Mme Norbert Levavasseur', raised by
Kordes in Germany in 1960.

ROSE 'GERTRUDE JEKYLL'   An
English Rose that grows to 5ft (1.5m) tall
and 3ft (90cm) wide, with a vigorous,
lanky habit. Flowers with a superb scent
bloom throughout summer. Tolerant to
-20°F (-29°C), US zones 5–10 with good
disease resistance. A cross between 'Wife
of Bath' and 'Comte de Chambord',
raised by David Austin in Britain and
launched in 1986. It is named after the
great English gardener Gertrude Jekyll
who wrote *Roses for English Gardens*.

ROSE 'PRIMA BALLERINA'
A Hybrid Tea that grows to 4ft (1.25m)
tall and 2ft (60cm) wide, with a strong,
upright habit. The scented flowers that
bloom continuously throughout summer
are deep pink in bud. Hardy to -10°F
(-23°C), US zones 6–10, but susceptible
to mildew. A cross between a seedling and
'Peace', raised by Tantau in Germany and
launched in 1957.

ROSE 'WENDY CUSSONS'
(right)   A Hybrid Tea
that grows to 2ft (60cm)
tall and as wide,
although the climbing
variety can reach 7ft
(2m). Scented flowers
open throughout
summer. Tolerant of
poor soils, hardy to
-10°F (-23°C), US
zones 6–10, but hates
wet weather when in flower.
A cross between a seedling of
'Independence' and probably
'Eden Rose', raised by Gregory in
Britain in 1959 and launched in the US
by Ilgenfritz in 1963.

ROSE 'RAUBRITTER'   A Hybrid
Macrantha that grows to 3½ft (1m) tall
and 7ft (2m) wide. The semi-double, in-
curving blooms, which flower profusely in
clusters around midsummer, have a good
scent. This variety will tolerate poor soils,
some shade and temperatures of -20°F
(-29°C), US zones 5–10, but it is
susceptible to mildew. A cross between
'Daisy Hill' and 'Solarium', raised by
Kordes in Germany and launched in 1936.

ROSE 'REGENSBERG'   A 'hand-
painted' Floribunda that grows to 2ft
(60cm) tall and 1½ft (45cm) wide, with a
compact, bushy habit. Free-flowering and
well-scented, repeating throughout
summer, it is hardy to -30°F (-35°C), US
zones 4–10. A cross between 'Geoff
Boycott' and 'Old Master' raised by
McGredy in New Zealand and launched
in 1979.

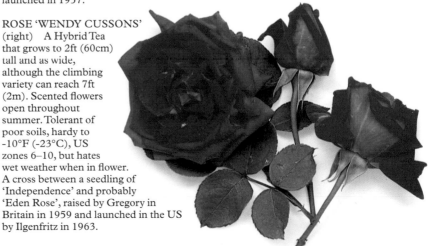

157

Roses grown beautifully between topiary walls and buttresses

**ROSE 'THE TIMES'** A Floribunda that grows to 2ft (60cm) tall and as wide, with a bushy habit and some scent. Very free-flowering and repeating throughout summer. Flowers may be pale pink in cold weather. The leaves are dark green and very healthy. Hardy to -30°F (-35°C), US zones 4–10, with good disease resistance. A cross between 'Tornado' and 'Redgold', it was raised by Kordes in Germany and launched in 1985.

**ROSE 'PAPA MEILLAND'** A Hybrid Tea that grows to 3ft (90cm) tall and 2ft (60cm) wide, with a bushy upright habit and excellent scent. It blooms repeatedly throughout summer. Hardy to -10°F (-23°C), US zones 6–10, but susceptible to blackspot and mildew. A cross between 'Chrysler Imperial' and 'Charles Mallerin', raised by Meilland in France and launched in 1963.

**ROSE 'PROSPERO'** An English Rose that grows to 2ft (60cm) tall and 3ft (90cm) wide. The medium, fully double blooms flower throughout summer and have a strong Old Rose scent. Thrives in good soil, hardy to -20°F (-29°C), US zones 5–10, but susceptible to mildew and blackspot. A cross between 'The Knight' and 'Château de Clos Vougeot', raised by David Austin in Britain and launched in 1982.

**ROSE 'RUBY WEDDING'** A Hybrid Tea that grows to 2ft (60cm) tall and as wide with a bushy spreading habit and some scent. It blooms abundantly throughout summer. Tolerant of poor soils and hardy to 10°F (-12°C), US zones 7–10, but susceptible to some blackspot. A cross between 'Mayflower' and an unknown rose, raised by Gregory in England and launched in 1979.

**ROSE 'MARJORIE FAIR'**, 'Red Ballerina', 'Red Yesterday' A Modern Shrub rose that grows to 4ft (1.25m) tall and 3ft (90cm) wide, with a bushy habit and some scent. Repeat-flowering throughout the summer. Tolerant of poor soils, some shade and hardy to -20°F (-29°C), US zones 5–10. A cross between 'Ballerina' and 'Baby Faurax', raised by Harkness in Britain and launched in 1978.

**ROSE 'HANNAH GORDON'** (right) A Floribunda that grows to 3ft (90cm) tall and 2ft (60 cm) wide. Very free-flowering, repeating throughout summer and hanging in big clusters with some scent. Tolerates poor soils and hardy to -30°F (-35°C), US zones 4–10. A cross between a seedling and 'Bordure', it was raised by Kordes in Germany and launched in 1983.

**ROSE 'MODERN ART'**, 'Prince de Monaco' A Hybrid Tea that grows to 3¹/₂ft (1m) tall and 2ft (60cm) wide, blooming abundantly throughout the summer. This variety is hardy to -10°F (-23°C), US zones 6–10. Rose 'Modern Art' was raised by Poulson in Denmark and launched in 1984.

'Prospero'

'Ruby Wedding'

'Marjorie Fair'

ROSE 'ALEC'S RED'   A Hybrid Tea that grows to 4ft (1.25m) tall and 2ft (60cm) wide, although the climbing variety can reach 8ft (2.5m) tall. Beautifully scented flowers bloom throughout summer. Tolerant of poor soils and hardy to -10°F (-23°C), US zones 6–10. A cross between 'Fragrant Cloud' and 'Dame de Cœur', raised by Cocker in Scotland and launched in 1973.

'Papa Meilland'

'Alec's Red'

ROSE 'MAGIC CARROUSEL' (above) A Miniature or patio rose that grows to 12in (30cm) tall, with an upright habit. The slightly scented flowers bloom in small clusters throughout the summer. Hardy to -10°F (-23°C), US zones 6–10 and inclined to leggy growth unless pinched back. A cross between 'Little Darling' and 'Westmont', raised by Moore in the US and launched in 1972.

'Modern Art'

'The Times'

# CLIMBING ROSES

'Mme Alfred Carrière'

**ROSE 'Mme ALFRED CARRIÈRE'**
A Noisette climber or sprawling shrub
that grows to 20ft (6m) tall and 10ft (3m)
wide. Beautifully scented blooms appear
in late spring and early summer, and are
produced intermittently after the main
crop. Tolerates poor soils, some shade and
hardy to 0°F (-18°C), US zones 7–10.
Raised by Schwartz in France and
launched in 1879.

**ROSE 'SALLY HOLMES'**  A Modern
Shrub rose that grows to 5ft (1.5m) tall
and 4ft (1.25m) wide, with an upright
habit. Single blooms repeat almost
continuously throughout summer and
have a slight scent. Will grow in some
shade and is hardy to -20°F (-29°C), US
zones 5–10, with good disease resistance.
A cross between 'Ivory Fashion' and
'Ballerina', raised by Holmes in Britain
and launched in 1976.

**ROSE 'ADÉLAIDE D'ORLÉANS'**
A Rambler that grows to 15ft (4.5m) tall
and 10ft (3m) wide, with a long, lax habit.
Produces scented flowers in midsummer
with an occasional few late blooms.
Tolerant of poor soils and some shade, but
hardy to only -15°F (-26°C), US zones
5/6–10 and susceptible to mildew. A *Rosa
sempervirens* hybrid Rambler, raised by
Jacques in France and launched in 1826.

**ROSE 'ALBÉRIC BARBIER'**
A Rambler that grows to 17 ft (5.25m) tall
and 10ft (3m) wide, and has a good scent,
reminiscent of apples. Although flowering
mainly in summer, many blooms are
produced through the season to autumn.
Hardy to -10°F (-23°C), US zones 6–10.
A cross between *R. wichuraiana* and
'Shirley Hibbard', raised by Barbier in
France and launched in 1900.

**ROSE 'AIMÉE VIBERT'**, 'Bouquet de
la Mariée, 'Nivea'  A Noisette climber or
sprawling shrub that grows to 15ft (4.5m)
tall and 10ft (3m) wide. Flowers, with a
fragrant, musky scent, appear after midsummer and repeat in a good season.
Tolerant of poor soils, some shade and
hardy to 0°F (-18°C), US zones 7–10. A
cross between 'Champneys' Pink Cluster'
and a *Rosa sempervirens* hybrid, raised by
Vibert in France and launched in 1828.

**THE BUTTONHOLE ROSE**
**ROSE 'CÉCILE BRÜNNER'**
**CLIMBING**   A very vigorous Climbing
Polyantha that grows to 24ft (7m) tall and
20ft (6m) wide. The small double flowers
bloom in summer, growing in clusters
with good scent. Tolerant of poor soils,
some shade, a northerly aspect and hardy
to -10°F (-23°C), US zones 6–10. A sport
of 'Cécile Brünner', raised by Pernet-
Ducher in France and launched in 1981.

*ROSA FILIPES* 'KIFTSGATE'
A selection of the wild rose species *Rosa
filipes* that reaches up to 40ft (12m) tall
and 20ft (6m) wide. The small single
blooms flower in late summer and
autumn, growing in huge, well-scented
clusters. Tolerant of poor soils, some
shade, a northerly aspect and hardy to
-10°F (-23°C), US zones 6–10. Native to
China, 'Kiftsgate' was planted at Kiftsgate
Court in Gloucestershire in 1938.

**ROSE 'ICEBERG'**, 'Fée des Neiges',
'Schneewittchen'  A Floribunda that
grows to 3ft (90cm) tall and 2ft (60 cm)
wide. Very free-flowering, repeating
almost continuously throughout the
summer, with some scent. Tolerant of
poor soils and hardy to -30°F (-35°C),
US zones 4–10, but susceptible to

'Sally Holmes'

'Wedding Day'

'Rambling Rector'

'Aimée Vibert'

*Rosa filipes* 'Kiftsgate'

blackspot. A cross between 'Robin Hood' and 'Virgo', raised by Kordes in Germany and launched in 1958.

ROSE 'RAMBLING RECTOR'
A rampant Rambler that grows to 20ft (6m) tall and 15ft (4.5m) wide, producing a superb show of scented flowers once only in summer. Will tolerate poor soils, some shade, a northerly aspect and hardy to -10°F (-23°C), US zones 6–10. A hybrid of unknown origin, it has been grown since 1912.

ROSE 'WEDDING DAY'   A rampant Rambler that grows to 24ft (7m) tall and 15ft (4.5m) wide. Flowers only once in summer, but makes a superb show and the scent is good. Will tolerate poor soils, some shade, a northerly aspect and is hardy to -10°F (-23°C), US zones 6–10. The flowers are spoiled by rain, becoming spotted with dull red. Raised from a seedling by Sir Frederick Stern in Britain and introduced in 1950.

'Iceberg'

*Rosa filipes* 'Kiftsgate'

'Adélaide d'Orléans'

'Cécile Brünner'

'Albéric Barbier'

# CLIMBING ROSES

'Lady Hillingdon'

'Maréchal Neil'

'Golden Showers'

ROSE 'MERMAID' (right)
A Hybrid of *Rosa bracteata* that grows to 30ft (9m) tall and 20ft (6m) wide. It is a vigorous, almost evergreen climber, tolerating some shade, a northerly aspect and temperatures of 0°F (-18°C), US zones 7–10. Although resistant to disease it is not very hardy and may be cut down to the ground in cold winters. A cross between a Tea rose and *Rosa bracteata*, it was raised by Paul in Britain and launched in 1918.

ROSE 'ALCHYMIST',
'Alchemist','Alchymiste'
A large-flowered Climber or giant shrub rose with some scent that reaches to 18ft (5.5m) tall and 8ft (2.5m) wide. Although flowering only once in summer, it makes a beautiful show and will tolerate poor soils and some shade. Hardy to -10°F (-23°C), US zones 6–10, but susceptible to blackspot. A cross between 'Golden Glow' and a *Rosa rubiginosa* hybrid, raised by Kordes in Germany and launched in 1956.

ROSE 'GOLDEN SHOWERS'
A large-flowered Floribunda climber with some scent that can also be grown as a free-standing shrub. It reaches 12ft (3.5m) tall and 6ft (1.8m) wide, flowering throughout summer. Tolerates poor soils and is resistant to disease. Hardy to -10°F (-23°C), US zones 6–10. A cross between 'Charlotte Armstrong' and 'Captain Thomas', raised by Lammerts in the US and launched in 1956.

ROSE 'MAIGOLD'   A Modern Climber or large shrub with a rampant, climbing habit and a good scent that grows to 20ft (6m) tall and 8ft (2.5m) wide. Tolerates poor soils, some shade and a northerly aspect. Hardy -20°F (-29°C), US zones 5–10. A cross between 'Poulsen's Pink' and 'Frühlingstag', raised by Kordes in Germany and launched in 1953. One of the first of the modern roses to burst into flower.

ROSE 'DESPREZ À FLEURS
JAUNES'   A Noisette climber that grows to 15ft (4.5m) tall and 10ft (3m) wide, and can also be grown as a shrub. It has beautifully scented flowers in late spring to early summer, repeating intermittently thereafter. Tolerant of poor soils and some shade and hardy to 0°F (-18°C), US zones 7–10. A cross between 'Blush Noisette' and 'Parks' Yellow China', raised by Desprez in France.

ROSE 'BREATH OF LIFE'   A Hybrid Tea climber that grows to 9ft (2.75m) tall and 6ft (1.8m) wide with a pleasant scent. Needs good drainage and, if possible, full sun. This variety tolerates temperatures of -10°F (-23°C), US zones 6–10. Rose 'Breath of Life' is a cross between 'Red Dandy' and 'Alexander'. It was raised by Harkness in Britain and launched in 1982.

ROSE 'MARÉCHAL NEIL'
A slightly tender Tea Noisette that grows to 15ft (4.5m) tall. Very popular in Victorian conservatories, this repeat-flowering rose is very fragrant. Hardy to 0°F (-18°C), US zones 7–10. A seedling from 'Cloth of Gold', raised by Pradel in France and launched in 1864.

ROSE 'GLOIRE DE DIJON', 'The Old Glory Rose'   A climbing Tea with a good scent that grows to 13ft (4m) tall and 8ft (2.5m) wide. Blooms repeatedly throughout the summer and will tolerate 0°F (-18°C), US zones 7–10, but is slightly susceptible to blackspot. A Tea-Bourbon hybrid created by crossing a yellow Tea rose with 'Souvenir de la Malmaison'. Raised by Jacotot in France in 1853.

ROSE 'LADY HILLINGDON'
A climbing Tea with purple leaves and a fine scent that grows to 13ft (4m) tall. Repeat flowering and not really tender except in very cold areas. Hardy to 0°F (-18°C), US zones 7–10. A cross between 'Papa Gontier' x 'Mme Hoste'. Raised by Lowe & Shawyer in Britain and launched in 1910.

'Maigold'

'Desprez à Fleurs Jaunes'

'Breath of Life'

'Alchymist'

'Alchymist'

'Gloire de Dijon'

'American Pillar'

'Complicata'

'Zéphirine Drouhin'

'Alexandre Girault'

'Mme Grégoire Staechelin'

ROSE 'ALEXANDRE GIRAULT'
A Rambler that grows to at least 20ft (6m) tall and 12ft (3.5m) wide. Flowers, with a scent reminiscent of apples, bloom once in summer. Tolerates poor soils, some shade and hardy to -10°F (-23°C) US zones 6–10. A cross between *Rosa wichuraiana* and 'Papa Gontier', raised by Barbier in France and launched in 1909.

ROSE 'AMERICAN PILLAR'
A robust Rambler that grows to 17ft (5.25m) tall and 10ft (3m) wide. Flowers have a light scent and bloom only once in summer. Tolerates poor soils, some shade and is hardy to -10°F (-23°C), US zones 6–10. Susceptible to mildew. A cross between *R. wichuraiana* and *R. setigera* 'Red Letter Day', raised by Van Fleet in the US and launched in 1902.

ROSE 'Mme GRÉGOIRE STAECHELIN'   A climbing Hybrid Tea that grows to 16ft (5m) tall and 10ft (3m) wide. Flowers with a good scent produced in late spring. Tolerates poor soils, some shade, a northerly aspect and hardy to -10°F (-23°C), US zones 6–10, with good disease resistance. This Hybrid Tea is a cross between 'Frau Kark Druschki' and

'Château de Clos Vougeot', raised by Dot in Spain and launched in 1927.

ROSE 'BLAIRII NO. 2'   A Hybrid China that grows to 12ft (3.5m) tall and 6ft (1.8m) wide. Can be trained as a climber. Semi-double scented blooms flower mainly in summer, with a few scattered flowers occurring later. Hardy to 0°F (-18°C), US zones 7–10, but susceptible to mildew. A cross between a China rose and 'Tuscany', raised by Blair in Britain and launched in 1845.

ROSE 'COMPASSION', 'Belle de Londres'   A climbing Hybrid Tea that grows to 10ft (3m) tall and 6ft (1.8m) wide. Beautifully scented flowers bloom repeatedly throughout summer. This variety will tolerate poor soils and is hardy to -10°F (-23°C), US zones 6–10, with good disease resistance. One of the most popular modern climbers. A cross between 'White Cockade' and 'Prima Ballerina', raised by Harkness in Britain and launched in 1972.

ROSE 'COMPLICATA'   A Gallica that grows to 10ft (3m) high and 6ft (1.8m) wide. It is a large, vigorous shrub with a climbing habit. Blooms up to 5in (12cm) across, with a wonderful scent, flower in summer. Tolerant of poor soils, some shade and hardy to -30°F (-35°C), US zones 4–10. Lovely planted to grow up through a small tree. Possibly a cross between *Rosa gallica* and *Rosa canina*, its origins are unknown.

### ROSE 'CONSTANCE SPRY'
An English Rose that makes a climber or large shrub, reaching 20ft (6m) tall and 10ft (3m) wide. The large double blooms appear only once in the summer and have a very good scent, likened to myrrh. Tolerates poor soils, some shade and is hardy to -20°F (-29°C), US zones 5–10, with good disease resistance. A cross between 'Belle Isis' and 'Dainty Maid', raised by David Austin in Britain and launched in 1961.

### ROSE 'HANDEL'
A large-flowered Floribunda climber that grows to 12ft (3.5m) tall and 8ft (2.5m) wide. The semi-double slightly scented blooms which flower repeatedly throughout the summer into winter, are pale pinky-cream edged with pink. Tolerates poor soils and -20°F (-29°C), US zones 5–10. A cross between 'Columbine' and 'Heidelberg', raised by McGredy in Northern Ireland and launched in 1965.

### ROSE 'Mme ISAAC PEREIRE' (above)
A Bourbon that grows to 6ft (1.8m) tall and 4ft (1.25m) wide. Can be grown as a bush or a climber, when it can reach 10ft (3m). Flowers with a rich scent bloom from midsummer to autumn. Tolerant of poor soils, some shade and hardy to -20°F (-29°C), US zones 5–10. Raised by Garçon in France and launched in 1881.

### ROSE 'WILLIAM LOBB', 'Old Velvet Moss'
A Damask Moss that grows to 10ft (3m) tall and 5ft (1.5m) wide and forms a tall lank shrub. Flowers bloom at midsummer and only have a very good scent in sun. This variety will tolerate poor soil and temperatures of -20°F (-29°C), US zones 5–10. A Damask Moss with a quarter China in its ancestry, raised by Laffay in France and launched in 1855.

### ROSE 'ZÉPHIRINE DROUHIN'
A climbing Bourbon that grows to 8ft (2.5m) tall and 6ft (1.8m) wide, but can be trained to 13ft (4m). Sweetly scented flowers from midsummer to autumn. Tolerant of poor soil, shade and a northerly aspect. Hardy to -20°F (-29°C), US zones 5–10, but suffers slightly from blackspot and mildew, especially if grown on a wall. Raised by Bizot in France and launched in 1868. The best climber for a shady spot.

'Constance Spry'

'William Lobb'

'Handel'

'Blairii No. 2'

'Compassion'

'Ena Harkness'

'Danse du Feu'

ROSE 'VEILCHENBLAU' (above)
A vigorous Rambler that grows to 13ft
(4m) tall and 12ft (3.5m) wide.
Numerous flowers appear only once
during the summer, growing in large
clusters, with a scent reminiscent of
apples. Tolerant of poor soils, some shade,
a northerly aspect and hardy to -10°F
(-23°C), US zones 6–10. A cross between
'Crimson Rambler' and 'Erinnerung an
Brod'. It is a Hybrid Multiflora Rambler,
raised by Schmidt in Germany and
launched in 1909.

ROSE 'PAUL'S SCARLET CLIMBER'
This is a large-flowered Climber that
grows to 20ft (6m) tall and 8ft (2.5m)
wide. Flowers, with a scent reminiscent of
apples, bloom mainly in summer but with
many later flowers through the season to
early winter. One of the healthiest
climbers, tolerant of poor soils, some
shade, a northerly aspect and hardy to
-10°F (-23°C), US zones 6–10. A cross
between *Rosa wichuraiana* and a Hybrid
Tea, raised by Paul in Britain and
launched in 1916.

ROSE 'DANSE DU FEU', 'Spectacular'
A large-flowered Floribunda climber that
grows to 16ft (5m) tall and 8ft (2.5m)
wide. Free-flowering, with little scent and
largish double blooms repeating
throughout summer. This variety will
tolerate some shade and -20°F (-29°C),
US zones 5–10 , but susceptible to black
spot. A cross between 'Paul's Scarlet
Climber' and a *Rosa multiflora* seedling,
raised by Mallerin in France and
launched in 1953.

ROSE 'ENA HARKNESS' CLIMBING
A climbing Hybrid Tea that grows to 12ft
(3.5m) tall and 8ft (2.5m) wide. Large
double flowers, with an excellent old-rose
scent, bloom abundantly throughout
summer. Hardy to -10°F (-23°C), US
zones 6–10. A climbing sport of 'Ena
Harkness', it was introduced by Murrell
in 1954.

ROSE 'FRED LOADS'   A low climbing
Floribunda that reaches up to 5ft (1.5m)
tall and 4ft (1.25m) wide, with an upright
habit. Free-flowering, repeating almost
continuously throughout the summer,
with some scent. Hardy to -30°F (-35°C),

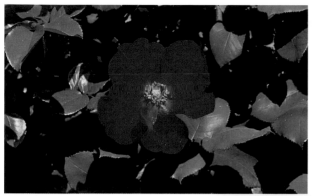

'Altissimo'

'Masquerade'

US zones 4–10. A cross between 'Orange Sensation' and 'Dorothy Wheatcroft', raised by Holmes and launched in 1967.

ROSE 'DUBLIN BAY' A large-flowered Floribunda climber that grows to 12ft (3.5m) tall and 8ft (2.5m) wide. Flowers with some scent repeat throughout summer and grow in clusters. Hardy to -20°F (-29°C), US zones 5–10. A cross between 'Bantry Bay' and 'Altissimo', raised by McGredy in Northern Ireland and launched in 1976.

ROSE 'ALTISSIMO' A Floribunda climber or large shrub that grows to 12ft (3.5m) tall and 6ft (1.8m) wide. Flowers with some scent repeat throughout the summer. Tolerant of poor soils and hardy to -10°F (-23°C), US zones 6–10. A cross between 'Tenor' and an unknown seedling, raised by Delbard-Chabart in France and launched in 1966. This particular variety is suitable for growing as a pillar rose or on a trellis.

ROSE 'MASQUERADE' CLIMBING A climbing Floribunda that grows to 13ft (4m) tall and 8ft (2.5m) wide; a shrub variety grows to 4ft (1.25m) tall and 3ft (90cm) wide. Flowering only once in summer but with some later blooms hanging in big clusters, with only a little scent. Hardy to -30°F (-35°C), US zones 4–10. A climbing sport of the familiar Floribunda ' Masquerade', introduced by Dillon in 1958.

ROSE 'SUMMER WINE' A large-flowered Climber that grows to 10ft (3m) tall and 6ft (2.5m) wide, with a bushy upright habit. Well-scented flowers, growing in clusters, bloom throughout summer. Tolerates poor soils and is hardy to -20°F (-29°C), US zones 5–10. A Modern Climber, raised by Kordes in Germany and launched in 1985.

'Paul's Scarlet Climber'

'Dublin Bay'

'Fred Loads'

'Summer Wine'

*Helleborus orientalis*

*Helleborus foetidus*

CHAPTER FOUR

# Perennials

*In this chapter all the hardy plants are arranged by their flowering times, starting with the very early ones – hellebores to peonies, irises and on to daylilies – through to the very late-flowering plants such as daisies and asters. A selection of tender plants are found at the end of the chapter.*

CORSICAN HELLEBORE *Helleborus argutifolius* (syn. *H. corsicus*)   An evergreen perennial that grows up to 2ft (60cm) tall, forming clumps of erect leafy stems, rather wider than tall. It produces large, branched clusters of pale yellow-green, cup-shaped flowers, each about 1½in (4cm) wide, in late winter. Hardy to 0°F (-18°C), US zones 7–9. Native to Corsica and Sardinia.

STINKING HELLEBORE *Helleborus foetidus*   An evergreen perennial that grows to 2½ft (75cm) tall, forming clumps of erect stems rather wider than tall. In late winter it produces large, branched clusters of flowers, each about ¾in (2cm) wide. Hardy to -10°F (-23°C), US zones 6–9. Native to much of western Europe, where it has long been cultivated. When planted among the large simple leaves of hostas, it makes an effective contrast of textures.

*Helleborus niger*

CHRISTMAS ROSE *Helleborus niger*   An evergreen perennial that grows to 1ft (30cm) tall, bearing flowers up to 3in (8cm) wide, sometimes tinged pink on the outside, in late winter. The fruit is a cluster of light green pods whose sap can blister the skin. Needs a fertile limy soil and a partially shaded position. Hardy to -30°F (-35°C), US zones 4–8. Native to central and eastern Europe. Not always easy to grow well and may need some protection from slugs and snails.

*Helleborus niger*

*Helleborus argutifolius*

*Ranunculus aconitifolius*

*Caltha palustris* var. *alba*

*Caltha palustris*

*Caltha palustris* 'Flore Pleno'

**LENTEN ROSE** *Helleborus orientalis*
An evergreen perennial that grows to 1ft (30cm) tall, forming clumps of handsome foliage. Flowers about 2in (5cm) wide appear in late winter. Fruit sap can blister the skin. Hardy to -20°F (-29°C), US zones 5–9. The leaves may be infected by a fungus disease causing black spots. Native to Greece, Turkey and the Caucasus.

**MARSH MARIGOLD** *Caltha palustris*
An herbaceous perennial that grows up to 2ft (60cm) tall and is as wide. It produces loose clusters of brilliant yellow flowers, each about 1½in (4cm) wide, in early spring. It should have a sunny position and is hardy to -30°F (-35°C), US zones 4–10. Native to North America, Europe and much of Asia and has long been in cultivation, often growing as a common wildflower.

*Caltha palustris* var. *alba* Loose clusters of milk-white flowers for much of the spring and often into early summer. Thought to originate in the Himalayas, this variety is well established in cultivation, being happy to grow in the wettest ground.

*Caltha palustris* 'Flore Pleno' This variety grows to 1ft (30cm) tall and usually a little wider. Flowers, 1in (2.5cm) wide, with many petals. A compact and long-flowering form, it is equally happy growing by a pond or stream.

*Ranunculus aconitifolius* A perennial that grows to 2ft (60cm) tall, bearing flowers, up to ½in (1cm) across, in summer. Hardy to -20°F (-29°C) or less, US zone 5. Native to Europe, growing in subalpine meadows and by streams at up to 8750ft (2500m).

169

Dicentra formosa 'Zestful'

Dicentra spectabilis var. alba

Dicentra formosa

Dicentra 'Bountiful'

Dicentra 'Langtrees'

Dicentra eximea

Dicentra spectabilis

Dicentra 'Adrian Bloom'

Dicentra formosa 'Stuart Boothman'

½ life size. Specimens from Wisley, 14 April

Dicentra eximea 'Alba'

**Anemone sylvestris** An herbaceous perennial that grows to 1½ft (45cm) tall, spreading gently by the roots to form compact colonies. Erect stems of flowers, each about 1½–2½ (4–6cm) wide, in spring or early summer. Best in a lightly shaded position and hardy to -20°F (-29°C), US zones 5–10. Native to much of northern Europe.

**Dicentra eximea** A plant that forms compact patches with a creeping rhizome, flowering throughout summer. Flowers ¾in (2cm) long, pinkish or white with reflexed outer petals. Prefers moist but well-drained soil, growing well on shaded rock outcrops. Hardy to -30°F (-35°C), US zones 4–10. Native to eastern North America.
  **Dicentra eximea 'Alba'** Produces pure white flowers.

**Dicentra formosa** A slow creeping herbaceous perennial that grows to about 1½ft (45cm) tall and rather wider, forming small patches in forest and woodland, in shaded dry or damp places. Loose, drooping sprays of locket-shaped flowers, each ½in (1cm) long, in late spring and early summer. Plant in autumn or spring in a cool, partially shaded position. Hardy to -20°F (-29°C), US zones 5–8. Native to western North America.
  **Dicentra formosa 'Alba'** Produces pure white flowers.
  Dicentra formosa 'Stuart Boothman' Light pink flowers, each about ½in (1cm) long. Raised in Britain in this century.
  **Dicentra formosa 'Zestful'** Flowers paler pink and does better in full sun due to the paler greyer leaves.
  **Dicentra 'Adrian Bloom'** Narrow greyish leaves and deep pink flowers.
  **Dicentra 'Bountiful'** Deep purplish-red flowers.
  Dicentra 'Langtrees' (syn. 'Pearldrops') Pink-tipped white flowers, each nearly ¾in (2cm).

BLEEDING HEART **Dicentra spectabilis** A clump forming herbaceous perennial that grows to 2ft (60cm) tall, rather wider than tall. Sprays of flowers about 1in (2.5cm) long appear in late spring. It prefers a cool, partially shaded position and is hardy to -20°F (-29°C), US zones 5–8. Native to northern China.
  **Dicentra spectabilis 'Alba'** Produces flowers that are pure white.

**Epimedium x youngianum 'Niveum'** An herbaceous perennial plant that grows to 8in (20cm) tall. Flowers, each ¾in (2cm) wide, appear in early spring. Sun or partial shade and hardy to -10°F (-23°C), US zones 6–9. Excellent ground-cover plant for damp, shady places and is one of the most elegant of epimediums.

*Epimedium* x *perralchicum* 'Fröhnleiten' An evergreen perennial that grows to 1¹/₂ft (45cm) tall, forming spreading clumps wider than tall. Flowers about ³/₄in (2cm) wide appear in early spring. Happy in sun or partial shade and hardy to 0°F (-18°C), US zones 7–10.

PASQUE FLOWER *Pulsatilla vulgaris* (syn. *Anemone pulsatilla*) An herbaceous perennial that grows to 1ft (30cm) tall. Rich purple flowers, each about 2in (5cm) wide, in spring. Can be planted in autumn or spring in well-drained soil in a sunny position. Hardy to -10°F (-23°C), US zones 6–8. Native to northern Europe, this perennial, beautiful both in flower and in fruit, has long been cherished in gardens. It is easily grown either in a rock garden or in the front of a border.

*Pulsatilla vulgaris* f. *alba* Produces pure white flowers.

*Pulsatilla vulgaris* f. *rubra* Produces red flowers.

*Epimedium* x *youngianum* 'Niveum'

*Epimedium* x *perralchicum* 'Fröhnleiten'

*Pulsatilla vulgaris*

*Anemone sylvestris*

*Pulsatilla vulgaris* f. *alba*

*Pulsatilla vulgaris* f. *rubra*

171

*Euphorbia characias* subsp. *characias*

*Euphorbia griffithii* 'Fireglow'

*Euphorbia amygdaloides* 'Rubra'

LADY'S SMOCK *Cardamine pratensis* 'Flore Pleno'   An herbaceous perennial that grows to 1ft (30cm) tall, producing flowers ³/₄in (2cm) wide. Best in a sunny position and hardy to -20°F (-29°C), US zones 5–9. Grows wild in much of Europe and North America. Very ornamental for some months in early spring.

*Erysimum* 'Bowles' Mauve'   An evergreen perennial or sub-shrub that grows to 3ft (90cm) tall. From spring and for much of the summer, it produces a succession of flowers each about ³/₄in (2cm) wide. Best in a warm, sunny position and hardy to 0°F (-18°C), US zones 7–10.  It has a wonderful combination of flower and foliage colour over a very long season.

*Erysimum cheiri* 'Harpur Crewe'
An evergreen perennial that grows to 1¹/₂ft (45cm) tall and usually as wide. In spring it produces sweet-scented flowers, each about 2cm wide, with a mixture of yellow, buff and bronze. Best in a warm, sunny position and hardy to 0°F (-18°C), US zones 7–10.

DAME'S VIOLET *Hesperis matronalis*
An herbaceous perennial that grows to 4ft (1.25m) tall, producing open clusters of white or pink flowers with a strong sweet evening scent, in early summer. Hardy to -30°F (-35°C), US zones 4–8. Native to southern Europe but commonly naturalized elsewhere.

*Euphorbia characias* subsp. *characias*
An evergreen perennial that grows to 5ft (1.5m) tall. In early spring each stem ends in a large broad cluster of bright light-green long-lasting flowers, each about

³/₄in (2cm) wide. Hardy to 10°F (-12°C), US zones 8–10 or a little lower. Native to much of the Mediterranean region, from where it was introduced into cultivation in the 19th century.
*Euphorbia characias* subsp. *wulfenii*   The flowers are a much more yellow-green.

*Euphorbia griffithii* 'Dixter'
An herbaceous perennial plant that grows to 2ft (60cm) tall, spreading at the root to form colonies considerably wider than tall. In early summer the erect leafy stems bear clusters of bright reddish-orange flowers, about ³/₄in (2cm) wide. Reddish-purple leaves with dark red bracts. Hardy to -10°F (-23°C), US zones 6–10. Native to the Himalayas.
*Euphorbia griffithii* 'Fireglow'   Dark green leaves with a pale midrib. This variety is a recent selection and is a most useful colonizer for a border. It is equally suitable for a semi-wild area in the garden, planted along with ferns and other foliage plants.

WOOD SPURGE *Euphorbia amygdaloides* (right)   An evergreen plant that grows to 2ft (60cm) tall, spreading gently at the root to form colonies wider than it is tall. Erect, reddish-purple stems with clusters of small yellow flowers, each held within a collar of bright yellow-green bracts, ³/₄in (2cm) wide, are produced in spring. Thrives in partial shade but foliage colour is brighter in sun. Hardy to 0°F (-18°C), US zones 7–9 or a little lower. Grows wild in much of Europe.
*Euphorbia amygdaloides* 'Rubra'   Deep purple leaves. This plant brings unusual foliage colouring to the border, the leaves contrasting well with the flowers.

Euphorbias under birches in Beth Chatto's garden

*Euphorbia characias* subsp. *wulfenii*

*Euphorbia griffithii* 'Dixter'

*Hesperis matronalis*

*Erysimum cheiri* 'Harpur Crewe'

*Erysimum* 'Bowles Mauve'

*Cardamine pratensis* 'Flore Pleno'

*Bergenia purpurascens*

*Bergenia* 'Beethoven'

*Bergenia cordifolia*

*Bergenia* 'Bressingham White'

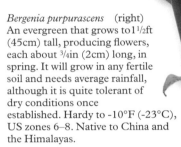

*Bergenia* 'Sunshade'

*Bergenia purpurascens* (right) An evergreen that grows to 1¹⁄₂ft (45cm) tall, producing flowers, each about ³⁄₄in (2cm) long, in spring. It will grow in any fertile soil and needs average rainfall, although it is quite tolerant of dry conditions once established. Hardy to -10°F (-23°C), US zones 6–8. Native to China and the Himalayas.

*Bergenia cordifolia* An evergreen that grows to 1¹⁄₂ft (45cm) tall, forms low clumps and produces dense heads of mauve-pink flowers, each about ³⁄₄in (2cm) wide, in spring. Hardy to -40°F (-40°C), US zones 3–8. Native to Siberia, from where it was introduced into cultivation in the 18th century.

*Bergenia* 'Bressingham White' An evergreen that grows to 1ft (30cm) tall, producing dense heads of white flowers, each about ³⁄₄in (2cm) wide, on short, stout stems. It prefers a cool position in partial shade. Hardy to -40°F (-40°C), US zones 3–8. It is a hybrid raised in Britain in the 20th century.

*Bergenia* 'Sunshade' An evergreen that grows up to 1ft (30cm) tall, producing dense heads of lilac-pink flowers, each about ¹⁄₂in (1cm) wide, on stout stems. Hardy to -40°F (-40°C), US zones 3–8. A garden hybrid raised in Britain in the 20th century. This plant is useful for planting under small shrubs and for the front of a shady border.

*Bergenia* 'Sunningdale' An evergreen that grows to 15in (40cm) tall, producing dense heads of bright rose-pink flowers, each ³⁄₄in (2cm) wide, on stout stems. The leaves take on bronze or purple tints in autumn and winter. Tolerant of dry conditions once established and hardy to -40°F (-40°C), US zones 3–8.

*Bergenia* 'Beethoven'   An evergreen that grows to 1ft (30cm) tall, producing dense heads of white flowers, $3/4$in (2cm) wide, contrasting with a reddish calyx. Tolerant of dry conditions once established, it prefers a cool position in partial shade. Hardy to -40°F (-40°C), US zones 3–8. A hybrid raised in Britain in this century.

*Viola cornuta*   Up to 9in (23cm) tall, this perennial produces a succession of deep violet flowers, each about $1 1/4$in (3cm) wide, in summer. Hardy to -10°F (-23°C), US zones 6–8. Native to the Pyrenees, this is an important parent of many attractive perennial violas.
   *Viola cornuta* 'Lilacina'   A perennial that grows up to 9in (23cm) tall. In summer it produces a succession of pale blue-violet flowers. Native to the Pyrenees.
   *Viola cornuta* 'Boughton Blue' A perennial that grows up to 10in (25cm) tall, flowering in summer. Especially sought after for its beautiful pale blue flowers.

*Viola corsica* (syn. *Viola bertolonii*) A long-lived perennial with flowers to $1 1/4$in (3cm), violet, rarely yellow in spring and early summer. Hardy to 25°F (-4°C), US zone 9. Native to Corsica and Sardinia.

*Viola* 'Irish Molly'   A reliable perennial pansy that grows up to 9in (23cm) tall, producing a succession of slightly scented, rounded flowers, each about 1in (2.5cm) wide, with a curious but attractive combination of bronze and green with a dark centre in summer. The colouring of the flowers is unique. Hardy to -10°F (-23°C), US zones 6–8.

   *Viola* 'Ardross Gem' (left) A perennial that grows up to 6in (15cm) tall, producing a succession of purple and yellow flowers, each about 1in (2.5cm) wide, in summer. Hardy to -10°F (-23°C), US zones 6–8. This is one of many attractive and reliably perennial violas now available. All are useful for edging or for planting among other low perennials.

*Viola* 'Irish Molly'

*Viola cornuta*

*Bergenia* 'Sunningdale'

*Viola cornuta* 'Lilacina'

*Viola cornuta* 'Boughton Blue'

*Pachysandra terminalis* 'Variegata'

*Vinca minor* 'Argenteo-variegata'

*Vinca minor* 'Alba Variegata'

*Pachysandra terminalis*

*Pachysandra terminalis* An evergreen perennial that grows to 1ft (30cm) tall, flowering in spring. Hardy to -20°F (-29°C), US zones 5–9. Native to China and Japan, from where it was introduced into cultivation in the 19th century. It is a useful ground-cover plant for dry, shady places, valued for its neat, dense foliage.
*Pachysandra terminalis* 'Variegata' This has leaves edged with white.

*Phlox pilosa* An herbaceous perennial forming a clump of sprawling stems about 1ft (30cm) tall and usually wider. In spring and early summer it produces many flowers, each about 1in (2.5cm) wide, which may be light purple, pink or white. Hardy to -20°F (-29°C), US zones 5–9. Native to eastern North America.

*Phlox maculata* 'Alpha' An herbaceous perennial forming a clump of erect stems up to 3ft (90cm) tall. In early summer it produces cylindrical heads of slightly fragrant lilac-pink flowers, each about 1in (2.5cm) wide. Hardy to -20°F (-29°C), US zones 5–9. *Phlox maculata* is native to eastern North America.

*Phlox* 'Chattahoochee' An herbaceous perennial forming a clump of sprawling stems up to 8in (20cm) tall and wider. In spring and early summer it produces a succession of red-eyed, light lavender-blue flowers, each about 1in (2.5cm) wide. Hardy to -20°F (-29°C), US zones 5–9. Found in Florida in the mid-20th century and may be a natural hybrid.

*Pulmonaria angustifolia* An herbaceous perennial spreading to form mats up to 10in (25cm) tall. In spring it produces clusters of bright blue flowers, each about 1/2in (1cm) wide. The leaves become larger after the flowers fade. Hardy to -20°F (-29°C), US zones 5–8. Native to much of central Europe, where it was introduced into cultivation early in the 18th century.

*Pulmonaria officinalis* 'Sissinghurst White' An herbaceous perennial spreading slowly to form mats to 1ft (30cm) tall. In spring it produces clusters of flowers nearly 1/2in (1cm) wide. Hardy to -30°F (-35°C), US zones 4–8. Native to much of western and central Europe and introduced into cultivation by the late 16th century.

*Pulmonaria longifolia* 'Bertram Anderson' An herbaceous perennial forming clumps to 10in (25cm) tall. In spring it produces clusters of bright blue flowers, each about 1/2in (1cm) wide and opening from purple buds. Hardy to -10°F (-23°C), US zones 6–8. Native to much of western Europe.

*Pulmonaria rubra* 'David Ward' Usually the earliest pulmonaria to flower, making a clump up to 1ft (30cm) tall. In early spring it produces clusters of light coral-red flowers, each about 1/2in (1cm) wide. Hardy to -10°F (-23°C), US zones 6–8. *Pulmonaria rubra* is native to much of eastern Europe.

*Pulmonaria vallarsae* 'Margery Fish' An herbaceous perennial spreading to form mats up to 1 1/2ft (45cm) tall. In spring it produces clusters of bright coral-pink flowers, each over 1/2in (1cm) wide and turning purplish with age. Striking silvery leaves. Hardy to -10°F (-23°C), US zones 6–8. Native to Italy.

*Vinca minor* 'Alba Variegata' A creeping evergreen perennial forming extensive mats up to 6in (15cm) tall, the stems rooting as they go. A succession of small white flowers, each about 1in (2.5cm) wide, are produced in spring. Hardy to -10°F (-23°C), US zones 6–8. The blue flowered species is native to Europe and the Caucasus. An excellent ground-cover plant for shady places but can be invasive. Forms with variegated leaves, like 'Alba Variegata', tend to be less vigorous.
*Vinca minor* 'Argenteo-variegata' This variety has silver-edged leaves.

*Pulmonaria officinalis* 'Sissinghurst White'

*Pulmonaria vallarsae* 'Margery Fish'

*Pulmonaria longifolia* 'Bertram Anderson'

*Pulmonaria angustifolia*

*Pulmonaria rubra* 'David Ward'

*Phlox pilosa*

*Phlox* 'Chattahoochee'

*Phlox maculata* 'Alpha'

*Brunnera macrophylla*

*Brunnera macrophylla* 'Hadspen Cream'

*Lamium maculatum* 'Pink Pearl'

*Mertensia virginica*

*Ajuga reptans* 'Atropurpurea'

*Lamium maculatum* 'White Nancy'

Lamium maculatum 'Silbergroschen'

Ajuga reptans 'Atropurpurea'

Lamium maculatum 'Chequers'

Lamium maculatum 'Roseum'

Lamium maculatum 'Aureum'

Ajuga reptans 'Multicolor'

½ life size. Specimens from Eccleston Square, London, 12 April

**VIRGINIA COWSLIP or BLUE BELLS**
*Mertensia virginica* A perennial with a thick fleshy root and flowers about 1in (2.5cm) long in spring. The plant dies down soon after flowering and is completely dormant by midsummer. It prefers peaty soil in part shade or sun. Native to North America, found in wet meadows and along streams. Hardy to -40°F (-40°C), US zones 3–9.

*Ajuga reptans* 'Atropurpurea' A creeping evergreen perennial that grows to 6in (15cm) tall, producing erect spikes with several small, tubular, light-blue flowers arranged among large, leafy bracts, in spring. It grows equally well in sun or shade, although the leaves colour best in an open situation. Hardy to -20°F (-29°C), US zones 5–10. Native to most of Europe except for the far north, also North Africa and western Asia.
*Ajuga reptans* 'Multicolor' (syn. 'Tricolor', 'Rainbow') Leaves variegated with pink and white.

*Brunnera macrophylla* A clump forming herbaceous perennial that grows up to 1½ft (45cm) tall and is usually wider than it is tall. Sprays of small, intense blue flowers, each about ½in (1cm) wide, are produced in early spring. Hardy to -20°F (-29°C), US zones 5–8. Native to the Caucasus, from where it was introduced into cultivation early in the 18th century.
*Brunnera macrophylla* 'Hadspen Cream' The broad, heart-shaped leaves are boldly variegated with a rather narrow, creamy-white margin and enlarge after flowering to 6in (15cm) or longer.

*Lamium maculatum* 'Roseum' An herbaceous perennial that grows up to 10in (25cm) tall, with creeping stems forming mats much wider than it is tall. In spring and early summer it produces flowers, each about 1in (2.5cm) long. The leaves are heart-shaped and marked with a central silvery blotch. Hardy to -40°F (-40°C), US zones 3–8.

*Lamium maculatum* 'Aureum' Grows up to 8in (20cm) tall with leaves that are a bright greeny-yellow with a central silvery stripe.
*Lamium maculatum* 'White Nancy' Silvery leaves with a narrow, dark green margin.
*Lamium maculatum* 'Silbergroschen' (syn. 'Beacon Silver') Pinkish-purple flowers and white leaves, often with purple blotches caused by disease.
*Lamium maculatum* 'Chequers' A perennial that grows to 8in (20cm) tall with bright greenish-yellow leaves that have a broad central silvery stripe.
*Lamium maculatum* 'Pink Pearl' A new variety that grows up to 8in (20cm) tall, with the most delicate pearly-pink flushed flowers. 'Pink Pearl' bears green leaves with a broad central silver stripe.

*Lysichiton camtschatcensis*

*Lysichiton americanus*

*Acorus calamus* 'Variegatus'

*Acorus calamus* 'Variegatus'
An herbaceous perennial that grows to 3½ft (1m) tall, forming clumps wider than tall. In early summer it produces narrow, cone-like cream flower spikes about 2½in (6cm) long. The leaves have a pleasant spicy scent when crushed. Best in a sunny position and hardy to -10°F (-23°C), US zones 6–10. Native to eastern Asia and western North America.

## YELLOW SKUNK CABBAGE
*Lysichiton americanus* An herbaceous perennial that grows to 4ft (1.25m) tall. In spring it produces spectacular flowers, each consisting of a large bright yellow spathe, up to 8in (20cm) long, within which the true flowers form a yellowish column. Both flowers and foliage have a rather unpleasant scent. Hardy to 20°F (-7°C), US zones 5–9. It is free from pests and diseases, but young seedlings may be attacked by slugs. Native to western North America.

*Lysichiton camtschatcensis* A perennial that grows to 2½ft (75cm) tall, producing spectacular flowers in spring; each consists of a large white spathe, to 8in (20cm) long, within which the true flowers form a light green column. Unlike the American species, the flowers have a pleasant sweet scent. Plant in autumn or late spring in wet soil by a pond or stream. It should have a sunny position and is hardy to -10°F (-23°C), US zones 6–9. Young seedlings may be attacked by slugs.

*Aquilegia caerulea* An herbaceous perennial that grows to 2ft (60cm) tall, forming compact clumps, taller than wide. In summer it produces many flower about 2½in (6cm) wide. Hardy to -40°F (-40°C), US zones 3–10 or lower. Native to mountainous parts of southern North America and introduced into cultivation in the 19th century. This plant is a parent of many garden strains of long-spurred aquilegias.

*Lysichiton americanus* at Chyverton, Cornwall

*Aquilegia* 'Hensol Harebell' (left) An herbaceous perennial that grows to 2¹/₂ft (75cm) tall, producing flowers, each about 2in (5cm) wide, in summer. Hardy to -10°F (-23°C), US zones 6–10 or lower. Sometimes afflicted with aphids. A hybrid between *A. alpina* and *A. vulgaris*, which were both native to Europe and raised in Scotland early in the 20th century.

*Aquilegia* 'Mrs Scott Elliot' Hybrids' (above) A hybrid of *Aquilegia caerulea*. The state flower of Colorado, rather darker and more purple in colour than the typical wild type. Height to around 2¹/₂ft (75cm). Hardy to -20°F (-29°C), US zones 5–10 or lower.

*Aquilegia canadensis* Perennial that grows up to 2ft (60cm) tall, producing flowers, each about 1¹/₄in (3cm) long, in summer. It can be planted in autumn or early spring and is hardy to -40°F (-40°C), US zones 3–10 or lower. May be infested by aphids. Native to North America, from where it was introduced into cultivation in the 17th century. Like other species of aquilegia, this is an elegant and attractive plant and is suitable for a cool corner in a rock garden.

COLUMBINE *Aquilegia vulgaris* An herbaceous perennial that grows up to 3ft (90cm) tall, producing flowers, each about 1¹/₂in (4cm) wide, in summer. It prefers a sunny or partially shaded position with some shelter. Hardy to -30°F (-35°C), US zones 4–10 or lower. It is free from diseases but is sometimes afflicted with aphids. Native to much of Europe, it has long been cultivated in cottage gardens, showing interesting variations in colour when it is raised from seed.

*Aquilegia caerulea*

*Aquilegia vulgaris*

*Aquilegia canadensis*

*Aquilegia vulgaris* red seedling

*Helianthemum* hybrids, *Geranium sanguineum* and *Alchemilla mollis* at Barnsley House, England

*Corydalis flexuosa* An herbaceous perennial that grows to 15in (40cm) tall, spreading by stolons to form extensive patches, producing clusters of blue or sometimes mauve-blue flowers, about 1in (2.5cm) long, over a long period in spring and early summer. Hardy to -10°F (-23°C), US zones 6–9. Native to western China.

*Linum narbonense* An herbaceous perennial that grows up to 1¹/₂ft (45cm) tall and wider, producing a succession of bright blue flowers, 1¹/₂in (4cm) wide. Prefers a sunny position and is hardy to -20°F (-29°C), US zones 5–10. Native to southern Europe and North Africa.

*Helianthemum* 'Henfield Brilliant' A dwarf evergreen shrub of spreading habit that grows up to 1ft (30cm) tall. From early summer it has a succession of rich orange-brown flowers, each about 1in (2.5cm) wide. A sunny position where it can trail over a wall is ideal. Hardy to -10°F (-23°C), US zones 6–8. A hybrid of *Helianthemum nummularium*.

*Helianthemum* hybrids Dwarf evergreen shrubs of speading habit that grow up to 1ft (30cm) tall, but usually less, forming mats wider than tall. From early summer they produce a succession of flowers that may be white, yellow, pink or red, single or double. Hardy to -10°F (-23°C), US zones 6–8.

*Thalictrum aquilegiifolium* An herbaceous perennial that grows to 4ft (1.25m) tall. In early summer it produces frothy sprays of cream, pale or deep purplish-pink flowers. The individual flowers are small but abundant and showy, although they consist of little except stamens. Hardy to -20°F (-29°C), US zones 5–8. Native to much of Europe.

*Thalictrum flavum* subsp. *glaucum* An herbaceous perennial that grows to 5ft (1.5m) tall. In midsummer it produces frothy sprays of very pale creamy-blue flowers. The leaves and stem are bluish-green. Hardy to -20°F (-29°C), US zones 5-8. Native to North Africa, Spain and Portugal.

*Thalictrum delavayi* 'Hewitt's Double' (syn. *T. dipterocarpum*) An herbaceous perennial that grows to 5ft (1.5m) tall, producing airy sprays of light purple, fully double flowers about ¹/₂in (1cm) wide, but abundant and showy in early summer. Hardy to -20°F (-29°C), US zones 5–8. *Thalictrum delavayi* is native to south-west China.

*Linum narbonense*

*Thalictrum delavayi* 'Hewitt's Double'

*Thalictrum flavium* subsp. *glaucum*

*Helianthemum* 'Henfield Brilliant'

*Thalictrum aquilegiifolium*

*Corydalis flexuosa*

# PERENNIALS

*Paeonia lactiflora*
An herbaceous peony from which most of the large garden peonies have been bred. Flowers 2½–4in (6–10cm) wide in the wild, white to pink, in early summer. Prefers good, sandy, well-drained soil, but moist in summer. Hardy to -30°F (-35°C) or less, US zones 4–9. Native to Siberia, from south of Lake Baikal, eastwards to Vladivostock, and from north-west China and Mongolia to Beijing, growing on steppes and in scrub.

*Paeonia lactiflora* cultivars A perennial well-developed in Chinese gardens by the 18th century, these cultivars reached the peak of their popularity in the West at the beginning of the 20th century. They are very hardy and tolerate -60°F (-50°C), US zones 1–9 or lower. Best planted in heavy soil with good drainage, moist in summer. The crowns should be placed just under the surface; if planted too deeply, the plant will not flower freely.

'Beacon Flame' (left) Stems grow to 2½ft (75cm). Raised by Kelways.

'Bowl of Beauty' Flowers scented, mid- to late season. Probably the commonest of the 'Imperial' peonies in which the stamens are replaced by narrow petaloid filaments.

'Festiva Maxima' (right) Robust stems grow to 3ft (90cm). Scented white flowers with crimson blemishes. Raised by Miellez in 1851.

'Sarah Bernhardt' Stems grow to 3ft (90cm). Flowers very large, in mid- to late season. Raised by Lémoine in 1906.

'Shirley Temple' (below) Stems grow to 2½ft (75cm). Highly scented flowers, palest pink to white.

*Paeonia mlokosewitschii*
An herbaceous perennial that grows to 2ft (60cm) tall and usually wider. Large long-stalked, pale yellow flowers, about 5in (12cm) wide, in spring. Plant in autumn or spring in a sheltered position in sun or part-shade. Hardy to -10°F (-23°C), US zones 6–8, but flower buds may be damaged by late spring frosts. Native to the Caucasus.

*Paeonia obovata* var. *alba* Up to 2ft (60cm) tall and wider, this herbaceous perennial produces large, cup-shaped, pure white flowers, each about 3in (8cm) wide, in spring and early summer. Plant in autumn or spring in a sheltered position in part-shade. Hardy to -10°F (-23°C), US zones 6–8. It is free from pests and diseases, but the flower buds may be damaged by late spring frosts.

*Paeonia mlokosewitschii*

*Paeonia obovata* var. *alba*　　　'Sarah Bernhardt'　　　'Bowl of Beauty'

*Paeonia lactiflora*

*Geranium pratense* 'Mrs Kendall Clark'

*Geranium sanguineum*

*Geranium phaeum* 'Album'

*Geranium* x *oxonianum* 'Claridge Druce'

*Geranium sanguineum* var. *striatum*

*Geranium phaeum* (right)
An herbaceous
perennial that grows
to 2ft (60cm) tall,
forming good
clumps of foliage. In
summer it bears many
deep maroon flowers on
erect stems. Each flat
flower is about 1in (2.5cm)
wide. Hardy to -10°F (-23°C),
US zones 6–8 or lower. Native
to much of Europe and has been
grown in England since the 16th
century. This is a most useful plant for
really shady places, being quite drought-
tolerant once established.

*Geranium phaeum* 'Album'  This white
form  is a most useful plant for really
shady places, perhaps mixed with the
deep purple form for contrast.

*Geranium himalayense* 'Gravetye'
A perennial forming spreading mats by
underground rhizomes, with rich blue
flowers produced in summer. This is a
good garden plant, tolerant of drought
conditions and a certain amount of shade.
Hardy to -20°F (-29°C), US zones 5–10.

*Geranium renardii*  An herbaceous
perennial that grows to 2½ft (75cm) tall.
In early summer it bears many white
flowers, about 1¼in (3cm) wide with
deep purple veins. Best grown in
a sunny position. Hardy to
-10°F (-23°C), US zones
6–8 or lower. Native to
the Caucasus.

*Geranium* x *oxonianum* 'Claridge Druce'
An herbaceous perennial that grows to 2ft
(60cm) tall, forming good clumps of
foliage. From early summer to late
autumn it bears many flowers, each about
2in (5cm) wide. Hardy to -10°F (-23°C),
US zones 6–8 or lower. This variety is very
drought-resistant.

*Geranium pratense* 'Mrs Kendall Clark'
An herbaceous perennial that grows to
2½ft (75cm) tall, bearing a succession of
pale mauve flowers, each about 1½in
(4cm) wide with white veins, for several
weeks from early summer. Hardy to -10°F
(-23°C), US zones 6–8 or lower. Native to
much of Europe and Asia.

*Geranium sanguineum*  About 1ft (30cm)
tall and forming sprawling mats of foliage,
this herbaceous perennial bears flowers,
each 1in (2.5cm) wide, in summer. Best
grown in a sunny position and hardy to
-20°F (-29°C), US zones 5–8 or lower.
Native to much of Europe.

*Geranium sanguineum* var. *striatum*  Up to
6in (15cm) tall, this herbaceous perennial
forms sprawling mats of foliage bearing

*Geranium sylvaticum*

many flowers, about 1in (2.5cm) wide, in summer. In autumn some leaves turn crimson. Best grown in a sunny position. Hardy to -20°F (-29°C), US zones 5–8.

*Geranium sylvaticum* An herbaceous perennial that grows to 2½ft (75cm) tall. In late spring or early summer it bears many violet-blue flowers, 1in (2.5cm) wide with a white centre. Hardy to -20°F (-29°C), US zones 5–8 or lower. Native to much of Europe. An excellent plant in partial shade.

*Geranium* x *cantabrigiense*
An herbaceous perennial that grows to 9in (23cm) tall, bearing flowers, each about 1in (2.5cm) wide, in early summer. Hardy to -10°F (-23°C), US zones 6–8. A hybrid first raised in England in this century, but also found wild in the Balkans.

*Geranium* 'Johnson's Blue' This is almost certainly a hybrid between *Geranium himalayense* and *Geranium pratense*, with flower petals to 1in (2.5cm) long. Because it is sterile it has a longer flowering season than *Geranium pratense*, generally in summer. Hardy to -20°F (-29°C), US zones 5–9.

*Geranium* x *cantabrigiense*

*Geranium renardii*

*Geranium himalayense* 'Gravetye'

*Geranium* 'Johnson's Blue'

*Tiarella wherryi*

*Houttuynia cordata* 'Variegata'

*Rheum ribes*

*Saxifraga hirsuta*

*Saxifraga spathularis*

*Rheum palmatum* 'Atrosanguineum'

*Heuchera cylindrica* 'Greenfinch'
A perennial that forms mats of wavy-edged leaves. Green flowers, $\frac{1}{2}$in (1cm) wide with stiff upright stems, in spring and summer. Hardy to -30°F (-35°C), US zones 4–10. Prefers sun or partial shade in well-drained soil. Native to North America, growing on cliffs and rocks.

*Heuchera micrantha* 'Palace Purple'   A perennial that forms mounds of striking leaves, 8in (20cm) high, purplish-black with a metallic sheen. Those produced in winter are nearly round, whereas summer leaves are lobed. Flowers white. Hardy to -20°F(-29°C), US zones 5–10. Native to North America, growing in rocky places to 2800ft (800m).

*Heuchera sanguinea* (right)
A perennial that forms mats of dark green leaves and numerous red flowers, up to $\frac{1}{2}$in (1cm) long. Flowers from spring to autumn. Requires sun or partial shade in cooler, northern climates. Hardy to -30°F (-35°C), US zones 4–10. Native to North America, growing on moist, shady rocks.

*Houttuynia cordata* 'Variegata' (syn. 'Chameleon')   Perennial with slender creeping rhizomes. Flowers minute in an elongated head. Multicoloured leaves and flowers in summer. Leaves can be eaten raw or cooked like spinach; in western China they are sold in local markets. Hardy to 5°F (-15°C), US zones 7–10.

*Heuchera micrantha* 'Palace Purple'

*Rheum palmatum*

*Rheum palmatum*   A huge plant from a very stout woody stock, with leaves up to 3ft (90cm) long. Flowers, usually white, appear in late spring. All rheums require very rich moist soil, well-manured each year, to grow and flower to their full potential. Native to western China, in scrub and rocky places, and by streams at 8750–14,000ft (2500–4000m). Hardy to -10°F (-23°C), US zones 6–9.

*Rheum palmatum* 'Atrosanguineum' (syn. 'Atropurpureum')   Rich crimson-purple young leaves and pink flowers.

*Rheum ribes*   A perennial with a very stout woody rhizome and prickly leaves. Flowers in early summer. Suits a dry position, where it is very long-lived. The stalks are eaten raw by local people. Hardy to -10°F (-23°C), US zones 6–10 or less. Native to Asia, growing in dry gorges among rocks.

*Saxifraga hirsuta*   A perennial that forms mats of loose rosettes, with hairy leaves and petals, flowering from May to July. Easily grown in a moist shaded or partially shaded position, but not tolerant of drought. Hardy to -30°F (-35°C), US zones 4–10. Native to Europe.

*Saxifraga spathularis*   A perennial that forms loose clumps of rosettes. Flowers from May to July. Hardy to 5°F (-15°C), US zones 7–10. Native to Europe, growing among shady rocks, in woods and on shaded cliffs in acid soils.

*Tiarella wherryi*   An herbaceous perennial that grows to 1ft (30cm) tall, producing short, erect spikes of starry white flowers, each about ½in (1cm) wide, in summer. Prefers cool, moist soil and a partially shaded position. Hardy to 0°F (-18°C), US zones 7–8. Native to the south-eastern regions of the US.

*Heuchera cylindrica* 'Greenfinch'

# PERENNIALS

*Lupinus* 'The Chatelaine'

*Lupinus* 'Magnificence'

*Lupinus* 'My Castle'

*Thermopsis caroliniana*

*Baptisia australis*

*Lychnis coronaria* 'Oculata'

*Lychnis chalcedonica* 'Rosea'

*Baptisia australis*   An herbaceous perennial that grows to 4ft (1.25m) tall, producing flowers, each about 1in (2.5cm) long, in early summer. Plant in autumn or early spring in any fertile and deep soil, except shallow chalk. Hardy to -20°F (-29°C), US zones 5–9. Native to the eastern parts of the United States.

LADY'S MANTLE *Alchemilla mollis* An herbaceous perennial that grows to 1¹/₂ft (45cm) tall and rather wider, producing airy sprays of tiny yellow flowers in summer. Hardy to -20°F (-29°C), US zones 5–10. As it may self-seed freely, it is wise to cut off the flower heads as they turn brown. Native to eastern Europe and western Asia, this plant is cherished for its fine foliage.

*Lupinus* 'The Chatelaine'   An herbaceous perennial that grows to 4ft (1.25m) tall. In early summer it produces flowers, each about ³/₄in (2cm) long, with a characteristic scent. Best in a sunny position. Hardy to -10°F (-23°C), US zones 6–9. Sometimes affected by a large aphid. A hybrid of *L. polyphyllus*, it was raised in Britain in the 20th century.

*Lupinus* 'My Castle'   A perennial that grows to 4ft (1.25m) tall, producing erect spikes of deep salmon-pink flowers, each ³/₄in (2cm) long, with a characteristic scent in early summer. Best in a sunny position. Hardy to -10°F (-23°C), US zones 6–9. May be affected by aphids. A hybrid of *L. polyphyllus*, raised in Britain.

*Lupinus* 'Magnificence'   A perennial that grows to 4ft (1.25m) tall, producing spikes of flowers, each about ³/₄in (2cm) long, in early summer. Hardy to -10°F (-23°C), US zones 6–9. It can be affected by aphids. This hybrid is derived from *L. polyphyllus*, raised in Britain in the 20th century.

JERUSALEM CROSS *Lychnis chalcedonica*   An herbaceous perennial that grows to 3ft (90cm) tall, forming clumps rather wider than tall. Summer flowering. Hardy to -30°F (-35°C), US zones 4–8. Native to northern Asia, it was introduced into cultivation in the 16th century.

*Lychnis chalcedonica* 'Rosea'   It has pale salmon-pink flowers and can look wishy-washy near strong colours. It is perhaps best planted among white flowers and silvery foliage.

DUSTY MILLER *Lychnis coronaria* 'Oculata'   Perennial that grows to 3ft (90cm) tall, producing flowers in summer. Best in a sunny position and easily grown in poor soils. Hardy to -20°F (-29°C), US zones 5–8. Native to southern Europe, it was introduced into cultivation in the 16th century.

RAGGED ROBIN *Lychnis flos-cuculi*   An herbaceous perennial that grows up to 2¹⁄₂ft (75cm) tall, and forms spreading clumps rather wider than tall. In summer it produces clusters of clear pink flowers, each about 1¹⁄₂in (4cm) wide. It prefers moist soil. Hardy to -20°F (-29°C), US zones 5-8. Native to much of Europe.

*Silene schafta*   A spreading herbaceous perennial that forms mats up to 6in (15cm) tall. In early summer it produces an abundance of flowers, ³⁄₄in (2cm) wide. Hardy to -10°F (-23°C), US zones 6–8. Native to Iran.

*Thermopsis caroliniana*   A plant producing clusters of flowers in spring. Prefers good soils in full sun or partial shade. Hardy to -30°F (-35°C), US zones 4–10. Native to North America, where it grows in open woods and on river banks.

*Alchemilla mollis* at Fitz House, Teffont Magna, Wiltshire, England

*Lychnis flos-cuculi*

*Alchemilla mollis*

*Lychnis chalcedonica*

*Silene schafta*

**Geum coccineum** An herbaceous perennial that grows to 1ft (30cm) tall and usually wider, producing a succession of flowers, each about 1¼in (3cm) wide, in summer. Plant in autumn or early spring. It prefers a sunny position and is hardy to -20°F (-29°C), US zones 5–8. Native to the Balkans.

**Geum 'Mrs J Bradshaw'** An herbaceous perennial that forms clumps, rather wider than tall. In summer it produces a succession of bright orange-red, semi-double flowers, each about 1¼in (3cm) wide. Best in a sunny position and hardy to -20°F (-29°C), US zones 5–8. Thought to be a hybrid of *G. chiloense*, it was raised in the early 20th century.

**Geum 'Lemon Drops'** An herbaceous perennial that grows to 1ft (30cm) tall and produces pale yellow, bowl-shaped flowers in summer. Best planted in spring or autumn in a moist, peaty soil in sun or partial shade. Grows well in northern Europe and eastern North America. Hardy to 0°F (-18°C), US zones 6–9.

**Geum montanum** An herbaceous perennial that forms clumps with flower stems up to 1ft (30cm) tall. In summer it produces a succession of flowers, each

about 1½in (4cm) wide. Plant in autumn or early spring in a sunny position. Hardy to -20°F (-29°C), US zones 5–8. Native to the mountains of Europe.

**Geum 'Georgenberg'** An herbaceous perennial that forms clumps, usually wider than tall. It produces a succession of flowers, each about 1¼in (3cm) wide, in summer. Prefers a sunny position and hardy to -20°F (-29°C), US zones 5–8. Thought to be a hybrid of *G. chiloense*, it was introduced into cultivation in the late 20th century.

**Geum rivale** f. *album* Perennial that forms low mats, flowering in early summer. Its stems and flowers are pale yellow green. Hardy to -25°F (-32°C), US zones 4–8. Native to most of Europe except the far south, to the Caucasus and northern Turkey, northern Asia and North America.

**Geum rossii** Perennial that forms dense clumps to 1ft (30cm) across and petals to ½in (1cm) long, flowering in summer. Easily grown in well-drained soil and hardy to -30°F (-35°C), US zones 3–10. Native to North America and eastern Asia, growing in arctic tundra and on stony meadows in mountains.

**Geum rivale 'Leonard's Variety'** A perennial with flower stems that grow to 1½ft (45cm) tall and usually wider. It produces many nodding, slightly bell-shaped flowers, each about ¾in (2cm) wide. Best in a sunny position and hardy to -30°F (-35°C), US zones 4–8. *Geum rivale* is native to much of Europe, growing in damp places.

**Potentilla atrosanguinea** An herbaceous perennial that grows to 2ft (60cm) tall, the stems somewhat sprawling. In summer it produces many deep red to crimson, or sometimes yellow flowers, each about 1½in (4cm) wide. Best in a sunny position and hardy to -20°F (-29°C), US zones 5–8. Native to the Himalayas.

**Potentilla 'Gibson's Scarlet'** An herbaceous, somewhat sprawling perennial that grows to 1½ft (45cm) tall, producing many flowers, each about 1½in (4cm) wide, in summer. Thrives in a sunny position and hardy to -20°F (-29°C), US zones 5–8. A hybrid derived from *P. atrosanguinea*, it was raised in England in the 20th century.

**Potentilla nepalensis** Perennial that forms a loose mass of wiry branching stems with flowers ½–1in (1–2.5cm), dark crimson to bright pink or orange, produced in summer to early autumn. Easily grown in any good, moist soil. Native to the Himalayas, from Pakistan eastwards to central Nepal, in alpine meadows and fields up to 9450ft (2700m).

**Potentilla rupestris** (syn. *Potentilla foliosa*) A tufted perennial that flowers in summer. Flower petals ½in (1cm) long. Easily grown in well-drained soil in full sun. Hardy to -12°F (-25°C), US zones 5–10. A characteristic species of dry, rocky slopes in the foothills in Europe. Native to most of Europe, growing on dry sunny rocky slopes in the mountains,

*Geum coccineum*

*Geum rivale* 'Leonard's Variety'

*Potentilla* 'Gibson's Scarlet'

*Geum* 'Mrs J Bradshaw'

*Geum* 'Lemon Drops'

*Potentilla rupestris*

*Geum rivale* f. *album*

*Potentilla atrosanguinea*

*Geum rossii*

*Geum* 'Georgenberg'

*Geum montanum*

*Potentilla nepalensis*

*Potentilla atrosanguinea*

²/₅ life size. 9 June

Primula 'Groeneken's Glory'

Primula florindae

Primula 'Guinevere'

DRUMSTICK PRIMULA *Primula denticulata* An herbaceous perennial that grows to 8in (20cm) tall. In summer it produces dense heads of flowers, each about ¹/₂in (1cm) wide. Hardy to -10°F (-23°C), US zones 6–8. Native to the Himalayas and introduced into cultivation early in the 19th century. Suitable for a bog garden or pool-side, but will grow well in an ordinary border if not too dry.

OXLIP *Primula elatior* subsp. *elatior* An herbaceous perennial that grows up to 1ft (30cm) tall, producing a loose cluster of flowers, about ³/₄in (2cm) wide, in spring or early summer. Hardy to -10°F (-23°C), US zones 6–8. Native to northern Europe and long grown in gardens, it thrives in rich chalky soils.

*Primula florindae* An herbaceous perennial that grows to 4ft (1.25m) tall, producing a loose cluster of fragrant, bright yellow, occasionally orange or red, flowers, each about ³/₄in (2cm) wide, in summer. Hardy to -10°F (-23°C), US zones 6–8. Native to western China and introduced into cultivation early in the 20th century. This is a spectacular plant for massing in a bog garden or pool-side.

*Primula* 'Lady Greer' An herbaceous perennial that grows to 5in (12cm) tall, producing numerous pale primrose-yellow flowers, each about ³/₄in (2cm) wide in a cluster on a single stalk, in spring. Plant in autumn or spring in a partially shaded position. Hardy to -10°F (-23°C), US zones 6–8.

*Primula* 'Groeneken's Glory' A perennial that grows to 6in (15cm) tall and produces numerous flowers, each about 1¹/₄in (3cm) wide, in spring. It can be planted in autumn or spring in any fertile soil that is not too dry, in a partially shaded position. Hardy to -10°F (-23°C), US zones 6–8. A recent introduction which was raised in the 20th century.

*Primula* 'Guinevere' A perennial that grows to 6in (15cm) tall and produces numerous flowers, about 1¹/₂in (4cm) wide, in spring. The leaves become larger after flowering and strongly tinged with purple. Hardy to -10°F (-23°C), US zones 6–8. Raised in Ireland early in the 20th century, it is an attractive and unusually coloured plant.

*Primula vulgaris*

*Primula elatior* subsp. *elatior*

*Primula* 'Lady Greer'

*Primula sikkimensis*

*Primula sikkimensis* An herbaceous perennial that grows to 2¹/₂ft (75cm) tall, producing flowers, each about ³/₄in (2cm) wide, in summer. Plant in autumn or spring in moist or wet, peaty soil. Hardy to -10°F (-23°C), US zones 6–8. Native to the eastern Himalayas and western China.

PRIMROSE *Primula vulgaris* (yellow and pink forms) These herbaceous perennials grow to 6in (15cm) tall and produce numerous pale yellow or light dusky pink flowers, about 1in (2.5cm) wide, in early spring. Plant in any moist, fertile soil in partial shade in autumn or spring. Hardy to -20°F (-29°C), US zones 5–8. Native to much of Europe and western Asia.

*Primula denticulata*

*Primula japonica* 'Miller's Crimson'

*Primula rosea*

**Primula japonica 'Miller's Crimson'**
An herbaceous perennial that grows to 2ft (60cm) tall, producing red flowers about ³/₄in (2cm) wide. Best in a partially shaded position as the flowers can bleach in full sun. Hardy to -10°F (-23°C), US zones 6–8. *Primula japonica* is native to Japan and Taiwan and was introduced into cultivation in the late 19th century.
**Primula japonica 'Postford White'** Has white flowers with a yellow eye.

**Primula bulleyana** A perennial that grows to 2¹/₂ft (75cm) tall, producing flowers, each about ³/₄in (2cm) wide, opening from reddish buds in summer. Plant in a partially shaded or, if the soil is wet, a sunny position. Hardy to -10°F (-23°C), US zones 6–8. Native to western China,

from where it was introduced into cultivation early in the 20th century.

**Primula rosea** A perennial that grows to 8in (20cm) tall and produces vivid rose-pink flowers on a short stalk, about ³/₄in (2cm) wide, in early spring. Plant in autumn or spring in a moist or wet, lime-free soil in a sunny position. Hardy to -10°F (-23°C), US zones 6–8. Native to the western Himalayas and introduced into cultivation in the 19th century.

**Primula pulverulenta** An herbaceous perennial that grows to 3ft (90cm) tall, producing flowers, each about ³/₄in (2cm) wide, in spring. The leaves become larger after flowering. Hardy to -10°F (-23°C), US zones 6–8. Native to western China,

Primula pulverulenta

Primula vialii

Primula chionantha

Primula bulleyana

Primula beesiana

from where it was introduced into cultivation early in the 20th century.

CANDELABRA PRIMULA *Primula beesiana* An herbaceous perennial that grows to 2¹/₂ft (75cm) tall and produces flowers, each about ³/₄in (2cm) wide, in summer. Hardy to -10°F (-23°C), US zones 6–8. Native to western China; it is one of the 'candelabra' primulas, so-called because of the tiered arrangement of its flowers.

*Primula vialii* An herbaceous perennial that grows up to 2ft (60cm) tall. Small lavender-blue flowers, each about ¹/₂in (1cm) wide, are produced in spring from red buds. Plant in autumn or spring in any moist, fertile soil in a partially shaded position. Hardy to -10°F (-23°C), US zones 6–8. *Primula vialii* is native to western China and was introduced into cultivation early in the 20th century. It is unique among primulas because of its appearance.

*Primula chionantha* An herbaceous perennial that grows to 2ft (60cm) tall and produces flowers, each about ³/₄in (2cm) wide, in summer. This perennial can be planted in the autumn or spring in a moist, lime-free soil, in a partially shaded or, if the soil is wet, a sunny position. Hardy to -10°F (-23°C), US zones 6–8. *Primula chionantha* is native to south-west China, from where it was introduced into cultivation early in the 20th century.

Primula japonica 'Postford White'

*Mimulus cardinalis*

*Mimulus* 'Andean Nymph'

*Asarina procumbens*  A low-growing perennial that reaches only 3in (8cm) tall, with stems trailing to 1ft (30cm) long or more. For several months in the summer it produces flowers, each about 1¹/₄in (3cm) long. Hardy to 0°F (-18°C), US zones 7–10. Native to south-west Europe.

*Mimulus cardinalis*  An herbaceous perennial that grows to 2¹/₂ft (75cm) tall, spreading slowly from a creeping root stock but usually taller than wide. Over a long period from early summer, it produces bright red, orange or yellow flowers, each about 2in (5cm) long. Hardy to -20°F (-29°C), US zones 5–9.

*Mimulus* 'Andean Nymph'
An herbaceous perennial that grows to 6in (15cm) tall. In summer it produces an abundance of flowers, each about 1in (2.5cm) long. Hardy to 0°F (-18°C), US zones 7–9. It is thought to be of hybrid origin, although introduced from Chile in the late 20th century.

FORGET–ME–NOT *Myosotis sylvatica*
*A* short-lived, often biennial plant. Flowers in summer, ¹/₃in (8mm) across, are pale blue or rarely white and often pink if the plants are moved while in flower. Often disfigured by powdery

mildew in dry conditions. Hardy to -5°F (-20°C), US zones 6–10 or less.

*Omphalodes cappadocica* 'Cherry Ingram'
An evergreen perennial that grows to 10in (25cm) tall and usually wider. Flowers, each about ¹/₃in (8mm) wide, in spring. It prefers a partially shaded position where it will get some frost protection. Hardy to 0°F (-18°C), US zones 7–9.

*Omphalodes verna*  A creeping perennial that grows to 6in (15cm) tall, spreading to form a wide mat. Flowers, each about ¹/₃in (10mm) wide, in spring. Hardy to -10°F (-23°C), US zones 6–9. Native to southern and central Europe, from where it was introduced into cultivation in the 17th century.

*Symphytum* x *uplandicum* 'Variegatum'
An herbaceous perennial that grows to 1¹/₂ft (45cm) tall. In summer it produces tubular pink and blue flowers, each about ³/₄in (2cm) long. Hardy to -10°F (-23°C), US zones 6–8. It is free from pests and diseases, but the leaves are liable to scorch in dry or sunny conditions.

*Symphytum* 'Hidcote Pink'
An herbaceous perennial that grows to 1¹/₂ft (45cm) tall. In summer it produces

*Symphytum* x *uplandicum* 'Variegatum'

*Symphytum* 'Hidcote Pink'

*Omphalodes cappadocica* 'Cherry Ingram'

*Omphalodes verna*

flowers, each about ³/₄in (2cm) long. Hardy to -10°F (-23°C), US zones 6–8. A hybrid of uncertain origin, easily grown and useful for suppressing weeds in a shady place.

*Veronica austriaca* 'Crater Lake Blue' An herbaceous perennial that grows to 1¹/₂ft (45cm) tall. Flowers, each ¹/₂in (1cm) wide, appear in summer. Hardy to -10°F (-23°C), US zones 6–8. Native to Europe and northern Asia from where it was introduced into cultivation early in the 16th century.

*Veronica gentianoides* An herbaceous perennial with flowering stems that grow to 2ft (60cm) tall. Flowers, each about ¹/₂in (1cm) wide, in summer. Best in a sunny position. Hardy to -20°F (-29°C), US zones 5–8. Native to the Caucasus and valued for its pallid blue flowers.

*Veronica spicata* 'Heidekind' A perennial that grows to 1ft (30cm) tall. Flowers, each about ¹/₄in (6mm), wide in summer. Best in a sunny position. Hardy to -30°F (-35°C), US zones 4–8. *Veronica spicata* is native to Europe and northern Asia. 'Heidekind' is a good selection with pink rather than blue flowers.

JACOB'S LADDER *Polemonium caeruleum* An herbaceous perennial that grows to 4ft (1.25m) tall. In summer it produces flowers, each about ³/₄in (2cm) wide. It prefers a sunny or lightly shaded position and is hardy to -30°F (-35°C), US zones 4–8.

*Myosotis sylvatica*

*Veronica austriaca* 'Crater Lake Blue'

*Veronica spicata* 'Heidekind'

*Polemonium caeruleum*

*Asarina procumbens*

*Veronica gentianoides*

*Polygonatum biflorum*

*Anthemis cretica* subsp. *cupaniana*

*Erigeron karvinskianus*

### ANGULAR SOLOMON'S SEAL

*Polygonatum odoratum* (above)
Perennial with long creeping rhizomes
forming colonies. Flowers, solitary or in
groups of 2–4, appear from April to July.
Hardy to -12°F (-25°C), US zones 5–10.
Native to Europe, including western
England, eastwards to the Caucasus,
northern Iran, Siberia and Japan, growing
in woods, usually on limestone.

*Polygonatum biflorum* Perennial
producing greenish flowers, usually in
pairs ¹/₂in (1cm) long, flowering from
April to July. The smaller of the two North
American species, it is usually found in
dryish places and in woods. Hardy to
-40°F (-40°C) US zones 3–9. Native to
North America, from New Brunswick
west to Michigan, south to Tennessee,
West Virginia and Florida, growing in
deciduous woods and scrub.

*Smilacina stellata* (syn. *Maianthemum
stellatum*) Perennial with creeping
rhizomes, forming extensive patches.
Flowers, 3 to 15 in a loose cluster, petals
¹/₄–¹/₃in (6–8mm) long, from April to
June. Hardy to -40°F (-40°C), US zones
3–8. Native to California, north to British
Columbia, and eastwards to New-
foundland, Virginia and Kansas, in wet
places in woods and scrub.

*Smilacina racemosa* An herbaceous
perennial that forms clumps of arching
leafy stems up to 3ft (90cm) tall. In spring
or early summer it produces frothy sprays
of tiny cream flowers at the tip of each
stem. Plant in autumn or spring in a
moist, lime-free soil in a partially shaded
or, if the soil is wet, sunny position. Hardy
to -30°F (-35°C), US zones 4–9. Native to
North America, introduced into
cultivation early in the 17th century. An
elegant plant for a cool, shady place.

*Maianthemum bifolium* Perennial that
forms spreading mats by creeping
underground rhizomes, flowering from
April to July according to altitude and
latitude. Flowering stems are hairy above,
usually around 6in (15cm) tall. A delicate
invasive plant, useful for ground-cover in
cool shady places. Hardy to -40°F
(-40°C), US zones 3–8. Native to Europe,
from England and Norway eastwards, and
to northern Japan, usually growing in
coniferous woods on acid soils.

### LILY-OF-THE-VALLEY *Convallaria
majalis* A perennial forming spreading
mats by rhizomes that creep on the soil
surface beneath the leaf layer. Stems with
1 to 4 leaves, 1–8in (2.5–20cm) long.
Flowers arise from the lower sheaths that
grow to 8in (20cm) tall, with 5–13
wonderfully scented flowers produced
from May to June. Hardy to -40°F
(-40°C), US zones 3–9. Several varieties
are found in the wild and other variants
are cultivated. Native to Europe from
northern England, south to the Caucasus
and north-eastern Turkey and eastwards

*Aster tongolensis*

*Aster falconeri*

to Japan. Also in North America in Virginia, and North and South Carolina, growing in woods, scrub, on limestone pavement and meadows in the mountains.

*Convallaria majalis* 'Fortin's Giant' A large clone.

*Convallaria majalis* 'Prolificans' Numerous small flowers on a branched infloresence.

*Convallaria majalis* var. *rosea*   Common to parts of central and eastern Europe and has small pinkish flowers.

*Speirantha convallarioides*   Plant with thick rhizomes, spreading by stolons. Scented flowers from April to May. Prefers leafy soil in shade. Hardy to 10°F (-12°C), US zones 8–10. Native of southeastern China, where it grows in woods

*Anthemis cretica* subsp. *cupaniana* An herbaceous perennial that grows to 2ft (60cm) tall from a woody base, much wider than tall. In late spring and early summer it produces many white daisies, each about 2½in (6cm) wide. It can be planted in autumn or early spring in a sunny position and grows particularly well in dry regions such as the Mediterranean or California. Hardy to 0°F (-18°C), US zones 7–10. Native to Sicily and introduced into cultivation in the 20th century. This plant has a long flowering season and attractive foliage.

*Aster tongolensis*   A perennial that forms mats of hairy, dark green leaves with numerous, almost leafless, flowering stems that grow to 1½ft (45cm), bearing flowers 2½in (6cm) across, in June. It prefers well-drained soil in full sun. Hardy to -5°F (-20°C), US zones 6–10. Native to western China, growing in stony alpine meadows at 12,250ft (3500m).

*Aster falconeri*   A perennial producing solitary flowers, to 3in (8cm) across, from June to August. Perfers moist, well-drained soil in full sun. Hardy to -10°F (-23°C), US zones 6–10 or less. Native to the Himalayas, from northern Pakistan to western Nepal, growing in alpine meadows up to 14,700ft (4200m).

*Erigeron karvinskianus* (*E. mucronatus*) A low-growing perennial with trailing stems that grows to 6in (15cm) tall and 1½ft (45cm) long. Throughout the summer it produces a succession of small pale pink flowers, ¾in (2cm) wide. Plant in autumn or spring in a sunny position. Once established, it thrives in the crevices of old walls. Hardy to 0°F (-18°C), US zones 7–10. Native to Mexico from where it was introduced into cultivation in the 19th century. This plant is good for softening old walls or edging paths.

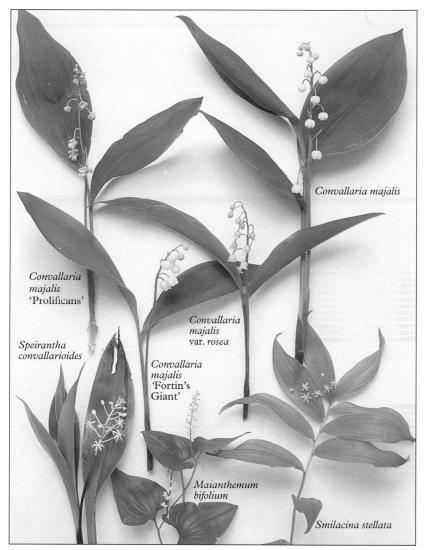

*Convallaria majalis*

*Convallaria majalis* 'Prolificans'

*Convallaria majalis* var. *rosea*

*Speirantha convallarioides*

*Convallaria majalis* 'Fortin's Giant'

*Maianthemum bifolium*

*Smilacina stellata*

¼ life size. Specimens from Wisley, 15 May

*Smilacina racemosa*

*Smilacina racemosa* in fruit

# PERENNIALS

'Green Spot'

'Canary Bird'

'Langport Wren'

'Langport Honey'

'Amethyst Flame'

'Florentina'

'Langport Chief'

'Langport Finch'

'Langport Chapter'

'Blue Pansy'

*Iris germanica*

*Iris germanica* 'Nepalensis'

¹/₅ life size. Specimens from Eccleston Square, 20 May

*Iris germanica* An excellent plant for dry town gardens, where it will flower happily in light deciduous shade in late spring and early summer. Scented, probably of hybrid origin, but perhaps native to the eastern Mediterranean. Hardy to -20°F (-29°C), US zones 5–10 or less if mulched with sand. Widely cultivated as an old garden plant and also for the perfume extracted from its rhizome. Commonly naturalized in dry, rocky places.

ORRIS ROOT *Iris germanica* 'Florentina' (syn. *Iris florentina*) An iris cultivated in Italy, especially around Florence, for its perfume. Fragrant flowers in late spring and easily grown in ordinary garden soil and full sun. Hardy to 10°F (-12°C), US zones 8–10. The root must be dried before the scent, which resembles violets, is released.

*Iris germanica* 'Nepalensis' (syn. *Iris germanica* 'Atropurpurea') An ancient scented variety that crops up in old gardens and can be found naturalized. Hardy to 5°F (-15°C), US zones 7–10.

*Iris* 'Austrian Sky' Dwarf bearded iris that grows to 1ft (30cm) tall, flowering in late spring and early summer. Hardy to 5°F (-15°C), US zones 7–10 or less if mulched with sand. Seedling x 'Welch'.

*Iris* 'Amethyst Flame' Tall bearded iris that grows to 3¹/₂ft (1m) high and flowers in late spring and early summer. 'Crispette' x ('Lavandesque' x Pathfinder'). Hardy to 5°F (-15°C), US zones 7–10 or less if mulched with sand.

*Iris* 'Autumn Leaves' Tall bearded iris that grows to 3¹/₃ft (1m), bearing several striking browny-purple flowers in late spring and early summer. Hardy to 5°F (-15°C), US zones 7–10. Take care when placing this iris in your garden as the colours are rather difficult to combine with other plants.

*Iris* 'Blue Pansy' Tall bearded iris that grows to 3¹/₂ft (1m) and flowers in late spring and early summer. 'Black Hills' x 'Knight Valiant'. Hardy to 5°F (-15°C), US zones 7–10 or less if mulched with sand.

*Iris* 'Brown Chocolate' Tall bearded iris that grows to 3¹/₃ft (1m) with several striking, rich-brown flowers, the upper petals (standards) being maroon-chocolate. Flowers in late spring and early summer. Hardy to 5°F (-15°C), US zones 7–10. Because of its unusual colour, this iris needs careful placing in the garden.

*Iris* 'Staten Island'

*Iris* 'Olympic Torch'

# BEARDED IRISES

A view of irises in Monet's garden at Giverney

*Iris* 'Canary Bird'   Tall bearded iris that grows to 3ft (90cm) and flowers in spring and early summer. 'Berkeley Gold' seedling. Hardy to 5°F (-15°C), US zones 7–10 or less if mulched with sand.

*Iris* 'Langport Chief'   Intermediate bearded iris that grows to 15ins (40cm) tall and flowers in late spring. Hardy to 5°F (-15°C), US zones 7–10 or less if mulched with sand.

*Iris* 'Langport Chapter'   Intermediate bearded iris that grows to 1½ft (45cm) tall and flowers in late spring. Hardy to 5°F (-15°C), US zones 7–10 or less if mulched with sand.

*Iris* 'Langport Finch'   Intermediate bearded iris that grows to 1½ft (45cm) tall and flowers in early spring. Hardy to 5°F (-15°C), US zones 7–10 or less if mulched with sand.

*Iris* 'Langport Honey'   Intermediate bearded iris that grows to 2ft (60cm) tall and flowers in early spring. Hardy to 5°F (-15°C), US zones 7–10 or less if mulched with sand.

*Iris* 'Langport Wren'   Intermediate bearded iris that grows to 2ft (60cm) tall, flowering in early spring. Hardy to 5°F (-15°C), US zones 7–10 or less if mulched with sand.

*Iris* 'Olympic Torch'   Tall bearded iris that grows to 3½ft (1m), bearing several unusual ruffled bright orange flowers in mid-season. Hardy to 5°F (-15°C), US zones 7–9 but will stand lower temperatures if mulched with sand.

*Iris* 'Green Spot'   Intermediate bearded iris that grows to 10in (25cm) tall and flowers in early spring. Seedling x yellow *pumila*. Hardy to 5°F (-15°C), US zones 7–10 or less if mulched with sand.

*Iris* 'Grace Abounding'   Tall bearded iris that grows to 3½ft (1m) in height. Lightly ruffled lemon-yellow flowers and brilliant yellow beard. Blooms in mid-season. Hardy to 5°F (-15°C), US zones 7–9 but will stand lower temperatures if mulched with sand.

*Iris* 'Staten Island'   Tall bearded iris that grows to 3½ft (1m). Derived from 'The Red Admiral' x 'City of Lincoln'. Blooms mid-season. Hardy to 5°F (-15°C), US zones 7–9 but will stand lower temperatures if mulched with sand.

*Iris* 'Austrian Sky'

*Iris* 'Grace Abounding'

*Iris* 'Autumn Leaves'

*Iris* 'Brown Chocolate'

*Iris innominata*

*Iris innominata*

*Iris unguicularis* (white form)

*Iris variegata*

*Iris japonica*

*Iris cristata* An herbaceous perennial that forms wide mats of foliage to 8in (20cm) tall. In spring it produces flowers about 1¹/₂in (4cm) wide. Best planted in a partially shaded position and benefits from regular division and replanting. Hardy to -20°F (-29°C), US zones 5–8. Often needs protection from slugs and snails. Native to the eastern US.

*Iris japonica* A perennial with a creeping aerial rhizome that roots at intervals, bearing flowers 2–2¹/₂ins (5-6cm) across, which open in succession in spring. Susceptible to damage by late spring frosts and will fail to flower after an exceptionally cold winter. Hardy to 20°F (-7°C), US zones 9–10. Native to Japan and China, as far west as Sichuan, on grassy and rocky slopes, in woods in the hills and among rocks by streams.

*Iris unguicularis* 'Walter Butt'
An herbaceous perennial that forms spreading clumps to 2ft (60cm) tall. It produces flowers, about 3in (8cm) wide, with the scent of sweet violets, intermittently between autumn and spring. Best in a sunny and even dry position and hardy to 0°F (-18°C), US zones 7–9. Native to parts of North Africa and south-east Europe, it was introduced into cultivation in the 19th century.
   *Iris unguicularis* (white form)
Its flowers are pure white, marked with yellow on the lower petals. Some white forms are infected by a virus, resulting in yellow-streaked leaves and poor flowers.

GLADDON *Iris foetidissima*
An evergreen perennial that forms spreading clumps to 1¹/₂ft (45cm) tall. Typical iris flowers, about 2in (5cm) wide, produced in early summer. The strongly veined flowers are dull purple in the common form but yellowish in others. The abundant, sword-like leaves have a curious scent when crushed. Plant in autumn or early spring in a partially shaded or sunny position. Hardy to 0°F (-18°C), US zones 7–9, although the leaves may be damaged by severe frost or cold winds. Native to western Europe, where it grows in open woods and hedge banks and has long been cultivated for its bright orange ornamental seeds, which are showier than the rather dull flowers.

*Iris innominata* An evergreen perennial that forms spreading clumps up to 8in (20cm) tall. Typical iris flowers, about 2in (5cm) wide, variable in colour from yellow to pale blue or purple, produced in spring. Plant in autumn or early spring in well-drained, lime-free soil. It prefers a sunny or lightly shaded position and is hardy to 0°F (-18°C), US zones 7–9.

Native to the western United States, where it grows in damp meadows and was introduced into cultivation in the 20th century.

*Iris variegata* An herbaceous perennial that forms dense clumps growing to 1ft (30cm) tall and branched at the top. Flowers, which appear in early summer, have yellow standards and white falls that are strongly veined in very dark red. Plant in autumn or late spring in moist, fertile soil in a sunny position. Hardy to 0°F (-18°C), US zones 7–9 or lower. Native to central and south-eastern Europe.

*Iris tectorum* 'Alba' An herbaceous perennial that can be found growing on old walls. The flowers are puplish blue or white (in the form 'Alba') and the stems are 1ft (30cm) tall. Plant in autumn or late spring in a well-drained fertile soil in a sunny position. It is best suited to cold dry winters and warm wet summers. Hardy to -10°F (-23°C), US zones 6–9 or lower. Native to Burma and south-west and central China.

*Iris cristata*

*Iris unguicularis* 'Walter Butt'

*Iris tectorum* 'Alba'

*Iris foetidissima*

*Iris foetidissima* seeds

*Iris ensata* 'Caprician Butterfly'

*Iris ensata* 'Flying Tiger'

*Iris ensata* 'Gusto'

*Iris ensata* 'Time and Tide'

JAPANESE IRIS *Iris ensata* (syn. *Iris kaempferi*)  A compact, clump-forming perennial that grows to 2ft (60cm) tall, with stems 15–33in (40–80cm), bearing purple flowers about 4in (10cm) wide, in early summer. Hardy to -5°F (-20°C) or less, US zones 6–10. Prefers wet soil or shallow water, if possible rather drier in winter. Native to Japan, China and Korea. In Japan many cultivars have been bred, particularly for exhibition. Other cultivars are more suitable for garden cultivation. Shown here are:

    *Iris ensata* 'Caprician Butterfly'.
    *Iris ensata* 'Flying Tiger'    Grows to 4ft (1.25m) tall. Hardy to -10°F (-23°C), US zones 6–9.
    *Iris ensata* 'Gusto'
Grows to 4ft (1.25m) tall. Hardy to -10°F (-23°C), US zones 6–9.
    *Iris ensata* 'Rose Queen'
Grows to 2ft (60cm) tall. Hardy to -10°F (-23°C), US zones 6–9.
    *Iris ensata* 'Time and Tide'
Grows to 3½ft (1m) tall.

*Iris monnieri*  A perennial that grows to 4ft (1.25cm) tall, producing fragrant lemon-yellow flowers with rounded falls, 1½in (4cm) wide, in summer. Hardy to -30°F (-35°C), US zones 4–9. Thought to be an ancient hybrid between *Iris orientalis* and Iris *xanthospuria*, introduced to France and known as 'Iris de Rhodes' when painted by Redouté in the early 19th century.

*Iris missouriensis*  A perennial that forms extensive dense clumps. Falls to 2½in (6cm) long, ¾in (2cm) wide, flowering in early to midsummer. Easily grown in a sunny position, if kept wet in spring. Hardy to -30°F (-35°C), US zones 4–9. Native to western North America, from Mexico northwards to British Columbia, eastwards to South Dakota and Alberta, and common in inland California.

*Iris spuria* cultivars  Strong-growing upright perennials that grow to 7ft (2m) tall, flowering mainly in midsummer, thriving in continental climates. Because of their hardiness and tolerance of heat, as well as saline or alkaline soils, they are popular in the inland parts of the United States. Most were raised in North America and the colour range and flower shapes are continually being improved. Hardy to -40°F (-40°C), US zones 3–9. Shown here are:
    *Iris* 'Cambridge Blue'.
    *Iris* 'Dawn Candle'.

*Iris pseudacorus*  An herbaceous perennial that forms spreading clumps to 4ft (1.25m) tall, producing flowers to 4in (10cm) wide, in early summer. Hardy to -20°F (-29°C), US zones 5–9. Native to much of Europe, Asia and North Africa, where it grows in damp meadows and lakesides.

*Iris chrysographes* (black form)
An herbaceous perennial that forms spreading clumps to 1½ft (45cm) tall. In early summer it produces typical small iris flowers, 2in (5cm) wide, 2 to each slender stem. The flowers are a rich blackish-purple marked with gold on the lower petals. Plant in autumn or early spring in a fertile, moist soil. Best in a sunny or partially shaded position. Hardy to 0°F (-18°C), US zones 7–9. Native to western China where it grows in damp meadows, it was introduced into cultivation early in the 20th century. The black forms are a beautiful sight when planted to catch the low morning or evening rays of sun.

*Iris forrestii*  An herbaceous perennial that forms compact clumps to 1½ft (45cm) tall. Typical, light buff-yellow flowers marked with fine brown lines or spots on the lower petals, about 2in (5cm) wide, appear in early summer. Plant in autumn or early spring in a fertile, moist peaty soil and a sunny position. Hardy to -20°F (-29°C), US zones 5–9. Native to western China where it grows in damp meadows. It was introduced into cultivation early in the 20th century.

*Iris sibirica*  An herbaceous perennial that forms spreading clumps to 3ft (90cm) tall. Typical flowers, clear blue-violet, strongly veined on the white and yellow haft of the lower petals, about 3in (8cm) wide on slender leafy stems, appear in early summer. Plant in autumn or late spring in a moist, fertile soil in a sunny position. Hardy to -20°F (-29°C), US zones 5–9 or lower. Native to Europe and northern Asia, it was introduced into cultivation in the 16th century. There are now named selections in various colours.

*Iris monnieri*

*Iris* 'Dawn Candle'

*Iris forrestii*

*Iris ensata* 'Rose Queen'

*Iris* 'Cambridge Blue'

*Iris missouriensis*

*Iris sibirica*

*Iris pseudacorus*

*Iris chrysographes*

*Stipa gigantea* with *Cotinus coggyria* 'Folis Purpureis' at Withersdane Hall, Kent, England

*Carex elata* 'Aurea'

BOWLES' GOLDEN SEDGE *Carex elata* 'Aurea'  Perennial that grows to 2ft (60cm) tall, forming tufts of erect or arching long, grass-like leaves, slender but stiff, bright yellow in spring, becoming greener by late summer. Hardy to -10°F (-23°C), US zones 6–9. Native to Europe, North Africa and the Caucasus.

*Carex morrowii* 'Evergold' (also known as *C. oshimensis* 'Evergold')  An evergreen perennial that grows to 1½ft (45cm) tall, forming tufts of arching foliage, wider than tall. Grass-like leaves, 1ft (30cm) long, slender but rather stiff and green with a broad cream centre. Hardy to 0°F (-18°C), US zones 7–9. Native to Japan.

*Carex ornithopoda* 'Variegata'  An evergreen perennial plant that grows to 9in (23cm) tall, forming tufts of grass-like leaves up to 8in (20cm) long, slender and green with a white central stripe. Hardy to -10°F (-23°C), US zones 6–9. Native to much of Europe. The variegated form was introduced in the 20th century.

*Glyceria maxima* 'Variegata'  An herbaceous perennial that grows to 5ft (1.5m) tall, forming dense spreading clumps, wider than tall, producing sprays of small greenish flowers on stems well above the foliage. Arching narrow strap-like leaves are 2–3ft (60–90cm) wide and handsomely striped with green and cream. Hardy to -20°F (-29°C), US zones 5–9. Native to most of Europe, extending well into Asia.

*Helictotrichon sempervirens*  An evergreen perennial forming dense clumps of leaves to 2ft (60cm) tall and usually wider, producing small pale brown flowers on stems up to 4ft (1.25m) tall, in summer. The bright, blue-grey leaves are narrow and at first upright, later arching. Hardy to -10°F (-23°C), US zones 6–10. Native to the Alps of southern Europe.

*Miscanthus sinensis* 'Zebrinus'  A perennial that grows to 8ft (2.5m) tall, producing flowers in late summer; the flower head may be over 1ft (30cm) in length. Leaf blades are up to ³⁄₄in (2cm) wide, with regular, transverse cream patches. Hardy to -10°F (-23°C), US zones 6–9. Grows wild in Japan, Taiwan and China.

*Stipa gigantea*  An herbaceous perennial that grows up to 8ft (2.5m) tall, producing sprays of oat-like flowers, at first purplish, later turning to yellow-brown in summer. Arching grassy narrow leaves, to 2½ft (75cm) long. Hardy to -10°F (-23°C), US zones 6–9. Native to Spain and Portugal. One of the more striking of ornamental grasses.

*Carex elata* 'Aurea' at Longstock Park Gardens, Hampshire, England

*Carex ornithopoda* 'Variegata'

*Carex morrowii* 'Evergold'

*Miscanthus sinensis* 'Zebrinus'

*Helictotrichon sempervirens*

*Glyceria maxima* 'Variegata'

*Delphinium brunonianum*

*Delphinium brunonianum* A glandular, hairy plant with few stems and a stout rootstock. Flowers 1–2in (2.5–5cm) long, purplish with a broad, blunt spur are produced from July to September. Hardy to -30°F (-35°C), US zones 4–10. Native of the Pamirs and the Himalayas.

*Delphinium* x *belladonna* These delicately branched delphiniums are the result of crossing *Delphinium elatum* hybrids and a branching species, such as *Delphinium grandiflorum*. From Siberia and northern China. Shown here are 'Lamartine', raised by Lémoine in 1903 and 'Moerheimii'. Hardy to -40°F (-40°C), US zones 3–9. Raised by Rays in 1906.

*Delphinium elatum* A perennial that grows to 7ft (2m), flowering from June to August. This is the main species from which garden delphiniums have been raised. Hardy to -40°F (-40°C), US zones 3–9. Native to Europe from the eastern Pyrenees and Provence, east to the Caucasus, and central Asia, Siberia and north-west China. Introduced into cultivation in 1597, probably from Siberia via St Petersburg.

*Delphinium* x *ruysii* 'Pink Sensation' (syn. *D.* 'Rosa Uberraschung') A hybrid between a garden delphinium and *Delphinium nudicaule*. Stems branching to 3ft (90cm). Hardy to -10°F (-23°C), US zones 6–10.

*Delphinium glaucum (*syn. *Delphinium scopulorum)* A perennial with upright stems that grows up to 8ft (2.5m), from a stout woody rootstock. Flowers, 3/4–1in (2–2.5cm) wide, are produced from July to September. Hardy to -5°F (-20°C), US zones 6–10. Native to California and north up to Alaska, and also native to the Rockies.

*Delphinium pyramidale* Flowers, about 1in (2.5cm) long and hairy, are produced from July to September. Hardy to -5°F (-20°C), US zones 6–10. Native to the Himalayas, from Pakistan to central Nepal, and common in Kashmir growing on many stony slopes, by streams and in scrub up to 12,600ft (3600m).

SCARLET LARKSPUR *Delphinium cardinale* (syn. *Delphinium coccineum*) Flowers, scarlet, rarely yellowish, about 1in (2.5cm) wide, appearing from May to July. Prefers well-drained soil in a warm position, dry in summer. Hardy to 15°F (-10°C), US zones 8–10. Native to southern California.

*Delphinium semibarbatum* syn. *Delphinium zalil* Flowers and spurs, about 1/2in (1cm) wide, appear from April to July. This unusually coloured species should be perfectly hardy to the cold, but can be damaged by warm, damp conditions in winter and summer. Prefers a hot dry position and water only in spring. Hardy to -5°F (-20°C), US zones 6–10.

*Delphinium glaucum*

*Delphinium pyramidale*

*Delphinium elatum*

*Delphinium cardinale*

*Delphinium* x *belladonna* 'Moerheimii'

*Delphinium* x *belladonna* "Lamartine'

*Delphinium semibarbatum*

*Delphinium* x *ruysii* 'Pink Sensation'

Blackmore and Langdon's hybrid

Delphinium 'Polarnacht'

Delphinium 'Loch Maree'

*Delphinium* 'Butterball'   A perennial that grows to 7ft (2m) tall and 3ft (90 cm) wide, with a stout, woody rootstock. Flowers in summer and again in early autumn. Hardy to -40°F (-40°C), US zones 3–9. One of the so-called 'yellow' cultivars raised by Blackmore and Langdon in England before 1969.

*Delphinium elatum* hybrid   A perennial that grows to 7ft (2m) tall and 3ft (90cm) wide, with a stout, woody rootstock. Flowers in summer and again in early autumn. Hardy to -40°F (-40°C), US zones 3–9. This hybrid was grown from Blackmore and Langdon seed in the 1950s, and is reliably perennial but has much smaller flowers than more recent, named cultivars.

*Delphinium* 'Turkish Delight'
A perennial that grows to 6ft (1.8m) tall and 3ft (90cm) wide, with a stout, woody rootstock. It produces medium-sized flowers in summer and again in early autumn. Hardy to -40°F (-40°C), US zones 3–9. One of the new cultivars raised by Blackmore and Langdon in England in 1967.

*Delphinium* 'Purple Triumph'
A perennial that grows to 2.5ft (75cm) tall and 2ft (60cm) wide, with a stout, woody rootstock. Flowers in summer and again in early autumn. Hardy to -40°F (-40°C), US zones 3–9. One of the new hybrids raised by Blackmore and Langdon in England in 1960.

*Delphinium* 'High Society'   A perennial that grows to 5ft (1.5m) tall and 3ft (90cm) wide. Very large flowers in summer and again in early autumn. Hardy to -40°F (-40°C), US zones 3–9. A cultivar raised by Pye in England before 1985.

*Delphinium* 'Lilian Bassett'   A perennial that grows to 5ft (1.5m) tall and 3ft (90cm) wide, with a stout, woody rootstock. Large flowers in summer and again in early autumn. Hardy to -40°F (-40°C), US zones 3–9. One of the new hybrids raised by Bassett in England in 1984.

*Delphinium* 'Loch Maree'
A tall perennial that grows to 8ft (2.5m) tall and 3ft (90cm) wide, producing large flowers in summer and again in early autumn. Large delphinium hybrids like full sun or partial shade. Hardy to -40°F (-40°C), US zones 3–9. One of the newer hybrids raised by Cowan in England in 1968.

*Delphinium* 'Polarnacht'   A perennial that grows to 8ft (2.5m) tall, with a stout, woody rootstock. Produces flowers in summer and again in early autumn. Hardy to -40°F (-40°C), US zones 3–9.

*Delphinium* 'Leonora'   A perennial that grows to 5ft (1.5m) tall and 3ft (90cm) wide, with a stout, woody rootstock. It produces flowers in summer and again in early autumn. Hardy to -40°F (-40°C), US zones 3–9. One of the new hybrids raised by Latty in 1969.

*Delphinium* 'Strawberry Fair'
A perennial that grows to 7ft (2m) tall and 3ft (90cm) wide, with a stout, woody rootstock. Large flowers in summer and again in the early autumn. Hardy to -40°F (-40°C), US zones 3–9. One of the new hybrids raised by Blackmore and Langdon in England in 1967.

# DELPHINIUMS

*Delphinium* 'Butterball'

*Delphinium* 'Lilian Bassett'

*Delphinium* 'Turkish Delight'

*Delphinium* 'Strawberry Fair'

Delphiniums in the herbaceous boarder at Pitmedden, Aberdeenshire, Scotland

*Delphinium* 'Leonora'

*Delphinium* 'Purple Triumph'

*Delphinium* 'High Society'

# PERENNIALS

*Nymphaea* 'Norma Gedye'

*Nymphaea* 'American Beauty'

*Nymphaea* 'Norma Gedye'   A vigorous perennial, best grown in water to 1½ft (45cm) deep. Flowers, about 5in (12cm) wide, are produced in summer. Hardy to -20°F (-29°C), US zones 5–10.

*Nymphaea* 'Gladstoniana'   An aquatic perennial producing flowers, each about 10in (25cm) wide, in summer. Needs a rich soil and a sunny position in the pool, with a water depth to 2½ft (75cm). Hardy to -20°F (-29°C), US zones 5–10.

*Nymphaea* 'American Beauty'   A tender summer-flowering perennial with scented flowers, about 10in (25cm) wide. Best in a sunny position with a water depth to 3ft (90cm). Not frost-hardy and needs a heated pool in most temperate regions.

*Nymphaea* 'Gonnère'   An aquatic perennial producing flowers, each about 10in (25cm) wide, in summer. Needs a rich soil, a sunny position in the pool and a water depth to 2½ft (75cm). Hardy to -20°F (-29°C), US zones 5–10.

*Nymphaea* 'James Brydon'   A vigorous aquatic perennial producing slightly scented flowers, each about 10in (25cm) wide, in summer. Needs a sunny position and a water depth of 1½– 3ft (45–90cm). Hardy to -20°F (-29°C), US zones 5–10.

*Nymphaea* 'Laydeckeri Fulgens'   A perennial producing flowers, each about 3in (8cm) wide, in summer. Best in a sunny position in the pool and a water depth of up to 2ft (60cm). Hardy to -20°F (-29°C), US zones 5–10.

*Nymphaea* 'Marliacea Carnea'   A vigorous perennial producing scented summer flowers, about 8in (20cm) wide. Hardy to -20°F (-29°C), US zones 5–10. Raised in France in the 19th century.
*Nymphaea* 'Marliacea Chromatella'   An aquatic perennial producing flowers, each about 6in (15cm) wide, in summer. Hardy to -20°F (-29°C), US zones 5–10. Raised in France in the late 19th century and remains a most popular variety.

*Nymphaea* 'Mrs Richmond'   A perennial producing flowers, each about 10in (25cm) wide, in summer. Best planted in the spring or summer in a rich soil, in a sunny position with a water depth of up to 2½ft (75cm). Hardy to -20°F (-29°C), US zones 5–10.

WATER FRINGE   *Nymphoides peltata*   An aquatic perennial with creeping rhizomes producing summer flowers held above the water, each about 1½in (4cm) wide. Best in a water depth of 2ft (60cm). Hardy to -10°F (-23°C), US zones 6–9.

*Nymphaea* 'Pink Opal'   A perennial that produces flowers, each about 10in (25cm) wide, opening from globose buds and held above the water in summer. Best in a sunny position with a water depth of up to 2½ft (75cm). Hardy to -20°F (-29°C), US zones 5–10.

*Nymphaea* 'Gladstoniana'

*Nymphaea* 'Laydeckeri Fulgens'

*Nymphoides peltata*

*Nymphaea* 'Marliacea Chromatella'

*Nymphaea* 'Gonnère'

*Nymphaea* 'Mrs Richmond'

*Nymphaea* 'Marliacea Carnea'

*Nymphaea* 'Pink Opal'

*Nymphaea* 'James Brydon'

Eschscholzia californica

*Eschscholzia californica* 'Cherry Ripe'

*Eschscholzia californica* 'Double Balarian' mixed

*Eschscholzia californica* 'Purple-Violet'

*Eschscholzia californica* 'Milky-White'

¹/₃ life size. Specimens from Eccleston Square, London, 8 July

Meconopsis cambrica 'Flore Pleno'

Meconopsis cambrica

CALIFORNIAN POPPY *Eschscholzia californica* An herbaceous perennial, most often grown as an annual, that reaches 2ft (60cm) tall. Flowers, each about 3in (8cm) wide, appear in late spring and summer. Best in a sunny position and hardy to 10°F (-12°C), US zones 8–10. Native to the United States. Cultivars shown here are:

*Eschscholzia californica* 'Cherry Ripe' Grows to 1ft (30cm) with flowers about 2¹/₂in (6cm) wide.

*Eschscholzia californica* 'Double Balarian' Grows to 1ft (30cm) tall with flowers about 2¹/₂in (6cm) wide.

*Eschscholzia californica* 'Milky-White' Grows to 1ft (30cm) with flowers about 2¹/₂in (6cm) wide.

*Eschscholzia californica* 'Purple-Violet' Grows to 1ft (30cm) tall with flowers about 2¹/₂in (6cm) wide.

HIMALAYAN BLUE POPPY *Meconopsis betonicifolia* An herbaceous perennial that grows to 4ft (1.25m) tall. Flowers, about 4in (10cm) wide, appear in early summer. Prefers a partially shaded position in acid soil. Hardy to 0°F (-18°C), US zones 7–9. Native to Burma and western China.

WELSH POPPY *Meconopsis cambrica* An herbaceous perennial that grows to 2ft (60cm) tall, producing a succession of solitary yellow flowers, about 2¹/₂in (6cm) wide, in summer. Hardy to -10°F (-23°C), US zones 6–9. Native to western Europe.

*Meconopsis cambrica* 'Flore Pleno' Semi-double yellow or orange flowers.

*Meconopsis* x *sheldonii* Many of the finest blue poppies in cultivation at present probably belong to this cross between *Meconopsis grandis* and *Meconopsis betonicifolia*. It was first raised at Oxted in Surrey in 1937 and is a strong and vigorous perennial, with stems that grow up to 5ft (1.5m) tall. Easy to grow, but liable to die if it becomes too hot and dry in summer. In warmer climates a cool, shaded and sheltered position is required if it is to survive. Hardy to -10°F (-23°C), US zones 6–9. Several named clones or forms are grown in gardens.

'Crewson Hybrids'
A good form with a neat habit derived from *Meconopsis betonicifolia*. Bears dark-blue flowers.

ORIENTAL POPPY *Papaver orientale* 'Mrs Perry' An herbaceous perennial that grows up to 3ft (90cm) tall and usually is wider than it is tall. It produces flowers, each about 4in (10cm) wide, in early summer. this poppy prefers a sunny position. Hardy to -20°F (-29°C), US zones 5–9. Native to south-west Asia.

*Papaver orientale* 'Black and White' Grows to 2¹/₂ft (75cm) tall, producing white flowers, about 4in (10cm) wide, with 4 overlapping petals and a large black blotch at the base.

*Papaver orientale* 'Beauty of Livermere' Grows up to 4ft (1.25m) tall. Rich blood-red flowers.

*Papaver orientale* 'Beauty of Livermere'

*Papaver orientale* 'Black and White'

*Papaver orientale* 'Mrs Perry'

*Meconopsis betonicifolia*

*Meconopsis* x *sheldonii*

*Meconopsis* 'Crewson Hybrids'

*Clematis texensis*

*Alcea rosea*

*Althea officinalis*

*Clematis integrifolia*

*Romneya coulteri*

HOLLYHOCK *Alcea rosea* (syn. *Althaea rosea*) A biennial that grows to 10ft (3m) tall (although there are dwarf varieties), producing a succession of showy, single or double flowers, about 3in (8cm) wide and of varying colours, in summer and autumn. Prefers a sunny position. Hardy to -40°F (-40°C), US zones 3–10.

MARSH MALLOW *Althea officinalis* An herbaceous perennial that grows to 7ft (2m) tall, producing flowers, about 1in (2.5cm) wide, over a long period in summer. Best in a sunny position. Hardy to -10°F (-23°C), US zones 6–10 or lower. Native to much of Europe.

*Clematis integrifolia* An herbaceous perennial that grows to 3ft (90cm) tall, usually making a clump about as wide as tall. In summer it produces flowers, each with four petal-like sepals, about 2in (5cm) long. Best in a sunny position. Hardy to -30°F (-35°C), US zones 4–9. Native to central and eastern Europe and western Asia.

*Clematis texensis* Stems often annual, although sometimes persistent near the base in warm winters. Grows to 10ft (3m) from a stout rootstock. Flowers, 3/4–1in (2–2.5cm) long and scarlet to reddish-purple, appear from July to September. Prefers a warm position. Hardy to -20°F (-29°C), US zones 5–10. Native to eastern North America.

*Lavatera* 'Barnsley' Vigorous sub-shrub that grows to 5ft (1.5m) tall, producing a succession of flowers, 3in (8cm) wide, in summer. Prefers a sunny position. Hardy to -10°F (-23°C), US zones 6–9. Probably

*Malva moschata*

*Malva moschata* 'Alba'

*Lavatera* 'Barnsley'

of hybrid origin and is one of several varieties introduced late this century.

MUSK MALLOW *Malva moschata* 'Alba' An herbaceous perennial that grows to 3ft (90cm) tall. In summer it produces pure white flowers, 2in (5cm) wide. Best in a sunny position. Hardy to -30°F (-35°C), US zones 4–8. Native to much of Europe. The wild type has mallow-pink flowers, but the variety 'Alba' is the more garden-worthy.

*Polygonum vacciniifolium* (syn. *Persicaria vacciniifolia*) A creeping herbaceous perennial that grows to 6in (15cm) tall, spreading to form wide mats. Flowers in late summer and autumn. Hardy to -10°F (-23°C), US zones 6–9. Native to the Himalayas and introduced into cultivation in the 19th century.

BISTORT *Polygonum bistorta* 'Superbum' (syn. *Persicaria bistorta* 'Superba') An herbaceous perennial that grows to 2¹/₂ft (75cm) tall, spreading to form substantial clumps. In early summer it produces short spikes of flowers. Hardy to -30°F (-35°C), US zones 4–9. Native to much of Europe and Asia.

MATILIJA POPPY *Romneya coulteri* An herbaceous perennial that grows to 7ft (2m) tall, spreading by underground rhizomes. In summer and autumn it produces a succession of dazzling white poppy flowers, each about 8in (20cm) wide, with a prominent tuft of yellow stamens in the centre. Hardy to 0°F (-18°C), US zones 7–10. Native to California.

*Polygonum bistorta* 'Superbum'

*Polygonum vacciniifolium*

*Gypsophila* 'Rosenschleier'

*Gypsophila repens* 'Letchworth Rose'

*Saponaria ocymoides*

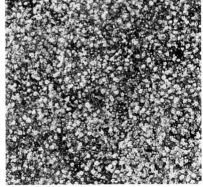

*Gypsophila paniculata* 'Bristol Fairy'

*Dianthus* 'Constance Finnis'
An evergreen perennial that grows to 10in (25cm) tall, forming a compact mat rather wider than tall. In summer it produces flowers 1½in (4cm) wide. Best in a sunny position. Hardy to -20°F (-29°C), US zones 5–9. A hybrid of garden origin, raised in England in the 20th century.

MAIDEN PINK *Dianthus deltoides*
A perennial with sprawling stems that grows to 1½ft (45cm) from a slender, creeping rootstock. Solitary flowers, ¾in (2cm) wide, appear in mid- to late summer. Prefers light soil in full sun. Hardy to -40°F (-40°C), US zones 3–8. Native to most of Europe, from Scotland eastwards to Finland and northern Russia, growing in dry grassy places.

*Dianthus* 'Doris'   An evergreen perennial that grows to 10in (25cm) tall, forming a compact mat wider than tall. In summer it produces strongly fragrant double flowers, 2in (5cm) wide. Best in a sunny position. Hardy to -20°F (-29°C), US zones 5–10. A hybrid of garden origin, raised in England in the 20th century.

*Dianthus deltoides*

*Dianthus* 'Constance Finnis'

*Dianthus* 'Laced Joy'

*Dianthus* 'Doris'

*Dianthus* 'Laced Joy'   An evergreen perennial that grows to 1ft (30cm) tall, producing scented double flowers with attractively laced petals, 2in (5cm) wide, in summer. Best in a sunny position. Hardy to -20°F (-29°C), US zones 5–9. A hybrid of garden origin, raised in England in the 20th century.

*Dianthus* 'Pink Mrs Sinkins'   Grows to 10in (25cm) tall, forming a compact mat rather wider than tall, producing flowers, 1¹/₂in (1cm) wide, of untidy form but very fragrant. Best in a sunny position and hardy to -20°F (-29°C), US zones 5–9. A hybrid of garden origin.

*Gypsophila paniculata* 'Bristol Fairy'
An herbaceous perennial that grows to 4ft (1.25m) tall, usually rather wider than tall. In summer it produces large airy sprays of small double white flowers, about ¹/₂in (1cm) wide. Best in a sunny position. Hardy to -20°F (-29°C), US zones 5–9. Native to eastern Europe and northern Asia.

*Gypsophila* 'Rosenschleier' ('Rosy Veil')
An herbaceous perennial that grows to 1ft (30cm) tall and wider, with trailing stems, producing flowers, about ¹/₂in (1cm) wide,

in summer. Best in a sunny position and hardy to -20°F (-29°C), US zones 5–9. A hybrid between *G. paniculata* and *Gypsophila repens* 'Rosea'.

*Gypsophila repens* 'Letchworth Rose'
An herbaceous perennial that grows to 8in (20cm) tall and wider, with trailing stems, producing flowers, about ¹/₂in (1cm) wide, in summer. Best in a sunny position. Hardy to -20°F (-29°C), US zones 5–9. Raised in England in the early 20th century.

SOAP-WORT, BOUNCING BET
*Saponaria officinalis* 'Rosea Plena'
A rather invasive herbaceous perennial that grows to 2¹/₂ft (75cm) tall, producing delicately scented flowers, about 1in (2.5cm) wide, in summer. Hardy to -20°F (-29°C), US zones 5–8. Native to Europe and western Asia.

*Saponaria ocymoides*   A perennial that grows to 6in (15cm) tall, forming dense mats much wider than tall. In late spring and summer it bears abundant small bright pink flowers, each about ¹/₂in (1cm) wide. Best in a sunny position. Hardy to -10°F (-23°C), US zones 6–9. Native to southern Europe.

*Dianthus* 'Pink Mrs Sinkins'

*Saponaria officinalis* 'Rosea Plena'

*Filipendula* in a mixed perennial bed

## QUEEN OF THE PRAIRIES
*Filipendula rubra* 'Venusta'  A robust herbaceous perennial that grows to 8ft (2.5m) tall, forming clumps taller than wide. In summer it produces large frothy sprays of tiny, bright pink flowers. Hardy to -30°F (-35°C), US zones 4–8. Native to eastern North America.

*Filipendula rubra* 'Venusta'

## GOLDEN MEADOW-SWEET
*Filipendula ulmaria* 'Aurea'  A perennial that grows to 3ft (90cm) tall, producing frothy sprays of small, creamy-white flowers in summer. The leaves are bright golden-yellow when they open in the spring. Hardy to -30°F (-35°C), US zones 4–8. Native to Europe and Asia.

GOAT'S RUE *Galega officinalis* 'His Majesty'  An herbaceous perennial  that grows to 5ft (1.5m) tall, forming loose clumps as wide as tall, producing flowers, $\frac{1}{2}$in (1cm) wide, in summer. Hardy to -30°F (-35°C), US zones 4–9.

EVERLASTING PEA *Lathyrus latifolius*
A vigorous climbing herbaceous perennial that grows to 10ft (3m) tall. In summer it produces unscented flowers, $1\frac{1}{2}$in (4cm) wide, vivid magenta-pink and, less commonly, pale pink. Hardy to -20°F (-29°C), US zones 5–10.
  *Lathyrus latifolius* 'White Pearl' Bears pure white flowers.

STONECROP *Sedum acre*  A small, succulent perennial that grows to 3in (8cm) tall, producing flowers, $\frac{1}{2}$in (1cm) wide, in summer. The leaves have a

*Filipendula ulmaria* 'Aurea'

*Galega officinalis*

peppery taste if chewed. Best in a sunny position. Hardy to -30°F (-35°C), US zones 4–9. Native to much of Europe.

*Sedum aizoon* 'Aurantiacum'   A succulent perennial that grows to 1¹/₂ft (45cm) tall, producing clusters of flowers, 2¹/₂in (6cm) wide, with each flower about ¹/₃in (8mm) wide, opening from reddish buds in late summer and autumn. Hardy to -30°F (-35°C), US zones 4–9. Native to northern China and Japan.

*Sedum alboroseum* 'Medio-variegatum' A perennial that grows to 2ft (60cm) tall. In summer and autumn it produces flat heads, up to 5in (12cm) wide, containing many starry, whitish flowers, each about ¹/₃in (8mm) wide, which are attractive to butterflies. The fleshy leaves are heavily splashed in the centre with creamy white, producing a showy foliage. Hardy to -10°F (-23°C), US zones 6–9. Native to north-east Asia.

*Sedum* 'Ruby Glow'   An herbaceous perennial that grows to 10in (25cm) tall producing flowers, about ¹/₂in (1cm) wide, in summer. Hardy to -10°F (-23°C), US zones 6–9. A hybrid of garden origin, raised early in the 20th century.

*Sedum spectabile* 'Carmen'   A perennial that grows to 2ft (60cm) tall, producing flat heads to 5in (12cm) wide, containing many starry, rosy-pink flowers, each about ¹/₃in (8mm) wide, in summer and autumn. Hardy to -10°F (-23°C), US zones 6–9. The species is native to north-east China and Korea.

*Sedum* 'Sunset Cloud'   A succulent perennial that grows to 1ft (30cm) tall. In summer and autumn it produces domed heads to 3in (8cm) wide, containing many flowers, each about ¹/₃in (8mm) wide. Best in a sunny position but not too dry in summer. Hardy to -10°F (-23°C), US zones 6–9.

*Sedum acre*

*Sedum aizoon* 'Aurantiacum'

*Sedum alboroseum* 'Medio-variegatum'

*Sedum* 'Sunset Cloud'

*Sedum* 'Ruby Glow'

*Sedum spectabile* 'Carmen'

*Lathyrus latifolius* 'White Pearl'

*Lathyrus latifolius*

*Astilbe* 'Jo Ophorst'

*Astilbe* x *arendsii* 'Fanal' An herbaceous perennial that grows to 2½ft (75cm) tall, producing compact, much-branched panicles of dark crimson flowers in early summer. Each flower is tiny but they are packed densely on the stems and the effect is very showy. The reddish-brown fruiting stems are attractive in their own right. A good pool-side plant. Hardy to -10°F (-23°C), US zones 6–9. *Astilbe* 'Fanal' belongs to the complex hybrid group called *A.* x *arendsii* raised in Germany in the 20th century.

*Astilbe* at Trebah Garden in Cornwall, England

*Astilbe* x *arendsii* 'Weisse Gloria' (right) Dense, narrow panicles of creamy-white flowers. Belongs to the same hybrid group as *Astilbe* 'Fanal'.

*Astilbe* 'Deutschland'

*Astilbe* x *arendsii* 'Granat'   Deep red flowers, bronze-tinged leaves. Belongs to the same hybrid group as *Astilbe* 'Fanal'.

*Astilbe* 'Glut' (syn. 'Glow')   Grows to 3ft (90cm) tall with deep red flowers. Belongs to the same hybrid group as *Astilbe* 'Fanal'

*Astilbe* 'Bronce Elegans' (syn. 'Bronze Elegance')   An herbaceous perennial that grows to 1ft (30cm) tall, producing open panicles of densely packed, tiny, salmon-pink flowers in early summer. The effect is most attractive. The glossy leaves are pretty even when the plant is not in flower and the reddish-brown fruiting stems are quite attractive in their own right. Hardy to 0°F (-18°C), US zones 7–9.

*Astilbe chinensis* 'Pumila'   A perennial that grows to 1½ft (45cm) tall, producing branched spikes of densely packed, tiny flowers in late summer. The fruiting stems are reddish-brown and attractive in their own right. Hardy to -10°F (-23°C), US zones 6–9. Native to eastern China. The variety 'Pumila' is an attractive dwarf form and a good ground-cover plant by water or around shrubs.

*Astilbe* 'Deutschland'   An herbaceous perennial that grows to 2½ft (75cm) tall, forming a slowly spreading clump about as wide as tall. In early summer it produces large, much-branched panicles of tiny, densely packed, creamy-white flowers. Hardy to -10°F (-23°C), US zones 6–9. A hybrid of *A. japonica*, it is native to Japan.

*Astilbe* x *hybrida* 'Jo Ophorst' An herbaceous perennial that grows to 3ft (90cm) tall, producing compact, erect branched panicles of tiny, strong, rosy-pink flowers densely packed on the stems, in early summer. Hardy to -10°F (-23°C), US zones 6–9. *Astilbe* 'Jo Ophorst' belongs to the complex hybrid group called *A.* x *hybrida* and was raised in the Netherlands early in the 20th century.

*Astilbe* x *arendsii* 'Granat'

*Astilbe* x *arendsii* 'Fanal'

*Astilbe* 'Glut'

*Astilbe* 'Bronce Elegans'

*Astilbe chinensis* 'Pumila'

Epilobium angustifolium f. albiflorum

Aruncus dioicus

Limonium latifolium

Rodgersia aesculifolia

Rodgersia pinnata 'Superba'

GOAT'S BEARD *Aruncus dioicus*
An herbaceous perennial that grows to 7ft (2m) tall, producing flowers in summer. Individual plants are either male or female – the males are more attractive in flower, but the female plants are also attractive in fruit. Hardy to -20°F (-29°C), US zones 5–8. Native to much of the Northern hemisphere including Europe, North America and Asia.

ROSEBAY WILLOW-HERB, FIREWEED *Epilobium angustifolium* f. *albiflorum* A rhizomatous herbaceous perennial that grows to 5ft (1.5m) tall, spreading rapidly and can be invasive. In late summer it produces tall spires of pink or occasionally, white flowers, each about 1½in (4cm) wide. Hardy to -30°F (-35°C), US zones 4–8. Native to Europe, northern Asia and North America.

*Limonium latifolium* An evergreen perennial that grows up to 2½ft (75cm) tall and produces lavender-blue flowers, each about ½in (1cm) long, in late summer. Although the foliage is coarse, the flower heads are elegant and long-lasting. Best in a sunny position and hardy to -30°F (-35°C), US zones 4–9 or lower. *Limonium latifolium* is native to south-eastern Europe.

PURPLE LOOSESTRIFE *Lythrum salicaria* 'Feuerkerze' ('Fire Candle')
An herbaceous perennial that grows to 5ft (1.5m) tall and produces erect spires of bright rose-red flowers, each about ¹⁄₂in (1cm) wide, in summer. Best in a sunny position. Hardy to -20°F (-29°C), US zones 5–9. Native to Europe, North Africa and northern Asia.

*Rodgersia aesculifolia*   A robust herbaceous perennial that grows to 5ft (1.5m) tall in flower. It produces broad sprays of small, creamy-pink or white flowers in summer and is valued for its handsome foliage. Best in a partially shaded or, in wet soil, sunny position. Hardy to -10°F (-23°C), US zones 6–8. Native to western China.

*Rodgersia pinnata* 'Superba'   A robust herbaceous perennial that grows to 5ft (1.5m) tall in flower, producing broad sprays of small, rosy-pink flowers in summer. The leaves are tinged purple when young. Hardy to -10°F (-23°C), US zones 6–8. Native to western China, from where it was introduced into cultivation early in the 20th century. A colourful plant for a bog garden or pool-side, with very fine foliage.

*Rodgersia podophylla*   A rhizomatous perennial that grows to 3ft (90cm) tall, producing small flowers on stems up to 4ft (1.25m) tall, in summer. Each flower is ¹⁄₂in (1cm) wide. In autumn, the leaves turn to bronze, purple or deep crimson. Best in a partially shaded position, but will stand full sun if growing by water and will then colour more brightly in autumn. Hardy to -10°F (-23°C), US zones 6–9. Native to Japan and Korea.

*Lythrum salicaria* 'Feuerkerze'

*Rodgersia podophylla*

*Rodgersia podophylla* in autumn

Astrantia major subsp. *carinthiaca* 'Shaggy'

Astrantia major subsp. *major* 'Rubra'

*Lysimachia vulgaris*

*Lysimachia ciliata*

*Lysimachia clethroides*

*Lysimachia punctata*

1/3 life size. Specimens from Sellindge, Kent, England, 20 August

*Astrantia major* subsp. *carinthiaca* 'Shaggy' An herbaceous perennial that grows to 2ft (60cm) tall, forming tidy clumps as wide as tall when in flower. In summer it produces flower heads, about 2½in (6cm) wide. Hardy to 0°F (-18°C), US zones 7–9 or lower. Native to south-west Europe, and introduced into cultivation by the 16th century.

*Astrantia major* subsp. *major* 'Rubra' Grows to 2ft (60cm) tall, forming clumps and producing erect, branched stems bearing several flower heads, about 1½in (4cm) wide, which remain decorative when the plant is in fruit. Hardy to 0°F (-18°C), US zones 7–9 or lower. Native to south-west Europe. 'Rubra' is a selection with more strongly coloured flowers.

*Gunnera manicata* An herbaceous perennial that grows to 7ft (2m) tall, forming enormous clumps wider than tall. In summer strange cone-like green flower heads, 2–3ft (60–90cm) long and bearing minute flowers, grow from the rhizomes. Best in a sunny position. Hardy to 10°F (-12°C), US zones 8–10, with some protection in cold areas; the old leaves should be inverted over the rhizomes in late autumn to achieve this. Native to southern Brazil.

*Lysimachia ciliata* An herbaceous perennial that grows to 4ft (1.25m) tall, spreading by rhizomes to form colonies wider than tall. In summer it produces many small, nodding yellow flowers in airy sprays, each about ¾in (2cm) wide. Hardy to -30°F (-35°C), US zones 4–9 or lower. Native to North America.

*Lysimachia clethroides* An herbaceous perennial that grows to 3ft (90cm) tall, spreading to form colonies wider than tall. In late summer it produces many small, off-white flowers, ½in (1cm) wide. Hardy to -30°F (-35°C), US zones 4–9. Native to China and Japan and introduced into cultivation in the 19th century.

*Lysimachia ephemerum* An herbaceous perennial that grows to 3ft (90cm) tall, spreading to form colonies wider than tall. In late summer it produces flowers ½in (1cm) wide. Hardy to 0°F (-18°C), US zones 7–9. Native to south-west Europe and introduced into cultivation in the 19th century.

CREEPING JENNY *Lysimachia nummularia* 'Aurea' An herbaceous perennial that grows to 3in (8cm) tall, with creeping stems that root as they go. Can be invasive in heavy soils. Over a long period, from spring to late summer, it produces a succession of small yellow flowers, each about ½in (1cm) wide. Hardy to -20°F (-29°C), US zones 5–9. Native to Europe and western Asia.

*Lysimachia punctata* An herbaceous perennial with stems that grow up to 5ft (1.5m) tall. Flowers from late spring to early autumn. Can be planted at any time of year and prefers a damp area. Hardy to -30°F (-35°C), US zones 4–8. Native to eastern Europe but can be found growing in damp places all over North America.

YELLOW LOOSESTRIFE *Lysimachia vulgaris* Stems grow to 4ft (1.25m) from a creeping rootstock, spreading by stolons. Flowers, up to ¾in (2cm) wide, throughout spring and summer. Hardy to -12°F (-25°C), US zones 5–8. Native to most of Europe, north-west Africa and Asia, and naturalized in North America.

*Oenothera fruticosa* An herbaceous perennial that grows to 3ft (90cm) tall. For most of the summer it produces a succession of bright yellow flowers about 2in (5cm) wide. Best in a sunny position and hardy to -20°F (-29°C), US zones 5–9. Native to the eastern United States.

*Oenothera macrocarpa* (syn. *O. missouriensis*) An herbaceous perennial with flopping stems that grow to 1ft (30cm) long, making a mat wider than tall and producing a succession of flowers, about 4in (10cm) wide, for most of the summer. Best in a sunny position. Hardy to -20°F (-29°C), US zones 5–9. Native to the southern United States.

EVENING PRIMROSE *Oenothera speciosa* An herbaceous perennial with flowering stems that grows up to 1ft (30cm) tall, spreading by a rhizome to make a patch wider than tall. In the summer it produces a succession of large white flowers with a yellow eye, fading to pink. Each flower is up to 3in (8cm) wide. Hardy to -10°F (-23°C), US zones 6–9. Native to the southern United States.

Gunnera by the lake at Stancome Park, Gloucestershire, England

*Oenothera fruticosa*

*Oenothera macrocarpa*

*Lysimachia ephemerum*

*Lysimachia nummularia* 'Aurea'

*Oenothera speciosa*

*Eryngium variifolium*

*Nepeta* 'Six Hills Giant'

*Eryngium* x *tripartitum*

*Eryngium agavifolium*

Specimens ¼ life size

*Eryngium planum*

*Eryngium bourgatii*

**BUTTERFLY WEED** *Asclepias tuberosa*
A tuberous-rooted perennial that grows to 3ft (90cm) tall and usually wider, producing flowers, ½in (1cm) wide and of curious shape. All parts of this plant contain a milky white latex which is an irritant to the skin. Plant in autumn or early spring in a sunny position. Hardy to -30°F (-35°C), US zones 4–10. Native to North America.

*Eryngium bourgatii* An evergreen perennial with branched flower stems that grow to 2ft (60cm), arising from a rosette of leaves. In summer it produces egg-shaped, greenish-blue flower heads, up to 2in (5cm) long, each sitting in a rosette of narrow spiny, bright, metallic-blue bracts. Best in a sunny position. Hardy to -10°F (-23°C), US zones 6–9. Native to south-west Europe and North Africa.

*Eryngium* x *tripartitum* An evergreen perennial that grows to 2½ft (75cm) tall, arising from a rosette of leaves. In summer it has several flower heads, up to ¾in (2cm) long, in rosettes of a few narrow spiny, blue-green bracts. Best in a sunny position. Hardy to -20°F (-29°C), US zones 5–9. A hybrid of garden origin related to *Eryngium planum*, it has become widely grown in the 20th century.

*Eryngium variifolium* An evergreen perennial with erect flower stems, producing tall stems, 1½ft (45cm) tall, with several rounded greenish flower heads, about ½in (1cm) long in a rosette of spiny white bracts, in late summer. Hardy to 10°F (-12°C), US zones 8–10. Native to Morocco.

*Eryngium planum* An evergreen perennial with branched flower stems that grow to 3ft (90cm), arising from a rosette of leaves. It produces flower heads, ¾in (2cm) long, each sitting in a rosette of narrow spiny, blue-green bracts, in summer. Hardy to -10°F (-23°C), US zones 6–9. Native to much of Europe and introduced into cultivation by the 16th century.

*Eryngium agavifolium* An evergreen perennial with erect flower stems arising from a rosette of leaves. In summer it produces tall stems, up to 6ft (1.8m), with several egg-shaped, greenish flower heads, about 2in (5cm) long. Hardy to 10°F (-12°C), US zones 8–10. Native to Argentina in South America.

*Phlomis russeliana* A spreading herbaceous perennial that forms mats of foliage about 1ft (30cm) tall and rather

wider. In summer it produces erect stems up to 3ft (90cm) tall, with whorls of flowers 1in (2.5cm) long. Best in a sunny position. Hardy to -10°F (-23°C), US zones 6–9. Native to Turkey and introduced into cultivation in the early 19th century.

*Nepeta* 'Six Hills Giant' (syn. *N. gigantea*)
A perennial that grows to 3ft (90cm) tall and usually as wide. For most of the summer it produces small tubular flowers in large sprays. The greyish oval, aromatic leaves are up to 2in (5cm) long. Hardy to -20°F (-29°C), US zones 5–9. A hybrid of unrecorded origin, now well-established in gardens as one of the tougher catmints.

*Asclepias tuberosa*

*Phlomis russeliana*

*Stachys byzantina* 'Primrose Heron'

*Stachys byzantina*

*Stachys macrantha*

*Stachys officinalis* 'Grandiflora'

HYSSOP *Hyssopus officinalis*   A partially evergreen sub-shrub that grows to 2ft (60cm) tall, with aromatic leaves, producing deep violet-blue flowers, each about ¹/₂in (1cm) long, in summer. Hardy to -30°F (-35°C), US zones 4–9. Native to southern Europe and parts of western Asia and cultivated since the 16th century for its medicinal and culinary qualities but also makes a good dwarf hedge.

*Hyssopus officinalis* forma *roseus* Has deep rose-pink flowers.

*Phlox paniculata* 'Cherry Pink' An herbaceous perennial forming a clump of erect stems that grows to 3ft (90cm) tall, rather taller than wide. In late summer it produces broadly conical heads of slightly fragrant deep rosy-pink flowers. Plant in autumn or spring in a sunny or partially shaded position. Hardy to -30°F (-35°C), US zones 4–9. Native to eastern North America and introduced into cultivation early in the 18th century.

*Phlox paniculata* 'Fujiyama'   Grows to 4ft (1.25m) tall with pure white flowers, each about 1in (2.5cm) wide. 'Fujiyama' is a recent American introduction, rather later-flowering than the others.

*Phlox paniculata* 'Mother of Pearl' Grows to 4ft (1.25m) tall, bearing flower heads to 8in (20cm) long, of blush-pink flowers with a white centre, each about 1¹/₂in (4cm) wide. 'Mother of Pearl' is a recent British introduction.

*Phlox paniculata* 'Rijnstroom'   Grows to 3ft (90cm) tall with deep rosy-pink flowers, each about 1¹/₂in (4cm) wide. 'Rijnstroom' is a fairly old introduction, but remains reliable and popular.

LAMB'S EARS *Stachys byzantina* A low-growing evergreen perennial forming dense mats of foliage with erect stems that grow to 1¹/₂ft (45cm) tall. In summer it produces small, purplish-rose flowers, each about ¹/₂in (1cm) long, in whorls on the stems. Plant in autumn or spring in a warm, sunny position. Hardy to -10°F (-23°C), US zones 6–8. Native to the Caucasus and Iran and introduced into cultivation in the 18th century.

*Stachys byzantina* 'Primrose Heron' Leaves are pale yellow-green under the soft white hairs. 'Primrose Heron' has the uneasy combination of slightly sickly looking yellow older leaves and grey new growth.

*Stachys macrantha*   An herbaceous perennial with erect flower stems that grows to 2ft (60cm) tall, producing purplish-rose flowers, each about 1¹/₂in (4cm) long in summer. Plant in autumn or spring in a sunny or partially shaded position. It is hardy to -20°F (-29°C), US zones 5–8. Native to the Caucasus and Iran.

WOOD BETONY *Stachys officinalis* 'Grandiflora'   An herbaceous perennial with erect flower stems that grow to 2ft (60cm) tall, producing dense spikes of soft pink flowers, each about ³/₄in (2cm) long, in summer. Plant in autumn or spring in a sunny or partially shaded position. Hardy to -20°F (-29°C), US zones 5–8. The species is native to much of Europe.

*Hyssopus officinalis*

*Hyssopus officinalis* forma *roseus*

*Phlox paniculata* 'Cherry Pink'

*Phlox paniculata* 'Rijnstroom'

*Phlox paniculata* 'Mother of Pearl'

*Phlox paniculata* 'Fujiyama'

233

*Monarda didyma* 'Praerienacht'

*Monarda didyma*

**Salvia buchananii** An erect herbaceous perennial that grows to 2ft (60cm) tall. In summer and autumn it produces clusters of velvety-hairy, rose-purple flowers, each about 2in (5cm) long. Best in a sunny position. Hardy to 10°F (-12°C), US zones 8–10. Native to Mexico and introduced early in the 20th century.

**Salvia microphylla** var. *neurepia* A bushy sub-shrub that grows to 4ft (1.25m) tall, producing clusters of intense scarlet flowers, each about 1in (2.5cm) long, arising from red-purple bracts in summer and autumn. Best in a sunny position and generally needs the shelter of a warm wall. Hardy to 10°F (-12°C), US zones 8–10. Native to Mexico.

**Salvia nemorosa** 'Superba' An erect herbaceous perennial that grows to 3ft (90cm) tall, producing flowers, about ¹/₂in (1cm) long, in summer and autumn. Best in a sunny position and hardy to -10°F (-23°C), US zones 6–10. Native to eastern Europe and western Asia.

**Salvia patens** A bushy sub-shrub that grows to 2ft (60cm) tall, producing clusters of intense blue flowers, about 1in (2.5cm) long, in summer and autumn. Best in a sunny position and generally needs the shelter of a warm wall. Hardy to 10°F (-12°C), US zones 8–10. Native to Mexico and introduced into cultivation early in the 19th century.
**Salvia patens** 'Cambridge Blue' Clear, light blue flowers.

**CLARY SAGE** *Salvia sclarea* A biennial or short-lived perennial that grows to 3¹/₂ft (1m) tall. In summer it produces flowers, each about 1¹/₂in (4cm). Thrives in a warm, sunny position. Hardy to -10°F (-23°C), US zones 6–9. Native to south-east Europe and south-west Asia, it was introduced in the 16th century.

**Salvia uliginosa** A bushy perennial that grows to 5ft (1.5m) tall, producing flowers in autumn, each about ³/₄in (2cm) long. Prefers a sunny position and generally needs moist soil. Hardy to 10°F (-12°C), US zones 8–10 and native to eastern South America

**Salvia forskahlei** Perennial forming large, almost woody, ground-covering clumps bearing flowers with violet-blue centres, in spikes to 3¹/₂ft (1m) high, in mid- to late summer. Prefers rich soil in sun or partial shade. Hardy to 5°F (-15°C), US zones 7–10. Native to Bulgaria and northern Turkey along the Black Sea, growing on dry hillsides, bare meadows and in deciduous woodland, at up to 6650 ft (1900m).

**OSWEGO TEA, BERGAMOT** *Monarda didyma* An herbaceous perennial that grows to 4ft (1.25m) tall, producing sage-like red flowers, each about 1¹/₂in (4cm) long, and pleasantly aromatic leaves. Hardy to -20°F (-29°C), US zones 5–8. Can suffer from mildew in dry conditions. Native to the eastern United States.
*Monarda didyma* 'Croftway Pink' Grows to 3ft (90cm) tall with rose-pink flowers. 'Croftway Pink' is slightly more compact than the wild type.
*Monarda didyma* 'Praerienacht' Grows to 3ft (90cm) tall with rich purple flowers. 'Praerienacht' is slightly more compact than the wild type and is rather more tolerant of dry conditions.
...*Monarda didyma* 'Cambridge Scarlet'(right) Grows to 3ft (90cm) tall with flowers sitting within a purple calyx. Several cultivars have resulted from hybridization in gardens. 'Cambridge Scarlet' is one of the brightest.

*Monarda didyma* 'Croftway Pink'

*Salvia sclarea* in Mary Glasson's garden, NSW, Australia

*Salvia forskahlei*

*Salvia nemorosa* 'Superba'

*Salvia buchananii*

*Salvia patens*

*Salvia uliginosa*

*Salvia microphylla* var. *neurepia*

*Salvia patens* 'Cambridge Blue'

*Penstemon barbatus* 'Coccineus'

*Penstemon* 'Alice Hindley'   An erect perennial that grows to 4ft (1.25m) tall, making a compact clump and producing flowers, each about 1½in (4cm) long, in summer. Plant in autumn or spring in a sunny position. Hardy to 20°F (-7°C), US zones 9–10 or slightly lower. A hybrid raised in Scotland early this century.

*Penstemon heterophyllus*   An erect evergreen shrub that grows to 1½ft (45cm) tall, making a clump taller than wide. In summer it produces trumpet-shaped, blue and purple flowers, each about 1½in (4cm) long. Best in a sunny position and hardy to 10°F (-12°C), US zones 8–10 or slightly lower. Native to California and introduced into cultivation in the early 19th century.

*Penstemon heterophyllus* subsp. *purdyi* An evergreen shrub that grows to 1ft (30cm) tall, making a compact mat, wider than tall. Blue or mauve flowers, each about 1½in (4cm) long, are produced in summer. Plant in autumn or spring in a sunny position. Hardy to 10°F (-12°C), US zones 8–10 or slightly lower. Native to California.

*Penstemon barbatus*   An erect perennial that grows to 3ft (90cm) tall. Tubular bright red flowers, each about 1½in (4cm) long, produced in summer. Plant in autumn or spring in a sunny position Hardy to -30°F (-35°C), US zones 4–9 or slightly lower. Native to the Rocky Mountains of North America and introduced into cultivation in the 18th century.
   *Penstemon barbatus* 'Coccineus' A perennial producing bright scarlet flowers. This variety has greyer leaves and deep red flowers. It is an attractive and relatively hardy plant for a sunny, well-drained border.

*Penstemon* 'Hidcote Pink'   A bushy perennial that grows to 2½ft (75cm) tall, making a compact clump. In summer and

*Penstemon heterophyllus*

*Penstemon barbatus*

*Penstemon* 'Alice Hindley'

*Penstemon* 'Stapleford Gem'

*Penstemon heterophyllus* subsp. *purdyi*

autumn it produces flowers, each about 1½in (4cm) long. Prefers a sunny position. Hardy to 10°F (-12°C), US zones 8–10. A hybrid raised at Hidcote in England, during the 20th century. Hardier than many large-flowered hybrids.

*Penstemon glaber* (below)   A perennial that grows to 2ft (60cm) tall. In midsummer it produces flowers, 1½in (4cm) long. Plant in autumn or spring in a sunny position. Hardy to -30°F (-35°C), US zones 4–9 or slightly lower. Native to the prairies of North America, it was introduced into cultivation in the 19th century. Hardier than most hybrid penstemons.

*Penstemon* 'Rubicunda'   A perennial that grows to 2ft (60cm) tall and wide, producing large flowers in late summer. Hardy to 25°F (-4°C), US zones 9–10. Raised at Lyme Park, Chesire, England.

*Penstemon* 'Stapleford Gem'   A bushy perennial that grows to 3½ft (1m) tall, making a tall clump. In summer and autumn it produces flowers, each about 1½in (4cm) long. Plant in autumn or spring in a sunny position. Hardy to 10°F (-12°C), US zones 8–10 or slightly lower. A hybrid raised at Hidcote, in England, in the 20th century.

*Penstemon* 'Rubicunda'

*Penstemon* 'Hidcote Pink'

*Diascia barberae* 'Blackthorn Apricot'

*Diascia fetcaniensis*

*Diascia fetcaniensis* An herbaceous perennial that grows to 1 1/2ft (45cm) tall, forming loose mats of foliage rather wider than tall. In summer and early autumn it produces clusters of flowers, 3/4in (2cm) wide. Hardy to 10°F (-12°C), US zones 8–10 and native to South Africa. Like other diascias, this plant has recently become rather popular, although it is sometimes short-lived.

*Diascia integerrima* An herbaceous perennial that grows to 1 1/2ft (45cm) tall, forming loose mats of foliage rather wider than tall. In summer and early autumn it produces clusters of flowers, 3/4in (2cm) wide. Best in a sunny position. Hardy to 10°F (-12°C), US zones 8–10. Native to South Africa and introduced into cultivation in the 20th century. Probably the hardiest species.

*Diascia barberae* 'Blackthorn Apricot' c.f 'Hopley's Apricot' An herbaceous perennial that grows to 1 1/2ft (45cm) tall. Clusters of flowers, nearly 1in (2.5cm) wide, are produced in summer and early autumn. Best in a sunny position. Hardy to 10°F (-12°C), US zones 8–10. Native to South Africa and long-established in cultivation but has enjoyed a surge of interest recently.

*Diascia vigilis* Up to 1 1/2ft (45cm) tall, forming loose mats of foliage rather wider than tall, with somewhat sprawling flowering stems. In summer and early autumn it produces clusters of flowers, 3/4in (2cm) wide. Best in a sunny position. Hardy to 10°F (-12°C), US zones 8–10. Native to South Africa and introduced into cultivation in this century.

*Diascia rigescens* Grows up to 1ft (30cm) tall, with erect flowering stems. In

*Diascia vigilis*

*Diascia integerrima*

*Diascia rigescens*

*Verbascum* 'Helen Johnson'

*Verbascum chaixii*

summer and early autumn it produces dense spikes of flowers, nearly ³/₄in (2cm) wide. Best in a sunny position. Hardy to 10°F (-12°C), US zones 8–10. Native to South Africa, from where it was introduced to Britain in the 20th century. Cherished for its unusual colour and long flowering season.

NETTLE-LEAFED MULLEIN
*Verbascum chaixii*   A grey hairy perennial that grows to 3ft (90cm) tall, making a clump taller than wide. In summer it bears small purple-eyed yellow flowers, each about 1in (2.5cm) wide, in slender branched spikes. Best in a sunny position and is hardy to -10°F (-23°C), US zones 6–9. Native to southern and central Europe.
   *Verbascum chaixii* 'Album'   Purple-eyed white flowers. 'Album' is an attractive perennial for a sunny border.

*Verbascum* 'Helen Johnson'   A perennial with stems that grow to 4ft (1.25m), flowering in summer. Best in well-drained warm soil, thrives in chalk. Hardy to -5°F (-20°C), US zones 6–9. One of a group of hybrids raised by crossing *Verbascum phoeniceum* with a yellow species. They are not long-lived and should be propagated regularly by root cuttings.

*Linaria dalmatica*   An herbaceous perennial that grows to 3ft (90cm) tall, wider than tall. It produces flowers, 1¹/₂in (4cm) long, in summer. Hardy to -20°F (-29°C), US zones 5–9. Native to south-eastern Europe and introduced into cultivation in the 18th century. Although uncommon in gardens, a good clump is a fine sight; one of the showier plants for poor, dry conditions.

*Verbascum chaixii* 'Album'

*Linaria dalmatica*

*Mimulus luteus*

*Mimulus* 'Wisley Red'

*Mimulus luteus* A plant that usually has yellow flowers but sometimes creamy or pinkish ones in summer, in the wild as well as in selected cultivars. Hardy to -5°F (-20°C), US zones 6–9. Native to Chile and naturalized in Scotland, growing in streams and wet places.

*Mimulus* 'Wisley Red' Possibly a form or hybrid of *Mimulus cupreus*, raised at Wisley in England. Stems to about 6in (15cm) tall and flowering in summer. Hardy to 10°F (-12°C), US zones 8–10.

*Digitalis grandiflora* An evergreen perennial that grows to 3ft (90cm) tall. Flowers, each about 1¹⁄₂in (4cm) long, are produced in summer. Plant in autumn or spring in a sunny or partially shaded position. Hardy to -30°F (-35°C), US zones 4–9. Native to central and eastern Europe and introduced into cultivation by the 16th century.

COMMON FOXGLOVE *Digitalis purpurea* An herbaceous biennial or perennial that forms clumps up to 7ft (2m) tall. Purplish-pink flowers, each about 2in (5cm) long, in summer. Plant in autumn or spring in a sunny or partially shaded position. Hardy to -20°F (-29°C), US zones 5–9. Native to most of Europe.
  *Digitalis purpurea* 'Sutton's Apricot'

Grows to 6ft (1.8m) tall. Pale apricot-pink flowers. Hardy to -10°F (-23°C), US zones 6–9.

*Phygelius aequalis* 'Yellow Trumpet' A woody-based perennial that grows to 3ft (90cm) tall. In summer it produces large clusters of flowers, 1¹⁄₂in (4cm) long. Best in a sunny, sheltered position and hardy to 10°F (-12°C), US zones 8–10. *P. aequalis* is native to South Africa and normally has coral-pink flowers. 'Yellow Trumpet' is a recent introduction from the wild.

*Phygelius* x *rectus* 'Winchester Fanfare' A woody-based perennial that grows to about 3¹⁄₂ft (1m) tall. From summer to autumn it produces flowers, each about 1¹⁄₂in (4cm) long. Hardy to 0°F (-18°C), US zones 7–10. *Phygelius* x *rectus* is a hybrid between *P. aequalis* and *P. capensis*, both native to South Africa.

*Phygelius capensis* A woody-based perennial that grows to 7ft (2m) tall. From summer to autumn it produces large branched clusters of slender, tubular bright red flowers, each about 1¹⁄₂in (4cm) long. Best in a sunny, sheltered position. Hardy to 0°F (-18°C), US zones 7–10. Native to South Africa, introduced into cultivation in the 19th century.

*Digitalis purpurea* photographed at Warley Place, Essex, England

*Phygelius* x *rectus* 'Winchester Fanfare'

*Digitalis grandiflora*

*Phygelius capensis*

*Digitalis purpurea* 'Sutton's Apricot'

*Phygelius aequalis* 'Yellow Trumpet'

*Valeriana phu* 'Aurea'

*Acanthus mollis*

*Acanthus spinosus*

*Valeriana phu* 'Aurea'

and colours ranging from yellow to purple, blue and pink. Flowering in spring and early summer, this plant prefers sandy soil in full sun. Hardy to -10°F (-23°C), US zones 6–10. Native to south-east North America. 'Wyoming' is shown here.

*Valeriana phu* 'Aurea'   An herbaceous perennial that grows to 5ft (1.5m) tall, producing insignificant white flowers, each less than 1/4in (6mm) long, in summer. Hardy to -10°F (-23°C), US zones 6–8. Native to parts of the Caucasus and Europe and introduced into cultivation in the 16th century. Grown for its fresh yellow leaves in spring.

*Acanthus mollis*   A vigorous perennial that grows to 7ft (2m) tall, forming wide clumps. In summer it produces erect stems with many white flowers, 2in (5cm) long. Hardy to 10°F (-12°C), US zones 8–10 or lower. Native to south-west Europe. Var. *latifolius* has broader leaves.

*Acanthus spinosus*   A vigorous herbaceous perennial that grows to 5ft (1.5m) tall, forming wide clumps and producing erect stems with many white flowers, each about 2in (5cm) long, in summer. Hardy to 10°F (-12°C), US zones 8–10 or a little lower. Native to the eastern Mediterranean area.

*Centranthus ruber*   An herbaceous perennial that grows to 2 1/2ft (75cm) tall and wider, sometimes spreading quite freely by seed. Over a long period in the summer it produces tiny, deep pink flowers borne in compact rounded sprays. Hardy to -20°F (-29°C), US zones 5–8. Native to the Mediterranean region.

SWEET WOODRUFF *Galium odoratum* An herbaceous perennial that grows to about 9in (23cm) tall, with erect stems arising from its slender, spreading rhizome. In spring and early summer it produces loose heads of small white flowers, each about 1/4in (6mm) wide. Hardy to -20°F (-29°C), US zones 5–8.

*Phuopsis stylosa*   An herbaceous perennial, spreading underground into extensive patches up to 1ft (30cm) tall and much wider. Over a long period in summer and early autumn it produces rounded heads 2 1/2in (6cm) wide, composed of many small, tubular flowers. Hardy to -10°F (-23°C), US zones 6–9. Native to Iran and the Caucasus.

*Stokesia laevis*   Perennial with stems that grow to 1 1/2ft (45cm), usually woolly. Cultivars include varieties varying in size

SCABIOUS *Scabiosa caucasica* 'Clive Greaves' (left)   An herbaceous perennial that grows to 2ft (60cm) tall, producing large pale lavender-blue flowers, each about 2in (5cm) wide, over a long period in summer. Hardy to -20°F (-29°C), US zones 5–8. Native to the Caucasus.

*Centranthus ruber*

*Phuopsis stylosa*

*Acanthus mollis* var. *latifolius*

*Galium odoratum*

*Stokesia laevis*

*Campanula lactiflora*

*Campanula glomerata* 'Superba'

*Campanula carpatica*

*Campanula alliariifolia*  An herbaceous perennial that grows to 2ft (60cm) tall, producing many flowers, each about ³/₄in (2cm) long, in summer. Plant in autumn or early spring in a sunny position. Hardy to -30°F (-35°C), US zones 4–8. Native to the Caucasus and Asia Minor and introduced into cultivation early in the 19th century.

*Campanula punctata* 'Rubra'
A rhizomatous perennial that grows to 2ft (60cm) tall and can sometimes prove rather invasive. Flowers, each about 2in (5cm) long, produced throughout summer. Hardy to -20°F (-29°C), US zones 5–8, but, like other campanulas, may be attractive to slugs. Native to Japan. 'Rubra' is a selection with more deeply coloured flowers than normal.

*Campanula takesimana*  A rhizomatous perennial that grows to 2ft (60cm) tall, forming clumps with basal rosettes of leaves. Flowers, about 2in (5cm) long, that can be single or double in white, blue or pink, are borne throughout summer. Hardy to -20°F (-29°C), US zones 5–8. May be damaged by slugs. Native to Korea and introduced into cultivation in the late 20th century.

*Campanula carpatica*  An herbaceous perennial that grows to 1ft (30cm) tall, forming low clumps wider than tall. In summer it produces many flowers, each about 1¹/₂in (2.5cm) wide, that can vary in colour from white to pale and deep violet-blue. Best in a sunny position. Hardy to -20°F (-29°C), US zones 5–8. Native to eastern Europe.

*Campanula persicifolia*  An evergreen perennial that grows to 2¹/₂ft (75cm) tall and produces flowers over a long period in summer. Each flower is about 2in (5cm) wide and variable, with single or double flowers in white, blue or pink. Plant in autumn or early spring in any fertile soil. Hardy to -30°F (-35°C), US zones 4–8. Native to much of Europe.
   *Campanula persicifolia* 'Alba'  Pure white flowers. The white form is most appealing and looks fine with old roses as well as being an excellent border plant.

*Campanula latiloba*  A perennial plant that grows to 3¹/₂ft (1m) tall and makes good ground-cover. Over a long period in summer it produces stiffly erect stems crowded with flowers, each about 2in (5cm) wide, for most of their length. Hardy to -20°F (-29°C), US zones 5–8.

Native to northern Turkey and grown in gardens since the early 19th century.

*Campanula latiloba* 'Hidcote Amethyst'
A perennial that grows to 3¹/₂ft (1m) tall and produces flowers, each about 2in (5cm) wide, over a long period in summer. Hardy to -20°F (-29°C), US zones 5–8. *Campanula latiloba* is native to northern Turkey and 'Hidcote Amethyst' originated at the National Trust's Hidcote garden in England.

*Campanula glomerata* 'Superba'
A particularly robust herbaceous perennial that grows to 2ft (60cm) tall, spreading underground to form small colonies. Over a long period in summer it produces many flowers, each about ³/₄in (2cm) long. Best in a sunny position. Hardy to -30°F (-35°C), US zones 4–8. Native to much of Europe and Asia Minor.

*Campanula lactiflora*   An herbaceous perennial that grows to 4ft (1.25m) tall, forming compact clumps, producing clusters of flowers, each about ³/₄in (2cm) long, over a long period in summer. Plant in autumn or early spring in a sunny position. Hardy to -20°F (-29°C), US zones 5–8. Native to the Caucasus and Asia Minor.

*Campanula persicifolia* 'Alba'

*Campanula latiloba*

*Campanula alliariifolia*

*Campanula takesimana*

*Campanula punctata* 'Rubra'

*Campanula latiloba*

*Campanula latiloba* 'Hidcote Amethyst'

# PERENNIALS

*Lobelia siphilitica*

*Lobelia* x *gerardii* 'Vedrariensis'

*Lobelia cardinalis*

*Rudbeckia fulgida* var. *sullivantii*

*Liatris spicata*

*Liatris spicata* 'Alba'

*Achillea* Galaxy Hybrids   A group of hybrids between *A. millefolium* and *A.* 'Taygetea', raised in Germany in the late 20th century. Collectively known as Galaxy Hybrids, they come in a range of colours from sulphur-yellow to red and are colourful and easily grown plants, very suitable for a dry, sunny border. Hardy to -10°F (-23°C), US zones 6–10 or lower.

*Achillea millefolium* 'Cerise Queen' An herbaceous perennial that grows to 2ft (60cm) tall, forming a lax, spreading clump rather wider than tall and producing flower heads in summer. The very finely dissected leaves give an attractive feathery effect. Hardy to -40°F (-40°C), US zones 3–10 or lower. Native to Europe and western Asia.

*Achillea ptarmica*   An herbaceous perennial that grows to 2ft (60cm) tall, producing a succession of flower heads, each about 1/2in (1cm) wide, in summer. Hardy to -20°F (-29°C), US zones 5–10 or lower. In hot dry situations, the foliage may be afflicted by mildew. Native to much of northern Europe.

*Liatris spicata*   An herbaceous perennial that grows to 2ft (60cm) tall, forming compact clumps. In summer it produces stiffly erect spikes of bright mauve-pink or rosy-purple flowers. The flowers are small, but abundant and giving a showy effect. Plant in autumn or early spring in any well-drained but moist soil. Best in a sunny position and hardy to -30°F (-35°C), US zones 4–9. Native to the eastern United States.
   *Liatris spicata* 'Alba'   Has attractive fluffy white flowers.

*Ligularia stenocephala* 'The Rocket' An herbaceous perennial that grows to 5ft (1.5m) tall, forming robust clumps. In summer it produces a succession of abundant and densely packed flowers, about 1 1/2in (4cm) wide, giving a spectacular, rocket-like effect. Hardy to -20°F (-29°C), US zones 5–8. Native to China and Japan.

*Ligularia dentata* 'Desdemona'   An herbaceous perennial that grows to 4ft (1.25m) tall, forming robust clumps of foliage. In summer it produces clusters of flower heads, 4in (10cm) wide, on dark purple-brown stems. The leaves are bronze-green above and a striking rich mahogany-red on the underside. Hardy to -20°F (-29°C), US zones 5–8. Native to China and Japan.

CARDINAL FLOWER *Lobelia cardinalis* A perennial that grows to 3ft (90cm) tall, forming clumps taller than wide and

*Achillea millefolium* 'Cerise Queen'

*Achillea* Galaxy Hybrids

*Achillea ptarmica*

*Ligularia dentata* 'Desdemona'

producing spires of flowers, each about 1½in (4cm) long, over a long period in summer and autumn. Hardy to -40°F (-40°C), US zones 3–9. Native to North America.

*Lobelia* x *gerardii* 'Vedrariensis' A clump-forming herbaceous perennial that grows to 4ft (1.25m) tall. Throughout summer and autumn it produces spires of flowers, each about 1½in (4cm) long. Prefers a sunny position. Hardy to -20°F (-29°C), US zones 5–9.

*Lobelia siphilitica* An herbaceous perennial that grows to 3ft (90cm) tall, producing spires of flowers, each about 1in (2.5cm) long, over a long period in summer. Hardy to -20°F (-29°C), US zones 5–9. Native to the eastern United States and introduced into cultivation in the 17th century.

*Rudbeckia fulgida* var. *sullivantii* 'Goldsturm' An herbaceous perennial that grows to 2ft (60cm) tall, producing flowers, each about 4in (10cm) wide with a blackish centre, in summer. Best in a sunny position and hardy to -30°F (-35°C), US zones 4–9. Native to eastern North America and introduced into Britain in the 18th century.

*Ligularia stenocephala* 'The Rocket'

*Kniphofia* 'Spanish Gold'

*Kniphofia rooperi*

*Kniphofia* 'Little Maid'

*Asphodeline lutea*

*Artemisia absinthium* 'Lambrook Silver' An herbaceous perennial that grows up to 2¹/₂ft (75cm) tall, forming clumps a little wider than tall. In summer it may produce small brownish flowers, less than ¹/₂in (1cm) wide, but these are of no ornamental value. This plant can be planted in autumn or early spring in a sunny position and in cooler areas will benefit from a sheltered site by a south- or west-facing wall. Hardy to -20°F (-29°C), US zones 5–10. Selected in Britain in the 20th century, this plant is valued for its silvery foliage .

WESTERN MUGWORT *Artemisia ludoviciana* An herbaceous perennial with stems that grow to 3¹/₂ft (1m), forming spreading colonies wider than tall. In summer it may produce small brownish flowers, each less than ¹/₂in (1cm) wide, but they are of no ornamental value. The fruiting heads are insignificant and are best cut off. Plant in autumn or early spring in a sunny position. Hardy to -10°F (-23°C), US zones 6–10. Native to much of central and western North America.
    *Artemisia ludoviciana* 'Silver Queen' To 2¹/₂ft (75cm) tall. It was selected in Britain in the 20th century.

*Artemisia* 'Powis Castle' A woody-based perennial that grows to 2¹/₂ft (75cm) tall, forming compact rounded clumps. Best in a sunny position and in cooler areas will benefit from a sheltered site by a south- or west-facing wall. Hardy to 0°F (-18°C), US zones 7–10. May be short-lived in rich soils. Selected in Britain in this century.

YELLOW ASPHODEL *Asphodeline lutea* A perennial that grows to 4ft (1.25m) tall, producing slightly fragrant flowers, each about 2in (5cm) wide, in late spring. Plant in autumn or early spring in a sunny position. In cooler areas will benefit from a sheltered site by a south- or west-facing wall. Well-adapted to dry summer conditions, thriving in poor soils. Hardy to 10°F (-12°C), US zones 8–10 or lower.

CORN-FLOWER *Centaurea montana* 'Alba' A perennial that grows to 1¹/₂ft (45cm) tall, sometimes spreading extensively by its rhizomes. In early summer it produces flower heads, about 2in (5cm) wide. Plant in a sunny position as it tends to flop when shaded. Hardy to -30°F (-35°C), US zones 4–8. May suffer from slug damage. Native to mountain meadows in Europe and introduced into cultivation by the 16th century.

*Centaurea macrocephala* A perennial that grows to 3ft (90cm) tall, producing flowers borne in compact heads, about 3in (8cm) wide, in summer. The fruiting head is sometimes treated and used in dried flower arrangements. Tends to flop in a shaded position and is not drought-tolerant. Hardy to -30°F (-35°C), US zones 4–8. Native to the Caucasus, it was introduced into cultivation by the early 19th century. Although the flowers are a good colour, this plant has a coarse and wild appearance and is better suited to a less formal part of the garden.

RED-HOT POKER *Kniphofia* 'Little Maid' An herbaceous perennial that

*Artemisia absinthium* 'Lambrook Silver'

*Artemisia ludoviciana* 'Silver Queen'

*Artemisia* 'Powis Castle'

*Artemisia ludoviciana*

*Centaurea montana* 'Alba'

grows to 2ft (60cm) tall, producing flowers, opening from yellow-green or pinkish buds, in late summer. Each tubular flower is about 1in (2.5cm) long. Best in a sunny position. Hardy to -10°F (-23°C), US zones 6–9. Raised in Britain in the late 20th century, this excellent small poker is more gently coloured than most of the larger ones.

RED-HOT POKER *Kniphofia rooperi* (often sold as 'C M Prichard')   Grows to 4ft (1.25m) tall, forming dense clumps and producing flowers which open from deep red buds in autumn and fade abruptly to greenish-yellow. Best in a sunny position. Hardy to 0°F (-18°C), US zones 7–9. Grows wild in South Africa and was introduced into cultivation in the middle of the 20th century.

*Kniphofia* 'Spanish Gold'   An herbaceous perennial that grows to 6ft (1.8m) tall, producing flowers opening from green-tinted buds in summer. Best in a sunny position. Hardy to 0°F (-18°C), US zones 7–9. Raised in Britain in the 20th century, this is a fine plant of attractive colouring, most effective when mass-planted.

*Centaurea macrocephala*

*Hosta*
'Ginko Craig'

*Hosta decorata*
forma *decorata*

*Hosta fortunei*
'Phyllis Campbell'

*Hosta montana*
'Aureo-marginata'

*Hosta* 'Gold Standard'

*Hosta fortunei*
'Green Gold'

½ life size. Specimens from Savill Gardens, England, 17 July

*Hosta fortunei* 'Aurea'

*Hosta fortunei* var. *aureomarginata*

*Hosta* 'Betsy King'

*Hosta fortunei* 'Albopicta'

*Hosta* 'Betsy King'   A variegated perennial that forms a mound that grows to 14in (35cm) tall and 20in (50cm) wide. The flat, oval leaves are medium green and the flowers bloom in early summer. Hardy to -40°F (-40°C), US zones 3–9.

*Hosta decorata* forma *decorata*
A perennial that grows to 10in (25cm) tall, producing flowers in late midsummer and seed heads used in flower arranging. Hardy to -30°F (-35°C), US zones 4–10.

*Hosta fortunei* 'Albopicta'   A perennial that grows to 2ft (60cm) tall, producing bright yellow leaves edged with pale green which gradually fade until the yellow is nearly the same as the edge. Grows in shade to three-quarters shade and bears flowers in early to late midsummer. Hardy to -30°F (-35°C), US zones 4–10.

*Hosta fortunei* 'Aurea'   A perennial that grows to 14in (35cm) tall and 2ft (60cm) wide, producing vivid, soft yellow leaves that slowly turn green, and pale lavender flowers in midsummer. Hardy to -40°F (-40°C), US zones 3–9.

*Hosta fortunei* 'Green Gold'   A perennial producing leaves with a gold margin that fades gradually with age, and pale lavender flowers that appear in late midsummer. Hardy to -30°F (-35°C), US zones 4–10.

*Hosta fortunei* var. *aureomarginata*
A perennial that grows to 14in (35cm) tall and 2ft (60cm) wide, bearing dark green leaves with distinct wide, golden edges, and violet flowers in midsummer. Hardy to -40°F (-40°C), US zones 3–9.

*Hosta fortunei* 'Phyllis Campbell'
A perennial with firm leaves, splashed with yellow in the centre, and lavender flowers that appear in late midsummer, growing in shade to half-sun. Hardy to -30°F (-35°C), US zones 4–10.

*Hosta* 'Ginko Craig'   A perennial that grows to 4in (10cm) tall and 10in (25cm) wide if divided to keep the juvenile form, or up to three times bigger if allowed to mature. Leaves medium to dark green with clear white margins. Purple-striped flowers bloom in midsummer. Hardy to -40°F (-40°C), US zones 3–9.

*Hosta* 'Gold Standard'   A perennial that grows to 2ft (60cm) tall and 2¹/₂ft (75cm) wide, producing yellow leaves with green edges that tend to green in shade, and pale lavender flowers in midsummer. Hardy to -40°F (-40°C), US zones 3–9.

*Hosta montana* 'Aureo-marginata'
A perennial that grows to 2ft (65cm) tall and 3¹/₄ft (95cm) wide, bearing large rich green leaves with irregular yellow margins and densely grouped, pale lavender flowers in late midsummer. Hardy to -30°F (-35°C), US zones 4–10.

*Hosta* 'Birchwood Parky's Gold'

*Hosta sieboldiana* var. *elegans*

*Hosta undulata*

**Hosta 'Halcyon'** A ground-cover perennial that grows to 20in (50cm) tall and 3ft (90cm) wide. The leaves are blue-green and the bell-shaped flowers are violet, blooming in midsummer. This variety grows best in full shade, otherwise it fades in colour. Hardy to -40°F (-40°C), US zones 3–9. A cultivar that has won many awards and remains enduringly popular.

**Hosta 'Royal Standard'** A ground-cover perennial that forms a mound up to 2ft (60cm) tall and 15in (40cm) wide, with heart-shaped leaves and fragrant white funnel-shaped flowers in late summer. Grows in shade to three-quarters sun. Hardy to -40°F (-40°C), US zones 3–9. A cultivar of *Hosta plantaginea* registered by Wayside Gardens in the US in 1986.

**Hosta 'Shade Fanfare'** A ground-cover perennial that forms a mound up to 18in (45cm) tall and 2ft (60cm) wide, with leaves varying from light green to yellow, edged with a cream margin. The funnel-shaped flowers are lavender and bloom in midsummer. This particular variety will grow in shade to full sun and is hardy to -40°F (-40°C), US zones 3–9. A cultivar derived from *Hosta* 'Flamboyant'.

**Hosta sieboldiana var. *elegans***
A ground-cover perennial that forms a mound to 2½ft (75cm) tall and 3½ft (1m) wide. The heavily puckered leaves are bluish and the flowers, borne on short stems that nestle in the leaves, bloom in midsummer. Grows in full and half-shade. Hardy to -40°F (-40°C), US zones 3–9. A variety of *Hosta sieboldiana*.

**Hosta undulata var. *albomarginata*** (syn. *Hosta* 'Thomas Hogg') A ground-cover perennial that grows to 1½ft (45cm) tall and 3ft (90cm) wide, which bears funnel-shaped lilac flowers in mid-summer. Grows in shade to half-sun. Hardy to -40°F (-40°C), US zones 3–9. This old Japanese cultivar was brought to the West from Japan via the United States by Thomas Hogg in 1875.

**Hosta undulata** A varied assemblage of garden clones, characterized by twisted leaves with cream centres and olive green margins. The flowers are pale purple. Hardy to -40°F (-40°C), US zones 3–9.

**Hosta ventricosa** A perennial that forms a mound to 2ft (60cm) tall, growing in shade and half-shade. In late summer deep lilac-mauve flowers appear, up to 3in

(8cm) wide, rising above leaves that are heart-shaped, lustrous dark green above and glossy mid- to dark green beneath. Hardy to -40°F (-40°C), US zones 3–9. Native to China.

**Hosta ventricosa 'Aureo-marginata'** Grows to 1½ft (45cm) tall and persists until the first frosts. It has violet flowers and leaves with an irregular yellowish margin that turns white.

**Hosta 'Birchwood Parky's Gold'**
A ground-cover perennial that forms a mound up to 1½ft (45cm) tall and 2½ft (75cm) wide. The leaves are gold and the bell-shaped flowers are lilac and bloom in summer. Grows in shade to three-quarters sun. Hardy to -40°F (-40°C), US zones 3–9.

**Hosta 'Wide Brim'** A ground-cover perennial that forms a mound to 20in (50cm) tall and 3ft (90cm) wide. The wide leaves are green with yellow margins turning whitish. The funnel-shaped pale lavender flowers bloom in midsummer. Grows in shade to three-quarters sun. Hardy to -40°F (-40°C), US zones 3–9. 'Wide Brim' is a cultivar developed by crossing *Hosta* 'Bold One' with *Hosta* 'Bold Ribbons'.

*Hosta undulata* var. *albomarginata*

*Hosta* 'Wide Brim'

*Hosta ventricosa* 'Aureo-marginata'

*Hosta* 'Halcyon'

*Hosta* 'Royal Standard'

*Hosta ventricosa*

*Hosta* 'Zounds'  A ground-cover perennial that forms a mound up to 20in (50cm) tall and 2¹/₂ft (75cm) wide, with puckered leaves of a golden metallic colour. Funnel-shaped pale lavender flowers bloom in midsummer. Grows in a quarter to three-quarters sun. Hardy to -40°F (-40°C), US zones 3–9. A cultivar developed from a *Hosta sieboldiana* 'Elegans' hybrid.

*Hosta* 'Shade Fanfare'

*Hosta* 'Zounds'

*Agapanthus* 'Loch Hope'   A perennial that grows to 5ft (1.5m) tall, bearing large clusters of flowers, each about 2½in (6cm) long. Best in a sunny position and in cooler areas will benefit from the shelter of a south- or west-facing wall. Hardy to 10°F (-12°C), US zones 8–10.

*Agapanthus campanulatus* subsp. *campanulatus* (left)   A deciduous perennial that forms clumps of thick fleshy roots in gardens but is usually solitary in the wild. Stems, up to 3½ft (1m) or more, bearing blue flowers, about 1in (2.5cm) long, in summer. Prefers rich, well-drained sandy soil in full sun. Hardy to 5°F (-15°C), US zones 7–10 or less if the rhizomes are protected. Native to South Africa, growing in grassy and rocky places.

*Agapanthus* 'Ben Hope'   An herbaceous perennial that grows to 4ft (1.25m) tall, forming compact clumps. In summer it produces tall stems, well above the foliage, bearing large rounded clusters of trumpet-shaped, rich blue flowers, 2in (5cm) long. Hardy to 10°F (-12°C), US zones 8–10. Native to southern Africa.

*Agapanthus* 'Delft'   An herbaceous perennial that grows up to 3½ft (1m) tall, bearing flowers, each about 1½in (4cm) long in summer. Hardy to 10°F (-12°C), US zones 8–10. Native to southern Africa and introduced into cultivation in the 18th or 19th century.

PERUVIAN LILY *Alstroemeria aurea* (syn. *Alstroemeria aurantiaca*)   An herbaceous perennial that grows to 2½ft (75cm) tall, spreading underground to form wide colonies. In summer it bears flowers, each about 1½in (4cm) wide, speckled with maroon on the two upper inner petals. Hardy to 0°F (-18°C), US zones 7–10. Native to southern Chile.

*Alstroemeria ligtu*   A perennial that spreads widely by underground fleshy roots. Stems, 2–3½ft (60–100cm) tall, bear flowers, 1in (4cm) long, that are variable in colour, usually pinkish-lilac, reddish or whitish, in summer. Prefers well-drained soil in full sun. Hardy to 5°F (-15°C), US zones 7–10. Native to Chile.

ADAM'S NEEDLE *Yucca filamentosa*   An evergreen perennial that grows to 6ft (1.8m) tall when in flower. In summer it produces flowers, each about 2½in (6cm) long, with a pleasant fragrance in the evenings. Best in a sunny position and hardy to -10°F (-23°C), US zones 6–8. Native to coastal parts of the eastern United States. There is also a good form with variegated leaves.

*Yucca flaccida*   An evergreen perennial that grows to 5ft (1.5m) tall when in flower. In summer it produces widely branched stems with many cream bell-shaped flowers, about 2½in (6cm) long, tinged green in bud. Best in a sunny position. Hardy to -10°F (-23°C), US zones 6–8. Native to the south-eastern United States and introduced into cultivation early in the 19th century. There is also a form with variegated leaves.
   *Yucca flaccida* 'Ivory'   Grows to 4ft (1.25m) tall, with flowers about 2½in (6cm) long. 'Ivory' is a compact form raised in England in the 20th century.

*Agapanthus* 'Loch Hope'

*Agapanthus* 'Ben Hope'

*Agapanthus* 'Delft'

*Yucca flaccida* 'Ivory'

*Yucca flaccida*

*Yucca filamentosa*

*Alstroemeria aurea*

*Alstroemeria ligtu*

*Hemerocallis* 'Frans Hals'

*Hemerocallis* 'Ed Murray'

*Hemerocallis* 'Catherine Woodbery'

*Hemerocallis* 'Chicago Petticoats'

*Hemerocallis* 'Starling'

*Hemerocallis* 'Luxury Lace'

*Hemerocallis* 'Chicago Royal Robe'

DAY LILY *Hemerocallis* 'Burford' A perennial that grows to 3ft (90cm) tall. Flowers about 4in (10cm) wide, in midsummer. Hardy to -10°F (-23°C), US zones 6–9.

*Hemerocallis* 'Catherine Woodbery' Grows to 2¹/₂ft (75cm) tall, bearing flowers about 6in (15cm) wide, in summer. Hardy to -10°F (-23°C), US zones 6–9.

Hemerocallis 'Chicago Royal Robe' Grows to 2ft (60cm) tall, bearing flowers about 5¹/₂in (14cm) wide, in early summer. Hardy to -10°F (-23°C), US zones 6–9.

*Hemerocallis* 'Chicago Petticoats' Grows to 2ft (60cm) tall, bearing flowers about 5in (12cm) wide, in midsummer. Hardy to -10°F (-23°C), US zones 6–9.

*Hemerocallis* 'Ed Murray' Grows to 2¹/₂ft (75cm) tall, bearing flowers about 4in (10cm) wide, in midsummer. Hardy to -10°F (-23°C), US zones 6–9.

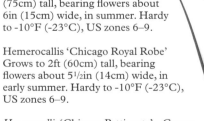

*Hemerocallis* 'Pink Damask' (left) Grows to 3¹/₂ft (1m) tall, producing flowers about 5in (12cm) wide, in early summer. Hardy to -20°F (-29°C), US zones 5–9.

*Hemerocallis* 'Hyperion' Grows to 3ft (90cm) tall, bearing sweet-scented flowers about 4in (10cm) wide, in midsummer. Hardy to -10°F (-23°C), US zones 6–9.

# DAY LILIES

*Hemerocallis* 'Hyperion'

*Hemérocallis fulva*

*Hemerocallis* 'Burford'

*Hemerocallis* 'Joan Senior'   Grows to 2ft (60cm) tall, bearing flowers about 6in (15cm) wide, in early and midsummer. Hardy to -10°F (-23°C), US zones 6–9.

*Hemerocallis* 'Frans Hals'   Grows to 2½ft (75cm) tall, bearing flowers about 5in (12cm) wide, in summer. Hardy to -10°F (-23°C), US zones 6–9.

*Hemerocallis fulva*   Grows to 4ft (1.25m) tall, bearing flowers about 4in (10cm) wide, in late summer. Hardy to -30°F (-35°C), US zones 4–9.

*Hemerocallis* 'Luxury Lace'   Grows to 2½ft (75cm) tall, bearing flowers about 4in (10cm) wide, in midsummer. Hardy to -10°F (-23°C), US zones 6–9.

*Hemerocallis* 'Starling'   Grows to 2½ft (75cm) tall, bearing flowers about 6in (15cm) wide, in early or midsummer. Hardy to -10°F (-23°C), US zones 6–9.

*Hemerocallis* 'Joan Senior'

*Gentiana asclepiadea*

*Gentiana septemfida*

*Aconitum* x
*cammarum* 'Bicolor'

*Aconitum henryi*
'Spark's Variety'

¹/₂ life size. Specimens from Wisley, 20 July

WILLOW GENTIAN *Gentiana asclepiadea* An herbaceous perennial that grows to 2ft (60cm) tall. In late summer it bears flowers about 2in (5cm) long. Plant in autumn or spring in any fertile, moist soil in a partially shaded position. Hardy to -10°F (-23°C), US zones 6–10. Native to the mountainous areas of Europe.

*Gentiana septemfida* An herbaceous perennial that grows to 1ft (30cm) tall. In summer each stem bears a cluster of flowers, each about 1¹/₂in (4cm) long. Plant in autumn or spring in any fertile, peaty soil in a sunny or partially shaded position. Hardy to -30°F (-35°C), US zones 4–9. Native to the Caucasus and northern Turkey.

*Aconitum x cammarum* 'Bicolor' An herbaceous clump-forming perennial that grows to 4ft (1.25m) tall, producing flowers, 1¹/₂in (4cm) long, in late summer. Plant in autumn in moist soil. Hardy to -30°F (-35°C), US zones 4–10. All parts of the plant are potentially harmful and it should be handled with care.

*Aconitum henryi* 'Spark's Variety' A perennial with tuberous roots and

stems, that twine or scramble up to 5ft (1.5m). Flowers with short, broad helmets appear in late summer. Plant in any good soil in partial shade. Hardy to -5°F (-20°C), US zones 6–9. Native to China, in Hubei and Sichuan, growing in scrub.

*Aconitum septentrionale* 'Ivorine' (syn. *A. lycoctonum* 'Ivorine') A perennial that grows to 3ft (90cm) tall, with flowers, each about 1¹/₂in (4cm) long, in early summer. Hardy to -30°F (-35°C), US zones 4–10. All parts of the plant are potentially harmful. Native to northern Europe.

JAPANESE ANEMONE *Anemone* x *hybrida* 'Königin Charlotte' ('Queen Charlotte') An herbaceous perennial that grows to 2¹/₂ft (75cm) tall, spreading at the root to form extensive colonies. In early autumn it produces flowers, about 3in (8cm) wide. Plant in autumn or early spring. Hardy to -10°F (-23°C), US zones 6–10.

JAPANESE ANEMONE *Anemone* x *hybrida* 'Honorine Jobert' (right) An herbaceous perennial that grows to 4ft (1.25m) tall, spreading to form colonies

and producing flowers, each 3in (8cm) wide, in early autumn. Plant in autumn or early spring in a sunny position. Hardy to -10°F (-23°C), US zones 6–10.

*Aconitum septentrionale* 'Ivorine'

*Anemone* x *hybrida* 'Königin Charlotte'

*Anemone* x *hybrida* 'Königin Charlotte'

*Anemone* x *hybrida* 'Honorine Jobert'

*Anemone* x *lesseri*  An herbaceous
perennial that grows up to 1¹/₂ft (45cm)
tall, forming a neat clump and producing
flowers, each about 1¹/₂in (4cm) wide,
over a long period from early summer to
autumn. Plant in autumn or early spring
in any soil. Hardy to -30°F (-35°C), US
zones 4–10 or lower.

*Gaura lindheimeri*  An herbaceous
perennial that grows to 4ft (1.25m) tall,
forming elegant clumps taller than wide.
For a long period in summer and autumn
it produces flowers, 1in (2.5cm) wide.
Planted in autumn or spring in any well-
drained soil in a sunny position. Hardy to
-10°F (-23°C), US zones 6–10.

*Anemone* x *lesseri*

*Gaura lindheimeri*

*Perovskia* 'Blue Spire'

*Perovskia* 'Blue Spire' An herbaceous perennial that grows to 4ft (1.25m) tall. In late summer it produces large airy sprays of small lavender-blue flowers. Aromatic leaves up to 6in (15cm) long. Best in a sunny position and hardy to -10°F (-23°C), US zones 6–9. A hybrid between two species, both native to the western Himalayas.

ANISE HYSSOP *Agastache foeniculum* (syn. *A. anethiodora*) An herbaceous perennial that grows to 3ft (90cm) tall, producing flowers, about 4in (10cm), in late summer. Best in a sunny position. Hardy to -30°F (-35°C), US zones 4–10. Native to central North America.

*Aster ericoides* 'Blue Star' A perennial that grows to 2½ft (75cm) tall, bearing an abundance of tiny flowers, each about ½in (1cm) wide, in late summer and early autumn. Best in a sunny position. Hardy to -30°F (-35°C), US zones 4–9. Native to much of North America.

*Aster amellus* 'Lady Hindlip' A perennial that grows to 2ft (60cm) tall, producing an abundance of flowers, about 2in (5cm) wide, in late summer and early autumn. Best in a sunny position. Hardy to -30°F (-35°C), US zones 4–9. May be afflicted by mildew in dry areas. Native to much of Europe and has long been cultivated.

*Aster lateriflorus* 'Horizontalis' A perennial that grows to 5ft (1.5m) tall. In late summer and early autumn, spreading branches bear an abundance of tiny flowers, each about ½in (1cm) wide. Best in a sunny position. Hardy to -30°F (-35°C), US zones 4–9. Native to eastern North America.

*Aster novae-angliae* An herbaceous perennial that grows to 7ft (2m) tall, producing flowers, about 2in (5cm) wide, in late summer and early autumn. Best in a sunny position. Hardy to -40°F (-40°C), US zones 3–9. Can be affected by mildew in dry areas. Native to much of eastern and central North America.

*Helenium autumnale* An herbaceous perennial forming clumps of erect stems up to 5ft (1.5m) tall. In late summer it produces flowers, each about 2½in (6cm) wide. Best in a sunny position. Hardy to -30°F (-35°C), US zones 4–9. Native to eastern North America.

WILD MARJORAM *Origanum vulgare* A woody-based perennial that grows to 3ft (90cm) tall. In summer it produces sprays of pale purple flowers, nearly ¾in (2cm) long, in clusters within deep purple bracts. The leaves are aromatic. Hardy to

*Helenium autumnale*

*Leucanthemum* x *superbum* 'Mount Everest'

*Agastache foeniculum*

*Leucanthemella serotina*

-40°F (-40°C), US zones 3–9. Native to much of Europe and Asia and has long been cultivated as a culinary herb.

GOLDEN MARJORAM *Origanum vulgare* 'Aureum'   The leaves are bright golden-yellow. The variety 'Aureum' is grown for its colourful foliage, which will brighten up any sunny border.

*Leucanthemella serotina*
(syn. *Chrysanthemum serotinum*)
A robust herbaceous perennial that grows to 6ft (1.8m) tall. In late summer or autumn it produces an abundance of large white daisies, each about 2¹/₂in (6cm) wide. Hardy to -10°F (-23°C), US zones 6–9. Native to eastern Europe.

SHASTA DAISY *Leucanthemum* x *superbum* 'Mount Everest' (*syn. Chrysanthemum maximum*)   A robust herbaceous perennial that grows to 3ft (90cm) tall, producing an abundance of flowers, each about 4in (10cm) wide. Hardy to -20°F (-29°C), US zones 5–9. A hybrid between two allied European species.

*Origanum vulgare*

*Origanum vulgare* 'Aureum'

*Aster novae-angliae*

*Aster amellus* 'Lady Hindlip'

*Aster lateriflorus* 'Horizontalis'

*Aster ericoides* 'Blue Star'

# PERENNIALS

*Cortaderia selloana* 'Aureolineata'
A perennial that grows to 8ft (2.5m) tall.
In early autumn it produces flower heads
about 1 1/2ft (45cm) long. The leaves have
rough edges and can cut the skin if
handled carelessly. Hardy to -20°F
(-29°C), US zones 5–10. Native to South
America.

*Cortaderia selloana* 'Pumila'  Grows to 5ft
(1.5m) tall, forming bold clumps of
foliage about half this height. In early
autumn it produces flowers, to 15in
(38cm) long. The leaves are up to 4ft
(1.25m) long with rough edges which are
able to cut the skin if handled carelessly.
Hardy to -20°F (-29°C), US zones 5–10.
Native to South America.

HARTS-TONGUE FERN *Asplenium
scolopendrium*  A perennial fern that
grows to 2ft (60cm) tall, forming clumps
as wide as tall. Like all ferns it has no
flowers. The leaves are up to 2ft. Hardy to
-20°F (-29°C), US zones 5–8. Native to
Europe, Asia and North America

GOLDEN-SCALED MALE FERN
*Dryopteris affinis*  A semi-evergreen
perennial that grows to 4ft (1.25m) tall,
forming 'shuttlecocks' of slightly arching
leaves, about as wide as tall. The leaves are
often a striking bright yellow-green in the
early summer. Hardy to -10°F (-23°C),
US zones 6–9 or lower. Native to Europe.

OSTRICH PLUME FERN *Matteuccia
struthiopteris*  An herbaceous perennial
that grows to 3ft (90cm) tall, spreading to
form colonies by means of stolons. Hardy
to -30°F (-35°C), US zones 4–8. Grows
wild in North America, Europe and Asia.

*Miscanthus sinensis*  A magnificent
specimen grass that grows to 8ft (2.5m)
tall, producing clusters of tiny silky
flowers, cream or pink-tinged in late
summer. The whole flower head may be
1ft (30cm) or more in length. Hardy to
-10°F (-23°C), US zones 6–9. Grows wild
in Japan, Taiwan and China.

SENSITIVE FERN *Onoclea sensibilis*
A deciduous perennial fern that grows up
to 2 1/2ft (75cm) tall, with a rhizome
spreading to form an extensive colony in
good conditions. Hardy to -30°F (-35°C),
US zones 4–9. Native to North America
and north-east Asia.

MAIDENHAIR FERN *Adiantum
pedatum*  A deciduous, clump-forming
perennial that grows to 1 1/2 ft (45cm) tall,
with delicate leaves. Best in shade. Hardy
to -30°F (-35°C), US zones 4–9. Native to
North America and north-east Asia.

*Matteuccia struthiopteris*

*Dryopteris affinis*

*Adiantum pedatum*

*Cortaderia selloana* 'Aureolineata'

*Cortaderia selloana* 'Pumila'

*Miscanthus sinensis*

*Asplenium scolopendrium*

*Onoclea sensibilis*

*Lampranthus haworthii*

*Dendrobium nobile*

*Streptocarpus* 'Holliday White'

*Streptocarpus* 'Holliday Blue'

*Columnea arguta* A trailing perennial for a greenhouse or conservatory that grows to 2ft (60cm) long, bearing flowers 2½in (6cm) long, from spring through summer. Plant in autumn or spring in a moist but well-drained leafy soil in partial shade. Hardy to 60°F (15°C), US zone 10. Native to Central America.

JADE TREE *Crassula ovata* (syn. *Crassula portulacea*) An easily grown plant for a cool greenhouse or conservatory, valued mainly for its foliage and tree-like habit, reaching to 7ft (2m) tall and wider. Mature specimens bear flowers ½in (1cm) wide, in autumn and early winter. Hardy to 40°F (5°C), US zone 10. Native to South Africa.

*Cymbidium* 'Nederhorst' An evergreen herbaceous perennial with bulbous leaf bases, growing to 2½ft (75cm) tall, producing scented waxy flowers, each about 5in (12cm) wide, in winter or early spring. Hardy to 28°F (-3°C), US zones 9–10. Native to eastern Asia. Many new garden hybrids are raised in Europe and North America for greenhouse decoration in winter or for use as cut flowers.

*Dendrobium nobile* A tender perennial that grows to 1ft (30cm) tall and wider, bearing flowers 2in (5cm) wide, in early summer. The leaves arise from a cane-like stem called a pseudobulb. This orchid can be planted in autumn or spring in special compost and benefits from regular spraying. Hardy to 50°F (10°C), parts of US zone 10. Native to eastern Asia.

*Lampranthus haworthii* An upright or spreading succulent shrub with stems that grow to 4ft (1.25m) tall, bearing magenta to pale silvery purple flowers, 2¾in (7cm) wide in spring. Prefers sandy well-drained soil, dry in summer. Hardy to 25°F (-4°C), US zones 9–10. Native to South Africa, on dry hills and in semi-desert scrub.

*Neoregelia carolinae* 'Flandria' An evergreen perennial with distinctive foliage that grows to 1ft (30cm) tall. Violet-blue flowers appear throughout the year in a dense cluster in the centre of the rosette. Plant in autumn or spring in a partially shaded position. Hardy to 50°F (10°C), parts of US zone 10. Native to South America.

*Primula obconica* 'Salmon' A perennial that grows to 9in (23cm) tall, making a compact clump as wide as tall, bearing flowers 1in (2.5cm) wide, in winter and spring. All parts of the plant contain a potent allergen and contact with the plant, or even proximity to it, may cause a

Crassula ovata

Neoregelia carolinae 'Flandria'

Primula obconica 'Salmon'

Cymbidium 'Nederhorst'

Schlumbergera x buckleyi

Columnea arguta

Vriesea splendens

severe skin reaction in some people.
Hardy to 20°F (-7°C), US zones 9–10.
Native to China.

CHRISTMAS CACTUS *Schlumbergera*
x *buckleyi*   A leaf-cactus that grows to 9in
(23cm) tall and usually wider. In mid-
winter, often in time for Christmas, it
bears flowers, 2$1/2$in (6cm) wide. Best in a
partially shaded position and hardy to
50°F (10°C), parts of US zone 10. This is
a hybrid of garden origin, between species
native to South America.

CAPE PRIMROSE *Streptocarpus*
'Holliday Blue'   A member of the African
Violet family Gesneriaceae, this greenhouse perennial grows to 9in (23cm) tall,
bearing light violet-blue flowers with a

white throat, each about 1$1/2$in (4cm)
wide, intermittently throughout the year.
Hardy to 50°F (10°C), the warmer parts
of US zone 10, it requires a humid
atmosphere. The many species of
streptocarpus are native to South Africa.
Cape Primroses, the most commonly
cultivated, are of hybrid origin and there
is a wide range available, varying in habit
and flower colour.
   *Streptocarpus* 'Holliday White'   White
flowers marked with violet-blue.

FLAMING SWORD *Vriesea splendens*
A stemless perennial that grows to 3$1/2$ft
(1m) tall, producing floral bracts to 3in
(8cm) long in bright scarlet to orange.
Native to South America. Hardy to 32°F
(0°C), US zone 10.

*Pelargonium* 'Pink Aurore'

*Pelargonium* 'Black Velvet'

*Pelargonium* 'Green Woodpecker'

*Pelargonium* 'Moon Maiden'

*Pelargonium* 'Mr Henry Cox'

*Pelargonium* 'Lord Bute'

# PELARGONIUMS

PELARGONIUMS are members of the Cranesbill family Geraniaceae. They are tender evergreen perennials, usually grown in pots indoors, in a greenhouse or a conservatory although they can be planted outdoors after the risk of frost is past, but flowers may be damaged in bad weather. Plant in any fertile, well-drained soil in a sunny position. Hardy to 32°F (0°C), US zone 10. They are all complex hybrids derived from several South African species. Zonals are excellent plants for bedding out or for containers outdoors, whereas Regal pelargoniums are less suitable for bedding out; some Angel pelargoniums are suitable for hanging baskets. Unique pelargoniums are characterized by tall growth and relatively small flowers produced over a long season.

*Pelargonium* 'Black Velvet'  A slow-growing Regal that reaches 1½ft (45cm) tall and usually as wide, bearing flowers, each about 2½in (6cm) wide, in summer. Raised in the early 20th century.

*Pelargonium* 'Green Woodpecker' A strong-growing Regal that reaches 2ft (60cm) tall, bearing clusters of single flowers, each about 2½in (6cm) wide, in summer. Raised in the late 20th century.

*Pelargonium* 'Captain Starlight'  A slow-growing Angel that reaches 10in (25cm) tall and usually wider, bearing flowers, each about 1½in (4cm) wide, in summer.

*Pelargonium* 'Lord Bute'  A slow-growing Regal that reaches 1½ft (45cm) tall and usually as wide, bearing clusters of single flowers, each about 1½in (4cm) wide, in summer. Raised in the early 20th century.

*Pelargonium* 'Moon Maiden' An Angel that reaches 10in (25cm) tall and usually wider, bearing clusters of single flowers, each about 1½in (4cm) wide, in summer.

*Pelargonium* 'Wayward Angel'  A slow-growing Angel that reaches 10in (25cm) tall and usually wider, bearing clusters of single flowers, each about 1½in (4cm) wide, in summer. Raised in the late 20th century.

*Pelargonium* 'Pink Aurore'  A Unique that grows to about 2½ft (75cm) tall, erect in habit, bearing long-stemmed clusters of flowers, about 1in (2.5cm) wide, over a long period in summer.

*Pelargonium* 'Happy Thought' (left) (syn. 'A Happy Thought')  A variegated leaved Zonal that grows to about 1ft (30cm) tall and usually as wide, bearing long-stemmed clusters of flowers, each about 2in (5cm) wide, in summer. Raised in the late 19th century.

*Pelargonium* 'Mr Henry Cox' A decorative Zonal that grows to about 1ft (30cm) tall and usually as wide, bearing multicoloured leaves and flowers, each about 1½in (4cm) wide, in summer. Raised in the late 19th century.

*Pelargonium* 'Wayward Angel'

*Pelargonium* 'Captain Starlight'

*Crocus chrysanthus* 'Blue Peter'

*Crocus* x *luteus* 'Golden Yellow'

CHAPTER FIVE

# Bulbs

*In this chapter the plants have been divided by flowering time into five groups: spring-flowering, summer-flowering, autumn- and winter-flowering bulbs, and finishing with the tender bulbs.*

GREEK ANEMONE *Anemone blanda* A blackish bulb (corm) 1 in (2.5cm) in diameter, producing blue flowers, each about 1¼in (3cm) across, in early spring. Best planted in late summer or early autumn, in well-drained leafy soil, flourishing in sun or light shade, dormant in summer, Hardy to 0°F (-18°C), US zones 7–9. Native to the eastern Mediterranean and western Asia.

CYCLAMEN *Cyclamen coum* (syn. *C. atkinsii*, *C. orbiculatum*) A bulb (corm) 2in (5cm) in diameter, producing pink flowers, about ¾in (2cm) long, in early spring. Flourishes in sun or light shade. Hardy to 5°F (-15°C), US zones 7–9. Native to the Mediterranean and western Asia.

CROCUS *Crocus chrysanthus* A bulb that grows to 3in (8cm) tall, flowering in winter and early spring. Best planted in autumn in good, well-drained soil to a depth of about 3in (8cm). It is advisable to surround the corms with a layer of sand as this helps improve the drainage. Hardy to -20°F (-29°C), US zones 5–9. *Crocus chrysanthus* is native to western Asia and the Mediterranean areas of Greece and Turkey. It was introduced into cultivation during the 19th century and has since given rise to many garden varieties, in shades of white, yellow and blue. Shown here is 'Blue Peter'.

*Crocus* x *luteus* 'Golden Yellow' (syn. 'Dutch Yellow', 'Golden Mammoth', 'Large Yellow', 'Yellow Mammoth', 'Yellow Giant') A bulb that grows to 4in (10cm) tall, producing flowers in early spring. This plant thrives under deciduous trees and shrubs, or in short grass where it can be left undisturbed for many years. Hardy to -20°F (-29°C), US zones 5–9. This is an old garden hybrid, introduced into cultivation during the 17th century. It originated as a hybrid between two other yellow species and does not set seed. For this reason it needs to be planted in drifts and the clumps dug up and divided if they become crowded.

*Crocus vernus* A member of the Iris family Iridaceae, this bulb was bred for its large showy flowers which are produced in spring. Hardy to -40°F (-40°C), US zones 3–9. Many different varieties of crocus have been bred over the years, particularly in Holland. The cultivars of *Crocus vernus* are particularly tough, as they are derived from wild crocuses found in alpine meadows and in subalpine woods from the Pyrenees to Russia. They grow best in short grass, either in the open or under deciduous trees where the soil becomes a little dry in summer. Shown here is 'King of the Whites' with pure white flowers.

SNOWDROP *Galanthus nivalis* A small bulb forming a clump 3–8in (8–20cm) tall, depending on the quality of the soil, that can spread to cover large areas. Flowers in early spring. Hardy to -25°F (-32°C), US zones 4–8. Native to the Mediterranean and western Asia and naturalized in much of northern Europe.

RETICULATA IRIS *Iris reticulata* A dwarf bulb that grows to 6in (15cm), producing flowers which are usually dark violet-blue and measure up to 3in (8cm) wide, in early spring. There are many forms and hybrids of this iris, in an array of colours and some are scented. Hardy to -25°F (-32°C) US zones 4–8. Native to western Asia.

*Crocus vernus* 'King of the Whites'

*Anemone blanda*

*Cyclamen coum*

*Iris* 'Katharine Hodgkin'   This beautiful little iris grows up to 4in (10cm) tall and produces flowers 3in (8cm) across, in early spring. The leaves are small and insignificant at flowering time but elongate later. Best planted in autumn in well-drained, slightly limy soil in a sunny position. Hardy to -25°F (-32°C), US zones 4–8.

*Iris histrioides* 'Major'   A selected form of *Iris histrioides,* producing flowers 3in (8cm) wide, in early spring. The bulbs like to be kept dry in summer and do best if divided frequently. Hardy to -25°F (-32°C), US zones 4–8 and will survive snowy conditions. Native to western Asia and central Turkey and introduced into cultivation in the 19th century.

GLORY OF THE SNOW *Chionodoxa luciliae* (syn. *C. gigantea*)   This plant grows to 4in (10cm) tall and flowers in early spring. Best planted in late summer or early autumn to a depth of about 3in (8cm) in moist but well-drained soil. The plants are easy to grow in sun or partial shade. Hardy to about -10°F (-23°C), US zones 6–9. Native to the Mediterranean and western Asia.

STRIPED SQUILL *Puschkinia scilloides* var. *libanotica*   This plant grows to 4in (10cm) tall, producing flowers ¹/₂in (1cm) long, in spring. Hardy to -5°F (-20°C), US zones 6–9. *Puschkinia* is named after Count Puschkin, a Russian chemist who collected plants in the 18th century. Native to the Mediterranean and western Asia, growing in the mountains of Turkey and the Lebanon and flowering when the snow melts.

SCILLA *Scilla bifolia*   A low-growing bulbous plant that reaches 8in (20cm), producing flowers in colours ranging from pale violet to deep blue, in early spring. Hardy to about -10°F (-23°C), US zones 6–9. Native to eastern Europe, the Mediterranean and western Asia. It does well in a rock garden, short grass or among shrubs where it will often naturalize itself.

*Scilla mischtschenkoana* (syn. *Scilla tubergeniana*)   A bulbous plant that grows to 4in (10cm) tall, producing flowers in early spring. Best planted in late summer or early autumn to a depth of about 3in (8cm) in moist but well-drained soil, in sun or partial shade. Hardy to -10°F (-23°C), US zones 6–9. Native to the Mediterranean and western Asia and growing in the mountains of northern Iran.

*Puschkinia scilloides*

*Galanthus nivalis*

*Scilla bifolia*

*Scilla mischtschenkoana*

*Iris* 'Katharine Hodgkin'

*Chionodoxa luciliae*

*Iris reticulata*

*Iris histrioides* 'Major'

*Trillium grandiflorum*

*Trillium chloropetalum*

**WOOD ANEMONE** *Anemone nemorosa*
An elongated brown bulb (rhizome) to
1/3in (8mm) in diameter, producing small
white or pale blue flowers, each about 1in
(2.5cm) wide, in spring. This plant does
well in areas where the summers are wet.
Hardy to -20°F (-29°C), US zones 5–8
but dislikes extreme heat and drought.
Native to much of northern Europe.

*Arisaema sikokianum*   A rounded bulb
(tuber) that grows to 2in (5cm) in
diameter. It produces chocolate-brown
and green-striped flowers with a hooded
petal and a white knob (spadix) in the
centre. Flowers, each about 3–5in
(8–12cm) high, appear in late spring.
Hardy to 0°F (-18°C), US zones 7–9, but
dislikes late frosts. Native to central Japan
and should be treasured in a collection of
small shade-loving plants. It is now,
because of commercial collecting, rare in
places where it was formerly abundant.

*Corydalis solida*   A brown bulb (tuber)
that grows to 1in (2.5cm) in diameter. It
produces small pale purple, bright pink,
white or red flowers, each about 1/2–1in
(1–2.5cm) long, in early spring. Hardy to
-10°F (-23°C), US zones 6–9, but dislikes
extreme cold and wet. Native to northern
Europe, the eastern Mediterranean and
western Asia.

**YELLOW ADDER'S TONGUE,
TROUT LILY, AMBERBELL**
*Erythronium americanum*   A small bulb
that grows to 8ins (20cm) tall, producing
flowers that only open in warm sun, in
spring. Best planted immediately after
flowering before the bulb dries out and
thriving in rich soil in moist areas under
trees. Hardy to -30°F (-35°C), US zones
4–8. Native to eastern North America.

*Arisaema sikokianum*

*Anemone nemorosa*

*Crocus tommasinianus*

## AMERICAN TROUT LILY

*Erythronium revolutum*   An elegant bulb that grows to 1ft (30cm) tall, producing nodding flowers of variable colour, usually pink, in spring; there are many named forms and hybrids. Best planted immediately after flowering before the bulbs dry out. Hardy to -15°F (-26°C), US zones 5–9. Native to North America.

## BLUEBELL, WILD HYACINTH

*Hyacinthoides non-scripta (Endymion non-scriptus; Hyacinthus non-scriptus; Scilla non-scripta)*   The common bluebell grows 8–20in (20–50cm) tall and produces one-sided drooping stems of fragrant tubular flowers, usually blue but occasionally white or pink, in spring. Hardy to -10°F (-23°C), US zones 6–8. Native to Britain and the western coasts of Europe, where it often grows in its millions in woods or shady meadows.

*Crocus tommasinianus*   This small bulb grows to 4in (10cm) tall and produces star-shaped flowers, with petals to 1½in (4cm) long, in winter and early spring. It is suitable for naturalizing, but happier in rock gardens and stony paths rather than grass. Hardy to -20°F (-29°C), US zones 5–9. Native to the Mediterranean and western Asia.

## SPRING SNOWFLAKE *Leucojum vernum*

This bulbous perennial grows to 9in (23cm) tall, producing groups of slightly scented flowers, each ¾in (2 cm) long. Best planted in late summer or autumn to a depth of 3–4in (8–10cm), in moist rich soil. Hardy to -30°F (-35°C), US zones 4–7. Native to northern Europe and western Asia.

## CALIFORNIAN TRILLIUM, STINKING BENJAMIN *Trillium chloropetalum*

A deciduous perennial with a rhizome that grows to 20in (50cm) tall. In spring it produces fragrant, greenish-yellow to purple flowers. Tolerant of some sun, thriving in partial shade, this plant needs shelter from strong winds. Hardy to -10°F (23°C), US zones 6–9. Native to western North America.

## WAKE ROBIN, WOOD LILY, BIRTHROOT *Trillium grandiflorum*

A deciduous perennial with a rhizome that grows to 1½ft (45cm) tall. It produces flowers, 2–3in (5–8cm) wide, that open white in spring and later become flushed with rose-pink. There are also forms with double or deep pink flowers. Hardy to -20°F (-29°C), US zones 5–8, thriving in areas with wet summers. Native to eastern North America where it can carpet the woods like bluebells do in England.

*Erythronium revolutum*

*Corydalis solida*

*Erythronium americanum*

*Leucojum vernum*

*Hyacinthoides non-scripta*

¼ life size. Photographed 12 January

**HYACINTH** *Hyacinthus orientalis*
A bulbous perennial that grows to 9in (23cm) tall, bearing erect clusters of very fragrant flowers, each about 1in (2.5cm) wide, in winter or early spring. Can be planted in autumn in well-drained soil or pots for displaying indoors. Best in a sunny position and hardy to 10°F (-12°C), US zones 8–10. It is seldom affected by pests and diseases. Native to western Asia and introduced into cultivation in the late 16th century. If grown indoors to flower during the winter, the bulbs should be put in a dark cool place at about 50°F (10°C), for at least two months while the roots develop. Shown here are:

'Bismarck'   Lavender flowers raised by D J Ziegler in the late 19th century.

'Carnegie'   White flowers raised by A Lefeber.

'L'Innocence'   White flowers raised in Holland in the 19th century.

'Pink Pearl'   Carmine-pink flowers raised in Holland in the 20th century.

'Rosalie'   A delicate early-flowering variety raised in 1948.

*Narcissus* 'Waterperry'   A bulbous plant that grows to 10in (25cm) tall, producing sweetly scented flowers in spring. Plant in late summer or autumn. Hardy to 5°F (-15°C), US zones 7–11. Raised in the 1950s derived from *Narcissus jonquilla*.

**DAFFODIL** 'Carlton'   A bulbous plant that grows to 2ft (60cm) tall, producing flowers in early spring. Plant in late summer or autumn, to a depth of 4in (10cm), in good rich soil, in partial shade. Hardy to -20°F (-29°C), US zones 5–9. A popular hybrid daffodil, commercially grown for cutting and forcing.

*Narcissus* 'Geranium'   Grows to 16in (42cm) tall, producing sturdy stems bearing a group of 4–6 flowers in spring. Hardy to 5°F (-15°C), US zones 7–11. 'Geranium' is a member of the 'poetaz' group of hybrids, derived from *N. tazetta* and *N. poeticus*.

*Narcissus papyraceus*

*Narcissus* 'Geranium'

*Narcissus* 'Peeping Tom'

DWARF DAFFODIL *Narcissus cyclamineus*  Grows to 8in (20cm) tall, producing flowers, about 2in (5cm) long, in early spring; these have recurved petals similar in shape to a cyclamen, hence the name. Hardy to -20°F (-29°C), US zones 5–9. Native to Spain and Portugal.

PAPER WHITE NARCISSUS *Narcissus papyraceus*  Grows to 15in (40cm) tall, bearing up to 20 strongly scented flowers from autumn to early spring. Hardy to 20°F (-7°C), US zones 9–11. Native to the Mediterranean region. In cooler areas, it is best grown in pots which can be brought into the house so that its scent can be fully appreciated.

*Narcissus* 'Peeping Tom'  Grows to 15in (40cm) tall, producing flowers in early spring. Hardy to -20°F (-29°C), US zones 5–9. This hybrid is derived from *Narcissus*

*cyclamineus*. It is an old favourite and was introduced into cultivation in the 1940s.

*Narcissus* 'Baby Moon'  Grows to 10in (25cm) tall, producing small sweetly scented flowers in spring. Plant in late summer or autumn, to a depth of about 4in (10cm), in good soil. Hardy to 0°F (-18°C), US zones 7–10.  A hybrid of *Narcissus jonquilla*, a species from the Mediterranean regions of Spain and Portugal.

*Narcissus* 'Erlicheer'  Grows to 1½ft (45cm) tall, producing flowers from autumn to early spring. Plant bulbs in summer to a depth of 4in (10cm), in good well-drained soil, preferably in a warm sheltered spot. Hardy to 20°F (-7°C), US zones 8–9. 'Erlicheer' is a double narcissus of garden origin, introduced into cultivation in 1951.

The Savill Gardens in spring

*Narcissus* 'Waterperry'

*Narcissus* 'Erlicheer'

*Narcissus* 'Carlton'

*Narcissus* 'Baby Moon'

*Narcissus cyclamineus*

Tulip 'Orange Nassau'

*Tulipa praestans*

*Tulipa fosteriana*

Tulip 'Heart's Delight'

Tulip 'Estella Rijnveld'

Tulip 'Jacqueline'

Tulip 'Spring Song'

TULIPS are members of the lily family Liliaceae, flowering in spring. They are best planted in autumn in a warm sunny position in good well-drained soil, to a depth of about 6in (15cm) and kept moist during the growing season. Hardy to -30°F (-35°C), US zones 3–9, thriving in cold winters, they are susceptible to viral diseases, aphids and slugs. In areas with wet summers the bulbs can be lifted when the foliage turns yellow, and stored in dry sand in a warm shed, until replanting time. The species from which garden tulips originate are native to the Mediterranean and western Asia and they have remained popular in Europe since their introduction into gardens from Turkey in the 16th century.

Tulip 'Apeldoorn' (a Darwin hybrid tulip) A bulb that grows to about 2ft (60cm) with flowers up to 7in (18cm) wide.

Tulip 'Estella Rijnveld' (a Parrot tulip) A bulb that grows to 20in (50cm). This sport of 'Red Champion' was raised in the early 20th century. Parrot tulips lend an exotic air to the garden, but unfortunately the flowers are sometimes almost too heavy for their stems. To prevent the plants flopping, it may be a good idea to grow them where they can come up through a low bush.

*Tulipa praestans* A small bulb that grows to about 1ft (30cm) tall, producing up to 5 flowers, measuring to 3in (8cm) wide when open, on each stem in spring. Best planted in late autumn in soil containing some leaf mould and grit. Hardy to -30°F (-35°C), US zones 3–9. Native to the Mediterranean and western Asia.

*Tulipa fosteriana* A small bulb that grows to about 8in (20cm) tall and produces slightly scented, single flowers, about 5in (12cm) long, in spring. The petals open out flat to reveal a black blotch margined with yellow inside. Best planted in late autumn and hardy to -30°F (-35°C), US zones 3–9. Native to western Asia and the Mediterranean.

Tulip 'Jacqueline'   A bulb that grows to about 2ft (60cm), raised in Holland in the early 20th century.

Tulip 'Heart's Delight' (a Kaufmanniana tulip)   Among the earliest of the tulips to flower in early spring, it grows to about 8in (20cm) tall, with leaves that are mottled with maroon. Hardy to -30°F (-35°C), US zones 3–9. Thriving in most areas where winters are cold, this tulip can do well when naturalized in grass. Raised in Holland in the early 20th century from a wild species from Uzbekistan.

Tulip 'Marilyn' (a Lily-flowered tulip) A bulb that grows to 22in (55cm), raised in Holland in this century.

Tulip 'Spring Song'   A bulb that grows to 2ft (60cm), raised in Holland in the early 20th century.

Tulip 'Peach Blossom'   A bulb that grows to 11in (28cm) tall, producing double, deep rose-pink flowers in early spring. Tulip bulbs should be kept moist during the growing season and until the leaves turn yellow after flowering, then the watering can be stopped. Hardy to -30°F (-35°C), US zones 3–9. 'Peach Blossom' is one of the old varieties of early double tulips and remains popular as a garden flower.

Tulip 'Orange Nassau'   This bulb grows to about 11in (28cm) tall and flowers in early spring. It is hardy to -30°F (-35°C), US zones 3–9. Tulip bulbs are best planted in autumn in a warm sunny position in good well-drained soil to a depth of about 6in (15cm). Popular in Europe for more than three hundred years, they were introduced from Turkey in the 16th century.

Tulip 'West Point' (a Lily-flowered tulip) A bulb that grows to 2ft (60cm) tall, it was raised in Holland in the early 20th century. 'West Point' is a particularly valuable plant in windy or exposed gardens because it has a very strong, sturdy stem that will withstand most weather conditions.

Tulip 'Apeldoorn'

Tulip 'Peach Blossom'

Tulip 'Marilyn'

Tulip 'West Point'

*Arum italicum* 'Pictum'

*Muscari armeniacum* 'Blue Spike'

*Ixia* hybrid

*Muscari armeniacum* 'Album'

*Muscari macrocarpum*

MARBLED ARUM *Arum italicum* 'Pictum'   A plant that grows to 2ft (60cm) tall, producing pale creamy-yellow flowers with a hooded spathe about 6in (15cm) tall, in spring. Hardy to 0°F (-18°C), US zones 7–9.  Attractive but poisonous, red fruiting heads are produced in late summer. Native to the Mediterranean and western Asia.

AFRICAN CORN LILY *Ixia* hybrid A plant that grows to 14in (35cm) tall, producing spikes of 5–15 red, pink, yellow or white cup-shaped flowers, 1½in (4cm) wide, in late spring. Hardy to 25°F (-4°C), US zones 9–11. Native to South Africa.

*Calochortus venustus* A member of the Lily family Liliaceae, this bulbous perennial grows to 2ft (60cm) tall, bearing flowers that can be white, pink, purple or dark red. Hardy to 20°F (-7°C), US zones 6–9. Native to California.

*Crinum* x *powellii* A large bulbous plant that grows to 5ft (1.5m) tall, producing flowers from summer to autumn. Plant in early spring, to a depth of 3in (8cm), in moist well-drained soil. This plant is easy to grow in a sunny position, best protected against a wall in cold areas. Hardy to 5°F (-15 C°), US zones 7–9.

## FIRECRACKER FLOWER
*Dichelostemma ida-maia* (syn. *Brodiaea ida-maia*) This bulb grows to 2ft (60cm) tall, producing scarlet (occasionally yellow) flowers, from spring to summer. Hardy to 25°F (-4°C), US zones 9–10. Native to western North America.

## SPRING STARFLOWER *Ipheion uniflorum* 'Rolf Fiedler' (syn. *Tritelia uniflora*)
This bulb grows to 8in (20cm) tall, producing beautiful star-shaped flowers, 2in (5cm) wide, in spring. The leaves smell of garlic if crushed. Best planted in autumn to a depth of about 2in (5cm) in well-drained gritty soil in sun or light shade, preferably in a sheltered position. Hardy to 10°F (-12°C), US zones 8–9. Native to South America.

## WHITE GRAPE HYACINTH
*Muscari armeniacum* 'Album' A member of the Lily family Liliaceae, this low-growing bulbous plant reaches up to 10in (25cm) high, producing flower stems bearing many small white flowers in spring. Hardy to -20°F (-29°C), US zones 5–9. This grape hyacinth is a form of *Muscari armeniacum*, which is native to the Mediterranean and western Asia.

*Muscari armeniacum* 'Blue Spike' Flower stems up to 10in (25cm) tall, with a mop of large double soft blue flowers.

## GRAPE HYACINTH *Muscari macrocarpum*
A low-growing, early flowering bulb that reaches 9in (23cm) high, bearing fragrant flowers. Hardy to 15°F (-10°C), US zones 8–10. Native to Turkey and the eastern Meditteranean.

## PEONY-FLOWERED
RANUNCULUS *Ranunculus asiaticus* A tuberous perennial plant reaching 15in (40cm) tall, producing single semi-double or double multicoloured flowers in red, pink, purple, yellow and white, to 2¹⁄₂in (6cm) across, from late spring to summer. Hardy to 20°F (-7°C), US zones 9–11.

*Crinum* x *powellii*

*Ipheion uniflorum* 'Rolf Fiedler'

*Ranunculus asiaticus*

*Dichelostemma ida-maia*

*Calochortus venustus*

**CAMASS** *Camassia leichtlinii* A whitish bulb, 2in (5cm) in diameter, with stems to 4ft (1.25m) with numerous flowers, about 1½–3in (4-8cm) wide, opening one at a time, in late spring. Hardy to 0°F (-18°C), US zones 7–9. Native to North America.

**QUAMASH, CAMOSH** *Camassia quamash* Stems 8in–2½ft (20–75cm), bearing clusters 2–12in (5–30cm), of flowers white to pale blue to deep violet-blue. Hardy to -20°F (-29°C), US zones 5–8. Native to the western United States, from Montana to Idaho.

**FOXTAIL LILY** *Eremurus* 'Cleopatra' A plant that grows to 6ft (1.8m) tall, bearing flowers in early summer and requiring plenty of sun. However, cold winters are necessary to produce good flowers. Hardy to -10°F (-23°C), US zones 6–9. A hybrid of *E. olgae* from Iran and Afghanistan.

**FRITILLARY, SNAKESHEAD** *Fritillaria meleagris* A plant that grows to 10in (25cm) tall, bearing hanging flowers in late spring. Best planted in late summer at a depth of about 3in (8cm) in rich well-drained soil. Hardy to about -20°F (-29°C), US zones 5–9. Native to western and southern Europe.

**BLACK FRITILLARY** *Fritillaria persica* 'Adiyaman' A bulbous plant that grows to 4ft (1.25m) tall, bearing flowers in late spring. Best planted in late summer or early autumn, to a depth of 3in (8cm), in sun or partial shade. Hardy to -10°F (-23°C), US zones 6–9. Native to Turkey, Iran and Israel.

**ENGLISH IRIS** *Iris latifolia* (syn. *Iris xiphioides*) Grows to 2½ft (75cm) tall, with flowers 5in (12cm) wide, on stems 20in (50cm). Unlike many other irises, this variety thrives in rich moist soil and does not need a dry period in summer. Hardy to -25°F (-32°C), US zones 4–9. Native to northern Spain.

**SUMMER SNOWFLAKE** *Leucojum aestivum* Grows to 2ft (60cm) tall, producing slightly scented flowers, each 1in (2.5cm) long, in spring. This plant thrives in waterlogged conditions, in sun or partial shade. Hardy to -25°F(-32°C), US zones 4–9. Native to Europe and western Asia.

**WHITE WATSONIA** *Watsonia borbonica* subsp. *ardernei* Grows up to 6ft (1.8m) tall, producing flowers, each 2½in (6cm) long, in early summer. Best in a sheltered sunny position and should not be allowed to dry out. Hardy to 12°F (-10°C), US zones 9–11. Native to South Africa.

*Camassia quamash*

*Fritillaria persica*

*Fritillaria meleagris*

*Watsonia borbonica* subsp. *ardernei*

*Iris latifolia*

*Camassia leichtlinii*

*Eremurus* 'Cleopatra'

**CROWN IMPERIAL**
*Fritillaria imperialis* (above)   Grows
to 4ft (1.25m) tall, bearing flowers,
sometimes red or yellow, in late spring.
It requires a position that is warm and
sheltered in spring, hot and dry in
summer. Hardy to -10°F
(-23°C), US zones 6–9. Native
to the Mediterranean and Asia.

*Leucojum aestivum*

Zantedeschia aethiopica 'Crowborough'

Crocosmia 'Emily McKenzie'

Eucomis bicolor

Crocosmia 'Lucifer'

MONTBRETIA, now properly called *Crocosmia,* is a member of the Iris family Iridaceae and grows from a pale brown bulb (corm), 1in (2.5cm) in diameter, into a fan of bright green leaves. Flowers open in succession in summer. Plant bulbs in early spring in moist fertile soil, in sun or light shade. Water from early summer to autumn. Crocosmias grow well in much of western Europe, eastern North America and the wetter parts of California. They are hardy to 15°F (-10°C), US zones 8–10. On the whole they are trouble-free, though the corms can be damaged by slugs.

*Crocosmia* 'Emily McKenzie'   Leaves 1ft (30cm) long and spikes of orange-yellow flowers with red markings, on stems to 2ft (60cm) tall. 'Emily McKenzie' is a hybrid of *Crocosmia* x *crocosmiflora,* raised by K McKenzie in the 20th century.

*Crocosmia* 'Lucifer'   Leaves 12–15in (30–40cm) long and spikes of orange-red flowers, about 1½in (4cm) wide, on stems to 4ft (1.25m) tall. 'Lucifer' is a hybrid between *Crocosmia masonorum* and *Crocosmia paniculata.* Raised by Alan Bloom in the 20th century.

*Crocosmia masonorum*   Leaves 12–15in (30–40cm) long and spikes of bright rich orange flowers, about 2in (5cm) wide, on stems to 5ft (1.5m) tall. Native to South Africa, in the southern Drakensberg mountains and introduced into cultivation in the 20th century.

ANGEL'S FISHING ROD *Dierama pulcherrimum*   An evergreen perennial with untidy leaves and elegant arching stems 6ft (1.8m) tall, bearing purplish-pink, occasionally pale pink or white, bell-shaped flowers, to 1in (2.5cm) long, in summer. Hardy to 12°F (-10°C), US zones 7–9 or less if the corms are well protected. Native to eastern South Africa.

*Galtonia candicans*

*Dierama pulcherrimum*

*Crocosmia masonorum*

*Gladiolus callianthus*

**SCENTED GLADIOLUS** *Gladiolus callianthus* This plant grows from a corm to about 6ft (1.8m) tall. It produces scented flower spikes, each 7in (18cm) long, in late summer. This plant needs plenty of water in summer and should not be allowed to dry out during dry weather. Hardy to 20°F (-7°C), US zones 9–11. Native to southern and tropical Africa.

**WILD GARLIC; SOCIETY GARLIC** *Tulbaghia violacea* This plant has a fleshy rhizome and looks similar to a small agapanthus. It grows to 2ft (60cm) and produces sweet-smelling flowers in summer; the leaves smell of garlic. Best planted to a depth of 2in (5cm) in good well-drained soil in a warm sunny position. Hardy to 10°F (-12°C), US zones 8–10. Native to South Africa.

**SUMMER HYACINTH** *Galtonia candicans* (syn. *Hyacinthus candicans*) A plant that grows to 4ft (1.25m) tall, producing stems that bear clusters of slightly scented flowers, each about 1½in (4cm) long, in summer. Galtonia bulbs thrive in deep, moist, sandy soil in full sun. Hardy to 5°F (-15°C), US zones 6–9. Native to South Africa and Lesotho.

*Gladiolus* 'Applause' A tender perennial that grows from a corm to 4ft (1.25m) tall. In summer it produces stiff spikes of bright pink flowers, each about 3½in (9cm) wide. Plant in autumn or early spring in a sunny position. Hardy to 20°F (-7°C), US zones 9–10. Native to the eastern Mediterranean.

**PINEAPPLE LILY** *Eucomis bicolor* A perennial bulb that grows to 2ft (60cm) tall, producing a flower spike in late summer. Hardy to 20°F (-7°C), US zones 9–10. Eucomis plants like plenty of light and water in summer and are native to South Africa. They were introduced into cultivation in the 19th century.

**ARUM LILY, CALLA LILY** *Zantedeschia aethiopica* 'Crowborough' A plant that grows to 3ft (90cm) tall with distinctive white flowers, 9in (23 cm) long, with one large petal folded round on itself, known as a 'spathe'. Hardy to 15°F (-10°C), US zones 8–10, for short periods, but if grown as an aquatic plant will often survive lower temperatures, particularly if it is protected from freezing by deep water. Native to South Africa.

*Gladiolus* 'Applause'

*Tulbaghia violacea*

281

*Lilium* Bellingham Hybrids

*Lilium pyrenaicum*

*Cardiocrinum giganteum*

*Lilium superbum*

*Lilium auratum*

spring or autumn to a depth of 1ft (30cm), in well-drained lime-free soil in a sunny position. Hardy to 15°F (-10°C), US zones 8–10. Native to Japan.

*Lilium* Bellingham Hybrids   A vigorous plant that grows to 8ft (2.5m) tall, producing flowers to 3in (8cm) wide, in summer. Best planted in spring or autumn when the ground is warm, to a depth of 6in (15cm), in light shade. Hardy to -20°F (-29°C), US zones 5–9. Raised in the US in the 1920s.

*Lilium* 'Black Beauty'   A bulbous plant that grows to 6ft (1.8m), producing maroon (not black) flowers, with reflexed petals, on long leaf stalks arising from the main stem, in late summer and autumn. Lily bulbs are best planted in spring or autumn, to a depth of 6in (15cm). Hardy to -5°F (-20°C), US zones 5–9.

*Lilium* 'Cover Girl'   One of the finest pink lily hybrids, growing to 7ft (2m) tall, producing flowers 10in (25cm) wide, in late summer and autumn, thriving in good, preferably lime-free well-drained soil in a sunny position. Hardy to -10°F (-23°C), US zones 6–9. Raised by Oregon Bulb Farms, in the US in 1967.

ORANGE SPECIOSUM LILY *Lilium henryi*   Grows to 10ft (3m) tall, producing orange, black-spotted flowers, in late summer. This lily does best in dappled shade, as the flower colour tends to bleach in full sun. Hardy to -20°F (-29°C), US zones 5–9. Native to China.

*Cardiocrinum giganteum*   A large bulb producing stems that grow to 12ft (3.5m) tall, bearing scented flowers, 9in (23cm) long, in summer. Best planted in late summer or early spring, in moist fertile soil, flourishing in light shade. Hardy to 0°F (-18°C), US zones 7–9. Native to the Himalayas and western China.

GOLDEN-RAYED LILY OF JAPAN, MOUNTAIN LILY *Lilium auratum*
A bulbous plant that grows up to 7ft (2m) tall, bearing fragrant flowers to 1ft (30cm) wide, from summer to autumn. Plant in

*Lilium henryi*

*Lilium* 'Black Beauty'

*Lilium pyrenaicum*  A bulbous plant that grows to 3ft (90cm), producing clusters of unpleasantly scented flowers, which are bright greenish-yellow with purplish-black spots and showy anthers covered with bright orange pollen. Hardy to -20°F (-29°C), US zones 5–7. Easy to grow in cool areas. Native to the Pyrenees, in France and Spain.

*Lilium regale*  A beautiful and popular plant that grows to 5ft (1.5m) tall. The bulb itself is distinctive, being deep red, and in summer it produces loose clusters of scented flowers that can be up to 5in (12cm) long. Hardy to -20°F (-29°C), US zones 5–9. Native to China, in north-western Sichuan, growing in its thousands on dry limestone cliffs where it was first collected by the famous plant hunter E H Wilson and introduced into cultivation in 1903.

TURK'S-CAP LILY *Lilium superbum* A bulbous plant that grows up to 8ft (2.5m) tall, producing flowers to 3in (8cm) wide. Best planted in the spring to a depth of 8in (20cm). Hardy to -20°F (-29°C), US zones 5–9. It is easy to grow in good moist (preferably lime-free) soil and partial shade. Native to North America.

*Lilium* 'Yellow Trumpet'  A bulbous plant that grows to 6ft (1.8m) tall, producing flowers up to 8in (20cm) wide, in late summer. Best planted in spring or autumn, when the ground is warm, to a depth of about 5–6in (12–15cm). Hardy to -10°F (-23°C), US zones 6–9.

*Lilium regale*

*Lilium* 'Yellow Trumpet'

*Lilium* 'Cover Girl'

*Colchicum speciosum* photographed above Trabzon, Turkey

*Colchicum speciosum*

*Colchicum speciosum* 'Album'

*Colchicum* 'Waterlily'

*Colchicum cilicium*

**MONKSHOOD** *Aconitum carmichaelii* 'Kelmscott' A tuber-rooted perennial forming a compact clump that grows to 6ft (1.8m) tall, bearing flowers, each about 1in (2.5cm) long, in late summer or early autumn. All parts of this plant contain highly poisonous substances and it should be handled with care. It flowers most freely in full sun, but the colour may be richer in a partially shaded position. Hardy to -20°F (-29°C), US zones 5–8. Native to China.

**NAKED LADIES** *Colchicum* Members of the Lily family Liliaceae these perennial cormous herbs produce flowers without leaves or any green stem in early autumn, and poisonous leaves in early spring. Best planted in late summer, to a depth of about 4in (10cm) in well-drained soil. The plant is easy to grow in a sunny position or in partial shade, requiring water in winter and spring. Hardy to about -10°F (-23°C), US zones 6–9, thriving in most of Europe and North America. Colchicum is not usually particularly prone to pests and diseases. Native to eastern Europe, North Africa and western Asia.

*Colchicum cilicium* Bright pink crocus-like flowers up to 7in (18cm) tall. Native to the Mediterranean and western Asia, growing in the mountains of southern Turkey among limestone rocks.

*Colchicum speciosum* Large bright pink, often white-throated, crocus-like flowers up to 7in (18cm) tall, 4in (10cm) wide. Native to the Mediterranean and western Asia, growing in the mountains of northern Turkey in alpine meadows.
  *Colchicum speciosum* 'Album' White goblet-shaped flowers, with exceptional purity of colour, up to 5in (12cm) tall. Plant bulbs to a depth of 3in (8cm).

*Colchicum* 'Waterlily' Bright pink, double crocus-like flowers to 7in (18cm) tall and 4in (10cm) across. A hybrid between a double *Colchicum autumnale* and *Colchicum speciosum*, raised by Kerbert in Holland around 1905.

**AUTUMN-FLOWERING CROCUS** *Crocus nudiflorus* A member of the Iris family Iridaceae, this small bulbous plant forms corms with a (stoloniferous) root system, which produces new corms at the tips. It grows up to 8in (20cm) tall, producing solitary flowers in autumn. The leaves are produced in spring long after the flowers have faded. Hardy to -10°F (-23°C), US zones 5–9. Native to the Mediterranean.

Aconitum carmichaelii 'Kelmscott'

Crocus speciosus

Cyclamen hederifolium

Nerine bowdenii

Crocus speciosus  One of the easiest and showiest crocuses to grow, it reaches 8in (20cm) high, producing flowers to 5in (12cm) wide in autumn. The leaves appear in spring after the flowers have died. Crocus speciosus is particularly suitable for naturalizing, thriving in sun or partial shade, under deciduous trees and shrubs or in short grass. Hardy to -10°F (-23°C), US zones 5–9. Native to the Mediterranean and western Asia.

WILD CYCLAMEN Cyclamen hederifolium (syn. C. neapolitanum) A corm that grows to 3in (8cm) in diameter, producing flowers about 1in (2.5cm) long, in early autumn and thriving in sun or light shade. The plants are dormant in summer and need little water then, unless earlier flowering is required. Hardy to -5°F (-20°C), US zones 6–9. Native to the Mediterranean and western Asia.

NERINE Nerine bowdenii  A bulbous perennial that grows to 2ft (60cm) tall, producing flowers in clusters up to 6in (15cm) wide. Best planted at the surface, or at most to a depth of about 1in (2.5cm), in a sunny position and preferably left undisturbed for several years. Hardy to 5°F (-15°C), US zones 7–11, although it will not survive low temperatures in wet conditions. Native to South Africa.

KAFFIR LILY, CRIMSON FLAG
Schizostylis coccinea (above)  This plant arises from a rhizome and grows to about 3ft (90cm) tall, producing spikes of 6–10 red, pink or white star-shaped flowers, each 1½in (4cm) across, in late autumn. Best planted in spring in moist fertile soil in a warm sheltered sunny position. Hardy to 12°F (-10°C), US zones 8–10. Native to South Africa, where it grows in gravel by streams in the Drakensberg mountains.

Begonia tuberhybrida

Lachenalia aloïdes

*Achimenes longiflora* 'Ambroise Verschaffelt' (syn. *A. verschaffeltii*) A perennial that grows from a scaly rhizome to 2ft (60cm) tall, bearing flowers 2¹/₂in (6cm) wide, in summer. The rhizome should be placed in well-drained compost in spring and kept moist with tepid water to start it into growth. Hardy to -10°F (-23°C), US zones 6–9. Native to Central America.

BELLADONNA *Amaryllis belladonna* A rather tender bulb that grows up to 2¹/₂ft (75cm) tall and usually rather taller than wide. In late summer and autumn its erect stems bear clusters of bright pink, widely trumpet-shaped flowers, each about 4in (10cm) wide and with a paler throat. Best planted in the autumn or spring in a sheltered, sunny position. Hardy to 10°F (-12°C), US zones 8–10. Native to South Africa.

*Begonia tuberhybrida* (syn. *Begonia tuberosa*) A tender perennial making a compact plant that grows to 1ft (30cm) tall and usually wider. Over a long period in summer it bears flowers, 6in (15cm) wide, in a range of shades of pink, yellow and red, clearly edged with a contrasting colour. Hardy to 32°F (0°C), US zone 10. The Tuberhybrida begonias are complex hybrids derived from various species native to South America.

*Canna* 'Dwarf Salmon' An herbaceous perennial that grows to 2ft (60cm) tall forming an erect clump, producing flowers about 2¹/₂in (6cm) wide, in summer. Plant in autumn or early spring in a rich peaty soil in a sunny sheltered position; in cold areas, in a cool greenhouse. Hardy to 10°F (-12°C), US zones 8–10. This is one of many named varieties, mostly belonging to the hybrid group called *Canna generalis*.

*Crinum asiaticum* var. *procerum* A plant that grows to 5ft (1.5m) tall, producing scented narrow-petalled spidery flowers, 10in (25cm) across, on a stalk often shorter than the leaves. It is easy to grow in a moist sunny position, in tropical areas. Hardy to 25°F (-4°C), US zones 9–10. Native to Asia and introduced into cultivation from Burma in the 18th century. It is used medicinally in Asia as a rather violent emetic.

*Cyclamen persicum* A tender perennial that grows to 8in (20cm) tall and wide, producing flowers in winter and early spring, each to 2¹/₂in (6cm) wide, in a range of red or pink tints or white. Dark green leaves are attractively marked with silvery marbling on the top and purple undersides. Plant in autumn in partial shade. Hardy to 20°F (-7°C), US zones 9–10. Native to eastern Mediterranean.

*Hippeastrum* 'Apple Blossom' A tender bulb that grows to 2ft (60cm) tall, with erect flowering stems bearing flowers, each about 6in (15cm) wide, in winter and spring. Plant in autumn or spring in a sunny position. Hardy to 50°F (10°C); 'Apple Blossom' requires a cool greenhouse except in parts of US zone 10. Derived from species native to South America.

*Lachenalia aloïdes* A tender bulbous perennial that grows to 1ft (30cm) tall, bearing narrow tubular flowers, varying in colour from yellow to red. Each flower is about 1in (2.5cm) long, produced in late winter and spring. Other species have flowers of red, purple, white, green or curious sea-blue tints and a few have fragrant flowers. Hardy to 20°F (-7°C), US zones 9–10. Most species of Lachenalia are native to South Africa.

GUERNSEY LILY *Nerine sarniensis* A bulbous perennial that grows to 2ft (60cm) tall, making a compact clump of foliage taller than wide. In autumn it bears flowers, each about 2¹/₂in (6cm) wide, up to 20 together on a slender stem. Best in a warm sunny position and hardy to 20°F (-7°C), US zones 9–10. Native to South Africa and introduced into cultivation in the middle of the 17th century.

*Hippeastrum* 'Apple Blossom'

Cyclamen growing at Château de la Guaroupe in France

*Amaryllis belladonna*

*Canna* 'Dwarf Salmon'

*Cyclamen persicum*

*Crinum asiaticum* var. *procerum*

*Achimenes longiflora* 'Ambroise Verschaffelt'

*Nerine sarniensis*

*Armeria caespitosa*

*Draba longisiliqua*

*Gentiana acaulis*

CHAPTER SIX

# Alpines

*The term alpines covers a number of small or low-growing plants that are suitable for growing on rock gardens or in a small, special place in the garden. Most, but not all, grow wild in mountain regions and they are grouped here so that those shown on the same page will be happy in roughly the same kind of conditions.*

*Androsace lanuginosa*

*Gentiana verna*

*Androsace lanuginosa*　A perennial with flower stems that grow to 1¹/₂in (4cm), bearing many pink flowers in summer and early autumn. Hardy to -5°F (-20°C), US zones 6–9. Native to the Himalayas.

*Armeria caespitosa*　A dense mat-forming perennial that grows to 3in (8cm) tall and wider, bearing flowers in spring or early summer. Hardy to 15°F (-10°C), US zones 8–9. Native to Spain, it is a fine plant for a rock garden or a wall crevice. Several selections are named, varying in size and flower colour.

*Draba longisiliqua*　A cushion perennial that grows to 2in (5cm) tall and 8in (20cm) wide, bearing flowers, each nearly

³/₄in (2cm) wide, borne in loose clusters on a 4in (10cm) stem in early summer. Best in a sunny position. Hardy to -5°F (-20°C), US zones 6–9. Susceptible to mildew in damp climates. Native to the Caucasus.

*Gentiana acaulis*　A low-growing perennial that only reaches 3in (8cm) tall, forming a mat wider than tall. Bears flowers, each about 2in (5cm) long, in spring or summer. Best in a sunny position. Hardy to -20°F (-29°C), US

zones 5–8, but is sometimes reluctant to flower freely. Native to the mountain regions of Europe.

SPRING GENTIAN *Gentiana verna*
A perennial that grows to 4in (10cm) tall, forming a tuft as wide as tall and bearing flowers to 1in (2.5cm) wide, in spring. Best in a sunny position. Hardy to -15°F (-26°C), US zones 5–9.

*Linaria alpina*　A small creeping alpine perennial forming a flat mat about 4in

Silene acaulis

Sempervivum montanum

Pulsatilla vernalis

Linaria alpina

Saponaria caespitosa

(10cm) across, of short stems with greyish fleshy leaves. In spring it bears numerous purple and orange snapdragon flowers. Needs a sunny, but not too hot position and very stony soil. Hardy to    -25°F (-32°C), US zones 4–8.

*Pulsatilla vernalis*  An herbaceous perennial that grows to 6in (15cm) tall, producing flowers about 2in (5cm) wide, in spring. At first they are nodding and bell-shaped, later becoming erect, opening wide to reveal a boss of golden stamens. Best in a sunny position. Hardy to -25°F (-32°C), US zones 4–8. Native to northern Europe and Siberia.

*Saponaria caespitosa*  A dense-growing perennial with a woody base that grows up to 6in (15cm) tall, flowering in late summer. Hardy to 5°F (-15°C), US zones 7–10.

HOUSELEEK *Sempervivum montanum* An evergreen perennial that grows to 8in (20cm) tall when in flower, forming clusters of rosettes rather wider than tall. In early summer it occasionally bears

spikes of flowers, each about 1in (2.5cm) wide. Hardy to -15°F (-26°C), US zones 5–9. Native to the mountains of central and southern Europe.

*Silene acaulis*  A cushion perennial that grows up to 1 1/2in (4cm) tall, bearing flowers 1/2in (1cm) wide, in early summer. Best in a sunny position and hardy to -40°F (-40°C), US zones 3–8. Native to the northern parts of North America, Europe and Asia. Although not always free-flowering in cultivation, it is an excellent rock garden plant.

*Armeria maritima*

## BEARBERRY, KINNIKINICK
*Arctostaphylos uva-ursi*   A creeping evergreen shrub forming extensive mats up to 10ft (3m) wide but only 3–6in (8–15cm) tall. In early summer it bears tiny flowers ½in (1cm) wide. Hardy to -35°F (-38°C), US zones 3–8. Native to North America, northern Europe and western Asia.

## SEA THRIFT *Armeria maritima*
A compact mat-forming perennial that grows to 1ft (30cm) tall and wider, bearing dense heads of flowers on short leafless stems to 1ft (30cm) tall, in spring or early summer. Best in full sun. Hardy to -15°F (-26°C), US zones 5–9. Native to Europe, Asia and North America.

*Gentiana* x *stevenagensis*   A low-growing perennial to 3in (8cm) tall, forming a mat wider than tall, performing best in acid peaty soil in areas with cool summers. In late summer or autumn it bears flowers 2½in (6cm) long. Hardy to -15°F (-26°C), US zones 5–9. Best divided fairly frequently to maintain vigour.

## FLOWERING WINTERGREEN
*Polygala paucifolia*   A stoloniferous perennial that grows to 6in (15cm) tall, forming colonies rather wider than tall. In late spring and summer it bears a succession of flowers ¾in (2cm) wide. Best in a sunny position and hardy to -40°F (-40°C), US zones 3–8. Native to the eastern US.

*Primula rosea*   An herbaceous perennial that grows to 8in (20cm) tall, producing flowers ¾in (2cm) wide, in early spring. Hardy to -10°F (-23°C), US zones 5–8. Native to the western Himalayas and introduced into cultivation in the 19th century, it is an attractive and colourful plant for a stream-side or bog garden.

*Parochetus communis*   A creeping herbaceous perennial that grows to 4in (10cm) tall, spreading to form wide mats.

*Rhododendron pemakoense*

*Arctostaphylos uva-ursi*

*Polygala paucifolia*

*Gentiana* x *stevenagensis*

*Saxifraga oppositifolia*

*Primula rosea*

Over a long period in summer and autumn it produces a succession of flowers ³/₄in (2cm) long. Hardy to 10°F (-12°C), US zones 8–9. Native to the Himalayas and introduced into cultivation in the 19th century.

*Rhododendron pemakoense*   A dwarf suckering evergreen shrub that grows to 3in (8cm) tall, making a compact mat wider than tall. In early spring it bears flowers 1in (2.5cm) wide and the leaves are covered with aromatic brownish scales on the underside. Hardy to -10°F (-23°C), US zones 6–9. Native to the eastern Himalayas and China.

RED STAR *Rhodohypoxis baurii*
A bulbous perennial with stems that grow to 6in (15cm) tall, producing flowers to 1in (2.5cm) wide, in late spring, varying in colour from white to deep red. Hardy to 5°F (-15°C), US zones 7–9. Native to Natal and Lesotho in the Drakensburg mountains.

PURPLE SAXIFRAGE *Saxifraga oppositifolia*   A creeping evergreen perennial forming mats scarcely 2in (5cm) tall, but much wider. Bears flowers ¹/₂in (1cm) wide in spring, pink to deep purple, fading to white. Hardy to -35°F (-38°C), US zones 3–8. Native to North America, northern Asia and northern Europe.

*Silene caroliniana*   A perennial that grows to 8in (20cm) tall, flowering in summer. Hardy to -15°F (-26°C), US zones 5–9. Native to eastern and central North America.

*Primula farinosa*   A perennial with short rhizomes that grows to 1ft (30cm) tall. Hardy to -25°F (-32°C), US zones 4–8. Native to Scotland, central Sweden to central Spain and Bulgaria.

*Primula farinosa*

*Parochetus communis*

*Rhodohypoxis baurii*

*Silene caroliniana*

*Dianthus freynii*

*Geranium cinereum* 'Ballerina'

*Aethionema armenum* 'Warley Rose'

*Iris lutescens*

*Aethionema armenum* 'Warley Rose'
An evergreen sub-shrub that grows to
10in (25cm) tall and usually wider. Bears
compact heads of small flowers in early
summer; clusters about 1in (2.5cm) wide
and elongating with age. Best in a sunny
position and hardy to -5°F (-20°C), US
zones 5–8. Native to western Asia.

*Alyssum saxatile* 'Citrina' (syn. *Aurinia
saxatilis*)   A perennial that grows to 9in
(23 cm), with profuse bright lemon
flowers produced in late spring. Hardy to
-35°F (-38°C), US zones 3–7. Native to
central and south-eastern Europe.

*Anacyclus pyrethrum* var. *depressus*
An attractive genus forming ground-
covering rosettes of feathery grey-green
foliage, bearing flowers often over long
periods in summer. Attractive in crimson
bud, closing up in dull weather and in
poor light. Suitable for rock gardens or on
scree. Although sometimes short-lived, it
is hardy to 0°F (-18°C), US zones 7–9,
but is intolerant of winter wet.

*Aubrieta* 'Oakington Lavender'   A dwarf
mat-forming perennial with four-petalled
flowers in spring. Other varieties are

*Alyssum saxatile* 'Citrina'

*Dianthus* 'Tiny Rubies'

*Iberis sempervirens*

*Dianthus* 'Inshriach Dazzler'

available in various shades of white, pink purple and carmine. Hardy to 15°F (-10°C), US zones 8–10. Most are derived from *Aubrieta deltoides*, native to Greece.

PINK *Dianthus freynii* A densely tufted perennial that grows to 4in (10cm) tall, bearing solitary pale pink or white flowers on short stems in summer. Hardy to -10°F (-23°C), US zones 6–9. Native to eastern Europe.

PINK *Dianthus* 'Inshriach Dazzler' A rock garden perennial that grows to 4in (10cm) tall, bearing flowers 1in (2.5cm) wide, in early summer. Hardy to -10°F (-23°C), US zones 6–9. A hybrid of *Dianthus pavonius* which is native to the mountains of southern Europe.

PINK *Dianthus* 'Tiny Rubies' A deep pink double-flowered alpine pink from North America. Hardy to -20°F (-29°C), US zones 5–9. A variety of the Cheddar pink, from Denver Botanic Gardens.

*Geranium cinereum* 'Ballerina' A rosette-forming perennial that grows to 6in (15cm) tall, bearing pink flowers, 1in (2.5cm) wide, tinged with purple-veined dark red in late spring and summer. Hardy to -15°F (-26°C), US zones 5–9.

*Iberis sempervirens* An evergreen spreading sub-shrub that grows to 1ft (30cm) tall, bearing white flowers in spring and summer. Native to southern Europe. Hardy to -25°F (-32°C), US zones 4–10.

*Iris lutescens* (syn. *Iris chamaeiris*) An evergreen plant forming dense mats with stems up to 8in (20cm) tall and flowers 2³⁄4in (7cm) across, in spring. Hardy to 5°F (-15°C), US zones 7–10. Native to north-eastern Spain, southern France and Italy.

*Anacyclus pyrethrum* var. *depressus*

*Aubrieta* 'Oakington Lavender'

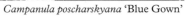

*Campanula poscharskyana* 'Blue Gown'

*Geum triflorum*

*Phlox subulata* 'Emerald Cushion Blue'

*Festuca glauca*

*Pseudofumaria alba*

**BLUE FESCUE** *Festuca glauca*
A perennial that grows to 6in (15cm) tall, bearing inconspicuous flowers in summer. The bright blue-grey leaves are bristle-like, up to 5in (12cm) long. Hardy to -10°F (-23°C), US zones 6–9 or lower. Native to Europe, this unusual foliage plant gives a unique combination of texture and colour.

*Geum triflorum* (syn. *Sieversia triflora*)
Plant forming clumps to 1ft (30cm) or more across, on stems to 1ft (30cm) tall, bearing 1–9 pale yellow to reddish or purplish flowers in summer. Hardy to -5°F (-20°C), US zones 6–9 or lower. Native to North America, growing in damp places and mountain scree.

MOSS PHLOX, MOUNTAIN PHLOX; MOSS PINK *Phlox subulata* 'Emerald Cushion Blue'  A perennial forming dense mats to 20in (50cm) tall, producing pink to lavender or white flowers in spring. Hardy to -40°F (-40°C), US zones 3–8. Native to eastern US.
  *Phlox* 'Red Wings'  Carmine-red flowers with dark centres.

*Phlox douglasii* 'Rosea'  A perennial that grows to 8in (20cm) tall. Hardy to -15°F (-26°C), US zones 5–8. Native to north-western US.

*Pseudofumaria alba* (syn. *Corydalis ochroleuca*)  A bushy perennial that grows to 15in (40cm) tall, producing white flowers in late spring and summer. Hardy to -10°F (-23°C), US zones 5–9. Native to Europe.

*Saxifraga* 'Garnet'  A hybrid mossy saxifrage with deep pink flowers in spring above crowded rosettes of soft leaves. Hardy to -15°F (-26°C), US zones 5–9.

*Thymus pannonicus*  An herbaceous perennial that grows to 8in (20cm) tall, producing pale pink or red flowers. Hardy to -15°F (-26°C), US zones 5–8. Native to central and south-western Europe.

*Veronica prostrata*  A mat-forming perennial that grows to 6in (15cm), producing pale to deep blue flowers in late spring and summer. Hardy to -20°F (-29°C), US zones 4–8. Native to Europe.

*Campanula poscharskyana* 'Blue Gown'  A perennial that grows to 10in (25cm) tall, producing clusters of large mid-blue flowers in summer and autumn. Hardy to -40°F (-40°C), US zones 3–8. *Campanula poscharskyana* is native to eastern Europe.

*Phlox* 'Red Wings'

*Thymus pannonicus*

*Phlox douglasii* 'Rosea'

*Veronica prostrata*

*Saxifraga* 'Garnet' at the Denver Botanical Gardens, Colorado

*Eriognum umbellatum*

*Eriogonum caespitosum*

*Gypsophila repens*

*Eriognum flavum*

*Helianthemum* 'Mrs C W Earl'

*Eriogonum caespitosum* A mat-forming perennial herb or sub-shrub that grows to 10in (25cm) flowering in summer. Hardy to 5°F (-15°C), US zones 7–10. Native to the western US.

*Eriognum flavum* A perennial with a woody base that grows to 8in (20cm) tall. Hardy to -5°F (-20°C), US zones 6–8. Native to the western US.

SULPHUR FLOWER *Eriognum umbellatum* A low spreading perennial herb or sub-shrub that grows to 3$^1$/$_2$ft (1m) tall. Sulphur or cream flowers on flower stalks to 1ft (30cm), in summer. Native to the eastern Rockies in the US and to south-western Canada. Hardy to -30°F (-35°C), US zones 4–10.

*Erodium cheilanthifolium* A tufted stemless perennial bearing white to pale pink flowers with red veins, to $^1$/$_2$in (1cm) wide, in summer. Hardy to -5°F (-20°C), US zones 6–9. Native to the mountains of southern Spain and Morocco.

*Gypsophila repens* (syn. *Gypsophila dubia*) A mat-forming perennial with arching flowering stalks growing to 8in (20cm)

*Erodium cheilanthifolium*

*Spraguea umbellata*

*Hymenoxys acaulis*

*Potentilla argentea*

*Penstemon fructicosus*

*Moltkia petraea*

tall. White, purple or pink-purple flowers produced in summer. Hardy to -25°F (-32°C), US zones 4–7. Native to the mountains of central and southern Europe.

ROCK ROSE; SUN ROSE
*Helianthemum* 'Mrs C W Earl'
A shrublet with short-lived double scarlet flowers flushed yellow at the base, produced in spring and late summer. Hardy to -5°F (-20°C), US zones 6–9. Most garden rock roses are hybrids of *Helianthemum appenninum, Helianthemum nummularium* and *Helianthemum croceum*.

*Hymenoxys acaulis* (syn. *Tetraneuris acaulis*) A perennial that grows to 6in (15cm) tall, producing yellow daisy-like flowers with orange veins. Hardy to -30°F (-35°C), US zones 4–8. Native to the central US.

*Moltkia petraea* A white, bristly, slender shrublet that grows to 15in (40cm) tall, producing blue or violet-blue flowers. Hardy to -5°F (-20°C), US zones 6–9. Native to Europe from the Balkans to central Greece.

SHRUBBY PENSTEMON *Penstemon fructicosus* A plant that forms shrubby clumps to 15in (40cm) tall, producing lavender-blue to pale purple flowers in spring and summer. Hardy to -25°F (-32°C), US zones 4–7. Native to North America.

HOARY CINQUEFOIL, SILVERY CINQUEFOIL *Potentilla argentea* A much-branched, somewhat woody-based perennial that grows to 20in (50cm) tall. Sulphur-yellow flowers 1/2in (1cm) across, produced in early summer. Hardy to -30°F (-35°C), US zones 4–7. Native to Europe and Asia Minor.

PUSSY-PAWS *Spraguea umbellata* A spreading annual or perennial that grows to 6in (15cm) tall, producing clusters 1/2–1 1/2in (1–4cm) wide, of white or pink flowers. Hardy to 0°F (-18°C), US zones 7–10. Native to western North America.

*Papaver rhoeas*

*Papaver nudicaule*

*Papaver somniferum* 'Pink Beauty'

CHAPTER SEVEN

# Annuals

*The annuals chosen here are a selection of the hundreds available; most are true annuals which can be sown in spring to flower throughout the summer. Some are perennials or soft shrubs which are usually grown as annuals; they are planted out as young plants and may need to be brought indoors as whole plants or cuttings if they are to survive the winter frosts.*

CORNFLOWER *Centaurea cyanus* An annual or biennial to 3ft (90cm) tall, producing intense blue flower heads, each about ³/₄in (2cm) wide, in summer. Best in a sunny position and hardy to -10°F (-23°C), US zones 6–9. Native to much of northern Europe.

WALLFLOWER *Erysimum cheiri* (syn. *Cheiranthus cheiri*) Grows to 2ft (60cm) tall and invariably as a biennial, this plant produces fragrant flowers in a wide range of colours, ³/₄in (2cm) wide, in late spring and early summer. Best in a sunny position and hardy to -10°F (-23°C), US zones 6–8. Native to much of southern Europe.

GARDEN STOCKS *Matthiola* (mixed) Hybridization in this genus has resulted in various races of hardy annuals and biennials that grow to 2ft (60cm) tall, producing highly scented single and double flowers in a wide range of pinks,

whites, reds and mauves, from spring to late summer or autumn. Each flower is about 1¹/₂in (4cm) wide. Hardy to 10°F (-12°C), US zones 8–10.

*Nigella hispanica* An annual that grows to 1¹/₂ft (45cm) tall, producing flowers, each about 1¹/₂in (4cm) wide, in summer. The fruit is a cluster of fused capsules and is ornamental in its own right. Hardy to 10°F (-12°C), US zones 8–10. Native to south-west Europe.

*Papaver nudicaule* A perennial, usually grown as an annual, that grows to 1ft (30cm) tall, making a clump taller than wide, producing long-stemmed flowers about 3in (8cm) wide, in shades of yellow and orange, in summer. Hardy to -20°F (-29°C), US zones 5–8 or lower. Native to subarctic Europe and Asia.

FIELD POPPY *Papaver rhoeas* A hardy annual that grows to 3ft (90cm) tall, producing solitary flowers about 2¹/₂in (6cm) wide, in summer. Best in a sunny position. Hardy to -20°F (-29°C), US zones 5–9. Native to most of Europe and western Asia.

*Papaver somniferum* 'Pink Beauty' An annual that grows to 3ft (90cm) tall, making a clump taller than wide, producing flowers, each about 4in (10cm) wide, in summer. Hardy to -20°F (-29°C), US zones 5–8. Native to south-east Europe and western Asia.

*Centaurea cyanus*

*Lathyrus odoratus* 'Sally Unwin'

Viola 'Prince John' is seen to good effect with *Muscari* 'Blue Spike'

*Viola tricolor*

Pansy 'Imperial Silver Princess'

SWEET PEA *Lathyrus odoratus*  A vigorous self-clinging annual that grows to 7ft (2m) tall, producing highly scented flowers, about 1¹/₂in (4cm) wide, over a long period in summer. Prefers a sunny position and wires or trelllis for support. Hardy to 20°F (-7°C), US zones 9–10. Native to Italy and Crete. Over the years, many forms have been selected, both for colour and habit and it is now one of the most popular bedding plants availablc. As well as the familiar tall climbing forms, there are also dwarf bushy varieties available, well-suited to small gardens or containers. Shown here are:

'Blue Danube'(above), 'Sally Unwin' (left) and 'Red Arrow'(below).

*Viola* 'Prince John'  An annual that grows to 6in (15cm) tall, producing flowers about 1in (2.5cm) wide. Hardy to 10°F (-12°C), US zones 8–10. *Viola* 'Prince John' is of complex hybrid origin. Here it is seen to good effect with *Muscari* 'Blue Spike'.

WILD PANSY; HEART'S EASE
*Viola tricolor*  An annual or biennial that grows to 1ft (30cm) tall with violet, yellow or bicoloured flowers. Hardy to -25°F (-32°C), US zones 4–8. Native to Europe and Asia.

PANSY 'Imperial Silver Princess'
An annual or biennial that grows to 6in (15cm) tall, producing flowers about 2¹/₂in (6cm) wide, in summer. Hardy to 10°F (-12°C), US zones 8–10. *Viola* 'Imperial Silver Princess' is of complex hybrid origin, raised in the 20th century.

Dwarf mixed Brompton stocks

*Nigella hispanica*

*Erysimum cheiri* growing with Forget-Me-Nots (see page 198)

*Lathyrus odoratus* 'Red Arrow'

'Princess White Purple-Eye'    'Liberty Yellow'    'Madame Butterfly Mixed'    'Cornette Scarlet'    'Cornette Crimson'    'Cornette White'    'Liberty Pink'    'Little Darling'

Modern snapdragon cultivars

*Lobelia erinus* 'Cambridge Blue'

*Antirrhinum majus* 'Double Madame Butterfly', showing the range of colours

*Nicotiana* 'Domino Salmon-Pink'

*Dianthus chinensis* 'Raspberry Parfait'

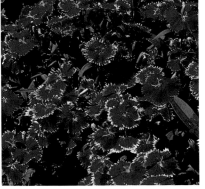

*Dianthus chinensis* 'Telstar Picotee'

SNAPDRAGON *Antirrhinum majus*
Grows to 6ft (1.8m) tall in the wild,
producing flowers in shades of purple or
pink, about 1½in (4cm) long, in summer.
Hardy to 10°F (-12°C), US zones 8–10.
Native to the Mediterranean region and
south-west Europe. Many popular garden
varieties have been raised. They are
generally more compact in growth with
flowers in a wide range of colours and are
invariably grown as annuals.
  'Double Madame Butterfly'   Grows to
2ft (60cm) tall, producing fully double
flowers about 1½in (4cm) long, in a range
of colours over a long period in summer.
Also illustrated here are:
  'Cornette Crimson', 'Cornette Scarlet',

'Cornette White', 'Liberty Pink', 'Little Darling', 'Liberty Yellow', 'Princess White Purple-Eye', 'Madame Butterfly Mixed'.

*Dianthus chinensis* 'Raspberry Parfait' Grows to 8in (20cm) tall, producing fragrant flowers 2in (5cm) wide, in summer. Hardy to 0°F (-18°C), US zones 7–10. *Dianthus chinensis* is native to China. It has produced many selected garden varieties, mostly of dwarf habit and in a range of colours.
  *Dianthus chinensis* 'Telstar Picotee' Grows to 10in (25cm) tall with fragrant flowers 1¹/₂in (4cm) wide.

*Godetia* 'Furora'  An annual, usually planted in spring. Hardy to 15°F (-10°C), US zones 8–10. Numerous cultivars of godetias have been raised in various shades of pink, purple and stripes; 'Furora' is a particularly bright red variety. Native to California.

*Lobelia erinus* 'Cambridge Blue'  This is a tender trailing perennial usually grown as an annual, to 6in (15cm) tall, producing flowers ³/₄in (2cm) wide, in summer. Hardy to 20°F (-7°C), US zones 9–10 Native to South Africa.

TOBACCO PLANT *Nicotiana* 'Domino Salmon-Pink'  A half-hardy, somewhat poisonous annual that grows to 1ft (30cm) tall, producing sweetly scented flowers 1¹/₂in (4cm) wide, in summer. Hardy to 10°F (-12°C), US zones 8–10.

*Nicotiana* 'Havana Apple Blossom' Grows to 15in (40cm) tall and somewhat poisonous, producing scented flowers 1¹/₂in (4cm) wide, in summer. Hardy to 10°F (-12°C), US zones 8–10.

PETUNIA *Petunia* cultivars  Trailing half-hardy annuals, with flowers about 4in (10cm) wide, produced in summer. Hardy to 20°F (-7°C), US zones 9–10. The garden petunias are of hybrid origin, their ancestors came from South America. Now very popular annuals, valued for their showy flowers produced over a long season. Shown here are:
  *Petunia* 'Frenzy Red Star'  An especially

compact cultivar that grows up to 8in (20cm) tall.
  *Petunia* 'Prime Time Red-Veined' Grows to 14in (35cm) tall. The Prime Time series comes in many colours, including veined and striped petals.
  *Petunia* 'Surfinia Pink Vein'  Grows to 1ft (30cm) tall, producing flowers about 3in (8cm) wide. The Surfinia series of petunias is raised from cuttings not seeds, for planting out in the early summer. They are especially vigorous and thus particularly suitable for baskets.

*Zinnia elegans* 'Fantastic Light Pink' A half-hardy annual that grows to 9in (23cm) tall and as wide. In summer and early autumn it produces flowers about 2in (5cm) wide. Hardy to 10°F (-12°C), US zones 8–10. *Zinnia elegans* is native to Mexico. The Fantastic series is a range of especially dwarf selections in various colours.
  *Zinnia elegans* 'Yellow Ruffles'  Grows to 2ft (60cm) tall. The Ruffles series is one of the taller selections, available in various colours.

*Nicotiana* 'Havana Apple Blossom'

*Zinnia elegans* 'Yellow Ruffles'

*Zinnia elegans* 'Fantastic Light Pink'

*Petunia* 'Surfinia Pink Vein'

*Petunia* 'Frenzy Red Star'
*Petunia* 'Prime Time Red-Veined'

*Godetia* 'Furora'

# ANNUALS

LIVINGSTONE DAISY *Dorotheanthus bellidiformis* (syn. *Mesembryanthemum criniflorum*) (mixed)   A creeping half-hardy annual that grows to 3in (8cm) tall, producing flowers about 1½in (4cm) wide, range of pastel colours, over a long period in summer. Hardy to 32°F (0°C), US zone 10. Native to South Africa.

BIRDS' EYES *Gilia tricolor*   An erect branching annual that grows to 15in (40cm) tall, producing clusters of flowers, each about ½in (1cm) wide, in early summer. Hardy to 0°F (-18°C), US zones 7–10. Native to California and introduced into cultivation in the early 19th century.

*Laurentia axillaris* 'Blue Stars' (syn. *Isotoma axillaris*)   A bushy perennial usually grown as an annual, with blue delicately scented starry flowers over the summer. Hardy to 25°F (-4°C), US zones 9–10. Native to Australia.

BABY-BLUE-EYES *Nemophila menziesii* (syn. *N. insignis*)   A spreading annual that grows to 6in (15cm) tall and wider, with an abundance of flowers each about 1in (2.5cm) wide in summer. Hardy to 10°F (-12°C), US zones 8–10. Native to California. Numerous selections are available, varying in colour and markings.

*Nolana paradoxa* 'Blue Bird'   An annual or short-lived perennial that grows to 10in (25cm) tall, producing flowers 2in (5cm) wide, in summer. Hardy to 32°F (0°C), US zone 10. Native to Chile and introduced into cultivation early in the 19th century.

SWAN RIVER DAISY *Brachycome iberidifolia*   A half-hardy annual that grows to 15in (40cm) tall and wider, bearing masses of small daisies, each about ¾in (2cm) wide, throughout summer and early autumn. These have yellow centres but the rays may be violet-blue, rose-pink, purple or white. Hardy to 10°F (-12°C), US zones 8–10. *Brachycome iberidifolia* is native to southern Australia.

STAR OF THE VELDT *Dimorphotheca sinuata*   A spreading annual that grows to 1ft (30cm) tall and wider, producing daisy-like flowers about 2in (5cm) wide, in summer. Hardy to 20°F (-7°C), US zones 9–10. Native to South Africa and introduced into cultivation in the late 18th century.

*Osteospermum* 'Tresco Purple'

*Nolana paradoxa* 'Blue Bird'

*Gilia tricolor*

*Osteospermum* 'Tresco Purple'  A tender perennial that grows to 1ft (30cm) tall and wider. Flowers, each about 2½in (6cm) wide, over a long period in summer. Hardy to 20°F (-7°C), US zones 9–10. 'Tresco Purple' is of hybrid origin, the parent species is native to South Africa. Although a popular hybrid, it is rather less hardy than most other *Osteospermum* cultivars.

ANNUAL PHLOX *Phlox drummondii*
An annual that grows to 1½ft (45cm) tall, producing flowers ¾in (2cm) wide, in summer and early autumn. They are available in a wide range of colours including whites, reds, pinks and purples, as well as intermediate tints. Hardy to 10°F (-12°C), US zones 8–10 or lower. Native to Texas in the southern US.

*Dorotheanthus bellidiformis*

*Nemophila menziesii*

*Phlox drummondii*

*Brachycome iberidifolia*

*Dimorphotheca sinuata*

*Laurentia axillaris*

*Plectranthus forsteri* 'Variegatus'

*Amaranthus caudatus*

**LOVE LIES BLEEDING** *Amaranthus caudatus*  A half-hardy annual that grows to 3ft (90cm) tall and as wide, bearing flowers to 1 1/2ft (45cm) long in summer and autumn. Best in a sunny position and hardy to 32°F (0°C), US zone 10. Native to the tropics of Southern Hemisphere.

**BORAGE** *Borago officinalis*  An annual that grows to 3ft (90cm) tall. In summer and autumn it produces flowers, each 3/4in (2cm) wide. Best in a sunny, sheltered position. Hardy to 0°F (-18°C), US zones 7–10. A valuable forage plant for bees.

*Heliotropium arborescens* 'Marine' A bushy compact perennial shrub to 1 1/2ft (45cm) producing clusters of sweetly scented deep violet flowers. Hardy to 32°F (0°C), US zone 10. Native to Peru.

**COCKSCOMB** *Celosia argentea* var. *cristata* 'Apricot Beauty'  A compact annual that grows to 9in (23cm) tall and as wide, producing large bright orange,

plumose flower heads in summer. Whilst the individual flowers are minute, the heads may be 6in (15cm) across. Best in a sunny position and hardy to 20°F (-7°C), US zones 9–10. Derived from a wild plant widespread in tropical America, Africa and Asia.

*Celosia argentea* var. *cristata* 'Golden Triumph'  Grows to 1ft (30cm) tall with bright yellow flower heads.

*Eryngium giganteum* 'Silver Ghost' Grows to 2ft (60cm) tall, bearing white flower heads tinged with blue, 1 1/2in (4cm) long, in summer, and similar fruiting heads, giving the plant a long season of interest. Hardy to -10°F (-23°C), US zones 6–9. Native to the Caucasus and northern Turkey.

**SEA LAVENDER** *Limonium sinuatum* (syn. *Statice sinuata*)  Grows to 2ft (60cm) tall, producing sprays of small flowers barely 1/2in (1cm) wide, each sitting within a coloured calyx, in

*Tanacetum ptarmiciflorum*

*Verbena* 'Novalis Deep Blue'

'Forever Gold'

'Blue Peter'

'Roselight'

'Sunset'

'Petite Bouquet White'

'Petite Bouquet Schuman'

'Petite Bouquet Blue'

*Limonium sinuatum*

*Verbena* x *hybrida* 'Sissinghurst'

summer. Hardy to 10°F (-12°C), US zones 8–10. Native to the Mediterranean region, it is grown mostly for picking, as the papery calyx retains its colour when dried. Many varieties are available with flowers in a range of colours. Shown here: 'Roselight', 'Blue Peter', 'Forever Gold', 'Petite Bouquet White', 'Sunset', 'Petite Bouquet Blue' and 'Petite Bouquet Schuman'.

*Plectranthus forsteri* 'Variegatus' (syn. *Plectranthus coleoides*)   An aromatic perennial that grows to 3½ft (1m) across, producing clusters of small white flowers and variegated cream leaves. Native to New Caledonia, Fiji and eastern Australia.

*Tanacetum ptarmiciflorum* (syn. *Pyrethrum ptarmiciflorum*) 'Silver Feather'   A sub-shrub that grows to 1ft (30cm) tall, usually treated as an annual and grown for its foliage. In summer it may produce small white daisies 1in (2.5cm) wide. Hardy to 20°F (-7°C), US zones 9–10. Native to the Canary Islands.

*Verbena* 'Novalis Deep Blue'   Grows to 1ft (30cm) tall, producing flowers about 3in (8cm) across, over a long period in summer and autumn. Hardy to 25°F (-4°C), US zones 9–10. Native to Mexico, where it covers the ground spectacularly after a forest fire.

*Verbena* x *hybrida* 'Sissinghurst' A perennial herb usually grown as an annual, forming mats 3½ft (1m) across, producing fragrant, magenta-pink flowers. Hardy to 25°F (-4°C), US zones 9–10.

*Celosia* 'Apricot Beauty'

*Eryngium giganteum* 'Silver Ghost'

*Celosia argentea* var. *cristata* 'Golden Triumph'

*Borago officinalis*

*Heliotropium arborescens* 'Marine'

*Helianthus annuus*

*Cineraria* 'Brilliant' (syn. *Senecio cruentes*, *Pericallis* x *hybrida*)   The florists' cineraria is a hybrid of species from the Canary Islands. Plants are available in a wide variety of colours. Seeds are sown in spring to flower the following winter. Hardy to 32°F (0°C), US zone 10.

*Cosmos bipinnatus*   Grows to 6ft (1.8m) tall, erect in growth and taller than wide, producing flowers, about 3in (8cm) wide, in shades of rosy-pink and lilac as well as white and even bicolored forms, in summer. Hardy to 32°F (0°C), US zone 10. Native to Mexico and the southern United States.

*Dahlia* 'Bishop of Llandaff'   A tender perennial that grows to 3ft (90cm) tall, producing flowers 3¹/₂in (9cm) wide, for much of the summer. The deep bronze-purple colour of the leaves forms a lovely contrast with the showy flowers. Hardy to 20°F (-7°C), US zones 9 or 10. Derived from *Dahlia coccinea*, native to Mexico.

*Gazania* cultivars   These tender perennials produce showy daisies, about 2¹/₂in (6cm) wide, in summer. In most areas they are tender and can be planted out only when all risk of frost is over. Best in a sunny position and hardy to 20°F (-7°C), US zones 9–10. The garden hybrid gazanias are derived from South African species. They are now available in a wide range of colours, some with multi-coloured flowers.
  *Gazania* 'Mini Star Series'   Grows to 8in (20cm) tall with flowers in a range of colours from white through yellow to tangerine-orange and bronze.
  *Gazania* 'Schofield Variegated'   Grows to 1ft (30cm) tall with dark-eyed orange flowers.

*Rudbeckia* Rustic Dwarfs

*Cosmos bipinnatus*

*Cosmos bipinnatus*

*Dahlia* 'Bishop of Llandaff'

# DAISY FAMILY

*Gazania krebsiana*  Grows to 3in (8cm) tall, producing flowers about 2¹/₂in (6cm) wide in summer. Hardy to 20°F (-7°C), US zones 9–10. Native to South Africa, this is less often grown than the numerous hybrids, which give a wider range of colours, but is nevertheless a good plant for a warm garden.

SUNFLOWER *Helianthus annuus* 'Sunspot'  An annual that grows to 2ft (60cm) tall, producing flowers as much as 10in (25cm) wide, in summer. The fruiting head may be used for dried flower decoration or left for the birds to take the seeds. Hardy to -10°F (-23°C), US zones 6–10. Native to South America.

*Rudbeckia* Rustic Dwarfs (mixed) Grow to 2ft (60cm) tall, producing golden-yellow, orange, bronze or mahogany flowers, sometimes bicoloured, in summer. Flowers each about 5in (12cm) wide. Hardy to 10°F (-12°C), US zones 8–10. *Rudbeckia* is a small genus native to North America.

FRENCH MARIGOLD *Tagetes* 'Aurora Fire'  A half-hardy annual that grows to 10in (25cm) tall, producing flowers each about 2in (5cm) wide, in summer. Hardy to 32°F (0°C). The French Marigolds are derived from *Tagetes patula*, native to Mexico.

SIGNET MARIGOLD *Tagetes tenuifolia* 'Golden Gem'  Grows to 6in (15cm) tall, producing flowers, each a little over ¹/₂in (1cm) wide, in summer. Hardy to 32°F (0°C), US zone 10. Native to Mexico and Central America.

AFRICAN MARIGOLD *Tagetes* 'French Vanilla'  Grows to 2ft (60cm) tall, producing flowers, each nearly 3in (8cm) wide, in summer. Hardy to 32°F (0°C), US zone 10. The African Marigolds are derived from *Tagetes erecta*, native to Mexico and Central America.

*Cineraria* 'Brilliant'

*Gazania krebsiana*

*Gazania* 'Schofield Variegated'

*Gazania* 'Mini Star Series'

*Tagetes tenuifolia* 'Golden Gem'

*Tagetes* 'Aurora Fire'

*Tagetes* 'French Vanilla'

Argyranthemum 'Jamaica Primrose'

'Showboat'

'Big Top'

'Spectra'

New Guinea Hybrids *Impatiens hawkeri*

*Argyranthemum* 'Jamaica Primrose'
Grows to 3ft (90cm) tall, bearing flowers
2¹/2in (6cm) wide throughout the
summer. Hardy to 20°F (-7°C), US zones
9–10. Probably a hybrid of *A. frutescens*,
native to the Canary Islands.

*Argyranthemum* 'Vancouver' Grows to
3ft (90cm) tall, bearing double candy-
pink flowers 2¹/2in (6cm) wide throughout
the summer. Hardy to 20°F (-7°C), US
zones 9–10. Probably a hybrid of *A.
frutescens*, native to the Canary Islands.

*Impatiens* 'New Guinea' hybrids
Members of the balsam family,
Balsaminaceae, these plants grow to 10in
(25cm) tall and form clumps wider than
tall, bearing flowers about 2in (5cm)
across, throughout the year. Hardy to
32°F (0°C), US zone 10. They can be
grown outside in the summer in colder
areas. This race of spectacular 'New
Guinea' hybrids was formed by crossing
*I. linearifolia* and a form of *I. hawkeri* with
exceptionally highly coloured leaves.
Shown here are:
'Big Top', 'Eclipse', 'Octavia', 'Showboat'
and 'Spectra'.

BUSY LIZZIE *Impatiens walleriana*
A tender perennial, usually grown as an
annual, that grows to 10in (25cm) tall,
producing flowers about 1¹/2in (4cm)
wide, for much of the summer. Hardy to
32°F (0°C), US zone 10. This variety is
derived from *Impatiens walleriana*, native
to tropical east Africa.

*Impatiens* 'Double Diamond Rose'
This is a new strongly coloured double
variety.

IVY-LEAFED PELARGONIUM
*Pelargonium* 'Decora Rose' A plant with a
strong trailing growth that will reach 1ft
(30cm) tall and usually wider. In summer
it bears clusters of flowers, each about
1¹/4in (3cm) wide. Hardy to 32°F (0°C),
US zone 10.

ZONAL PELARGONIUM *Pelargonium*
'Mrs Parker' Grows to 1¹/2ft (45cm) tall
and wider, producing flowers to 1in (3cm)
wide with variegated leaves, in summer.
Hardy to 32°F (0°C), US zone 10. The
Zonal Pelargoniums are of hybrid origin,
their wild ancestors come from South
Africa.
    *Pelargonium* 'Salmon Elite' A seed-
raised strain with particularly fine flowers
and black-zoned leaves. Scarlet, red and
white flowered varieties are also available
in the elite series.

*Begonia semperflorens* A perennial usually
grown as an annual; in the dwarf bedding

varieties shown here about 6in (15cm)
high, producing flowers in shades of red,
pink or white until the frost. Hardy to
32°F (0°C), US zone 10.

*Begonia tuberhybrida* Grows to 1ft
(30cm) tall and wider, bearing flowers,
5–6in (12–15cm) wide, in a range of
shades of pink, yellow and red, clearly
edged with a contrasting colour, over a
long period in summer. Hardy to 32°F
(0°C), US zone 10. The tuberhybrida
begonias are complex hybrids derived
from various species, native to South
America. Shown here is 'Pin Up' which
can be raised from seed to flower well in
one season.

POMPOM CHRYSANTHEMUM
*Dendranthema* 'Fairy Rose' Grows to 1ft
(30cm) tall, producing flowers, each
about ¹/2in (1cm) wide, in late summer
and autumn. Hardy to 12°F (-10°C), US
zones 8–10. Native to China.

*Argyranthemum* 'Vancouver'

*Dendranthema* 'Fairy Rose'

Impatiens 'Octavia'

Begonia tuberhybrida 'Pin Up'

Begonia semperflorens

Impatiens 'Double Diamond Rose'

Impatiens growing on an old tree trunk

Impatiens walleriana

Impatiens 'Eclipse'

Pelargonium 'Salmon Elite'

Pelargonium 'Mrs Parker'

Pelargonium 'Decora Rose'

*Cleome hassleriana* 'Violet Queen'

*Cleome* 'Pink Queen'

*Eustoma grandiflorum* 'Echo Pink'

SPIDER PLANT *Cleome* 'Pink Queen'
Grows to 4ft (1.25m) tall, producing pink
flowers 2in (5cm) wide in summer. Best in
a sunny position and hardy to 32°F (0°C),
US zone 10. *Cleome hassleriana* is native to
Uruguay in South America.
   *Cleome hassleriana* 'Violet Queen'
Violet-purple flowers.

MONKEY FLOWER *Mimulus*
'Magnifique'   Grows to 1ft (30cm) tall,
producing flowers 2¹/₂in (6cm) across in
summer and autumn. Hardy to 15°F
(-10°C), US zones 8–10. Native to North
and South America.

PRAIRIE GENTIAN *Eustoma
grandiflorum*   Grows to 2ft (60cm) tall,
producing white, mauve, pink or purple
flowers 2¹/₂in (6cm) wide in summer.
Hardy to 20°F (-7°C), US zones 9–10,
but is very susceptible to over-watering.
Native to the southern United States and
Mexico. Careful breeding has produced a

wide range of colours and both tall long-
stemmed varieties and dwarf bushy ones
are available.
   *Eustoma grandiflorum* 'Echo Pink'
Almost rose-like, fully double flowers.

SWAMP ROSE MALLOW *Hibiscus
moscheutos*   Grows to 3ft (90cm) tall,
producing white, pink or crimson flowers,
6in (15cm) across in summer. Hardy to
-20°F (-29°C), US zones 5–9. Native to
the eastern United States.

*Silene coeli-rosa* (syn. *Viscaria elegans*)
'Brilliant Mixture'   Grows to 15in
(40cm) tall, producing pink, white, red or
light violet-blue flowers, about 2in (5cm)
wide in summer. Hardy to 10°F (-12°C),
US zones 8–10. Native to the western
Mediterranean region.

*Salpiglossis* 'Festival Mixed'   Grows to 1ft
(30cm) tall, producing yellow, salmon, red
and purple flowers, 2¹/₂in (6cm) wide, all

*Eustoma grandiflorum*                    *Hibiscus moscheutos*

*Mimulus* 'Magnifique'

with prominent veining in the yellow throat in summer. Hardy to 10°F (-12°C), US zones 8–10. *Salpiglossis sinuata*, the parent of most of the garden varieties, is native to South America.

*Salvia coccinea* 'Lady in Red'   Grows to 15in (40cm) tall, producing flowers ³/₄in (2cm) lon, in summer. Hardy to 10°F (-12°C), US zones 8–10. Native to tropical South America.

*Salvia farinacea* 'Victoria'   Grows to 1¹/₂ft (45cm) tall, producing deep purple-blue flowers in summer. Hardy to 10°F (-12°C), US zones 8–10. Native to the southern United States and Mexico.

BUTTERFLY FLOWER or POOR MAN'S ORCHID *Schizanthus pinnatus* 'Giant Hybrids'   Grows to 2¹/₂ft (75cm) tall, producing flowers 1in (2.5cm) wide in a wide range of colours in late spring and summer. Hardy to 32°F (0°C), US zone 10. Native to Chile.

GARDEN NASTURTIUM *Tropaeolum majus* (mixed)   Grows to 6ft (1.8m) tall, producing yellow, orange or red, single or double flowers 2in (5cm) wide in summer. Hardy to 10°F (-12°C), US zones 8–10. Native to South America.

*Tropaeolum majus*

*Schizanthus pinnatus*

*Salpiglossis* 'Festival Mixed'

*Silene coeli-rosa*

*Salvia farinacea* 'Victoria' with *Helichrysum petiolare* 'Limelight'

*Salvia coccinea* 'Lady in Red'

# INDEX

The common names are set in ordinary roman type and the botanical names are all set in italic. Single quotes around a name or part of a name denote that it is a cultivated form (cultivar).

# INDEX

# INDEX

# INDEX

# INDEX